Jamie Lee Curtis:

Scream Queen

Jamie Lee Curtis:
Scream Queen

a biography by

David Grove

BearManor Media

2010

Jamie Lee Curtis: Scream Queen

© 2010 David Grove

For information, address:

BearManor Media
P. O. Box 71426
Albany, GA 31708

bearmanormedia.com

Typesetting and layout by John Teehan

Published in the USA by BearManor Media

ISBN—1-59393-608-7

TABLE OF CONTENTS

To Maureen

(1939-2009)

Michael Myers continues his relentless pursuit of Laurie Strode in a scene from *Halloween II* (1981). (Photo courtesy of Kim Gottlieb-Walker www.lenswoman.com)

ACKNOWLEDGEMENTS

Writing is often a draining and lonely job, but writing a book about a living subject is probably the most exhausting and obsessive task a writer can undertake. If I'd known how much time and work this book would require, I wouldn't have started the project. Once I did start, I couldn't stop until I finished.

Whoever said that no one writes a book alone clearly never wrote a biography before. The writing of a biography, especially one as extensive as this, is a lonely and maddening pursuit that requires a commitment and discipline that pushes the limits of a writer's endurance.

My only sustaining force throughout the seemingly endless process of completing this book has been my dream of this book transforming into the comprehensive, definitive, and important film biography I always envisioned. It takes a month to write a film biography that's forgotten instantly, but it took me over five years to write this one, and I hope it's remembered for many more to come. In terms of documenting the scream queen career of Jamie Lee Curtis, I wanted to describe this era through the memories and sights of the colleagues who worked closely with Jamie Lee Curtis during her scream queen era. This was the only way I could reconstruct the past and document the production histories of the films that established Jamie Lee Curtis as a genre icon.

Although I've interviewed Jamie Lee Curtis several times over the past decade, it seemed logical to me that the people who worked with Jamie Lee Curtis most closely during her genre career—in films like *Halloween, The Fog, Prom Night, Terror Train, Roadgames, Halloween II*—would have the clearest vision of who she was. I was right. Going back in time wasn't as difficult as I thought it would be.

In this regard, I've been overwhelmed by the number of Jamie Lee Curtis' colleagues who kindly took the time to be interviewed for my book. They helped me to reconstruct the past and create a portrait of the genre icon and scream queen that was, and is, Jamie Lee Curtis. I could list on one hand the number of people who declined to be interviewed for this book, and I'm eternally grateful to all of the people who took the time to share their memories and thoughts with me. I'm especially grateful to those interview subjects who are now deceased.

Although *Jamie Lee Curtis: Scream Queen* is an unauthorized biography, and wasn't authorized by Jamie Lee Curtis or anyone associated with Jamie Lee Curtis, I want to thank Jamie Lee Curtis for taking the time to answer my questions and for filling in the blanks I had regarding certain aspects of her career. I also want to thank Ms. Curtis' publicist, Heidi Schaeffer from PMK/HBH Public Relations, for making this possible and also for tolerating my constant intrusions into Ms. Curtis' past that must've come across as obsessive—and somewhat weird at times.

Jamie Lee Curtis' acting career began at Universal Studios in 1977 and I'd like to thank Chuck Binder, Jamie Lee Curtis' former manager, for shedding light on how Jamie Lee Curtis' acting career first came to be. I would also like to thank the late Thomas D. Tannenbaum who was instrumental in launching Ms. Curtis' acting career during his tenure at Universal Television.

Halloween is the staple of both Jamie Lee Curtis' scream queen career and her acting career in general. I would like to thank John Carpenter and the late Debra Hill for sharing their memories from the making of the film, and of working with Ms. Curtis. I would also like to thank the late Moustapha Akkad, Brian Andrews, Don Behrns, Nick Castle, Dean Cundey, Charles Cyphers, Kim Gottlieb-Walker, Louise Jaffe, Kool Marder, Tony Moran, P.J. Soles, Craig Stearns, Raymond Stella, Rick Wallace, Tommy Lee Wallace, James Winburn and Irwin Yablans for their input.

Although Donald Pleasence passed away in 1995, I'd like to thank Mr. Pleasence's longtime acting agent, Joy Jameson, for kindly sharing with me the details of Mr. Pleasence's involvement with the *Halloween* films, as well as his working relationship with Ms. Curtis.

I would like to thank Johnny Lee Schell, Jamie Lee Curtis' former boyfriend, for sharing his fond memories of Ms. Curtis during this period—the release of *Halloween*—as well as his memories of the warm relationship between Ms. Curtis and her mother, the late Janet Leigh.

The Fog reunited Jamie Lee Curtis with most of her colleagues from *Halloween*, as well as co-starring Jamie Lee Curtis' mother, Janet Leigh. In addition to thanking the cast and crew who'd previously worked on *Halloween*, I'd like to thank Tom Atkins and Adrienne Barbeau for sharing their memories from *The Fog*, and a special thanks to the late Janet Leigh, who I interviewed, for sharing her memories from *The Fog*, as well as her memories of working on classic films like *Psycho*, *The Manchurian Candidate* and *Touch of Evil*.

Prom Night was the first of two horror films that Jamie Lee Curtis filmed in Canada in 1979. I'd like to thank Paul Lynch, the director of *Prom Night*, for sharing his memories from the film and for putting me in touch with his sister, dance choreographer Pamela Malcolm, who gave Jamie Lee Curtis dancing lessons for the film and also provided me with many interesting details about *Prom Night*'s filming.

A special thanks to the late Peter Simpson for describing how Jamie Lee Curtis came to be involved with *Prom Night* and for providing invaluable production details.

I'd also like to thank William Gray, Karen Hazzard, Sheila Manning, Dwayne McLean, David Mucci, Robert New, Leslie Nielsen, Nancy Ramos, Mary Beth Rubens, Sheldon Rybowski, Joy Thompson, Michael Tough, George Touliatos and Steve Wright for sharing their memories with me.

A special thanks to Marty Galin and Gloria Martin for sharing their memories with me of their friend, the late Casey Stevens. Thanks also to Shirley Solway, Stevens' former agent, for making this possible.

The filming of *Terror Train* took place in Montreal and coincided with Jamie Lee Curtis' momentous twenty-first birthday. I'd like to thank Roger Spottiswoode for sharing his memories of working with Jamie Lee Curtis on the film, as well as Lamar Card and Daniel Grodnik for describing how Jamie Lee Curtis came to be involved with the project.

I'd also like to thank Howard Busgang, Glenn Bydwell, Don Carmody, the late Thomas Y. Drake, Penny Hadfield, Andrea Kenyon, Derek MacKinnon, Nadia Rona, Ray Sager and Timothy Webber for sharing their memories with me.

A special thanks to Mark D. Currie and the Currie family for providing me with details about the life and untimely passing of Sandee (Sandra) Currie.

Since *Roadgames* was filmed in Australia, it was much more difficult to locate cast and crew. I'd like to give a special thanks to the late Richard Franklin for sharing with me his memories of working with Jamie Lee Curtis on the film, and this is especially poignant since I spoke to Mr. Franklin just two weeks before he passed away.

I'd also like to thank Everett De Roche, Jon Dowding, Stacy Keach, Grant Page, Sue Milliken, Vincent Monton, Lisa Peers, Greg Ricketson and Richard Soames for sharing their memories with me.

Halloween II represented the end of Jamie Lee Curtis' scream queen career, and a turning point in her acting career. I would like to give special thanks to Rick Rosenthal for taking the time to recount, in detail, his work with Ms. Curtis on *Halloween II*. I hope this book serves to absolve Mr. Rosenthal of any blame regarding any of *Halloween II*'s perceived deficiencies or shortcomings, few of which were his making.

A special thanks to Mick Garris, Jamie Lee Curtis' former press agent, for sharing with me his memories of working with Ms. Curtis.

I'd also like to thank William S. Beasley, Jeffrey Chernov, Gloria Gifford, Lance Guest, Alan Howarth, Nancy Jacoby, Tawny Moyer, Pamela Susan Shoop and Dick Warlock for sharing their memories with me.

I'd like to thank Paul Pompian for sharing me with his memories of working with Jamie Lee Curtis on the film *Death of a Centerfold: The Dorothy Stratten Story*.

I'd like to thank Amy Holden Jones, the writer-director of *Love Letters*, for sharing with me her memories of working with Jamie Lee Curtis on what was Jamie Lee Curtis' first post-scream queen dramatic leading role.

I'd also like to thank the many people who spoke to me on the condition of anonymity.

I'd also like to thank the following group of people who either provided me with information, or helped me to get in touch with certain people, or who took the time to share with me their memories, opinions and thoughts about Jamie Lee Curtis and her career: Mark A. Altman, Jim Avey, James Berardinelli, Gilles Boulenger, Geoffrey Brandt, John Bruno, John Burnham, Mark Cerulli, Sean Clark, Rich Cline, Jason Paul Collum, Erin Connor, Tom De Simone, Roger Ebert, John Fallon, Stephen Farber, Brad Fuller, Mitchell Gabourie, Bradley Glenn, Ian

Greenberg, Lawrence Grobel, Simon Jackson, Alan Jones, Lisa King, Roy Lee, Carl Liberman, Tim Lucas, Anthony Masi, John McCarty, Stevan Mena, Brad Miska, John Kenneth Muir, Philip Nutman, Adam Rockoff, Richard Schmenner, Lois Siegel, Mike Simpson, David Skal, Bruce Smith, Paul Alan Smith, Anthony Timpone, Dante Tomaselli, Jovanka Vuckovic, Cori Wellins, Wynn Winberg, David Winning, Frank Wuliger and Mommy.

INTRODUCTION

Between 1978 and 1981, Jamie Lee Curtis established herself as the greatest scream queen in film history. Many years later, Curtis' status as a genre icon remains intact.

In 1978, nineteen year old Jamie Lee Curtis made her film debut in a low budget horror film called *Halloween*, and the rest was cinematic history—both for audiences and for Curtis. Playing the role of Laurie Strode, Curtis created the ultimate scream queen—with the invaluable friendship and help of director John Carpenter and producer Debra Hill—in what is now regarded as the greatest horror film in modern film history. Displaying a disarming combination of bottomless vulnerability, inner strength, and unconventional beauty, Curtis' Laurie Strode character represented cinema's definitive and ultimate scream queen.

With her performance as Laurie Strode, Curtis set a towering bar that no future actress—certainly none of the Jamie Lee Curtis impersonators that have tried and failed to copy Curtis since—would equal in terms of matching Curtis' brilliance. The fact that no other actress—no other "Jamie Lee Curtis wannabe"—has come close to matching Jamie Lee Curtis' impact since 1978 is a testament to both Curtis' enduring power and her uniqueness. There's only one true scream queen because there's only one Jamie Lee Curtis. There's no one else like her.

Of course, one horror film, no matter how great and immortal, doesn't make a great scream queen. If that were the case, Curtis' own mother, Janet Leigh, would be regarded as an immortal scream queen for her brilliant and unforgettable performance in 1960's *Psycho*. For Leigh, the iconic role of Marion Crane in *Psycho*, which earned Leigh a Best Supporting Actress Academy Award nomination, represented her lone scream queen role. This explains one of the key qualities that made Curtis such a definitive scream queen: longevity.

Perhaps Fay Wray, star of 1933's *King Kong*, is the Closest comparison to Curtis in this regard. Prior to *King Kong*, Wray had starred in films like *Doctor X* (1932), *Mystery of the Wax Museum* (1933), and *The Vampire Bat* (1933). There's no question that Wray made a powerful impact as a scream queen in *King Kong*, but although *King Kong* and Wray's performance remain enduring and iconic landmarks, both *Halloween* and Curtis' performance as Laurie Strode have surpassed them as genre vanguards. Ultimately, when people throw out the Scream Queen label, the first—and usually the only—name that's mentioned is Jamie Lee Curtis.

Also, Wray had distaste for the scream queen mantle and its typecasting, eventually taking her career to England to escape the bonds of the horror genre, while Curtis was much more philosophical about her scream queen persona and grateful for what the horror films, *Halloween* especially, ultimately did for her career in terms of giving her a film career.

Between 1978 and 1981, Jamie Lee Curtis starred in six horror films—from 1978's *Halloween* to *Halloween*'s 1981 sequel, *Halloween II*, a film that represented both the end of Curtis' scream queen career and the beginning of a new chapter in her acting career and her life.

In 1979, Curtis followed up *Halloween* with *The Fog*, a stylish ghost story which re-teamed Curtis with mentors Carpenter and Hill as well as her mother, Janet Leigh, who had a small supporting role in the film. Although not nearly the commercial or critical success that *Halloween* was, *The Fog* was a solid hit when it was released in 1980 and solidified Curtis' scream queen persona.

It's no coincidence that Jamie Lee Curtis' ascendance as a scream queen coincided with the horror movie boom that exploded between 1980 and 1981, an era defined by a flood of slasher films—most notably 1980's *Friday the 13th*—that were all inspired by the commercial success of *Halloween*. Curtis herself joined this fray, starring in two slasher films that were released in 1980: *Prom Night* and *Terror Train*. With the release of *The Fog*, *Prom Night*, and *Terror Train*, 1980 was definitely the year of the scream queen.

Curtis' roles in *Prom Night* and *Terror Train* demonstrated Curtis' undeniable star quality in the way that her involvement with these films gave the films respectability.

Although *Prom Night* and *Terror Train* were basically *Halloween* ripoffs, Curtis' mere presence gave these films a kind of legitimacy and validation that would make *Prom Night* and *Terror Train* staples of the slasher film genre. The fact that all of the genre films Curtis made between 1978 and 1981, save for 1981's *Roadgames*, have been remade is further proof of Curtis' strong influence over the horror genre—then and now.

Curtis' scream queen career crossed the entire trajectory of the horror genre between 1978 and 1981—the good, the bad, and the ugly. With *Halloween*, Curtis had the distinction of starring in what is unquestionably the Godfather, the vanguard, of modern horror films. *The Fog*, Curtis' *Halloween* follow-up, was one of the most commercially-successful of the post-*Halloween* horror films, and continues to enjoy a wide audience today. *Prom Night* and *Terror Train* established Curtis as the queen of the slasher films—or "The Queen of Crud," as Curtis used to refer to herself—as well as establishing Curtis as a measurable box office draw. She did it all.

In 1981, Curtis' scream queen career took an exotic detour with the release of the thriller *Roadgames*. Curtis shot *Roadgames* in Australia in 1980 and the film represented a departure for Curtis in that *Roadgames* was much more of a psychological-thriller than a horror film. Although *Roadgames*—which Curtis regards as the best film of her post-*Halloween* scream queen career—was the least commercially-successful genre film that Curtis made between 1978 and 1981, the film represents a colorful and interesting chapter in Curtis' career. As with Curtis' other genre films, *Roadgames* enjoys a strong following today.

1981's *Halloween II* was the end of Curtis' scream queen career, and represents the point in Curtis' career where the actress was determined to leave the horror genre; to abandon her scream queen persona in the hopes of becoming a respected and serious actress. That Curtis was able to do this, was able to move on from the horror genre and have an award-winning acting career, is the true testament of her greatness as a scream queen. Most scream queens never escape their typecasting because they simply can't act, but the fact that Curtis was able to reinvent herself outside of the horror genre is proof of what a durable actress she was, and continues to be.

Jamie Lee Curtis, like any human being, is more than just an iconic and legendary scream queen, more than any one label or stereotype. She's a daughter, a wife, a mother, a sister, a blogger, children's book author, pitch-woman, inventor, Grammy nominee, baroness, AIDS activist, Hollywood survivor. As an actress, Curtis has worked in various genres—action, comedy, drama, thriller—and proven herself capable in all of them.

Jamie Lee Curtis has had a very successful acting career and life by any standards, and that's wonderful, but it's not exactly the stuff that's worthy of a deep, serious, thoughtful biography, certainly not the kind of extensive film biography that I was determined to write. Jamie Lee Curtis has never won an Oscar, although she did win a British version of the award for her memorable supporting performance in 1983's *Trading Places*, and her acting career has never inspired any deep critical analysis or thesis projects (1).

In this regard Jamie Lee Curtis' acting career has mirrored that of her famous parents, Tony Curtis and Janet Leigh, in the sense that none of them has ever received the recognition as performers that they sought and deserved.

Jamie Lee Curtis is regarded as a screen icon today not because of her solid body of work or any awards she's won in her long acting career but rather a result of the enduring image of her scream queen persona.

It's this scream queen persona, even as contained in such primitive horror films like *Prom Night* and *Terror Train*, that will live on in the public consciousness far longer than Curtis' work in mainstream Hollywood films like *Freaky Friday* and *True Lies*. Jamie Lee Curtis is a good actress, and a very underrated actress, but it was as a scream queen that she reached greatness and immortality.

This is why I decided to write this book, *Jamie Lee Curtis: Scream Queen*. I wanted to write a book that covered not only Jamie Lee Curtis' scream queen career, but which also served as a detailed Making-Of document for films such as *Halloween, The Fog, Prom Night, Terror Train, Roadgames, Halloween II.*

As Curtis' scream queen reign also mirrored the horror boom between 1978 and 1981, this book is also a document of this era. Instead of writing a typical film biography, I set out to write a book that would also exist as an important film reference that will be studied for many years to come. I wanted to write a book that would be of as much interest to film historians as to fans of Jamie Lee Curtis.

In addition to covering her career and her films, I also sought to chronicle Jamie Lee Curtis' changing life during this period. The book also covers, in great detail, Curtis' post-scream queen genre career which began with the 1981 made-for-televison film *Death of a Centerfold: The Dorothy Stratten Story* and extends to Curtis' reprisal of her Laurie Strode character in 1998's *Halloween: H20* and 2002's *Halloween: Resurrection*.

I set out to write a detailed film biography on Jamie Lee Curtis' scream queen career—and all of the films that comprised this chapter of her career and life—but I think I ended up with more—much, much more. Too much. I conducted over 100 interviews for the purpose of writing this book and I also collected and studied thousands of pages of articles and documents. Several people I interviewed for this book are now dead, a painful reminder—along with the unbelievable arrival of Jamie Lee Curtis' 50th birthday on November 22, 2008—of how much time has passed since the height of Curtis' scream queen career.

Perhaps one day Jamie Lee Curtis will write her own biography, one that encapsulates the entire scope of her life—from her Hollywood upbringing to her arrival at 50 years of age. Ironically, if Curtis wrote such a biography, which she says she has no plans to do, she would probably spend very little time talking about her scream queen career—a career I've spent many years and many tens of thousands of words documenting and reconstructing. If she does write a biography one day, and does talk about her scream queen career in detail, she's certainly welcome to use this book as a reference in terms of jogging her memory about this period.

– David Grove
February 3, 2009

one

JAMIE LEE

On November 22, 1958, a future scream queen was born. Her name was Jamie Lee Curtis.

This wasn't just any birth. Jamie Lee Curtis' parents were Tony Curtis and Janet Leigh who were then two of the biggest movie stars in Hollywood, and certainly the most glamorous celebrity couple of their era. Curtis and Leigh, who'd been married since June 4, 1951, were to the 1950s what Elizabeth Taylor and Richard Burton were to the 1960s and what Angelina Jolie and Brad Pitt are in the present. They were Hollywood's undisputed golden couple.

With their picturesque, almost ungodly beauty and glittering star-power, Tony Curtis and Janet Leigh were, at the moment of Jamie Lee's arrival, the dream Hollywood couple that everyone—and certainly every paparazzi camera and movie magazine of the period—wanted to catch. Jamie Lee Curtis was, quite simply, born into Hollywood royalty—at the moment of its zenith—and while most births are greeted with maybe a sentence or two in a local newspaper, the *Associated Press* (AP) published the news of Jamie Lee's arrival all over the world. Just a few hours old, Jamie Lee Curtis had her first brush with celebrity and the inner-workings of the Hollywood publicity machine. HOLLYWOOD, November 22 (AP) —Actress Janet Leigh gave birth to her second daughter today at Cedars of Lebanon Hospital. The baby weighed 6 pounds 8 ounces. "Mother and daughter are doing fine," said Dr. Leon Krohn. Miss Leigh is married to actor Tony Curtis. Their first daughter, Kelly, is two years old.

Newsweek published details of the birth a few days later. Jamie Lee was the second—and would turn out to be the last—child for Curtis and Leigh, with Jamie Lee's older sister, Kelly Lee Curtis, having been born previously on June 17, 1956. Jamie Lee Curtis was born into a golden age of Hollywood—certainly a bygone era by today's standards—where gossip columnists like Louella Parsons and Walter Winchell could make or break careers with the tap of a typewriter key, and where Hollywood stars were forced to project a clean and healthy public appearance, especially in regards to their domestic life.

Where most children have their infancy documented through home movies or family photos, Jamie Lee Curtis' photo album, her early life, was documented in the public eye, in the Hollywood media. Just a few months after her birth, Jamie Lee Curtis' little face was plastered on the covers of all of the major movie magazines of the period—rags like *Photoplay* and *Screen Stories*—along with her smiling parents and older sister Kelly.

When Jamie Lee Curtis was just days old, Leigh noticed that Curtis had a pronounced swelling on her right side. Concerned, Leigh took her baby daughter, who measured twenty and a half inches at birth, to a specialist who diagnosed that little Jamie Lee had in fact suffered a hernia which was caused by a tear in the wall of the intestine. This required an immediate, and quite risky, operation that was nonetheless entirely successful.

Also, there was something strange about little Jamie Lee, in terms of the way she looked. Although it's difficult to look at a baby in their infant months and project their later appearance, it became quickly obvious that Curtis wasn't exactly the spitting image of her gorgeous celebrity parents. This was most evident during Curtis' infancy when it became obvious that her teeth were crooked and greyish, a condition that would haunt Curtis, and plague her self-esteem, throughout her early life and into the early part of her film career. This would contribute to the vulnerability that would be a key element of Curtis' scream queen persona. "My parents were such beautiful people and when I was growing up, I felt ugly in comparison," recalls Curtis. "I never felt good about how I looked."

Leigh had been taking the powerful antibiotic tetracycline—an antibiotic that's primarily used for the treatment of bacterial and respiratory infections, although some people, including celebrities, also use it to treat acne—while she was pregnant with Curtis, between March and November of 1958. This had the effect of making Curtis' teeth crooked and greyish, a condition that Curtis would endure up until she was twenty-one when Curtis would have her teeth capped and straightened. "I was always embarrassed about my teeth, from my early childhood to when I began my acting career" says Curtis. "Growing up, I learned to smile and talk without showing my teeth, because I was embarrassed. I developed a smirk."

Of course, the Jamie Lee Curtis of today is, like her mother, a very beautiful woman—gorgeous even—but it's an all-together different kind of beauty than Janet Leigh's natural and decidedly All-American beauty. Jamie Lee's beauty, as unconventional at it would turn out to be, would have to evolve, slowly but surely, over the course of her career and life whereas Janet Leigh's beauty was god-given. Still, there are other more direct resemblances between Curtis and her parents, if not in physical appearance than in terms of Curtis' eventual identity and personality.

Perhaps the greatest gift Jamie Lee Curtis received from both her parents was a tireless work ethic, something that would come in handy during the tough early years of Curtis' own acting career. Although Curtis was born into Hollywood royalty, both Tony Curtis and Janet Leigh had come from extremely humble, modest backgrounds, especially Tony Curtis whose rough-and-tumble Bronx upbringing was very visible in his early film career. "My parents, especially my mother, always taught me the value of money and taught me to work hard and to not expect to be handed things," recalls Jamie Lee. "My mother did everything she could to give me a grounded and normal childhood. I grew up around so many Hollywood stars that celebrity didn't impress me after awhile."

Janet Leigh was born Jeanette Helen Morrison on July 6, 1927 in Merced, California. The story of Leigh's acting career was the mirror of the classic Lana Turner Schwab's legend as Leigh was discovered, quite by chance, by screen legend Norma Shearer, one of MGM's biggest stars in the 1930s. In 1946, Shearer spotted Leigh's photo at a ski lodge in Soda Springs, California where Leigh's vagabond parents, Fred and Helen Morrison, were working. The rest would be history.

Leigh was attending the University of the Pacific at the time, in addition to being in the midst of her second marriage, and was subsequently put under contract by MGM—where Norma Shearer had ended her own career in 1942—after just a single screen test (1). In 1947, Leigh—who had no acting experience whatsoever—would make her film debut opposite leading man Van Johnson in the rustic drama *The Romance of Rosy Ridge*.

More film roles quickly followed for Leigh, but with a few notable exceptions, such as Leigh's fine performance as a housewife in director Fred Zinnemann's 1949 film noir *Act of Violence*, most of the films Leigh made between 1948 and 1955 featured the actress in undemanding roles. Because of her exquisite body and lovely face, Leigh found herself cast in the same peaches and cream ingenue roles over and over again. Leigh was more than just a pretty face; there was an edge and a gutsiness to her beauty that made her—in spite of the thin roles she was given early in her career—one of the most interesting screen sex symbols of the 1950s who transcended the stereotypes she was often pigeonholed in.

The most notable event for Leigh during this period was when Leigh met Tony Curtis at a Hollywood cocktail party that was held at the RKO studio in 1950. Curtis had recently been put under contract at Universal Pictures and was on the verge of breaking through in his own acting career when Curtis and Leigh first met (2). There were instant fireworks between Curtis and Leigh who eventually eloped to Greenwich, Connecticut and were married on June 4, 1951.

Curtis, whose real name is Bernard Schwartz, had made his screen acting debut in the 1949 thriller *Criss Cross*, where he appeared uncredited as a rumba dancer, and had since made nine films in the period between 1949 and 1951, mostly in crime movies like *City Across the River* (1949), *The Lady Gambles* (1949), *Johnny Stool Pigeon* (1949) and *I Was a Shoplifter* (1950).

From the period between Curtis' and Leigh's wedding—in June of 1951—to Jamie Lee Curtis' birth in November of 1958, Tony Curtis and Janet Leigh would transform into the most attractive and closely-watched young couple in Hollywood. This kind of heightened publicity—manifested through endless coverage in fluffy movie magazines—can be unwelcome for actors who want to be taken seriously for their work, but in fairness, Tony Curtis and Janet Leigh didn't become a golden Hollywood couple because of publicity stunts or scandals. Their adonis-like beauty played a part, certainly, but by the time of Jamie Lee's birth, Curtis and Leigh had become famous for their acting. The publicity stunts and scandals would arrive later.

Jamie Lee Curtis' birth coincided with the height, the peak, of her parents' respective film careers and their excellence as actors. It was during this general period surrounding Jamie Lee's birth—between 1957 and 1960—that Curtis and Leigh would appear in a series of films that would be enjoyed by audiences and critics—and later by film historians. This was the period, the period around Jamie Lee's birth, that would ultimately define Tony Curtis and Janet Leigh in terms of their legacies as screen actors.

Not only was Jamie Lee Curtis born into Hollywood royalty, she was also born into Hollywood power. Curtis' godfather was Lew Wasserman, the chairman of MCA (Music Corporation of America), the all-powerful entertainment corporation and talent agency that, at the time of Jamie Lee's birth, represented most of the top stars in Hollywood. MCA was a Hollywood juggernaut that earned the nickname "The Octopus" for the way it crushed competition by insisting, and ensuring, that its clients were booked exclusively into MCA- related productions.

Curtis and Leigh were very close friends with both Wasserman, and his wife, Edie Wasserman, who became Jamie Lee's godmother. Without question, Curtis and Leigh benefitted from their friendship with titan Wasserman and their association with MCA Inc. (the company was incorporated on November 10, 1958) as much as any of their acting contemporaries, although no more than other star MCA clients like Marlon Brando and James Stewart who were making the kinds of great and important films that both Curtis and Leigh aspired to. Not even Wasserman could force serious film- makers to hire actors like Curtis and Leigh if they weren't inclined, nor did Curtis or Leigh ever receive any such favors.

Tony Curtis' transforming moment as a serious actor came in 1957 with the release of the gritty drama *Sweet Smell of Success*. Playing the role of Sidney Falco, a seedy New York press agent who enters a vicious game of one-upmanship with a callous gossip columnist, played by Burt Lancaster, Curtis gave a brilliant, complex, layered performance. Although the film was somewhat of a commercial and critical disappointment upon its initial release in 1957, *Sweet Smell of Success* is now considered a masterpiece. Tony Curtis' excellent performance is regarded today as Oscar-worthy, if only in hindsight.

For Janet Leigh, the transition from ingenue to serious leading lady materialized in the form of the classic film noir thriller *Touch of Evil*, which Leigh began shooting in February of 1957. Written, directed, and co-starring Orson Welles, *Touch of Evil* paired Leigh with Charlton Heston and demonstrated a sharper edge to Leigh's acting that had rarely been showcased before. Released in the Spring of 1958, at the beginning of Leigh's pregnancy with Jamie Lee, *Touch of Evil* was, like many classic films of that period, misunderstood by audiences and critics upon its initial release but is today regarded as an undisputably-great American film.

In 1956, Curtis and Leigh had formed a production company, entitled Curtleigh, partially for business reasons and also for the purpose of finding quality film vehicles (3). In 1958, Curtis and Leigh starred together in *The Vikings*, a lavish and brutally-violent epic—almost shockingly-so for its period—that was a Curtleigh co-production. Directed by Richard Fleischer, the well-staged Viking adventure stands as the most successful—both commercially and critically—of Curtis' and Leigh's several screen collaborations (4).

Tony Curtis received his first and only Oscar nomination, in the Best Actor Category, for his performance in the 1958 escaped convict drama *The Defiant Ones*. Directed by Stanley Kramer, and co-starring Sidney Poitier, *The Defiant Ones* further distanced Curtis from his matinee idol image and further established him as a serious actor with surprising range. Curtis eventually lost the Best Actor Oscar—to David Niven in *Separate Tables*—which wasn't a surprise given that Poitier was nominated in the same category thus killing Curtis' chances, as well as Poitier's. Regardless, *The Defiant Ones* was a triumph.

Perhaps Tony Curtis' most iconic film, and most beloved, was the film he was making when Leigh was pregnant with Jamie Lee. This was 1959's *Some Like It Hot*, the comedy classic that is often listed as the greatest screen comedy in film history. Directed and co-written by Billy Wilder, and co- starring Jack Lemmon and Marilyn Monroe, *Some Like It Hot* featured Curtis in drag and showcased a deft comic timing that was unlike anything he'd done before.

Some Like It Hot was a massive hit upon its release in 1959, and earned several Oscar nominations, although Jack Lemmon was the only member of the cast to be nominated. Although Curtis' performance was hailed by critics, and deservedly so, his work in the film was subtly minimized, certainly in comparison to Lemmon's Oscar-nominated performance and Monroe's unforgettable presence, not to mention Billy Wilder's masterful direction.

Because Lemmon received an Oscar nomination for *Some Like It Hot*, and Curtis had been overlooked, the impression left was that Curtis had finished second best in the film, despite his terrific comic performance. It was the same with 1959's *Operation Petticoat*, a light submarine comedy that paired Curtis with the legendary Cary Grant. Although Curtis was the lead in the film, and had used his box office clout to secure Grant's appearance in the film, somehow Grant stole all of the good critical notices despite Curtis' own solid comedic work in the film.

Perhaps this is the price that Tony Curtis and Janet Leigh paid for their looks in that they weren't taken as seriously as actors as they deserved because of their physical beauty. Tony Curtis, in particular, deserves admiration for shunning his matinee idol image and seeking out challenging films like *Sweet Smell of Success* and *The Defiant Ones*. Leigh took the same approach in terms of downplaying her looks and seeking out more challenging material, like *Touch of Evil*. Curtis and Leigh took risks, but although the critics and the public recognized Curtis' and Leigh's skills as true actors, they would never get the appreciation and full recognition that they deserved.

Jamie Lee Curtis never faced such an enviable problem when she began her acting career in 1977. She had the opposite problem in terms of trying to convince herself that she was beautiful and was very mistrustful and shy about her physical appearance, primarily because of her crooked teeth. Curtis feels that her parents' handsomeness prevented them from receiving the critical acclaim, as actors, that they deserved. "I definitely feel that my parents weren't taken as seriously as actors because they were so beautiful," says Curtis. "I look at my father's films, and I'm amazed by how versatile he was. My favorite film of his was *Sweet Smell of Success*. I thought he gave a wonderful performance that was both funny and sad. I thought my mother gave some wonderful performances that were overlooked because people only paid attention to her beauty. I think they were both great actors."

Curtis' introduction to the horror genre—and to the scream queen mantle that would later make her famous in her own acting career—occurred in 1959 when Leigh was offered $25,000 to appear in Alfred Hitchcock's film version of author Robert Bloch's book *Psycho*. Leigh's established salary at the time was $100,000 per film, but Leigh didn't really care about the money or that her male co-stars—John Gavin and Anthony Perkins—were to be paid more money than her as she loved the book and desperately wanted to work with the great Alfred Hitchcock (5).

Leigh signed her contract for *Psycho* on October 28, 1959, just a few days before Halloween, which is ironic in many ways that would become obvious only many years later. Leigh's only concern was being away from Jamie Lee, who was less than a year old. "I would've done the film for nothing," Leigh later proclaimed. "I was paid less because I would only be working for three weeks whereas Tony Perkins and the other actors were going to be working for the whole two month shoot. That made me happy because it meant I wouldn't be away from Jamie for very long."

Jamie Lee Curtis, who was still less than a year old—although just barely—when *Psycho* began filming on November 11, 1959, says she was never taken by her mother to the Universal Studios back-lot where much of *Psycho* was filmed and instead was kept home with a nanny. Unlike actress Melanie Griffith, a later contemporary of Curtis' whose own mother—actress Tippi Hedren—would collaborate with Hitchcock on 1963's *The Birds*, Curtis has no cryptic memories—or any other memories—of meeting Hitchcock, either during the making of *Psycho* or in the years after (6). For Curtis, the doomed fate of her mother's character in *Psycho* would be enough.

Leigh had been approached for *Psycho*, whose production budget would end up being a tad above $800,000, just weeks before she signed her contract when Hitchcock had sent her a copy of Bloch's novel with the suggestion that Leigh consider the role of Mary Crane, later to be changed to Marion Crane. In the film, Marion Crane is a secretary in an Arizona real estate office who embezzles $40,000 from a client and heads to California for the purpose of being with her married lover, Sam Loomis, played by John Gavin, who runs a hardware store in Fairvale, California.

After driving for hours, Marion falls asleep on a lonely stretch of road and is awoken by a suspicious highway patrolman who seems to look right through her soul. Later, during a fierce rainstorm, Marion Crane misses the turnoff to Fairvale and is stranded at a remote motel, the Bates Motel, which is run by a schizophrenic, cross-dressing lunatic named Norman Bates, played by Anthony Perkins. Norman Bates is driven by the voice of his long-dead mother—who he emulates by donning her dress and wig—and ends up stabbing Marion Crane to death while she's taking a shower in what is one of the most famous and iconic scenes in film history.

Leigh sensed the role would change her life, but undoubtedly had no clue as to how it would change her image. "I read the novel the first time and my first reaction was that the material was very ugly and frightening," said Leigh whose iconic and gruesome shower scene was filmed between December 17 and December 23 of 1959. "Lew Wasserman was the President at MCA in 1959, and he was my agent and close friend, and he told me I was the first and only actress approached for the part. It was such an exciting and horrific story, and I was desperate to be a part of it even though I hadn't seen a script at that point. I wanted to see what Hitchcock would do with the material. When I got Joseph Stefano's script, I saw that my character's name was changed to Marion Crane because there was a real Mary Crane in Arizona so they had to change the name. I read the script and loved it. I was America's sweetheart at that time, a big star, and I knew it would shock people to see my character get savaged like she does halfway during the film."

Psycho was released in June of 1960, and was one of the top box office hits of the year. More importantly, the film would eventually, after initially mixed reviews, be regarded as, arguably, the greatest American thriller ever made, a true cinematic masterpiece. Leigh received her first, and only, Academy Award nomination for the film, in the Best Supporting Actress category, but eventually lost the award to Shirley Jones for Jones' performance in *Elmer Gantry*. Leigh, who was considered the odds-on favorite to win the Best Supporting Actress Oscar, had earlier won a Golden Globe award for her performance.

Psycho was a great triumph for Leigh as an actress, but in retrospect, the film may have hurt her career in terms of immortalizing her as a stabbing victim. Perhaps the image of Marion Crane being stabbed to death in the shower was too prominent for any actress to surmount, to move on from. It certainly marked the end of Leigh's working relationship with Hitchcock. "After the film came out, Alfred told me that he and I could never work together again after *Psycho*," recalled Leigh. "He explained that the audience would always see me as Marion Crane, the victim."

Just as *Psycho* would forever typecast Anthony Perkins as a jittery fruitcake, Leigh was typecast as a victim, and an especially gruesome one at that. The role of Marion Crane was so iconic—and Leigh gave such a haunting and memorable performance—that Hollywood—and perhaps also the public—could no longer see her as a leading lady, or even as an attractive woman anymore. In this respect, Leigh's performance—much like Perkins'—in *Psycho* had been too effective, too memorable. Although Leigh had the distinction of giving an unforgettable and Oscar-worthy performance in a truly great film that will live on for centuries, it seems clear—considering the scarce quality film roles Leigh would receive after *Psycho*—that *Psycho* actually hurt Leigh's career.

At the beginning of her own acting career, Jamie Lee Curtis would tell interviewers how much she loved *Psycho* in order to make herself seem more interesting, not to mention that *Psycho* was such a classic of its genre. It was a lie. The truth is that Curtis has scarcely watched *Psycho* from start to finish, which is also the case with sister Kelly. "When I first became an actress, I hadn't done anything so people would ask about my mother, about *Psycho*, and I finally made up a story about seeing the film," said Curtis. "I made up a story about being ten or eleven and sneaking downstairs to watch *Psycho* on *The Late Show*. I then told people that I was so scared after watching it that I ran into my mother's bedroom, screaming for her 'Mommy! Mommy!" because I was so disturbed by the shower scene where her character was stabbed to death. The truth is I've never seen *Psycho* because, ironically, I don't like watching horror movies and I never have. I think that's because I'm sensitive. I hate horror movies."

The seeds of Curtis' distaste for watching horror films were rooted outside of the genre. Curtis recalls the 1968 children's adventure film *Oliver!* as her most memorable early cinematic experience, but she also found the film—which won several Academy Awards and is now regarded as a classic—deeply disturbing. "It was the scene where Oliver Reed strangles Shani Wallis," recalls Curtis. "You see her legs twitch, and I was with my mother when I was watching it and she could see that it was upsetting me and she tried to cover my eyes. That was the first movie I remember seeing as a child and I found it really upsetting. I couldn't keep my eyes open watching that film."

The first genre films Curtis saw as a child, the ones that scared her the most and made her avoid the genre as a viewer, were the 1954 ant-thriller *The Naked Jungle* and the 1957 monster film *The Deadly Mantis*. "I remember the image, in *The Naked Jungle*, of seeing all of these killer ants – millions of them—marching along and it really freaked me out," says Curtis. "There's one scene in *The Naked Jungle* where a guy gets the killer ants in his hair and it really scared the hell out of me.

That was the scariest movie I'd ever seen. There was a part of me that was really drawn to those kinds of films, and another part of me that had to cover my eyes because I couldn't stand the shock of being scared like that. That's how I feel to this day."

It wasn't the gore aspect of horror films that Curtis found troubling but rather the shock aspect. In fact, Curtis was so transfixed by *The Exorcist* (1973) that she had the name "Dimmy"—which was a nickname used for actor Jason Miller's Damien Karras character in the film—put on a personalized license plate on what was Curtis' first car, a 1972 Mercury Capri. "I remember seeing *The Exorcist* with my girlfriends and then coming home and being so scared," recalls Curtis. "My girlfriends slept over and in the middle of the night, one of them woke me up and said, "Dimmy, Dimmy, why do this to me?" which was the line in the film that drove me crazy. Dimmy became my nickname for awhile after that. It's not that I didn't like *The Exorcist*; I thought it was a great film and still do. I just can't watch it ever again, and that's the same for all horror movies. It's not that I don't like them; I'm scared to hell of them. I have to keep my hands over my face."

Of what Curtis has seen of *Psycho* over the years, in bits and pieces, her favorite moment is the scene where Marion Crane is pulled over by a Highway patrolman, played by actor Mort Mills. Crane, in possession of thousands of dollars in stolen money, is understandably nervous of the patrolman who seems to look through Crane's guilty soul with icy detachment in the scene. "I thought that was the scariest scene in the film," says Curtis. "I thought it was scary because you felt like something bad was going to happen to this woman, but you didn't know what, and she's terrified of being caught. The way the cop looks at her in that scene is very scary. He's so cold, and you see how much she wishes, at that moment, that she could just go back in time and return the money, but she's caught in this trap now. I found it very disturbing."

The image of the perfect Curtis family that was continually splashed onto the covers of publications like *Photoplay* and *Screen Stories*—coupled with headlines that proclaimed "There will be no divorce"—was a Hollywood illusion. In 1957, Curtis had taken the advice of director and friend Blake Edwards, with whom Curtis had worked on 1957's *Mister Cory*, and began undergoing psychological therapy. In 1958, Curtis and Leigh both starred for Edwards in the army farce *The Perfect Furlough*. Curtis halted therapy in 1960 and by this time, the differences and the divide between Curtis—who would later admit to constant womanizing throughout his eleven year marriage to Leigh—and Leigh were palpable.

For several years, the fairytale Curtis-Leigh marriage had been plagued by reports of marital strife and looming divorce. Whenever these rumors picked up steam, MCA would arrange a cozy, happy, idyllic magazine photo spread with Curtis and Leigh—along with children Jamie Lee and Kelly—proclaiming their undying commitment to each other. By 1960, it had become increasingly difficult to maintain this mirage. "An emotional tumor was growing, infecting the tissue of our marriage," recalled Leigh. "It was not malignant as yet, but without preventive treatment, it could mushroom at any time. We were beginning to look at our life through different sets of mirrors."

1961 certainly started off well, especially for Leigh, beginning with Leigh's Golden Globe win for *Psycho* on March 16, 1961. This was quickly followed by the April 17, 1961 Academy Awards ceremony where Leigh was narrowly-defeated for the Best Supporting Actress Oscar by Shirley Jones for Jones' memorable if not long-lasting—certainly not compared to Leigh's impact in *Psycho*—performance in *Elmer Gantry*. Everything was downhill after this, and the period between the summer of 1961 and the Fall of 1963 would be filled with turmoil that would alter Jamie Lee Curtis' life forever.

The first traumatic event came on August 12, 1961 when Leigh's father, Frederick Morrison, was found dead in his real estate office. He'd committed suicide, for which he left an extended and tortured suicide letter to Leigh's mother, blaming their marital difficulties for his tragic fate. It was later revealed that Morrison was also having serious financial problems. Leigh had been attending the International Red Cross Ball in Monaco when Tony Curtis, who'd been unable to make the trip, called Leigh with the news of her father's passing. Frederick Morrison's funeral took place on August 15, 1961. Jamie Lee Curtis was still only two years old.

In September of 1961, the Curtis family—including Jamie Lee—traveled from New York to Argentina—aboard the *S.S. Argentina*—where Tony Curtis was to begin filming the action epic *Taras Bulba* for United Artists and director J. Lee Thompson. *Taras Bulba* was a lavish production, with the film's initial $3 Million budget eventually swelling to $10 Million. The Curtis family stayed mostly in Salta, Argentina during *Taras*

Bulba's filming. On a day off from filming, Curtis took two year old Jamie Lee to play at a nearby park where Jamie Lee took a bad fall and broke her clavicle, a bone in the shoulder. This would be a bad omen.

Taras Bulba teamed Curtis with screen legend Yul Brynner, but the film's most notable casting—in terms of the lives of the Curtis family—was that of Curtis' female co-star, a then seventeen-year-old Austrian-born actress named Christine Kaufmann. "I started seeing Christine during *Taras Bulba*, but she had nothing to do with the bust-up of my marriage," recalled Curtis. "It coincided, and there was a lot of heat that Christine caused it, but that wasn't true. My relationship with Janet had become untenable long before that."

On November 22, 1961, Leigh celebrated Jamie Lee's third birthday with a lavish birthday party in New York. By this time the Curtis-Leigh union was all but over, and by the end of 1961, Curtis and Leigh had decided to separate. On New Year's Day 1962, Leigh's grandmother, Kate Reeb Morrison, died. In the midst of all of this personal gloom, there was a ray of light in Leigh's film career in the form of a political thriller entitled *The Manchurian Candidate* which would team Leigh with Laurence Harvey and close friend Frank Sinatra.

Leigh shot *The Manchurian Candidate* between January and February of 1962 for director John Frankenheimer. Ironically, Leigh had read the Richard Condon best-selling novel on which the thriller was based just a year earlier with no inkling that she'd ever be involved with the film adaptation. Like *Psycho*, *The Manchurian Candidate* cast Leigh in a juicy supporting role, the difference being that Leigh appears midway through *The Manchurian Candidate*—with no apparent connection to the story—as opposed to *Psycho* where Leigh opened the film. "It was a difficult role because my character, Rosie, is plunked in the film midway through and you don't know what her purpose is," recalled Leigh. "Eventually, you realize that I'm trying to control and manipulate Frank and my character takes on a very interesting meaning in the film."

In a way, Leigh's performance in *The Manchurian Candidate* represented a grand finale to her film career as *The Manchurian Candidate*—and Leigh's complex and memorable Rosie character—would be the last quality and meaningful film role Leigh would be presented with in her acting career. Even this performance, and the film itself, would be overlooked for many years for reasons that would later become painfully obvious, and which would hit very close to Leigh's heart. Regardless, nothing Tony Curtis or Janet Leigh did on- screen between 1962 and 1963 would overshadow what was happening in their personal lives.

In March of 1962, Curtis and Leigh separated legally, which made news all over the world. A few days later, Leigh was found on the floor of a hotel bathroom in New York in a semi-comatose state that was later attributed to an accidental pill overdose. From here, events moved rapidly. By June of 1962, Leigh had begun dating stockbroker Robert "Bob" Brandt, and in September, Leigh traveled to Juarez, Mexico for a quick divorce decree. Brandt and Leigh were married the next day, on September 15, 1962, although Curtis' and Leigh's California divorce wouldn't be finalized until July of 1963. On February 8, 1963, Tony Curtis married Christine Kaufmann, his teenage co-star from *Taras Bulba*, at the Riviera Hotel in Las Vegas (7).

Leigh retained custody of both Jamie Lee and sister Kelly, both of whom saw little of their father—although Kelly would later spend a much greater amount of time with her father than Jamie Lee—in the period following the divorce. For Jamie Lee, this was the beginning of a close relationship with her new stepfather, Brandt, whom she adored, and the beginning of a prolonged alienation from her famous father. "I don't remember my father very much at all," said Curtis. "Robert really raised me and I've always felt like I grew up with two daddies, Robert and Tony. I barely saw Tony when I was growing up and barely saw him when I was beginning my acting career, mostly because he was going through a lot of problems. Bob is my father. He brought me up and raised me. Tony is my biological father, but I never lived with him when I was growing up, and I don't remember him very much when I was young. He was like a ghost."

Perhaps the most horrific irony of Jamie Lee Curtis' life was that her fifth birthday fell on the day of President John F. Kennedy's assassination in Dallas, Texas on November 22, 1963. Obviously, the Kennedy assassination was a tragedy that dwarfed the end of the Curtis-Leigh marriage but it was especially traumatic for Curtis and Leigh who had both befriended the Kennedy family and had been ardent Democratic supporters. Although Tony Curtis considered himself to be—besides his affection for the Kennedys—largely apolitical, Leigh was a lifelong Democrat who'd campaigned tirelessly for John F. Kennedy during his successful 1960 Presidential campaign.

Kennedy's assassination was a shocking blow to Leigh and an unforgettable vision for five year old Jamie Lee who would never speak about the event afterwards. On a less important note, the assassination was the reason why *The Manchurian Candidate*—which had been successfully-released in October of 1962—was subsequently pulled from circulation by star and Kennedy family friend Frank Sinatra (8). As a result, both Leigh's performance, and the film itself, would be forgotten for many years. In 1964, President Lyndon Johnson, Kennedy's successor, approached Leigh about becoming Ambassador to Finland, but Leigh felt that it was too early in her new marriage to Brandt and she declined.

By the mid-1960s, Tony Curtis' and Janet Leigh's acting careers were in various stages of decline. The seeds of this can be traced back to July of 1962 when the United States Justice Department crushed MCA Inc.'s Hollywood monopoly. This forced MCA, who were in the process of acquiring control of Universal Pictures, to dissolve its talent agency which, though formidable, was only accounting for roughly ten percent of MCA's revenue. Since MCA represented most of the top stars in Hollywood, the dissolving of the talent agency left many stars adrift and rudderless—especially Tony Curtis and Janet Leigh.

Things would never be the same for Curtis and Leigh—or Hollywood—following the agency's demise. By the mid-1960s, Leigh was becoming firmly-entrenched in television work, doing numerous episodic television guest appearances and made-for-television movies. Tony Curtis was still hanging onto his movie career, but his recent films—forgettable, mediocre efforts like *Boeing-Boeing* (1965), *Not with My Wife You Don't* (1966), *Arrivederci, Baby* (1966) —were destroying his box office credibility and revealing Curtis to be out-of- step with the edgier, more exciting kind of film-making that would define the end of the 1960s in such watershed films as *Bonnie and Clyde* (1967), *The Graduate* (1967), and *2001: A Space Odyssey* (1968).

Curtis' most substantial film role during this period—and his most notable contribution to the type of genre film- making that would largely define both Jamie Lee Curtis' and Janet Leigh's film careers—came in 1968 with Curtis' brilliant portrayal of serial killer Albert DeSalvo in the film *The Boston Strangler*. Curtis had first heard about the role in December of 1967 when producer Robert Fryer was looking everywhere for the right actor to play the infamous killer. "My career was losing momentum," said Curtis. "I needed a new challenge. I needed a new kind of movie. *The Boston Strangler* was it."

It was a role Curtis had to fight for. Curtis covered his face in putty and makeup, and dyed his hair black, to convince producer Fryer and 20th Century Fox's Richard Zanuck that he could be convincing in the role, that he could be the opposite of the blue-eyed Tony Curtis the public knew so well. Curtis also gained 40 pounds for the role, for which he drew upon his own numerous experiences with psychiatry in order to unlock the identity of DeSalvo's twisted mind. Even more difficult for Curtis, in terms of his performance, was that the film was structured so that DeSalvo doesn't appear on-screen until over 45 minutes into the film.

Directed by Richard Fleischer, and co-starring Henry Fonda, the film took a semi-documentary approach to DeSalvo's rampage with Curtis chillingly mimicking DeSalvo's multiple personalities, as well as acting out—in the film's most disturbing scenes—both the victims' deaths as well as DeSalvo's own sick sexual enjoyment from the murders. Released in 1968, *The Boston Strangler* was a box office success with strong critical praises for both the film and especially Curtis' adventurous and risky performance. *The Boston Strangler* represented Curtis' best acting in over a decade, so much so that he was considered a shoo-in for an Oscar nomination.

Shockingly, when the list of 1968 Oscar nominees was announced, Curtis' performance was overlooked. This may have been due to the political climate at the time, the film's subject matter, or the fact that Curtis doesn't appear on- screen for such a long period of time. Regardless, Curtis' omission was a clear oversight—and is considered to be one of the more glaring oversights in the Academy's history—and perhaps the clearest evidence of this is the fact that 1968's Best Actor Oscar winner turned out to be Cliff Robertson for his rather bland and forgettable performance in *Charly*. Worse, Curtis' triumph in *The Boston Strangler* didn't seem to revitalize his stalled film career. Although the film had earned Curtis his best notices in a decade, more good film roles didn't follow.

When a Hollywood star's career goes into decline—especially two stars who accomplished what Tony Curtis and Janet Leigh did in their careers—it's a merciless, slow, steady fall. This forces the star to pivot and transition into a new persona in order to stay in the Hollywood game and keep working. When the film career fades away, as it inevitably does for almost every Hollywood star, the star must transition to character roles, and then to television. When television roles dry up, the star must then consider theater. It's not a pretty sight.

By 1970, Jamie Lee Curtis' parents were both in various positions on this Hollywood carousel. By this time, Leigh had been working in television for several years, and now Tony Curtis was making the transition from film to television. In April of 1970, Curtis traveled to London for discussions on a proposed television series called *The Friendly Persuaders* (later re-titled *The Persuaders*) which would team Curtis with Roger Moore who was on the verge of donning the iconic James Bond persona that would make him a superstar.

At London's Heathrow Airport, Tony Curtis was detained and arrested for possession of marijuana. Curtis had recently been recruited by the American Cancer Society as national chairman for their anti-smoking campaign. It wasn't really a big deal—resulting in a $120 fine and no jail-time—but because of Curtis' notoriety, the tabloids were all over it. It was also difficult for Jamie Lee, who was eleven at the time and attending the John Thomas Dye school in Los Angeles (9). Predictably, the news of her father's arrest made Jamie Lee the target of ridicule by her fellow students. "The kids at school would joke with me with a stupid poem that went "Your father's Tony Curtis and your mother's Janet Leigh. Your father just got busted and your mother is free," recalled Curtis. "The kids teased me a lot about my parents but it wasn't so bad that I would run home crying every day."

Not surprisingly, being the child of famous parents made it difficult for Jamie Lee Curtis to establish her own identity. Curtis' self-consciousness—and her lack of confidence in her own abilities and fragile sense of self- worth—would haunt her into her early twenties, even after Curtis achieved film stardom with *Halloween* in 1978. "I remember my mother would take me and my sister on ski trips to Bear Valley and the press would be there and they'd spell my name wrong in the papers," recalls Curtis. "When I met somebody, I'd be introduced as Tony Curtis' and Janet Leigh's daughter, or people would just refer to me like that. It messed with my head. I was a kid trying to establish my own identity and I felt that Hollywood was making me wonder who I was. It wasn't until I got to be about twelve or thirteen —when children develop emotionally and sexually—that I began to adjust. High school was fucking hell for me."

Curtis began high school at the infamous and ultra-exclusive Beverly Hills High, a school that Curtis would recall as a "designer school chock-full of chowderheads." The school functioned as a home for the spoiled children of the Hollywood elite, a category that Curtis certainly didn't fit into. 1970s teen idol Shaun Cassidy was a fellow student of Curtis' during her time at Beverly Hills High. "When I grew up, I had nothing in common with anybody," recalled Curtis. "There was nothing binding us. No force, no important music. We had Shaun Cassidy. I mean, no offense to Shaun—because I knew him, went to school with him. But we had nothing. I mean, if we all went out to dinner, say five people, we'd have nothing to talk about to get us excited. No music, movies. Disco! Where were The Beatles, Elvis? All I had was David Cassidy. What else did we have in the seventies?"

Unlike the other kids at Beverly Hills High, Curtis had been living in a modest house in Benedict Canyon, located near a dirt road, a product of Leigh's attempts to raise Jamie Lee away from the limelight. "I was not a Hollywood child," said Curtis. "I've never been one. Even though I'd grown up with famous parents, my mother had always taught me to respect money, and where it came from, and how hard you have to work to get money. Mom encouraged me to be like a typical California girl and go to parties and join the cheerleading team, stuff like that. I used to wear my sister's hand-me-down dresses, and then we'd give our clothes to charity. My mother also raised me to have strong morals, and that was hard to maintain when I was going through high school."

Unhappy with the environment at Beverly Hills High, Leigh enrolled Curtis in the academic-based Westlake School for Girls in Los Angeles. Curtis stayed at Westlake, a school that Curtis felt much more comfortable in than she had at Beverly Hills High, until the Fall of 1975 when Janet Leigh relocated to New York City for the purpose of making her Broadway debut, opposite Jack Cassidy, in the Bob Barry play *Murder Among Friends* (10).

Unsure of leaving Jamie Lee unattended back in California, Leigh enrolled Curtis at the prestigious Choate- Rosemary Hall school, located in tony Wallingford, Connecticut. The preppie boarding school was quite a change of pace for sixteen-year-old Curtis who discovered, quite rudely, that her Hollywood pedigree gave her little currency amongst her fellow students. "The kids were all really snobbish and they weren't impressed with Bernie Schwartz's kid at all," recalls Curtis. "I was totally out of place at the school, from the first day I arrived. I showed up for my first day with my hair frosted, and I had bell-bottoms on. The other kids were all wearing preppie clothes. I went to Brooks Brothers and bought some clothes after my first day so I'd look like the other kids. I wanted to fit in. Whatever the other kids were doing, I would follow. There were also a lot of kids doing drugs, and it was my first time being around all of that. I wanted to be like everyone else."

Curtis' fellow students at Choate recall her as a bright, confused, willowy beauty who possessed a great deal of energy but lacked focus. Curtis felt completely ostracized and singled-out because of her famous last name. "I only had two friends at Choate, one of whom was one of the few Jewish girls at the school, and the other was an exchange student from Iran named Ali," recalls Curtis. "I was singled out as much as they were for being Iranian and Jewish. I was from Hollywood, the daughter of Bernard Schwartz and Janet Leigh. High school was a fucking killer."

Choate had an active theater program, but Curtis found the atmosphere restrictive and snobbish. Jamie Lee auditioned for a production of *Oklahoma!* that was being held at the school, and it was here that she won her first acting role: the non-speaking part of a lass who periodically scoots across the stage and lifts up her dress for the audience to see. This inglorious introduction to "real acting" no doubt contributed to Curtis' distaste for stage and theater acting, and the art form in general. "I don't think studying theater or acting on stage prepares you for a career in film and television, which is what I wanted," says Curtis. "It's not a realistic environment. The biggest thing is the way the camera moves in film and television and one of the biggest challenges I discovered with acting on television and film was acting when the camera was right in front of me. You don't learn any of that in theater."

Curtis also didn't believe in taking acting classes. In fact, throughout her early film and television career, Curtis would rely on Leigh for acting advice and support. "I never took many acting classes when I was younger," recalled Curtis. "When I was a child, mommy would take me to all the movie sets she was working on, all around the world. I tapped into those memories when I started acting. I didn't see how you could learn much from being taught by out-of-work actors. Why should I study with them when I can get lessons for free from a woman who's been in the business as long as my mother? I also sort of taught myself how to act. I learned on the job."

Curtis' reliance on her mother as an acting teacher was more a testament to the close bond between mother and daughter than it was an agreement on how acting should be approached. Leigh, a product of the MGM assembly line, subscribed to the conventional methods of acting study that Curtis would shun in her own career. "My mother learned a lot at those old MGM classes," said Curtis. "When she was under contract to the studio, they had all kinds of classes – acting, dancing, speech. My mother learned so much there that she is a firm believer in studying acting. I'm not."

At the end of Curtis' last year at Choate in 1976, Curtis' last year of high school, it came time for Curtis and her fellow students to create yearbook inscriptions. Curtis, whose time at Choate had been like a gauntlet of psychological tests, had a lot of strange feelings stored in her head when she wrote the following inscription for the 1976 Choate yearbook: "Weirdness is a virtue that only some can project successfully. My bosoms aren't big, but they're mine." "I look back on that and think I must've been crazy when I wrote that," recalled Curtis. "All of the other kids were writing all of these deep intellectual things, quoting famous writers, and I wrote about my tits. It was weird."

The odd yearbook inscription reveals both Curtis' fear of the future—the fear of the unknown in terms of what she was going to do for the rest of her life—as well as the continued sense of alienation that Curtis and many 1970s teenagers felt growing up in this most nonspecific decade. Although the 1970s would ultimately be regarded as a golden age in both film and music, especially film, it wasn't so great for the teenagers that were actually there. "The yearbook thing was my way of saying that I was lonely," recalls Curtis. "I was saying that only a few of us can be truly weird. I was also afraid of not making a mark in the world, of not making an important contribution to the world in some way. I had a huge identity crisis, a monster identity crisis."

As high school ended, Curtis had no intention of following in her parents' footsteps and pursuing an acting career. In 1976, after graduating from Choate, Curtis—whose combined SAT score was 840—enrolled at her mother's alma mater, the University of the Pacific, located in Stockton, California. Curtis' older sister, Kelly, was studying at Skidmore College, a liberal arts college in Saratoga Springs, New York (11). Curtis began classes in the Fall of 1976. Curtis was studying law at Pacific—with an eye on a possible career in working with troubled children—when she was confronted with her show business destiny, quite by chance. "Even though I grew up with Hollywood all around me, I stumbled into a show business career by accident," said Curtis. "The curriculum I was taking at college had a course in Drama, and that's how it started. That's when I started thinking about acting as a career. Looking back, I don't think I was very scholastic."

Curtis took some acting classes while at Pacific and was unimpressed with the experience. Curtis had never been a fan of theatrical acting and she discovered that college acting classes provided little practical training for screen acting, which was all that Curtis was interested in. "I don't think that college acting classes are suitable for film or television acting," said Curtis. "Nobody gives classes in film technique. I feel it's a very simple thing—acting. If you let it be, it really is very easy to do. But film acting should be taught and I didn't see any of that at college. I remember in college having to memorize a list of terms in theater—downstage, upstage. But nothing for film-talk. What is cheating for the camera? What is a close-up? What is an off-camera look? What is a two-shot? I respect theater actors, but acting for film is completely different."

The Drama course called for Curtis to write a paper on the topic of "How to Break into the Business." It was a subject perfectly suited for Curtis who'd grown-up amidst Hollywood royalty and had witnessed the ups and downs of her parents' acting careers. The subject was about to become Curtis' life.

During Christmas break from school, in December of 1976, Curtis decided to return to Los Angeles and attend some acting auditions. Although Curtis' stated purpose for this was research for her college paper, Curtis would quickly become intrigued with acting—screen acting—in terms of a possible career. The paper would have to wait. Leigh, who had always tried to raise Curtis outside of the Hollywood glare, was skeptical, and wary of Curtis quitting school. Leigh was excited about the prospect of Curtis graduating from college and pursuing a "normal career," anything but the business that had turned her own life upside down. Seeing how enthralled Curtis was with the idea of becoming a professional actress, Leigh gave her blessing, but only if Curtis won a screen role before her Christmas vacation was over. If she didn't land a paying role, Curtis would have had to resume her studies at Pacific.

Curtis went to Los Angeles in mid-December, anxious to go on auditions and try the acting game. Enter Chuck Binder, a fledgling tennis instructor and aspiring talent manager who would end up being Curtis' first manager, and would be largely-responsible for helping to kick-start Curtis' acting career. Binder and Curtis, who was an avid tennis player herself, were casual friends and when Curtis told Binder of her interest in pursuing an acting career, Binder had his inspiration (12). "I was giving tennis lessons at the time and I knew Jamie and her family a bit," recalls Binder. "I was getting older, and my Dad was forcing me to make a decision about a career, and when I met Jamie I decided to try being a talent manager because I felt she had talent and I thought I could help her get started."

Unquestionably, Jamie Lee Curtis had numerous advantages over the millions of other aspiring actors that have circled around Hollywood over the years. Having famous parents who'd both had illustrious careers translated to having powerful family friends. Curtis' godfather was Hollywood powerhouse Lew Wasserman, a close friend and former agent of Curtis' parents who was, by 1977, an entrenched Hollywood titan who operated with undiluted power from his domain at MCA/Universal. Wasserman, who died in 2002, wasn't just one of the most powerful people in Hollywood, but is also credited with nurturing the careers of many Hollywood greats, from Jamie Lee Curtis' parents to Steven Spielberg.

Still, being the child of famous parents is a real double-edged sword in terms of the child trying to make it on their own. In terms of getting a foot in the door—which can be an impossible feat for many aspiring actors—it's a great advantage. After crossing that threshold however, a famous last name is usually more of a curse than a blessing. Regardless, Curtis disputes that nepotism—in terms of being Wasserman's goddaughter—played any part in kick-starting her acting career. "He was in Europe when I got hired," said Curtis. "No one believes that of course, but it's true. When I started, I was just another actress."

Whatever influence Jamie Lee Curtis' family connections had on her early career, it's not a big surprise that Curtis' first successful audition took place during a casting session at Universal Studios. Actually, it was Chuck Binder who was responsible for Curtis' introduction to Universal, as well as her first audition. This was a result of Binder's relationship with Thomas D. Tannenbaum, the then-Vice-President of Universal Television whom Binder had also been giving tennis lessons to. "The same time that I was giving tennis lessons to Jamie, and talking to her about her career, I was giving tennis lessons to Tom Tannenbaum who ran Universal television," recalls Binder. "I put Jamie and Tom together and that's how Jamie's acting career really got started."

At the end of 1976, just days before Curtis' Christmas break from school was about to expire, Binder brought Curtis to Tannenbaum at Universal. "Tom looked at Jamie and he said, 'Well, I know her mother, I know her father...I don't care' and that was kind of it in terms of Jamie getting signed to a contract at Universal," recalls Binder. "Then Tom turned Jamie over to Monique James, the head of casting at Universal Studios, and I think Jamie met with her for two minutes and then she was signed to a contract. It all happened fairly quickly."

Although Curtis has always regarded the legendary Monique James as the person who provided her with her first acting break, it was really Chuck Binder and Thomas Tannenbaum who were most responsible for laying the groundwork for Curtis' fledgling acting career (13). When Curtis met with Monique James, Curtis read a scene from the play *Butterflies are Free* which was written by Leonard Gershe with whom Janet Leigh had a warm friendship. Ultimately, James would take a warm liking to Curtis and would become one of the first champions of Curtis' acting career. "She was there when I did my reading, and I was offered a contract," recalls Curtis who was living with her mother and stepfather at their Beverly Hills home at this point. "It all happened very quickly and I was very excited."

By the dawn of 1977, Jamie Lee Curtis was officially under contract to Universal Studios in the form of a seven year contract that would pay eighteen year old Curtis $235 a week, although this number quickly moved to $285 once Curtis started working. Curtis' contract, and Curtis was just one of a legion of young actors under contract to Universal at this time, represented the last days of the studio contract system in the late 1970s. Curtis called her godparents, Edie and

Lew Wasserman, after she'd signed her contract, although it would be naive—especially given Thomas Tannenbaum's role in Curtis being signed—to think that all-powerful and omniscient Lew Wasserman didn't already know. Regardless, Curtis' subsequent career would put to rest any notions of favoritism or nepotism.

One of the first roles Binder tried to book Curtis into was the title role in *Nancy Drew* (also known as *Nancy Drew Mysteries*), a series that would air in revolving tandem with *The Hardy Boys* between 1977 and 1978. *Nancy Drew* was being shepherded by Thomas Tannenbaum and would begin shooting in early January of 1977. This was an era where television episodes would be shot and then broadcast sometimes two, three weeks later. *The Hardy Boys/Nancy Drew Mysteries* debuted on January 30, 1977, but not with Curtis in the role of Nancy Drew. Although Curtis auditioned for the role of Nancy Drew, a part that Binder thought she'd be perfect for, the part went to actress Pamela Sue Martin (14).

This would be the first of many disappointments and false-starts in Curtis' long acting career to which Curtis was unfazed. It was 1977 and Jamie Lee Curtis, who was represented at the start of her acting career by Creative Artists Agency (CAA), was now officially an actress, a vocation for which rejection was an inexorable element (15). The period between February and June of 1977 would see Curtis, as dictated by her contract, make a series of guest appearances on American television shows, all under the Universal banner.

Jamie Lee Curtis' first credited acting appearance was as a glorified extra (she was credited as "girl in dressing room") in a 1977 episode of *Quincy M.E.* entitled *Visitors in Paradise*. That appearance, which aired on February 18, 1977, was followed by a guest role on an episode of, ironically enough, *Nancy Drew* and then a small part as a waitress in a *Columbo* television movie entitled *Columbo: The Bye-Bye Sky High I.Q. Case*.

In July of 1977, Jamie Lee Curtis landed her first major role in the form of a featured co-starring role on a prospective new television series from ABC entitled *Operation Petticoat*. Starring television veteran John Astin, the show was a television remake of the 1959 feature film *Operation Petticoat* that starred Tony Curtis and Cary Grant. Ironically, *Operation Petticoat* was the first film Tony Curtis made following Jamie Lee's November 1958 birth and, perhaps not coincidentally, it was also his last big hit.

Curtis was cast as Lt. Barbara Duran—a character that had been played by actress Dina Merrill in the feature film version—on the naval comedy series, one of several attractive female subordinates to Astin's wacky lieutenant commander character. The irony of starring in a television series based on a film starring her father wasn't lost on Curtis. "I told him about it and we both laughed about it," recalls Curtis. "I learned a lot from doing the show in terms of being on the set and learning my lines. I used to joke that doing *Operation Petticoat* was kind of incestuous for me because I was playing a character who romanced my father in the film version. That was weird."

Between August of 1977 and January of 1978, Curtis filmed twenty-two episodes of *Operation Petticoat* which would eventually air on ABC between September of 1977 and May of 1978. By February of 1978, Curtis was at the end of her run on *Operation Petticoat*, although she didn't know it at this time. The first season's ratings had been poor, the series' scripts were formulaic and tepid, and the show was burdened with an overpopulated cast. *Operation Petticoat* definitely hadn't been Jamie Lee Curtis' ticket to stardom.

By this time, Curtis had already grown bored and weary with episodic television and was facing the hard reality that her acting career didn't seem to be going anywhere. "It wasn't that I hadn't been getting parts because I'd been working on television fairly steadily since 1977, but I wasn't getting to do anything interesting," recalls Curtis "With *Operation Petticoat*, I was getting one line every week and I was one of eighteen people on that show, which is no fun. No one was going to give me a feature film, that's for sure, because television actors really had a tough time making the transition to movies back then. I was starting to wonder, before *Halloween* fell into my lap, if I would make it as an actor."

The contract with Universal, which had seemed like such a godsend—and which Curtis is eternally grateful for—just a year earlier, had now—by 1978—become an albatross, trapping Curtis in a hell of repetitive television guest roles. The initial excitement, felt by all aspiring actors, of just "working" had ebbed for Curtis. What Jamie Lee Curtis needed, in order to show Hollywood what she was truly capable of as an actress, was a movie.

It was the late 1970s, a time when being a "television actress" carried an awful stigma. Television actors weren't allowed to make the transition to feature films. It didn't happen back then. There were no

George Clooneys during this era, although John Travolta had done the impossible—in the 1970s—by escaping the sitcom *Welcome Back Kotter* and catapulting to film stardom with his great performance in 1977's *Saturday Night Fever*. For every John Travolta there were ten Henry Winklers. The situation was even worse for teenage actors like then-nineteen year old Jamie Lee Curtis.

Unlike today, where teenage actors can earn millions of dollars per film, and are given the freedom to move in all kinds of different creative directions, there were few teenage movie stars for Curtis to look up to for inspiration in 1978. Jodie Foster and Tatum O'Neal were probably the two most popular young movie stars in Hollywood at this moment.

Jodie Foster had recently scored a dramatic triumph, and an Oscar nomination, for her performance in the film *Taxi Driver* (1976). Tatum O'Neal, who'd previously won an Oscar for her performance in the film *Paper Moon* (1973), had recently established a new baseline for the salaries of young stars when she'd been paid a then-whopping $350,000 to star in the 1976 comedy film *The Bad News Bears*.

Given these prospects, it's maybe not surprising that Jamie Lee Curtis' first feature film, her screen debut, would arrive in the form of a low budget horror film from a largely unproven young film-maker who had only one cult feature film under his belt. Bored and exhausted with the repetitive and tired world of episodic television, Curtis was ready for any feature film opportunity that might come her way.

This was *Halloween*.

two

INTRODUCING LAURIE STRODE

Hollywood was a much different place in 1978—the year that Jamie Lee Curtis made her feature film and scream queen debut—than it is now, or certainly was years earlier when Curtis' parents were still major film stars. By 1978, Janet Leigh's film career was long over and her current acting career consisted of regular guest appearances on episodic television, not to mention an endless stream of made-for-television movies that seemed to define and dominate the 1970s television era (1).

By 1978, Tony Curtis' film career was in steep decline, although his well-received performance in 1976's *The Last Tycoon*, a film that starred Robert De Niro and was directed by Elia Kazan, had given his career a boost (2). He was hanging on. Regardless, the name Curtis still meant something in Hollywood, just like the name Curtis still means something in Hollywood today. Tony Curtis and Janet Leigh were, regardless of their current power status as of 1978, prestigious Hollywood celebrities with a storied list of film credits. Jamie Lee Curtis was a part of Hollywood royalty.

One of the biggest differences in comparing the Hollywood of this era to the Hollywood of today—in terms of the beginning of Curtis' own acting career—is in terms of the power of the celebrity media, the paparazzi. While the paparazzi were still powerful in the late 1970s, much more than they are today where celebrities can seemingly ignore them without any fear of retribution, they no longer had the power to make or break careers which had certainly been the case when Tony Curtis and Janet Leigh were at the height of their careers.

Still, Jamie Lee Curtis played along with the media, doing fluffy ingenue news pieces and arranged softball interviews with the various puff celebrity movie magazines that were still abundant in the 1970's, the last links to old, trashy Hollywood. Curtis also made the rounds of the Hollywood variety talk show circuit, most notably in October of 1977 when Curtis appeared, along with her mother, on Dinah Shore's self-titled variety show *Dinah!*

The Dinah Shore appearance had been a way of introducing Curtis, who'd just begun work on *Operation Petticoat*, to the American public. The subject of the show concerned the children of famous parents, a subject that Curtis was certainly qualified to be considered an expert on. One of the other guests was Robert Carradine, then known as Bobby Carradine, the son of legendary Hollywood character actor John Carradine and the brother of actors David and Keith Carradine. The Carradines, like the Curtis family, were Hollywood royalty and Robert Carradine, like Jamie Lee Curtis, was at the dawn of his own acting career.

Carradine and Curtis began dating shortly after their appearance on *Dinah!* but Curtis was focused on her acting career and the two young actors eventually parted amicably. Curtis also dated Jack Ford, the son of former American president Gerald Ford, during this period (3). By the dawn of 1978, Curtis was single and living alone in a small apartment Curtis had rented after she'd started working at Universal. Curtis' career was first and foremost.

On this front, things had become somewhat shaky. In February of 1978, Curtis wrapped filming on her first season of *Operation Petticoat*. By March of 1978, *Operation Petticoat* was on hiatus, which would turn out to be a permanent hiatus since Curtis and the rest of *Operation Petticoat*'s first season cast wouldn't be asked to return for the filming of the series' second and last season (4).

Even though the *Operation Petticoat* purge extended to the entire cast and not just Curtis, and represented a complete overhaul of the show, the dismissal was an embarrassment for Curtis given that the series was, after all, inspired by a film that Tony Curtis had made famous. Sure, *Operation Petticoat* was a terrible show, but why would ABC get rid of Tony Curtis' daughter? What about Lew Wasserman's influence at Universal, the company that was producing the series? Was Jamie Lee Curtis that bad of an actress? It made people wonder.

Curtis tried not to take her dismissal from *Operation Petticoat*, which wouldn't be made official until May of 1978—when Curtis' final episodes would air—as a personal failure, rationalizing herself as a "superficial casualty of the revamping of the show." Still, by March of 1978, Curtis was an out-of-work actress looking for a job again. The thought of a movie career seemed like a pipe dream.

Enter John Carpenter, a thirty year old film-maker who would turn out to be Curtis' cinematic benefactor and godfather. John Howard Carpenter was born in Carthage, New York on January 16, 1948 but grew up in Bowling Green, Kentucky, a million miles removed from Curtis' Hollywood upbringing. In 1968, Carpenter, the son of a music teacher, headed to California to study film at the University of Southern California (USC). Carpenter, whose contemporaries at USC included future genre icons like George Lucas and Robert Zemeckis, had left USC by 1972 and although Carpenter had failed to fulfill the school's degree requirements to officially graduate, he would certainly make his mark in cinema, and in Curtis' acting career.

Carpenter's time at USC was certainly productive, much more so than most film students who stay until graduation. In 1969, Carpenter had been one of the principals involved with the making of the western short film *The Resurrection of Bronco Billy*. In 1970, *The Resurrection of Bronco Billy* won a student Academy Award, in the Best Live-Action Short category, although school regulations—which were the cause of much conflict between Carpenter and USC – prevented Carpenter and his collaborators from receiving the award which went to the school.

That same year, Carpenter and a rag-tag group of fellow students—most notably Dan O'Bannon who would go on to co-author genre classics like *Alien* (1979) and *Total Recall* (1990) — began work on an ambitious science-fiction satire film entitled *Dark Star*. The film, which began as a short project but which was eventually expanded into a feature film due to a later investment of $50,000, was completed in 1974 and debuted at the 1974 Filmex festival. In January of 1975, *Dark Star* was released in the United States in 50 theaters but despite some glowing reviews, the film was destined to fade into cult obscurity. Carpenter had gotten his foot in the door of Hollywood, albeit barely.

Like Curtis, Carpenter faced tremendous challenges and obstacles in terms of trying to break into mainstream Hollywood feature filmmaking. Although Carpenter and Curtis had traveled from completely different points, and Curtis seemingly had many more advantages in her favor, neither Carpenter or Curtis conformed to the Hollywood paradigm for success. After deciding to leave USC in 1971, and while overseeing *Dark Star's* glacier-like progress, Carpenter paid the bills as a screenwriter-for-hire, an occupation in which Carpenter would flourish between 1973 and 1975.

With his long, stringy hair, and rail-like physique, Carpenter was, much like Curtis, very much an oddball in terms of appearance and image. In 1973, Carpenter, who grew up idolizing gruff old film-making mechanics like John Ford and Howard Hawks, was commissioned by John Wayne's production company, Batjac Productions, to write a script for the screen legend which turned out to be the dark western *Blood River*. While at the Batjac office, Wayne's son, Michael Wayne once joked that Carpenter reminded him of The Hillside Strangler.

Ultimately, *Blood River* wasn't made due to John Wayne's increasingly-failing health, but a script that Carpenter wrote in 1974, a psychological-thriller script entitled *Eyes*, was bought in 1975 and would eventually be turned into the 1978 thriller *The Eyes of Laura Mars*, directed by Irvin Kershner and starring Faye Dunaway. *Black Moon Rising*, another thriller script Carpenter sold during this period, was later made into a 1985 film that starred Tommy Lee Jones and Linda Hamilton. Another script, *Fangs*, was later made into a rather lame 2001 TBS cable movie. Even *Blood River*, the project Carpenter had written for John Wayne, was eventually resurrected as a 1991 made-for-televison movie.

By 1975, Carpenter's career as a screenwriter was certainly thriving, but Carpenter longed to be known as a director. Carpenter's next shot at directing came in November of 1975 when the four-week shooting of the street-western-thriller *The Anderson Alamo*—later renamed *Assault on Precinct 13*—commenced. Conceived by Carpenter as an urban-thriller updating of Howard Hawks' classic western *Rio Bravo*, the low budget feature was a showcase for Carpenter's film-making style which combined the re-imagining of fantasy elements with classic western sensibilities. *Assault on Precinct 13* would later be regarded as a classic—and a model for future "street-western" action films—but much like *Dark Star*, *Assault on Precinct 13* was virtually ignored upon its American theatrical release in September of 1976. Europe would be a different story.

When *Assault on Precinct 13* was screened at the London Film Festival, in December of 1977, it was greeted with thunderous applause from audiences and critics. It's here that the connection to *Halloween*—and Carpenter's connection to Curtis—begins to evolve. Producer Irwin

Yablans, whose distribution company, Turtle Releasing, had released *Assault* in America, was about to start a new company, Compass International, and was so impressed with Carpenter's talent that he offered Carpenter the chance to write and direct what would be the company's first theatrical feature, based on a rough concept Yablans had that was entitled *The Babysitter Murders*.

The premise was simple, very simple—concerning a psychopath who stalks a group of babysitters—but Yablans thought he was onto something special. After much thought, Yablans decided that the story should be set on Halloween night, and would feature the Halloween setting as a key element of the film's terrifying impact. "I just thought Halloween was such a great night on which to base a horror film, to make a horror film from," says Yablans. "I couldn't believe that no one had ever made a film called *Halloween* before. Because everyone can identify with babysitters and everyone can identify with Halloween, I thought it was a great formula."

Carpenter was joined by Debra Hill, Carpenter's girlfriend at this time, who'd been a script supervisor on *Assault on Precinct 13* and was an aspiring film producer. Carpenter and Hill, whose names would become synonymous with each other, wrote a script for *Halloween* in just two weeks. Carpenter would receive $10,000 for his directing and writing efforts, and both he and Hill—who were living together at this time—would receive a share of the profits from the project, which was going to be budgeted at $300,000. In addition, Carpenter would receive complete creative control, something unheard of for someone with Carpenter's feature directing experience. "I thought it was very bold for such a young director to ask for creative control, and that impressed me," recalls Yablans. "I figured, since we were hardly paying John anything to write and direct the movie, the least we could do was to let John and Debra make the movie according to their artistic vision."

The money for *Halloween*, the $300,000, came from a Syrian-born film producer named Moustapha Akkad who was approached by Yablans while Akkad, who was operating under a company called Filmco International, was already pre-occupied with several expensive Arab-themed projects he was mounting during this period. Akkad, who would ultimately become the gatekeeper of the *Halloween* film franchise, was indifferent when Yablans first approached him in early January of 1978. "Irwin told me he had an idea for this horror film called *Halloween* and that it would only cost $300,000," recalled Ak-kad who was killed by a terrorist bombing in 2005. "As a producer, I get very nervous if a film is too cheap or too expensive but I had some extra money, and I decided to give it a shot. I liked the pitch. The combination of Halloween and the babysitters seemed like a good mix to me. Every kid in America has had a babysitter and every kid has been out trick-or-treating on Halloween."

John Carpenter and Debra Hill began pre-production on *Halloween* in March of 1978. This was happening just a few weeks after Carpenter had completed directing chores on a made-for-television thriller entitled *Someone's Watching Me!*, which had starred Lauren Hutton as well as Adrienne Barbeau whom Carpenter would later marry. "I moved onto *Halloween* about two weeks after I'd shot *Someone's Watching Me!* and the pre-production on *Halloween* lasted about six or seven weeks," recalls Carpenter. "Because we had so little money, Debra and I, especially Debra, wanted to be as prepared as possible before we started shooting."

Jamie Lee Curtis first heard of *Halloween* in March of 1978. Although Curtis was being represented by CAA, the same agency that represented her mother, there was no way a respectable talent agency like CAA—where Curtis was being watched over by Leigh's agent and CAA co-founder Rowland Perkins—would be involved with a low budget project like *Halloween*. It was only reluctantly that CAA told Curtis about the *Halloween* project. "My agent received the script for *Halloween*, and he was reluctant to even tell me about it because there was so little money," recalls Curtis. "At that point I was ready to audition for anything, especially a movie. I'd just been fired from *Operation Petticoat* and I was basically a television actress who'd never made a movie before."

When Curtis read the *Halloween* script, her focus was on the role of Laurie Strode, *Halloween*'s seventeen year old heroine. All motion picture screenplays are essentially blueprints, and that was especially the case with the John Carpenter-Debra Hill *Halloween* shooting script that had been hastily completed by the beginning of February. Without the foresight of the artistic technique and visionary camera-work that Carpenter and the rest of the *Halloween* crew would ultimately reveal, *Halloween* seemed, at its basest form, like a primitive and simplistic horror-thriller about a group of babysitters being stalked by a psychotic killer.

That was Curtis' first thought upon her first reading of the *Halloween* script. She didn't care. *Halloween* was a feature film, and Curtis, who wasn't familiar with any of Carpenter's previous work other than being told of *Assault on Precinct 13*'s popularity in Europe, was willing to make any film. She was, despite the sporadic television work that was undoubtedly still available to her at Universal, an out-of-work actress. Her career was at a standstill. "I often wonder what would've happened in my career, or if I would've had a career, had *Halloween* not come along," recalls Curtis. "If it hadn't been for *Halloween*, I don't know if I could've stuck with it for much longer."

There was one strong quality Curtis observed in her reading of the *Halloween* script that stuck with the actress, and that was the fact that Laurie Strode—the part that Curtis would soon audition for— was the film's lead, and was a strong and resourceful character. "The *Halloween* script wasn't a gem by any means, but it's hard to think of *Halloween* without seeing Debra's and John's vision and what they did with the script," says Curtis. "What I did like when I read the script was that I was going to be the lead in this film, and that the character of Laurie Strode seemed to be the smartest character in the story, a very resourceful heroine. When I read the script, I kept turning the pages and seeing 'Laurie' on almost every page. I was shocked to see that my character would have so much to do in the film."

The plot of *Halloween* was very simple, deceptively so. The story opens on Halloween night, 1963, in the cozy Midwestern town of Haddonfield, Illinois. A six-year old boy named Michael Myers stabs his promiscuous older sister, Judith Myers, to death and is then sent to a mental institution, Smith's Grove, for fifteen years where he's watched over by an obsessive psychiatrist named Dr. Sam Loomis (5). On October 30, 1978, Myers escapes the institution and returns to Haddonfield, to his hometown, to once again wreak havoc—on Halloween night no less. Laurie Strode is babysitting that night, across the street from her girlfriend Annie who's also a babysitter, and they become Michael Myers' main targets, along with a third girlfriend, Lynda. Meanwhile, Dr. Sam Loomis drives to Haddonfield to frantically stop Michael Myers, his most dangerous patient, from unleashing his reign of bloody terror.

It all sounded, without any knowledge of the brilliant cinematic masterpiece that would eventually be created, so primitive and simple. Luckily for Carpenter and Hill at this moment, there weren't a legion of sleazy, cheapjack slasher movies from which to emulate. By 1978, horror films were at a low ebb, both artistically and commercially. The Amicus and Hammer lines of horror films had become decadent and stale. Alfred Hitchcock was near death, and the few talented genre film-makers that were around at this time—most notably Brian De Palma—seemed to view the genre as a stepping stone to bigger and better things, to "legitimate" film work. *Halloween* was going to break the mold. Basically, Carpenter and Hill didn't have to follow any rules because there were no rules to follow. *Halloween* would rewrite the rules of genre film-making.

By the end of March of 1978, John Carpenter and Debra Hill were well into *Halloween*'s planning and pre-production in anticipation of beginning filming in May of 1978. For this purpose, Yablans had rented out a small production office that was located on lower Cahuenga Blvd., a rundown, seedy section of Hollywood. The office would double for the purpose of *Halloween*'s casting which, by March, still hadn't been finalized. "Because I'd moved right from *Someone's Watching Me!* to *Halloween*, and Debra and I had written the script so quickly, I was very tired at this point," recalls Carpenter. "That didn't last long because we were all so full of energy back then. We were all young and excited about making this movie and what this movie could possible turn into."

Jamie Lee Curtis' introduction to Carpenter and Hill was made through Curtis' fledgling manager, Chuck Binder. When Curtis went to the office for the first time, for her audition, she met with Hill, both women completely unaware that this first meeting was going to be the basis for a life-long friendship. Curtis also brought advice from her mother to her meeting with Hill. "She said, 'Be yourself, Jamie,'" recalled Curtis. "You can't learn to act, but you can learn to lose your inhibitions. Find what you need inside. It's in you somewhere."

For this fateful first audition, Hill, who was twenty-seven at this point, asked Curtis to simulate one of the script's many phone conversations. Since Laurie Strode spent much of her time in the script talking to her girlfriends over the phone, Hill wanted to see how well Curtis could communicate in this awkward fashion. "I recall that when Jamie started reading the phone conversations that I was very impressed," recalled Hill. "Jamie really sold the dialogue and I could tell that she'd be believable as this young babysitter. I'd seen Jamie on television, in *Operation Petticoat*, so I knew what she looked like whereas John didn't know anything about her."

Curtis recalls that Hill wasn't entirely sold on whether she possessed the vulnerability that the Laurie Strode role required which is ironic since vulnerability would be the staple of Curtis' genre career. Hill found Curtis' mature physical appearance a bit disarming at first. "Debra didn't think I was suited for the role of an intelligent, repressed babysitter," said Curtis. "Because I am tall, angular, thin, and have a deep voice, I give the impression that I am ballsy and tough. That's not true. I am very vulnerable."

Carpenter hadn't met Curtis yet, but he was already skittish about using her, although he knew that Hill and Yablans—who also liked the marketing aspect of using Janet Leigh's kid in this horror film—were interested in Curtis. Carpenter, who would eventually become Curtis' biggest admirer and supporter, thought the idea was too gimmicky and that audiences might think that the *Psycho* connection was contrived and exploitative. "I hadn't seen Jamie Lee act before that," recalls Carpenter. "I didn't watch television, so I never would've seen *Operation Petticoat*, so I was completely ignorant when it came to Jamie Lee. I just knew that she was Tony Curtis' and Janet Leigh's kid, and I just could see a poster that said, 'Starring the daughter of *Psycho* star Janet Leigh,' something silly like that. As it turned out, I was absolutely wrong, but I didn't know that at the time."

Actually, Carpenter had his sights set on another actress for the part of Laurie Strode. This was Anne Lockhart, a young actress who, like Curtis, was a child of Hollywood as the daughter of former *Lassie* and *Lost in Space* television star June Lockhart. Anne Lockhart was a chestnut-haired young girl who, much like Curtis, was looking to escape ingenue roles and establish herself as a film actress (6). Like Curtis, Lockhart was, by early 1978, already a weary veteran of episodic television. Carpenter was drawn to Lockhart and wanted her to play Laurie Strode in *Halloween*, a character that was named after one of Carpenter's former girlfriends.

Carpenter also vaguely recalls considering an actress who would appear in 1978's *Jaws 2*, possibly Ann Dusenberry, but ultimately it was Anne Lockhart who was Carpenter's first choice to play Laurie Strode (7). Ironically, Carpenter and Lockhart never met, nor was Lockhart—as far as she recalls— ever even made aware of *Halloween*. "I never met John Carpenter, was never told I was offered this role and certainly wouldn't have said no," recalls Lockhart. "I had a manager at the time who I believe passed on the film without ever telling me. Only years later did I hear the story."

Carpenter and Hill then turned their attention to Curtis who was about to meet Carpenter for the first time. For his part, Carpenter was more concerned about the casting for the equally pivotal—although less substantial in terms of actual dialogue and screen time—role of Dr. Sam Loomis, the obsessed psychiatrist trying to stop his most dangerous patient, Michael Myers, from unleashing a murderous rampage upon the peaceful town of Haddonfield, Illinois, a town named after Hill's hometown of Haddonfield, New Jersey. The way *Halloween*'s scripting had unfolded was that Hill had focused on the teenage girl-related parts of the script—the interplay between Laurie Strode and her girlfriends—while Carpenter had focused on the psychiatrist and the story's manifestation of pure evil. As a result, Carpenter viewed the casting of the Loomis character as key to the film.

The *Halloween* script described Laurie Strode as a seventeen-year old girl who was pretty but very shy. Curtis considered herself at the time to be very much a smart-aleck and really couldn't understand how she could ever play such a role, or how anyone else could see her that way. "I was very much a smart aleck back then, the total opposite of Laurie Strode," says Curtis. "The only time I maybe felt that way was when I first went to Choate and I felt like the outsider. That's what I thought of. I was an actress, so I decided to create this character. That's what actors are supposed to do. I don't think anyone who knew me at that time thought I was shy, although I was shy in a way because of my teeth. I never wanted to smile because my teeth were crooked and grey so I would just smirk at people. I think that helped me in playing Laurie Strode."

Nor did Curtis think she was especially pretty, once jokingly referring to herself as "a six" in terms of her sex appeal. Curtis wasn't blonde, she didn't have extraordinarily large breasts, and she wasn't beautiful in the classic sense, certainly not like her mother. Although Curtis would later be regarded as a film sex symbol, in 1978, she was kind of an odd-looking young ingenue with a tomboyish appearance, creaky bone structure, bad teeth, and an androgynous quality that defied classification. Her look was, and is, completely original. She wasn't pretty exactly, nor ugly; she was Jamie Lee Curtis. She didn't look like any of the other young starlets of the period—although Jodie Foster and Kristy McNichol also had a tomboyish appeal—and no one else looked remotely like her.

As always, Curtis sought, and received, valuable advice and counsel from Leigh who understood better than anyone what it was like to be a young actress climbing the ropes in Hollywood. "The best advice my mother gave me was when I was doing *Operation Petticoat*," recalled Curtis. "I thought I was on top of the world. I was eighteen, living alone, and I thought I was great because I was working on this television series. I bought a jeep, wore sunglasses and got my hair frosted, acted like I was this big star. My Mom saw what I was doing and one day she said to me, 'Jamie, they're not going to want you to be 32. They want Jamie Lee Curtis at eighteen, so just be yourself.' That was the best advice I've ever gotten in my career. Those words changed my life."

For her first meeting with both Carpenter and Hill, Curtis, who usually wore tight jeans, decided to act and dress very conservatively in order to convince Carpenter and Hill that she could be Laurie Strode. "When I met with both Debra and John for the first time, I wore an old fashioned dress, very demure, and I had no makeup on at all," recalls Curtis who was aware that another actress, Anne Lockhart, was being considered for the role. "I knew that there was another actress who was being considered and who had done a few movies, and that she was really good, and I knew that John wanted her and Debra wanted me. I don't know how John and Debra ended up choosing me in the end, but I thank God they did."

Curtis, who says she was still a virgin by the time she was sixteen, was bemused that Carpenter would think she could play a character like Laurie Strode who is—as is clearly implied in the *Halloween* script—a sexually-repressed virgin. "If I'd been casting the part of Laurie in *Halloween*, and I knew who I was, I wouldn't have cast me as the shy, virginal babysitter," says Curtis. "The shy part was something I could identify with because it made me think of my time at Choate, so I knew how to walk and talk like a shy girl. Then when I read the script again, I realized that it never actually said that Laurie was a virgin. She certainly looked like she was a virgin, but I also considered the possibility that she'd actually had sex already. Still, I knew that playing Laurie would be an interesting challenge because I would be playing a character who was far away from me in terms of her life and her identity. I knew I would have to find a way to get to Laurie, to reach her."

Curtis met with Carpenter and Hill twice before Curtis was officially given the role of Laurie Strode, which would pay Curtis a mere $8,000. In the end, Carpenter recognized the hidden acting talent that Hill was drawn to when she'd first spoken to Curtis. Combined with the obvious commercial appeal of casting Janet Leigh's daughter, which Yablans was especially drawn to, and the decision to cast Curtis was quickly agreed to by all parties without any argument. "In a way, Jamie kind of reminded me of the kind of woman you'd see in a Howard Hawks film because she had that kind of offbeat beauty," recalls Carpenter. "Originally, I wanted the other girl, and I give Debra credit for pushing me to use Jamie. Debra kept saying, 'Let's try Jamie, let's try Jamie' and when I got to know Jamie, I knew Debra was right."

Ultimately, Carpenter was won over by Curtis' charm and unconventional beauty. Carpenter also saw in Curtis a certain vulnerability that Carpenter felt would be essential in terms of making the audience identify with the Laurie Strode character and the terror she has to endure in the film. "She was just one of several girls auditioning for *Halloween*," recalled Carpenter. "She came in to read. She had a tremendous quality, just tremendous. Different! Very tomboyish in a way. Yet very sexy—and very pretty, no matter what she says."

Carpenter and Hill believed in Curtis, and what she could bring to the film, but Curtis' casting was also, at least to some degree, somewhat of a publicity stunt, at least at the beginning. "It was before we all saw what a great actress she was," recalls Yablans. "At the beginning, all I could see was the name Jamie Lee Curtis, and her connection to Janet Leigh who starred in *Psycho* and how we could exploit that for *Halloween*. I could see the poster in my head. I had this idea that I would make a poster with a picture of Janet Leigh from *Psycho* and a picture of Jamie from *Halloween*, side by side, with a caption that said 'Like mother, like daughter.' I thought, at the time, that would be good publicity. Luckily, none of that ever happened. When I saw how great Jamie was, I realized we didn't need that kind of publicity."

Carpenter was actually more preoccupied in trying to find a name actor—which would be near impossible given *Halloween*'s minuscule budget—he could cast in the role of Dr. Sam Loomis, the driven and tormented psychiatrist who follows Michael Myers to Haddonfield to hopefully prevent his reign of terror. Loomis was, at this time, considered the lead role in *Halloween*. Initially, Carpenter and Hill had offered the role, along with a proposed $25,000 fee, to horror legends Peter Cushing and Christopher Lee, both of whom, to their eternal regret, declined.

Carpenter then turned his focus to Donald Pleasence, the veteran British actor best known for playing the iconic villain Ernst Stavro Blofeld in the 1967 James Bond installment *You Only Live Twice*, although that was just one of many genre roles the enigmatic and legendary actor had portrayed in his career prior to becoming Sam Loomis (8). In fact, it was Pleasence's villainous performance in the 1968 western *Will Penny* that convinced Yablans, who controlled the money, that Pleasence would be inspired casting for the part of Dr. Sam Loomis, part heroic psychiatrist, part crazed madman. "I was a big fan of Donald's work even before we met," recalls Carpenter. "In fact, I was in awe of him. When I mentioned Donald to Irwin, he mentioned seeing Donald in *Will Penny* and we both agreed that he'd be a good choice to play Loomis, if we could get him."

Getting Donald Pleasence to agree to star in *Halloween* was no easy task, although it helped that Pleasence's oldest daughter, Angela Pleasence, had seen *Assault on Precinct 13* at the 1977 London Film Festival and was a fan of Carpenter's work. She recommended *Halloween* to her father who balked at the idea, having found the script that Carpenter forwarded to Pleasence's London agent, Joy Jameson, ludicrous and silly. Eventually, Pleasence agreed to do the film, for a fee of $25,000 which would cover five days of work. Pleasence was actually offered a percentage of the film's profits in lieu of a salary but declined, convinced that *Halloween* would never be successful.

This stringent agreement would necessitate Carpenter and the *Halloween* crew filming Pleasence's scenes in quick succession, quickening what was already going to be a rushed schedule. 1978 was an extremely busy year for the British actor—the busiest period in Pleasence's long career—with the thespian committed to no less than ten different film and television projects. Pleasence, though very much a professional actor, would give *Halloween* no special consideration or thought (9).

Jamie Lee Curtis, who was nervously awaiting the start of filming on *Halloween* that would eventually commence in the first week of May of 1978, was keenly aware of how important Pleasence's casting was to *Halloween*, and how much the actor's involvement meant both to the survival of the project and to Carpenter himself. "I knew getting Donald Pleasence was a big deal for John and for the film," says Curtis. "They put him up at the Chateau Marmont hotel in Los Angeles, and I could see that Debra and John were very excited to have him in the film. Even though Laurie was the lead role in the film, in terms of action and dialogue, I knew they were looking for a big name to play Loomis, to carry the movie in terms of having a name actor in the film. I knew Donald would get top billing, and I understood that totally. I'd seen a few of Donald's films and was very excited about seeing him in the film, although I knew we would only have one scene together in the film."

With Curtis and Pleasence, Laurie Strode and Dr. Sam Loomis, *Halloween* would feature two protagonists. This would be even more intriguing since Curtis and Pleasence would only have one scene together in the entire film. Even though the two characters spend most of *Halloween*'s story apart, their characters are both unified, in a sense, by the fact that they're both fighting the evil presence of Michael Myers—Loomis purposefully and Laurie Strode quite involuntarily. This dual-protagonist relationship would eventually turn out to be just one of *Halloween*'s many innovations.

Even though Curtis and Pleasence would hardly share any screen time in the film, it would be a great challenge for the actors—and for Carpenter—to make the audience feel like Curtis and Pleasence are indirectly working together to fight the evil that's trying to destroy the town of Haddonfield, Illinois. "They had to compliment each other in the film, even though you never see them together until the end," says Carpenter. "They're completely unaware of each other but they have this deep connection, which is interesting. Since we only had Donald for five days, and would be shooting all of his scenes in a block, away from Jamie and the others, I knew this would be a big challenge."

The most important relationship for the Laurie Strode character in the *Halloween* script is, in terms of establishing Laurie Strode's character, the relationship between Laurie and her two best friends, the outgoing and distinctly non-virginal Annie Brackett and Lynda Van derklok. For the role of Annie, Carpenter and Hill created the part for actress and friend Nancy Louise Kyes who had appeared *in Assault on Precinct 13*. Kyes, who at this time went by the name of Nancy Loomis, was then living with future husband Tommy Lee Wallace, a childhood friend of Carpenter's who would perform triple threat duty on *Halloween*, serving as co-editor, production designer, and location scout.

For the part of Lynda, actress P.J. Soles was cast, a buxom blonde who'd recently co-starred in 1976's *Carrie* where she'd played one of the high school students who'd terrorized Sissy Spacek's title character at her own peril, as well as her doomed friends. Carpenter loved *Carrie*, which was directed by contemporary Brian De Palma, and was eager to cast anyone from that film. Carpenter also felt that Kyes and Soles would form a nice counterpoint to the reserved and shy Laurie Strode character which is what Hill, who handled all of the "girl scenes" in the *Halloween* shooting script, had envisioned.

Soles, who'd also been introduced to Hill by Chuck Binder, was married at the time to actor Dennis Quaid, then a rising young actor who was still about a decade away from true film stardom. Actually, Carpenter was interested in having Quaid assume the role of Bob, Lynda's boyfriend in the film. Since Quaid was about to travel to Indiana to work on *Breaking Away*, his breakthrough film role, the role went to an unknown young actor named John Michael Graham.

The relationship between Laurie, Annie, and Lynda would be crucial to the film in terms of establishing Laurie's character. Before the start of filming, Curtis, Kyes, and Soles met with Carpenter at the Hollywood Hills house he shared with Hill to not so much rehearse the script, Curtis recalls, but rather to let the three actresses get to know each other. "I met P.J. and Nancy before the start of filming at John's house and we hit it off right away and I could see we were going to have good chemistry together," recalls Curtis. "We didn't read the script as much as we just talked about the characters and how the three girls fit in with each other. I was the shy type, Annie and Lynda were much more outgoing. That's when John talked to me about the importance of projecting vulnerability in my performance. He told me he wanted the audience to shout at me while I'm on the screen. I didn't understand what he meant until we started filming."

The three actresses formed an interesting dynamic, given that Kyes and Soles were, by the start of *Halloween*'s filming, twenty-eight and twenty-seven years old, respectively, compared to nineteen year old Curtis. While Kyes and Soles undoubtedly had more real-life experiences than Curtis, Curtis was old beyond her years in terms of Hollywood.

As a result, the three girls, the three actresses, formed an interesting dynamic. Whatever their differences, the three actresses got along splendidly from their first meeting and would become like girlfriends on the set, essentially mirroring the relationship their characters would have in the film. "I just found Jamie to be really down-to-earth when I met her," recalls Soles. "She was just no nice and so hard-working and we got along right away."

It's certainly not rare in films for teenage characters to be portrayed by actors in their twenties, even thirties, but the fact that nineteen year old Curtis was close to her character's age helped the actress immeasurably in terms of getting into character as the start of shooting loomed. "Because I was just a year or so out of high school, it was easy for me to tap into those painful memories," recalls Curtis. "It was weird because when I began my acting career, all of my peers were still at college and here I was surrounded by a bunch of people in their late twenties and early thirties. The people I worked with on *Halloween* had been at Woodstock, and seen Vietnam, and I was the only one who'd really grown up in the 1970s."

One of the most important qualities Carpenter saw in Curtis was her ability to display vulnerability. Carpenter saw vulnerability as the key to unlocking the Laurie Strode character and this was something Carpenter and Curtis discussed in detail. "When Jamie was cast as Laurie Strode, we talked about how I felt Laurie had to show a lot of vulnerability in order to make the audience identify with her," recalls Carpenter. "I wanted the audience to identify with Laurie so deeply that they would shout advice at the screen—things like 'Don't go in that house' or 'Run away from there'—throughout the film. That's what a great horror movie heroine is supposed to elicit from the audience. I wanted the audience to love Jamie, and I didn't think the movie would work if they didn't."

Certainly the *Halloween* script was written to maximize Laurie Strode's vulnerability: from Laurie Strode's shy, virginal persona, to the mind-numbing terror that confronts her in the persona of Michael Myers, to the maternal instincts that consume Laurie Strode in protecting the two children in her care from the monster, to Laurie Strode's eventual realization that her best friends have been murdered. Although *Halloween* was a horror film, the role of Laurie Strode would represent an emotional decathlon for Curtis as an actress, and especially as a scream queen.

Curtis was able to grasp all of this from her multiple readings of the script—along with her discussions with Carpenter—and took Carpenter's ideas to heart. "The main discussions John and I had before the start of filming were all about vulnerability," recalls Curtis. "John was very serious when he told me that it was my job to get the audience to love Laurie. John said it would make or break the film which kind of scared me. It was quite a lot of responsibility."

When *Halloween* began filming in May of 1978, Curtis was living in a modest tract house in the San Fernando Valley with Tina Cassaday, a Dallas native who'd graduated from high school in 1975 with a degree in cosmetology and had subsequently traveled to Los Angeles to pursue her dream of becoming a celebrity hairstylist (10). Both women were at the beginning of their careers and looking ahead into the future. For Curtis especially, there was a much greater sense of urgency as the events of 1978, and the filming of *Halloween* especially, would go a long way in determining her future as an actress.

three

THE MAKING OF *HALLOWEEN*

Going into the filming of *Halloween*, no one—not Jamie Lee Curtis or any of the rest of the cast and crew—had any idea of what this project was going to turn into. There was no optimism, no pessimism, but more of a morbid curiosity as to what the final result would turn out to be. "When we began shooting, I had no feelings as to how the film was going to turn out," recalls Curtis. "It was my first film, my first leading film role, and I would've been thrilled to be doing anything. Anyone who says they knew that *Halloween* was going to be a great film is a liar because no one knew. I really thought, at the beginning, that I would either get fired or that because *Halloween* was such a low budget production, the film would get shut down or something like that. I didn't know what to expect."

Halloween began filming in the first week of May of 1978 in South Pasadena, California. The start of filming on *Halloween* would be especially significant because it marked the first screen appearance of Jamie Lee Curtis, and the first appearance of Laurie Strode, *Halloween*'s heroine. The location was Oxley Street, and the setting was the front of Laurie Strode's house, a pleasant two-story house that looked perfectly comfortable within *Halloween*'s fictional Midwestern setting. The fact that the front lawn and streets were peppered with leaves enhanced this illusion.

Of course this wasn't Haddonfield, Illinois but rather South Pasadena, California, and the leaves were fake and had been rustled-up by Carpenter friend and *Halloween*'s jack-of-all-trades Tommy Lee Wallace who also spray-painted the leaves brown for effect. For Curtis, this first day of shooting wasn't going to be very demanding from an acting standpoint. In the scene, Laurie walks out of her house for the purpose

51

of going to high school and says goodbye to her father, real estate agent Morgan Strode, who was played in the scene by actor Peter Griffith, the father of actress Melanie Griffith (1).

Curtis and Melanie Griffith would later become friends when, in 1981, they would co-star in the made-for-television movie *She's in the Army Now*, a film that would represent a much more tumultuous period in Curtis' career and life than the filming of *Halloween* did. The two actresses had another more ironic connection and that was the fact that Curtis' mother, Janet Leigh, had been immortalized by Alfred Hitchcock in *Psycho* while Melanie Griffith's mother, Tippi Hedren had starred in *The Birds* and *Marnie*. Now Jamie Lee Curtis was following in her mother's footsteps.

In the scene, Curtis' first filmed scene in *Halloween* and her first scene ever as a film actress, Laurie Strode's father asks her to drop off a key at the nearby Myers house, a haunted house that acts as the power source for the evil in *Halloween* as it's the birthplace of Michael Myers and the sight where he butchered his sister, Judith Myers, back on Halloween night 1963.

In the next scene, Curtis bumps into young Tommy Doyle, played by Brian Andrews, whom Laurie Strode is scheduled to babysit later that night. They both walk up to the front of the abandoned and creepy Myers house and then Laurie drops off the key while Tommy warns Laurie that the boogeyman lives there, which of course he does. Then Laurie walks down the street, and this is when Michael Myers— nicknamed 'The Shape' in the *Halloween* script, and played by Carpenter friend and aspiring film-maker Nick Castle—appears and silently watches Laurie walk away (2).

That was it. This was the first day of the rest of Jamie Lee Curtis' illustrious film career, and really her life as a future pop culture icon. It all seemed kind of innocuous, especially to Carpenter and Hill who were preoccupied with thoughts of their hurried twenty day production schedule. This included several problematic night shoots, the first scene of which they were planning to film later that night. From Curtis' point-of-view however this first day of filming represented a make-or-break moment in her acting career.

Curtis had arrived on the set—which is a generous description of the humble surroundings given that cinematographer Dean Cundey's Winnebago was the only production vehicle visible at the unsecured location—at seven in the morning, before she was needed, and was wearing a conservative dress with her hair neatly trimmed. She looked like a Midwestern teenage girl who dressed to make her parents happy. Carpenter was impressed. "She looked the part," says Carpenter. "When I'd first met Jamie, she was a real tomboy but when filming started she totally transformed into the character of Laurie, especially with her hair and the clothes she wore. She was the awkward, shy girl in the script."

Before the first day of shooting, Curtis had studied the script meticulously and had worked on "conceptualizing" the look of Laurie Strode. "She was a Midwestern girl and I envisioned that Laurie's mother probably took her to J.C. Penney's a few times a year, during the different seasons, and got all of Laurie's clothes in coordinates," says Curtis who actually bought the skirt and sweater that Laurie wears in the film at J.C. Penney's. "Everything she wore was mix-and-match, right down the line. When I put on the clothes, it really helped me find the character. Laurie was very repressed in a lot of ways, and it's like she's ready to explode. Her friends are very outgoing—in the way they dress and talk and their sexual behavior—and Laurie keeps everything inside, and you see that in the way she dresses."

Not only was Curtis extremely conscious and self-aware about her performance on that first day of filming, but she also had the pressure of trying to gain the confidence and respect of the cast and crew. This would come almost immediately after the cast and crew met Curtis, but at the beginning, Curtis was only recognized as the daughter of Tony Curtis and Janet Leigh which was the only point-of-reference *Halloween*'s cast and crew had for her. Ultimately, Curtis' talent would win over everybody, but at the start of shooting, Curtis' own self-doubt—and her self-consciousness regarding her famous parents—weighed on her heavily. After Curtis completed her first scenes, she retreated into her trailer, Dean Cundey's Winnebago which was nicknamed "The Movie Wagon," for sanctuary.

BRIAN ANDREWS, CO-STAR: When Jamie and I met to film the first scene in the film, she didn't treat me like a child actor, but instead she just treated me like a regular actor. I was very impressed by how present she was an actress, and how easily she could disappear into character. The script for *Halloween*, and especially the dialogue, was very plain, and when Jamie and I were walking towards the Myers house and were talking, it was really impressive how she would take the ordinary dialogue and put a spin on it and make it come to life. She did that throughout the filming.

DON BEHRNS, PRODUCTION MANAGER: She wasn't exactly beautiful in the classic sense but she had a great body, a great personality, and she was a very attractive girl. Every morning, she would walk out of the trailer, and the guys on the crew would line up and just stare at her because she had a great body. You couldn't put your finger on what made her special, on what made her standout from the other girls, but she was definitely an attractive girl.

JOHN CARPENTER, CO-WRITER/DIRECTOR: From the first day of shooting, I could tell that Jamie was going to be great in the film. At the beginning, part of the casting of Jamie was for publicity purposes; I thought it would be great publicity because her mother, Janet Leigh, had been in *Psycho*, but that all went away when we started working. She would've been the best actress for the part of Laurie even if she hadn't been Janet Leigh's daughter, although I don't know if she would've gotten the part. The first day went smooth, and Jamie and I would talk before every scene about what I was trying to do with the scene in terms of creating suspense, and she understood all of that. After the first day of shooting, I knew I didn't have to worry about Jamie, and whether she could do the part, so I could spend all of my time worrying about our schedule and the budget and getting all of Donald Pleasence's scenes filmed.

DEAN CUNDEY, CINEMATOGRAPHER: I think our reaction to Jamie's casting wasn't that it was any kind of a publicity stunt but rather that it represented a very courageous and interesting choice on Debra's and John's part. I'd shot several exploitation and genre films before *Halloween*, and the girls in those films were busty women, models, playboy playmate types. Here we were on *Halloween* casting a shy girl who'd only done some television and was looking to move into features and who didn't think she was pretty. Jamie's casting was an out-of-the-box choice and a very daring move by Debra and John.

KIM GOTTLIEB-WALKER, STILL PHOTOGRAPHER: The first time I met Jamie Lee was in the trailer. I was hired by Debra and John to take photographs, stills, for publicity purposes and so I was on the set all of the time. When I met Jamie, she was very reluctant to have me take her picture at first. She didn't like having her picture taken because she'd grown up with the paparazzi, the tabloids, and she didn't trust me at first. Then one day I walked into the trailer and I saw Jamie looking at my portfolio of work; I'd worked with a lot of great musicians and she saw some pictures I'd taken of Jimi Hendrix and really liked them. At that point, she was happy to have me take her picture, and we even talked about doing some portraits. My most vivid memory of Jamie was how enthusiastic and cooperative she was and how willing she was to pitch in to help in any way.

DEBRA HILL, CO-WRITER/PRODUCER: Since I focused on the female parts in the script, I spent a lot of time with Jamie, and what impressed me was that she was able to find the emotional meaning in all of the scenes, the stuff that existed between the lines. On that first day of shooting, I could see the vulnerability that I'd seen when I first met her.

LOUISE JAFFE, SCRIPT SUPERVISOR: I knew Jamie had been doing *Operation Petticoat*, which was a television show I'd never seen, and I knew she was Janet Leigh's and Tony Curtis' daughter and that everyone was excited that she was going to be in the movie. She had a "name." Jamie Lee was very professional, pleasant, and low-key. She probably had a lot more experience than I had. I think I was twenty-two at the time. We were all pretty young, but energetic and hardworking.

KOOL MARDER, ASSOCIATE PRODUCER: Jamie was very sweet, and she had a sweet sincerity about her. She was excited and happy about doing a movie and Debra and John were the perfect film-makers for her to work with because they brought her along slowly throughout filming which made her confidence grow.

RAYMOND STELLA, CAMERA/PANAGLIDE OPERATOR: When we started filming, we just knew her as Janet Leigh's daughter, but Jamie immediately impressed all of us. I was impressed by how professional she was, and how well she took direction, but what made her really special was that you could see she had a genuine star quality. Some actors have that star quality, that ability to take control of the camera, and most don't. Jamie definitely had that.

RICK WALLACE, ASSISTANT DIRECTOR: *Halloween* was a low budget film and Jamie was a star and her name was always on the top of the call-sheet. At the beginning we knew her as the child of Hollywood royalty, but she made us quickly forget she was the daughter of Tony Curtis and Janet Leigh. She arrived on *Halloween* without any baggage, and she was very open and she didn't have any sort of guile or Hollywood attitude about her. She was kind and genuine and you could tell she was a very innate and natural person.

TOMMY LEE WALLACE, CO-EDITOR/PRODUCTION DESIGNER: Jamie was very young, very aware of her Hollywood pedigree, and she wanted, very much, to be seen as a regular person and a team player. She was friendly and interested in everyone involved, and she went out of her way to chat and hang-out with the cast and crew alike. She seemed mature beyond her years, and had the listening skills and focus to put people at ease, and make them feel valued. I would describe Jamie's basic personality, as of *Halloween*, as a good girl scout, true-blue, forthright, unpretentious, unaffected and very likable. People imagine that it must've been really wonderful being the child of Hollywood royalty, but I suspect for Jamie it was probably something of a burden, for the most part. Jamie felt to me like a survivor of all that, who'd made the best of things, and not let any of it throw her too far off her course, and her goal, which, as she made clear more than once at the time, was nothing more complicated than to be a fairly upright, whole and useful human being.

After her first day of filming, Curtis was too nervous about her own work to really gauge her impression of *Halloween*'s cast and crew, but she was convinced she was around good people. She could sense, even at this point, a synergy, a sense of teamwork that she would ultimately regard as the finest working experience of her career. The *Halloween* set was very much a hippie culture; the crew members were friends, for the most part, and they'd grown up around Berkeley and USC and Woodstock in the late 1960s. They weren't lazy, far from it, but there was a casualness on the *Halloween* set that Curtis found disarming at first, but eventually embraced wholeheartedly.

With a few exceptions, most of *Halloween*'s crew were, like Curtis, at the beginning of their careers. With the exception of the teenage Curtis, most of the *Halloween* crew were in their early to late twenties and for them, like Curtis, *Halloween* represented their big chance to establish themselves as competent, skilled professionals. There was an energy and blissful naivety present amongst *Halloween*'s cast and crew which would result in the most communal and generous of filming experiences. "It was unlike any other set I've been on, and it was the best set I've been on," says Curtis. "Everyone was so cool. When we weren't filming, people would just lie around on the grass and chill. The teamwork was unbelievable. We all chipped-in, whether it was carrying equipment or painting a house, and it made you feel like you were part of something really special."

That first day of filming actually ended on a comic note for Curtis, as she was in Cundey's Winnebago and relaxing after filming her scenes. When she opened the trailer door and looked outside, Curtis was horrified to see that everyone had gone. "It was like a ghost town," recalls Curtis. "They were all gone. They'd all left. I couldn't believe they'd just go without telling me or something, and I took that as a very bad sign. I thought it meant that my performance had been so bad that Debra and John had decided to move on and do something else, or that I was going to be fired, which was honestly what I thought was going to happen after that first day. I remember I just drove around after that and then I went home."

Actually, the rest of the *Halloween* crew, under a tight schedule, had relocated to the Hollywood Hills, near Hollywood Dam, for the filming of a nighttime scene where Dr. Sam Loomis drives up to Smith's Grove Sanitarium—planning to remove Michael Myers and take him to trial—and discovers that Myers and his fellow inmates have escaped. In the next scene, Loomis watches while Myers, played by Nick Castle, commandeers Loomis' car and drives away from the sanitarium, on his way back to Haddonfield. These scenes marked Donald Pleasence's first night of work on *Halloween*, and the first day of his five day contractual obligation which forced Carpenter and Hill to shoot all of Pleasence's scenes consecutively for fear of not having the scenes completed and thus losing Pleasence which would've hamstrung the film.

The fact is that, as far as Carpenter and Hill were concerned, Curtis' performance was the least of their concerns, and this was a part of the reason they felt they could move around and shoot Pleasence's scenes out of sequence. "Debra and I were both very impressed with Jamie's work on the first day," recalls Carpenter. "I saw a star quality on that first day that I hadn't even noticed when I met her for her audition. I don't talk to actors, that's not my thing, so sometimes they'll wonder what I'm thinking, if I like what they're doing or not. I just leave them alone and let them do their thing. If I don't say anything, it means I'm happy. I don't recall ever having to talk to Jamie about changing her performance, or anything she did wrong. The only discussions we had were about where the camera was going to be and how I wanted us to maximize the suspense in the scenes."

Timing is everything in film-making, especially low budget film-making, and *Halloween* is the ultimate example of this in terms of the importance of the filming process getting off to a good start. By staging such an elementary scene on the first day of filming, the scene where Curtis leaves her house and walks down the street, it allowed the *Halloween* crew to find a rhythm, to get their legs. It was a nice, simple beginning for a filming process that would become increasingly more challenging and difficult over the course of *Halloween*'s twenty day filming schedule.

This was especially important since Carpenter and Cundey were utilizing the newly-minted Panaglide camera system for *Halloween*. The Panaglide system, which was Panavision's version of the Steadicam, was useful for Carpenter because the form allowed greater camera movement—and a greater use of all four corners of the screen—while still maintaining a clear, crisp picture. Since movement was one of the key techniques Carpenter wanted to utilize in *Halloween* for the purpose of creating suspense, the Panaglide, despite its burdensome 60 pound weight and shifting parts, was ideal. Carpenter had used the Panaglide on *Someone's Watching Me!* but with *Halloween*, Carpenter, through the efforts of Panaglide Operator Raymond Stella, was going to make the Panaglide a virtual character in the film.

Carpenter's ambitious plans for using the Panaglide would put *Halloween*'s crew to the test, especially in terms of the film's opening scene. This is the scene where young Michael Myers walks into his house, and then goes upstairs and stabs his sister to death. Carpenter planned to film this via one continuous Panaglide shot in what would be a direct nod to the great continuous opening shot in Orson Welles' *Touch of Evil*. It was very ambitious, startlingly-so for such a low-budget production, and would require enormous planning and preparation.

Instead of scheduling the filming of the scene during the start of filming, Carpenter and Hill wisely scheduled the filming of the scene for the last day of filming instead. They also needed time to paint and renovate the decrepit Myers house, located on Mission Street in South Pasadena, in order to make the house resemble the clean appearance it would've had back in 1963. It was a smart move, and an example of the ruthlessly-economical nature of *Halloween*'s filming. It was all about planning. "Having no money on *Halloween* was the best thing for the film," recalled Hill. "It forced us to think really fast, and just get the job done, or in some cases to not think at all. It was shocking how swiftly we would go through the scenes."

Halloween was destined to be all about the camera; the camera was one of the stars of the film. For her part, Curtis had a firm grasp and clear understanding of the camera, one of the few good things that she'd taken from the *Operation Petticoat* experience. "On *Operation Petticoat*, they did a million camera setups a day so I knew about acting in front of the camera, doing closeups, but I learned a lot more about acting in front of the camera on *Halloween*," recalls Curtis. "One thing I learned from a guy on the *Halloween* crew was how to hit a mark. What do you use? A sandbag. That's what I used to hit my marks in the film and it worked great."

When Curtis returned home to the small tract house in the San Fernando Valley her roommate, Tina Cassaday, told her that John Carpenter had called to talk to her. When Carpenter called Curtis back later that night, Curtis was shocked to learn that Carpenter was actually calling to congratulate her on her first day of work. "I thought he'd called to fire me," recalls Curtis. "John called me up and told me that he loved my performance and that he thought I was great, and I was just shocked. That's one of the greatest moments in my career. I just wanted to cry. No other director has every said that to me before. I was on cloud nine. When I showed up on the set the next day, I was a totally different person. I was full of confidence and I felt like I could do anything."

Curtis' next scenes, filmed the following day, revolved around Laurie Strode's persona as a high school student. The first scene took place inside a classroom at Garfield Elementary in Alhambra, California which doubled for a classroom at Haddonfield High School in the film. The school's exterior would later be filmed at South Pasadena High School. In the classroom scene, a daydreaming Laurie Strode is mesmerized by the image of The Shape, Michael Myers, who she sees watching her outside her classroom window.

In addition to wearing garage overalls, which Michael Myers stole from a truck driver he murdered during Myers' return to Haddonfield, Myers—The Shape—is wearing a William Shatner mask—modeled after Shatner's appearance in a 1975 horror film entitled *The Devil's Rain*—he took from a local store he'd broken into. The mask was discovered by Tommy Lee Wallace who'd bought the mask, and several more copies, at Burt Wheeler's Magic Shop on Hollywood Boulevard. Wallace widened the eye-holes and spray-painted the flesh a bluish-white to achieve the appearance that Carpenter had described in the *Halloween* script as having "the pale features of a human face." The result was a Michael Myers, a monster, who looked expressionless, merciless, chillingly remorseless. It was perfect (3).

Before this, Carpenter and Wallace had seriously considered having Michael Myers wear a clown mask in the film, but the visceral power of the whitened William Shatner version won out. The mask itself had a chilling effect on the cast and crew, despite Nick Castle's own lighthearted and pleasant demeanor on the set. "Seeing Nick in the mask was creepy, especially since Nick was such a fun guy to be around when he wasn't in costume," recalls Curtis. "When you see him with the mask on, it's like he's not human. He is the boogeyman."

The scene in the classroom reveals a lot about the Laurie Strode character in terms of telling us how smart Laurie is and what a good student she is as evidenced by the fact that Laurie's able to answer a teacher's question even after being preoccupied with the image of The Shape. The discussion in Laurie's classroom is about the subject of fate which is ironic given that fate, and the cruelty of fate, could be considered *Halloween*'s main theme given the preventable tragedy that ensues in the film.

The film's implication is that if Michael Myers hadn't escaped from Smith's Grove the night before, or if the bureaucrats had listened to Dr. Loomis' dire warnings about Michael Myers earlier, Laurie's life—and the lives of everyone in Haddonfield—would be immeasurably different. This would turn out to be especially true of Laurie's friends, Annie and Lynda. The fact that Michael Myers has escaped is a most unlucky stroke of fate that's about to change, and in many ways shatter, Laurie's life forever. The fact that Laurie's totally unaware of this as she stares transfixed at the specter of Michael Myers that seems to be following her everywhere is also ironic.

Nick Castle had been one of Carpenter's co-collaborators on *The Resurrection of Bronco Billy* while the friends were both at USC where Castle graduated from in 1970. An aspiring director and screenwriter, who would later go on to achieve a substantial career in each field, Castle had been circling the *Halloween* production—focused more on jump-starting his own then-fledgling career—when close friend Carpenter plucked him to play *Halloween*'s masked, silent killer. That wasn't the only reason. "My dad was a famed Hollywood choreographer and I grew up around dancing and performing and I knew a lot about movement," says Castle. "John didn't give me a lot of direction; he just told me to walk, move, stuff like that. I asked John if he wanted me to play Michael Myers like a guy who's been institutionalized for fifteen years, a lifelong mental patient, or to play him as an evil psychopath who's haunted by voices, and I ended up doing both. The key was the walk. I decided that The Shape should walk very deliberately, very slow."

Despite the fact that Castle, as Michael Myers, would torment Laurie Strode throughout the film, there was no tension between Castle and Curtis on the set. In fact, Castle and Curtis would often joke around on the set. The mood between the two was very light and playful, especially when Castle brought his kids to the set and introduced them, along with Castle's wife, to Curtis. When it came time for filming, Castle and Curtis both got into their characters quite effortlessly.

The relationship between Michael Myers and Laurie Strode is very complex and interesting. The key to the relationship, as many film critics and historians would later point out, is that both characters are suffering from deep sexual repression. They're both seemingly virgins and this explains the motivations of both characters. In this regard, Laurie Strode and Michael Myers could be viewed as two sides of the same coin.

The hypnotic trance that Laurie's in during the scene in the classroom, when her eyes are focused on Michael Myers, highlights the sexual repression that her character's virginity has embedded in her. While her girlfriends, Annie and Lynda, are consumed—and eventually distracted to their own peril—by sex, Laurie's virginity gives her a clarity and razor-like focus in *Halloween* in that she only has eyes for Michael Myers. She can see the evil that is around her.

Michael Myers is Laurie Strode's psychotic mystery man, her dark knight in shining armor except he believes that his destiny is not to rescue her but to brutally murder her. "Her girlfriends are obsessed with sex, and Laurie's never had sex so she can see everything that's happening around her more clearly," says Curtis. "It's not that the others are being punished for having sex; that's not it at all. It's that Laurie's more focused. She's not distracted. Of course, I maintain that it never actually says in the script that Laurie is really a virgin. We just assume that. She's sixteen, seventeen, and there's nothing wrong with being a virgin at that age. I was still a virgin at sixteen, but on the other hand, there's a chance that Laurie isn't a virgin."

Michael Myers and his myriad of psychological issues are a whole other story. Institutionalized for virtually all of his meaningful life, he's most certainly still a virgin, and perhaps this is yet another torment on his already crazed psyche. In fact, he's had no female contact for at least fifteen years and his last memory of female contact was when he stabbed his naked sister to death. In *Halloween*, Michael Myers is focused on Laurie Strode. Is he attracted to her?

In *Halloween II*, the 1981 sequel to *Halloween*, it's revealed that Laurie and Michael are long-lost brother and sister which would suggest an incestuous angle to their relationship except for the fact that this brother-sister relationship was an invention of Carpenter's when he was writing the *Halloween II* script in 1980 (4). Carpenter was desperate for new ideas and imagined Laurie and Michael as long-lost siblings, an idea that neither Carpenter or Hill envisioned when they were constructing *Halloween*.

Regardless, Michael's infatuation with Laurie in *Halloween*, which includes both his voyeuristic obsession with Laurie followed later by his relentless stalking, is indicative of some repressed sexuality—some kind of dormant sexual energy—that's buried inside of Michael Myers' psychotic persona.

JOHN CARPENTER: *Halloween* isn't about a guy in a mask who just runs around killing people. It's about violence and sex, and the idea that evil never dies. As for the criticism that sex equals violence in the film, I think that's stupid because Michael doesn't know that any of the victims are going to have sex, or have been promiscuous in the past. Teenage girls are very interested in sex, and when I met with Jamie and the other girls, they were interested in playing the characters that way. Debra and I based the girls on girls we knew growing up. They were girls I knew back in Bowling Green, Kentucky. Laurie represents the shy girls who weren't sexually active, who haven't found their identity yet. Annie and Lynda are sexually active and so they seem to be enjoying life more. Laurie's in pain because she doesn't have much of a social life, and that's more than just sex. The film starts out with young Michael seeing his sister fucking a guy in the upstairs bedroom and Michael killing her for it. In that scene, I viewed that Michael had some kind of incestuous feelings towards his sister, and that's what drove his rage in that scene. If Annie and Lynda were virgins like Laurie, it wouldn't have been believable because the audience can identify with these characters because we all went to high school with girls like this.

JAMIE LEE CURTIS: I felt like Laurie was the smartest character in the story, of the three girls, and that's the reason she survives in the end, not because she's a virgin. When I read the script, I never assumed she was a virgin, because it never said that. I thought maybe she'd had a bad experience with a guy and that had made her shy, or not.

DEBRA HILL: I think people missed the point on this subject. Laurie and Michael are both repressed characters and they both have a lot of repressed sexual energy that kind of drives them crazy. At the end of the film, when Laurie has the long knife and she stabs Michael, it's as if she's letting out all of that sexual energy. That's what's happening.

Curtis' next major scene in *Halloween* was very crucial to understanding the Laurie Strode character in terms of her relationship to friends Annie and Lynda, and the fragile psyche that causes Laurie to be so painfully shy and withdrawn. This is the scene where Laurie and her friends leave Haddonfield High School and walk home in preparation for the Halloween activities that are to occur that night for all of them, although in much different forms for each. Annie and Laurie are babysitting while Lynda has a date with the local jock Bob Simms.

For this scene, the *Halloween* crew moved from South Pasadena High School, where the girls walk out of the school, and went to

Fairview Avenue and Highland Street in South Pasadena. As the girls are walking down the street, they talk about boys, their plans for Halloween night, girl stuff. It all seems very benign, but like everything in *Halloween*, looks are deceiving.

Suddenly, Michael Myers, The Shape, appears. He drives past them on the street in the station wagon he commandeered from Smith's Grove the night before. Annie and Lynda, preoccupied with thoughts of boyfriends, don't take much notice except to yell at the speeding car, but Laurie, trapped in her own lonely world with nothing else to focus on, once again recognizes Michael Myers, The Shape, for the specter, the boogeyman, he is.

The filming of this scene was challenging for Curtis in that Nancy Louise Kyes and P.J. Soles, both of whom had extensive theater backgrounds, decided to use the scene as an opportunity for improvisation. This was something that, in Soles' words, "threw Jamie off a bit at first" as Curtis was used to following the rigid guidelines of a script and had no experience with improvisation. "Nancy and I both had a theater background, and we were both used to improvisation, and Jamie wasn't into that," recalls Soles. "When we filmed the scene, Nancy and I would improvise in the middle of the scene and Jamie would say something like "Are we allowed to be doing this?" John was great that way. If you did something and it worked good he'd use it."

This was the second day of *Halloween*'s filming and the three actresses were already bonding. The ad-lib in the scene was a product of the casual atmosphere that was already present on the *Halloween* set, which in turn was a representation of the freedom that an independent production like *Halloween* could have, even with a tight budget and a tight schedule. "Everyone was just so professional on the set and everyone was helping everyone else out to get the job done," says Curtis. "It was a wonderful environment to work in."

The *Halloween* script also lent itself to such improvisation, particularly in this scene which necessitated improvisation from the actresses given that there wasn't enough dialogue in the script to sustain the scene's extended duration. During one take, Soles, whose character's signature is the repeated use of the word "Totally," decided to pull out a cigarette and use it in the scene. Curtis herself was a smoker, a hobby that would last until the early 1980s. "Most of that scene was ad-lib, although the "Totally" saying I use over and over again was in the script," says Soles. "Jamie wasn't as comfortable with the ad-lib and that's why Nancy and I kind of dominated the conversation in the scene."

The scene where the girls are walking home is, like the effect of the finished film itself, deceptively-innocuous and simple. In terms of *Halloween*'s visual style, the scene is a prime example of the film's powerful use of contrast between daylight and darkness, almost in the vein of a German expressionist film. Although the girls are walking in daylight, they're surrounded by overhanging trees which engulfs them in shadows and makes these daylight images seem creepy and dark. The disturbing suggestion of this approach, which wasn't accomplished with any lighting tricks, is that the boogeyman is everywhere and there's no relief from this malevolent presence, not even in the glow of daylight.

DEAN CUNDEY: When we were filming *Halloween*, I tried to use as much natural lighting as possible, and we chose locations that had overhanging trees which would provide a lot of shadows. When the girls are walking down the street, there was no lighting on the trees, just the shadows from the trees contrasting the daylight. When the girls walked along, they fell under the shadows and that created a lot of menace in the scene, as if the shadows from the overhanging trees represented the monster in the film. We were looking for contrast and mood in terms of the visual look of the film and that scene is a prime example. In terms of Jamie and the other girls, the three actresses worked hard to create believable teenage characters. The relationship between the girls was the same off-screen as it was on-screen and the girls worked at that, and I think you felt a history between the characters in the film.

DEBRA HILL: I wrote all of the scenes between the girls, and when I was writing the girl characters I always went back to when I was a teenager growing up in New Jersey and I recalled the conversations I had with my girlfriends. I was a babysitter myself and I knew girls who were exactly like Annie, Laurie, and Lynda and I based the characters on them.

P.J. SOLES: The scene where the girls walk home, where the car is following us, was shot on our second or third day of production. A lot of it was ad-lib and the three of us were bonding. We all tried to do something different, so I had a cigarette. I remember Jamie wasn't up to the ad-lib thing at that point, so I dominated the on-screen conversation.

RICK WALLACE: There was an interesting dynamic with the three girls because Nancy and P.J. had more life experiences than Jamie did, but Jamie had grown up in Hollywood and had a lot more Hollywood experience. Jamie's Hollywood upbringing wasn't an issue because Jamie was very down-to-earth and she never lorded her Hollywood pedigree over the other girls or the rest of us. Jamie was the same to everybody. She was just like one of us.

TOMMY LEE WALLACE: My impression of the dynamic between Jamie, P.J. and Nancy was that the older and more experienced actresses (Nancy and P.J.) helped their little sister Jamie take on a few acting tools, such as improvising, as things went along. Everybody was young, but everybody was also professional. Good actors make that stuff look easy. That being said, there was also a lovely chemistry among the three girls, age gaps or not.

The scene also raises the question of how a shy wallflower like Laurie Strode could ever have been friends with two such outgoing and promiscuous social butterflies like Annie and Lynda. It's a fascinating question which wasn't explained in the *Halloween* script, but which was later explored in writer Curtis Richards' 1979 novelization of the film which explained that the girls had been friends ever since early childhood.

The relationship between Laurie and her friends offers a believable look at teenage friendships, particularly in the late 1970s when all teenagers had to look forward to was sex, drugs, and rock n' roll. Teenagers form groups, and they often go to school together for many, many years, and those friendships, however unlikely, are solid and grounded in reality. "I thought the friendship between the three girls was believable," says Curtis. "I think they'd known each other since they were three or four and just stuck together through high school. They were like the three musketeers."

At first glance, Annie and Lynda seem like the typical unsympathetic horror movie characters that the audience cheerfully wishes to be gruesomely murdered, and certainly wishes to be punished for their amoral behavior. This is another example of *Halloween*'s sly use of misdirection. Because the relationship between Annie, Laurie, and Lynda is so believable, in terms of the fact that everyone in the audience can relate to knowing someone who was like each of these girls in high school, the film is able to establish these teenage characters as real people.

This is something film critic Roger Ebert, one of *Halloween*'s greatest champions, would point out in his later review of *Halloween*. In his review, Ebert noted that none of the performances in *Halloween* were meant to be Oscar-worthy performances but instead were designed to establish ordinary teenage characters. When a teenager dies it should be powerful and tragic, and by creating believable teenage characters, especially in such obvious would-be victims like Annie and Lynda, *Halloween* makes these characters more interesting as potential victims (5).

At the start of *Halloween*'s filming, Jamie Lee Curtis had felt that she had little in common with Laurie Strode, but by the end of *Halloween*'s first week of filming the relationship between actress and character had grown much closer. Curtis realized that her own memories of her time at Choate, memories that she'd tried to bury, weren't that far removed from Laurie Strode's clearly difficult teenage existence.

"High school was rough for me," says Curtis. "I drew upon some of those memories, of having all of the kids look at me as Tony Curtis' kid, but I still never thought of myself as being exactly like Laurie, not even close. I would never have cast myself as Laurie Strode. For one thing, I would never dress like Laurie does, and I was also a cheerleader during my time in school, and I could do the splits too."

It's hard to believe, given how their characters are forever intertwined, that Curtis, Kyes, and Soles only appear together in the scene where the girls are walking home from school. The fact that the three characters only have one scene together in the film, and yet have grown to be regarded as synonymous by fans of *Halloween*, is a testament to the work of the three actresses. It's interesting, in retrospect, to look at the three actresses—Curtis, Kyes, Soles—and reflect on the subsequent careers they've had over the past thirty years.

Nancy Louise Kyes, who was credited in *Halloween* as Nancy Loomis, was an early member of the Carpenter-Hill repertory company, given her relationship with Tommy Lee Wallace, and would spend her later years raising the two children she had with Wallace. Kyes and Wallace were married in 1979 and have since divorced. Today, Kyes is a Los Angeles-based sculptress who occasionally makes appearances at autograph shows and fan conventions. In terms of her acting career, Kyes only made a few acting appearances in projects outside of the Carpenter-Hill umbrella and in retrospect this connection might've cast a shadow that Kyes found difficult to escape from in terms of finding other acting roles (6).

P.J. Soles' acting career has been another story. Soles had a more varied career than Kyes—outside of the Carpenter-Hill tree—and seemed poised for stardom after *Halloween*. In fact, it looked for a time, after the release of *Halloween* in 1978, that Soles' career prospects might surpass those of Curtis whose own film career would be slow to get out of the gate following *Halloween*'s release. In 1979, Soles achieved cult status when she starred as Riff Randell in the Roger Corman-produced musical-comedy *Rock 'n' Roll High School*, which was a minor hit (7). Soles followed this up with a key supporting role in the 1981 Ivan Reitman-directed comedy hit *Stripes*. By that time, she seemed poised for stardom, but it wasn't meant to be.

Prior to starting work on *Halloween*, Carpenter had written a script entitled *Zuma Beach*, a teen coming-of-age drama for which he envisioned Soles as the star. Soles signed onto the project—which was eventually broadcast as a made-for-television movie on NBC in September of 1978—immediately after finishing *Halloween*. Unfortunately, what was supposed to be a starring role for Soles in the film was eventually trimmed to a supporting part, in deference to actress Suzanne Somers. In reaction, an outraged Carpenter subsequently took his name off the film in protest.

In 1981, Curtis and Soles, who would stay in touch following *Halloween*'s filming, were briefly attached to star in a horror-spoof comedy film entitled *Thursday the 12th*. Later re-titled *Pandemonium*, to avoid obvious comparisons with 1980's *Friday the 13th*, the film was to be directed by Alfred Sole, best known for the acclaimed 1977 psychological-horror film *Alice, Sweet Alice*. However when it came time to finalize casting for the project, Sole inexplicably decided that he wasn't interested in this seemingly irresistible genre pairing and nixed the idea. *Pandemonium* was eventually released in April of 1982 and was a box office and critical flop (8).

Although stardom would be elusive for Soles, she's certainly had a productive and varied career since *Halloween*. She's been, for the most part, a steadily-working actress, which is no small achievement in Hollywood, a place full of graveyards—figurative and literal—for forgotten young stars. Soles could've been a big star, much like Jamie Lee Curtis, no doubt about it, but circumstances and luck worked against her in the period following *Halloween*, which is how such things go.

For her part, Kyes never aggressively pursued stardom, and most of her screen appearances were done as a favor to friends Carpenter and Hlll, a relationship that also made her an extremely-affordable actress. It's also important to note that neither Kyes or Soles are the least bit bitter about this, and nor would they be jealous—at least outwardly—by the fact that Curtis would get most of the acclaim and attention from *Halloween*. Still, it's interesting, and more than a little unfair, that Curtis would reach major stardom on the basis of *Halloween* while her co-stars—who fans and critics would later credit for playing their roles just as convincingly—wouldn't have the same kinds of career opportunities.

It's a fact of horror films, and of the larger film business in general, that the actress who plays the heroine in a horror film—or the lead in any film—benefits much more career-wise than the supporting players. On the other hand, if this rule was truly ironclad, why did Linda Blair's film career vanish almost immediately following the release of *The Exorcist* in 1973? Why did none of the heroines, feisty and plucky as they were, in the later *Friday the 13th* horror film series escape footnote status? Why is there only one Jamie Lee Curtis amidst a legion of scream queen pretenders who would try, and fail, to copy her?

The fact is that *Halloween* would make Jamie Lee Curtis a star, yes, but not the kind of star she would later become by her thirties in terms of being a mainstream film actress. *Halloween* would transform Curtis into a scream queen. This is a title that can destroy an actress' career, should she be interested in becoming a mainstream star, by typecasting her and trapping her in a box that can be, for any actress, a worse nightmare than any monster she might encounter in a horror film.

Ultimately, Jamie Lee Curtis would have to fight to be taken seriously as an actress and, in that respect, one could argue that *Halloween* would be as much a hindrance as help in that regard. In order to gain credibility as an actress in Hollywood, Curtis would still have to jump through the same hoops as every other young actress around at that time, and the scream queen status she would ultimately gain from *Halloween* probably made that task twice as difficult.

Just like *Psycho* was, in many ways, the beginning of the end for Janet Leigh's film career, in terms of the public's inability to divorce themselves from Leigh's bloody image in *Psycho*, the same thing could've happened to Curtis. A key difference is that Leigh's character was killed while Laurie Strode would turn out to be the ultimate survivor. Horror movies are dangerous for any young actress' career, and while Janet Leigh had already enjoyed a distinguished film career before *Psycho*, *Halloween* represented Jamie Lee Curtis' first film and the first impression she would make on the public and on Hollywood.

None of this was even a remote thought in Curtis' mind as she navigated the first few days of filming on *Halloween*. As the end of the first week of *Halloween*'s filming closed, Curtis had grown immeasurably more comfortable in her own skin—and Laurie Strode's—than just a few days earlier when she'd been convinced that she was going to be fired. The credit for this goes to Carpenter and Hill whose unwavering faith in Curtis' ability gave Curtis immeasurable confidence in herself. "Debra and John had a movie to make, Jamie was a smart, smart choice, and they did right by her," recalls Tommy Lee Wallace. "They did what any director-producer team would want to do for its star: They boosted her confidence, handed her a fine script, provided her with a safe and nurturing atmosphere in which to perform, and surrounded her with the best cast and crew they could come up with."

The dynamic of the relationship between Carpenter, Curtis, and Hill was interesting given that Carpenter and Hill, who'd been living together, were going through a kind of personal divorce on *Halloween*. Although they'd been living together prior to *Halloween*'s filming, Carpenter had recently fallen in love with actress Adrienne Barbeau who he'd met during the two week filming of *Someone's Watching Me!* in March of 1978. "*Halloween* did feel like a divorce for us as we were making it," recalled Hill. "That was the only sad part of making the film. Everything else was perfect. There weren't any problems."

If *Halloween* represented a kind divorce for the unmarried Carpenter and Hill—although not a professional divorce as the duo would collaborate on several more films after *Halloween*—then *Halloween* was, in a sense, their joint community property with Curtis perhaps representing their only child. Carpenter and Hill were Curtis' cinematic godparents and even to this day, Curtis credits Carpenter and Hill, and *Halloween*, for her subsequent acting career. "I owe my career to Debra and John and I'll always feel that way," says Curtis. "If they hadn't taken a chance on me, who would have? When I look back at my early career, I wonder what would've happened to me if I hadn't gotten *Halloween*. I think I would've left acting eventually. I'm sure I wouldn't have had a film career without *Halloween*."

In a way, Carpenter and Hill, Carpenter especially, gave birth to Jamie Lee Curtis, the actress and scream queen. That's not to suggest that this was any type of Svengali relationship, or that this trio was joined at the hip, or that Curtis would ever do anything for Carpenter that made her uncomfortable. For one thing, it was understood that Curtis would never do a nude scene in *Halloween*, not that Carpenter or Hill would've ever made such a request. This was a two-way relationship built on trust, a feeling that extended to the entire cast and crew. The cast and crew ate together on the set, often slept near each other when they had a break from filming, and worked hand-in-hand to prove that they could make *Halloween* a reality.

Ultimately, Carpenter and Curtis both needed each other, just as *Halloween* needed both of them. Would *Halloween* have been a great film, a commercially-successful film, if Carpenter had cast his first choice, Anne Lockhart, in the role of Laurie Strode instead of Jamie Lee Curtis? Certainly, just as 1981's *Raiders of the Lost Ark* undoubtedly would've been successful if first choice Tom Selleck had been cast in the lead role instead of Harrison Ford.

Jamie Lee Curtis—like Harrison Ford would do with the character of Indiana Jones—would make the Laurie Strode character iconic, make the character her own, and ultimately render the thought of another actress playing Laurie Strode as unimaginable. Likewise, *Halloween* almost certainly wouldn't have turned out to be the artistic and commercial triumph it became without Carpenter's and Hill's leadership and the harmonic cast and crew dynamic that their leadership engendered. Years later, many film critics and historians would credit Carpenter as being the real star of *Halloween*, which is a slight to Curtis' invaluable contribution to the film.

The truth is that *Halloween* wouldn't exist as the immortal classic it's regarded as today without Jamie Lee Curtis, just as Jamie Lee Curtis wouldn't exist today as a pop culture icon without *Halloween*. It's the same with John Carpenter. Although everyone associated with *Halloween* would benefit from the film's eventual success in some form, no one would benefit more than John Carpenter and Jamie Lee Curtis. *Halloween* would make stars of both of them, although for much different reasons.

four

THE BABYSITTER AND
THE BOOGEYMAN

The most difficult part of *Halloween*'s filming, certainly for Jamie Lee Curtis, was the filming of *Halloween*'s nighttime scenes. It's this part of the film which establishes that *Halloween* really exists as two films in one that move in parallel lines: the Laurie Strode story and the Dr. Sam Loomis story.

From this point, the arrival of night in *Halloween*, the rest of the film would follow a pattern of cutting back and forth between Laurie Strode, who's babysitting and only eventually becomes aware of the real presence of Michael Myers, and the dogged Sam Loomis who spends much of the film at the old Myers house, hoping to catch Myers before he can continue his murderous rampage in Haddonfield. It's interesting that while these two characters, these co-protagonists, both serve as adversaries for Michael Myers in *Halloween*, they're unaware of the other's existence for virtually the entire film.

Halloween's terrifying nighttime scenes were established by the daylight scenes which were full of creepy and terrifying suggestion due to the effective use of contrast and shadows. This is also where the Panaglide, with its advantage of greater movement, was put to great effect in tandem with *Halloween*'s wide-screen palate. The technique is simple, and one that would be copied in countless horror films that would follow *Halloween*: a character moves to the edge of the screen, and the audience expects to see the killer jump out, but there's actually nothing but a door or a wall, something innocuous. Once the audience relaxes, then the character turns around or opens a door and then the killer jumps out. If *Halloween* didn't invent this strategy, it would certainly perfect it.

One of the most notable examples of this occurs in a daylight scene where Laurie's walking home and is startled by the appearance of Leigh Brackett, played by Charles Cyphers. Brackett's Haddonfield's sheriff and also the father of Laurie's friend, Annie, which would later take on a grim double meaning given Annie's later fate and the fact that Brackett ends up assisting Loomis in trying to stop Michael Myers. Cyphers recalls Curtis being genuinely spooked the first time they shot the scene. "The first time I met Jamie, one of the few times I met her at all, was when we did that scene and she just bumped into me," recalls Cyphers. "I remember that she was a very polite and shy girl. When we did the first take, she bumped into me and then she said, 'I'm sorry, Mr. Cyphers.' She was very nice. Then we did the scene at the hardware store where I look in on Jamie and Nancy in the car, and they've been smoking pot, and I just wave goodbye. That was it. I just remember Jamie being a very beautiful girl."

Another striking daylight scene featuring Curtis is the scene where Laurie leaves her house with a big pumpkin in her lap. She walks down the street and sits on a perch, waiting for Annie's car to pick her up and take them both to their nighttime babysitting assignments. Curtis and John Carpenter both laughed when they shot the scene with Laurie holding the pumpkin, the ridiculousness of seeing a pumpkin in California in Spring not lost on them or any of the rest of the cast and crew. For this purpose the *Halloween* production had imported a dozen large, round green gourds from South America that they spray-painted orange and kept in cold storage for the film.

The image of a smiling Laurie, a smiling Jamie Lee Curtis, sitting on the street corner with the pumpkin in her lap is an iconic image in that it offers a snapshot of who Curtis was at this very moment in the Spring of 1978. It's a picture of a young, insecure woman with crooked teeth and an awkward self-image who's nonetheless bursting with enthusiasm both about *Halloween* and the future. Perhaps there's a double meaning to this image in that just as *Halloween* represents Laurie Strode's last days of high school life, and certainly the end of her innocence given what transpires in the film, *Halloween* represented a kind of farewell to nineteen year-old Curtis' own teenage existence.

There's a touching innocence in the image of Laurie Strode holding the large pumpkin and waiting idly that's very poignant. This image is especially poignant when comparing the Laurie Strode and the Jamie Lee Curtis of this time—in the Spring of 1978—with the Jamie Lee Curtis of today who has certainly transformed into a completely different actress and person. Additionally, the image of Laurie clutching the pumpkin illustrates Laurie's heightened sense of responsibility, in terms of bringing the pumpkin to her babysitting job, that figures prominently in the film's later scenes and in terms of defining Laurie Strode's rigid moral character. This is a babysitter who can be trusted.

This scene, and really all of *Halloween*'s exterior scenes, represented a series of logistical and technical challenges for the *Halloween* crew in terms of recreating a Midwestern Halloween climate in South Pasadena, California in May of 1978. Minimizing the sight of abundant palm trees was just one of many challenges in terms of trying to create this illusion. Because there were palm trees visible everywhere, the cast and crew would often have to remind themselves that the film was taking place in Haddonfield, Illinois instead of the Hollywood milieu that completely surrounded them.

This was yet another example of the almost superhuman synergy amongst the *Halloween* crew, and this included the cast members who would also chip-in and assist with chores when needed. Prior to the filming of every scene, Tommy Lee Wallace would spread the leaves he'd bought from a local decoration shop over the scene and then when the filming of a scene was completed, he'd promptly gather all of the leaves up in a bag for the next scene. Carpenter and the actors would also carefully block out scenes to avoid shots of the palm trees but no one's perfect and despite everyone's best, and mostly successful, efforts, the odd mistake would show. "There's a couple of scenes in the film where you see the palm trees," recalls Carpenter. "Other than that, I thought we did a good job of making it look like a Midwestern town."

The scene where Annie and Laurie drive to their babysitting jobs is also interesting because it serves as kind of a time capsule in terms of what it meant to be a teenager in the late 1970s, an existence that Curtis had loathed when she was at Choate. With no Internet, no home video, no groundbreaking innovations in terms of teenage media pop culture, teenagers from the 1970s were left to their own spare devices. 1970s teenagers had to talk to each other, to really communicate with each other, and besides that there wasn't much else to do except to listen to music, go cruising, smoke pot, or talk about sex.

It was this part of the film, the discussions and interaction between Laurie and her girlfriends, that represented Debra Hill's main influence in *Halloween* in terms of character and story. Sure enough as Annie and Laurie are driving along they listen to Blue Oyster Cult's *Don't Fear the Reaper*, a recent top 40 hit, and talk about boys, mostly Laurie who reveals that she's attracted to an unseen high school student named Ben Tramer (1). Annie and Laurie also smoke pot, another popular teen ritual of the period. "John let me handle all of the girl scenes in the film, because that's what I knew best," said Hill. "With Annie and Laurie, I thought back to my own time in high school in Haddonfield, New Jersey, and how things like boys and going out on dates seemed like colossal events at that time."

The interplay between Annie and Laurie as they're driving to their babysitting jobs is poignant because the dialogue between the two girls feels authentic and realistic, but more so because it's a snapshot of what it must've been like to be a teenager circa 1978. In this way, *Halloween* almost serves as an earlier companion piece to Richard Linklater's brilliant 1993 comedy *Dazed and Confused*, a film that chronicled the lives of various teenagers growing up in 1976. Like the teenagers in that film, the teenage characters in *Halloween* live in a world where the only options are sex, drugs, rock 'n' roll. Like the teenage characters in *Dazed and Confused*, there's a sense that the teenage characters in *Halloween* perhaps feel like they'd been born ten or twenty years too early.

The most endearing quality of the teenagers in *Dazed and Confused* and in *Halloween* is the way that they communicate and really talk to each other, a trait that's largely non-existent in today's teenagers. In Annie and Laurie, *Halloween* shows teenagers who exist in a much simpler age that doesn't include the Internet, mega shopping malls, or prolonged thoughts about grim subjects like terrorism and Armageddon. For these teenagers, the biggest things in life are getting a car, going to a Kiss concert, and especially talking on the phone, which was still a big deal back in 1978. Most of all, they have to talk to each other which leads to more interesting relationships amongst teenagers, as Linklater's film showed and which *Halloween* also effectively demonstrates. This portrait of a late-1970s teenager is powerfully represented in *Halloween*.

The final part of the scene where Annie and Laurie are driving to their babysitting jobs is the moment where Laurie confesses her secret adoration for a guy named Ben Tramer, a name that was an in-joke reference to one of Carpenter's USC classmates. This part was filmed on the second to last day of *Halloween's* filming, and was almost entirely improvised between Curtis and Nancy Kyes. Hill and camera operator Raymond Stella were in the backseat for the scene whose required improvisation Curtis found much easier than the previous instance between Curtis, Kyes, and P.J. Soles. It didn't hurt that Curtis and Kyes had been spending a lot of time hanging out together and talking during filming (2). "We hung-out together on the set and we worked at being believable as teenage girls, friends," recalls Kyes. "I acted like I was really trying to convince Jamie to ask this boy out. We just pretended that we were talking to each other, which we'd been doing all during the shoot, and the dialogue flowed."

Halloween's real terror begins when Annie and Laurie arrive at the film's main location which is the street where Annie and Laurie arrive at for their respective babysitting jobs. They're across the street from each other. Laurie's at the Doyle house, watching over young Tommy Doyle, played by Brian Andrews, while Annie's across the street at the Wallace house, watching over Lindsey Wallace, played by Kyle Richards. These scenes would be filmed at Orange Grove Avenue which is located off the Sunset Strip in Hollywood. From this point on in the film, the structure of *Halloween* would be to switch between Annie and Laurie—with the later re-introduction of P.J. Soles' Lynda—and their story, and then back to Donald Pleasence's Sam Loomis character as he hovers around the Myers house, looking for Michael Myers.

For *Halloween* to truly be effective, Jamie Lee Curtis and Donald Pleasence would have to come across in the film as a horror version of Batman and Robin, Holmes and Watson, Clark Gable and Spencer Tracy. While those famous tandems are inextricably linked, the bond between Laurie and Loomis is hard to define given that the characters are virtually never on-screen together in *Halloween*. As well, Curtis and Pleasence didn't get to spend much time together on the set, mostly due to the rush of filming Pleasence's scenes, which were totally separate from Curtis' scenes. Although both actors knew of each other, and of each other's existence in *Halloween*'s story, they were like two ships moving in different waters while headed for a similar destination.

Another reason for Pleasence's "separation" from Curtis and Laurie in *Halloween* was the fact that Pleasence maintained a distant presence on the set and would later be regarded by his colleagues, save for Carpenter who would befriend the actor, as eccentric and elusive. Given the flood of Pleasence's acting commitments between 1977 and

1978, perhaps he was simply tired. "Donald was in a whirlwind during the time of *Halloween*'s making," recalls Joy Jameson, Pleasence's long-time agent. "Because he had so many children and ex-wives to support, he was working non-stop and he would've missed *Halloween* if another film he'd been working on prior to *Halloween* had taken longer to shoot. He was very tired because he was working non-stop."

Pleasence would eventually warm-up to *Halloween*'s cast and crew, even taking the time on occasion to help with carrying equipment, and *Halloween* would eventually usher a resurgence in the actor's long career. The veteran thespian would, in his brief five-day stay on the *Halloween* set, eat lunch with the other crew members and occasionally make jokes. Although Curtis was very much aware of Loomis' importance in the film, as well as Pleasence's importance to *Halloween* as a whole, she wasn't sure just how Laurie and Loomis would fit together in the finished film. Curtis' impression of Pleasence? "He was very quiet, but polite, a very professional actor," recalls Curtis. "Very intense when he was working, but he would laugh occasionally, and I think he had a good sense of humor."

According to Carpenter, who would collaborate with Pleasence on three more films and become good friends with the actor until Pleasence's death in 1995, Pleasence's sometimes eccentric behavior on the set was due to his initial lack of understanding of the material. "When we started, he didn't know what to make of the material and he'd tell me that he didn't like the story and didn't understand any of it," says Carpenter. "That changed after the first few days because he really got into his character and we became great friends. Once Donald saw what the rest of us were doing, he really got into the film, and he would help carry equipment, and he did everything possible to help us stay on schedule. By the end of the shoot, he was just as enthusiastic about the film as we were, so he really changed a lot from the start of filming to the end."

Most of Pleasence's scenes in the film aren't with Curtis but with actor Charles Cyphers. When Sam Loomis first arrives in Haddonfield, he meets with Cyphers' Leigh Brackett character at the scene of a hardware store robbery, committed by Michael Myers. Later that night, Brackett and Loomis travel to the old Myers house and spend the rest of the film trying to find Michael Myers before he can kill again. "He was a brilliant actor, but kind of mysterious and weird," recalls Cyphers. "He was so into that character, it was unbelievable. One time, I tried to break the ice by mentioning that I'd appeared in a stage version of Harold Pinter's *The Caretaker*, since Donald had starred in the film version. I told him we'd changed it from the English version and he just looked at me and curled his eyebrow and said in this soft voice, 'I see. Well, I don't think Harold Pinter would've liked that very much.' He was a great actor, but a strange man."

There's no question that Pleasence brought a great deal of psychic weight to the character of Sam Loomis, for reasons that are obvious and some that are well-hidden. Perhaps Hill described it best when she described Pleasence, and Loomis, as "the moral center of *Halloween*," a recognition that Loomis is the only person who's trying to prevent this ungodly evil entity from wreaking havoc upon Haddonfield and the world. "Donald's leading the Greek chorus in *Halloween* in that he's the only one who really knows what's going on with Michael Myers," said Hill. "I really loved working with Donald on *Halloween* because he played Loomis as such an obsessive man, almost a maniac, but he did it in such a low-key way that was very interesting. Donald brought an intensity to the role of Sam Loomis that wasn't on the page. The Loomis character was an invention of John's, and so John and Donald worked almost by themselves during filming, whereas my focus was with Jamie and the other girls. I can't imagine *Halloween* without Donald or Jamie."

Pleasence brought something else of interest to the role of Sam Loomis, and to *Halloween*, and that was the trimmed goatee that Loomis wears in the film. Pleasence often wore a beard throughout his long career, but it was never as pronounced, or as darkened and occult-like, as it appears in *Halloween*. The effect of the goatee, which has a pronounced devilish tinge to it, serves to add a subliminal supernatural suggestion to *Halloween* that certainly wasn't visibly present in the Carpenter-Hill script. This supernatural suggestion eventually gains added significance by the end of the film which provides a supernatural explanation for Michael Myers' existence. The scenes at the Myers house were filmed on Mission Street in South Pasadena, where Loomis and Sheriff Leigh Brackett arrive at the decrepit house which Laurie's realtor father is trying to sell. It's here that they discuss the house's, and Haddonfield's, grim legend. This is epitomized by a great speech, written by Carpenter, where Loomis describes Michael Myers as "having the blackest eyes, the devil's eyes" and being a patient that he "spent eight years trying to reach and then another seven trying to keep him locked up." Before this, Brackett and Loomis discover the remains of a dead animal downstairs, as they first walk into the house. "The house gave me the creeps and being with Donald made it even creepier," recalls Cyphers. "We just had to look down and imagine we were seeing a dead dog, some kind of dead animal, so we just stood there and looked ahead."

Aside from locations like Alhambra, Hollywood, and South Pasadena, other locations in California used for filming were City of Industry, which was used for the scene where Loomis discovers the body of a dead truck driver near some railroad tracks. Rosemead and Sierra Madre were other filming locations. Many of the locations in the film were surprisingly close to each other, like the hardware store which was located on Mission Street in South Pasadena, less than a block away from the Myers house. Years later, the Myers house would be moved and deposited across the street from the old hardware store which is now an information office. "We were very lucky to find everything we needed in the film in terms of locations," says Carpenter. "I can't think of anything that we would've done differently if we'd been in the Midwest, except for not having to deal with all of the palm trees."

It's uncanny how good of a job the film does of passing for the Midwestern setting of Haddonfield, Illinois, although to be fair, the American Midwest is probably completely alien to anyone who's not from the Midwest. Much of the credit goes to Tommy Lee Wallace who in addition to his tireless work as production designer and co-editor, as well as an eventual cameo appearance as Michael Myers in a later scene, was *Halloween*'s defacto location scout. Wallace had driven around Hollywood and Pasadena prior to *Halloween*'s filming and carefully chose most of the locations that would be present in the film.

The magic of film-making also played a pivotal role of course, and in this case, like with everything in *Halloween*, the simplest things worked best. The specter of the leaves in almost every shot, combined with agreeably mild weather during filming, plant the Midwestern feel and look in the mind of the viewer. The look of the film is almost always convincing, especially during the scene that was filmed at City of Industry against the backdrop of barren fields and long country roads.

Curtis and the rest of the cast deserve credit as well in the way they convey the small-town attitudes and personalities of their characters in the film. This is especially embodied in the Laurie Strode character in terms of her bland clothes, plain hair, and the sense that she's almost like a repressed animal who's almost waiting for someone like Michael Myers to arrive and unleash her from her Midwestern, small-town doldrums. In contrast, the more outgoing Annie and Lynda seem, with the way they talk, like California teenagers at first, especially when Lynda repeats her "Totally" mantra over and over again.

Perhaps this represents more of an imitation of the teenagers that Annie and Lynda have undoubtedly seen and studied on television, and the fact that they're desperate to escape their small town trappings. What is the future for a character like Laurie Strode in a town like Haddonfield? She seems destined to have a boring life, and the film does a good job of establishing this motif. The Haddonfield in *Halloween* is the kind of small town that people dream of leaving, likely dreading the thought of spending the rest of their lives there. In this regard, Haddonfield is as much a nightmare for Laurie Strode and her friends as Michael Myers turns out to be.

The real acid test, from a nuts-and-bolts production standpoint, for the cast and crew of *Halloween* was the filming of the crucial nighttime scenes. These scenes in the film, the scenes where Michael Myers executes his bloody rampage upon Haddonfield, would have to terrify the audience. First and foremost in Carpenter's mind was the thought of shooting the difficult Panaglide sequence for the film's opening, a continuous sequence that Carpenter and his crew had decided to schedule for the last night of filming.

For Jamie Lee Curtis, the nighttime scenes were the scenes where she would establish herself as a scream queen icon. This could only work if Michael Myers, the Shape, was scary and that the audience could identify with the nightmare that Laurie Strode was about to endure. The vulnerability that Carpenter and Curtis had discussed prior to the start of *Halloween*'s filming, and Curtis' ability to make the audience love her character, would be crucial to the film's success.

It helped that Michael Myers himself was a daunting and terrifying figure, thanks to Nick Castle's nuance of movement and uncanny embodiment of Myers' twisted psyche. Castle's movements and eerily quiet gait were splendidly chilling, but the fact is that the trick might not have worked were it not for the chilling $1.98 William Shatner mask that he wears in the film. Expressionless and ghostly-white, the mask took away all of Michael Myers' human characteristics—a human identity that was no doubt there but which is invisible to the viewer—and turned the character into a genuine boogeyman (3). "Nick was terrific," recalls Carpenter. "All of the movements, like the way he tilts his head in the film, were his idea because I didn't give him much direction except to just walk. I was too busy with the rest of the filming so I left him alone, and so he really brought life to the character."

The dynamic of the nighttime sequences was simple in terms of character and story, but difficult in terms of the specifics of filming, especially with the Panaglide. The rest of the film would take place through Laurie Strode's eyes and ears, from her point-of-view. She's at the Doyle house, watching over Tommy Doyle, making popcorn and watching horror movies. Annie's across the street, watching Lindsey Wallace. Michael Myers is hovering around the Wallace house, and will try to first kill Annie, followed by Lynda, and then Laurie across the street.

Meanwhile, Loomis and Sheriff Brackett roam the streets of Haddonfield, circling the Myers house, desperately looking for Myers. This is a fool's errand that will eventually be revealed to be *Halloween*'s red herring, *Halloween*'s version of the Hitchcockian MacGuffin device. The rest of the film would inter-cut these different story arcs, but the center of the film—the audience's perspective—would exist through Laurie's eyes.

What makes Laurie Strode a great horror film heroine – and would establish Curtis as a scream queen after *Halloween*'s theatrical release—isn't just the ability to scream or to run from a masked killer, and nor is it merely the ability to show vulnerability. Every heroine seems vulnerable to the audience when they're being chased by a killer in a horror film. If these qualities, namely looking cute and having a great set of lungs, were the only test for scream queen stardom then surely each of the heroines in the later *Friday the 13th* horror film series—not to mention the legion of other horror films that would arise after *Halloween*—would've become screen icons.

What makes Laurie Strode special is the courage, decency, and extreme sense of moral responsibility that she demonstrates in the film. This is illustrated in the scenes where she's looking after young Tommy Doyle, and then Lindsey Wallace, after Annie brings Lindsey over to the Doyle house so Annie can go be with her boyfriend. It's at this point in the film that Laurie begins to take on the role of a defacto mother figure to the two children who are in her care. It's at this moment that the viewer begins to feel a psychic identification with Laurie Strode, in terms of caring about her well-being and becoming emotionally-invested in her life or death.

Laurie Strode is a good, decent, responsible teenage girl and those qualities shine through in the film. Besides vulnerability, these were the qualities that Curtis revealed in Laurie that made Curtis' performance special and unique. This was quite a stretch for an actress who was only nineteen and had felt little connection with the Laurie Strode character and had described herself as being somewhat of a smart-aleck. Watching Curtis in these scenes, the scenes where Laurie's watching over the children, there's a powerful sense that Laurie—and perhaps Curtis herself given how believable her performance is—would make an excellent mother (4).

By the end of *Halloween*, when Michael Myers has traveled from Laurie's imagination to grim reality, it becomes clear that Laurie would kill to protect these children. In a sense, these children become Laurie's children and whereas the viewer senses, probably correctly, that most other heroines—certainly most other scream queen heroines—would've run away screaming, it becomes obvious that Laurie is special. By the end of the film, Laurie's courage and her protectiveness of the children she's babysitting—along with the deep sense that Laurie is just a decent, good person—create powerful feelings of admiration and endearment in the viewer.

The Laurie Strode character, and the evolution of Jamie Lee Curtis during the filming of *Halloween*, reflects why Curtis has enjoyed such an enduring career in Hollywood. There's an underdog quality in both Curtis and Laurie, especially visible during the period of *Halloween*'s filming, that the audience can relate to. Whereas more celebrated and glamorous actresses that came from Curtis' generation—Jodie Foster and Michelle Pheiffer being prime examples—have always carried an air of exclusivity, audiences have always found Curtis extremely accessible. When the audience looks at Jamie Lee Curtis, especially the Jamie Lee Curtis from *Halloween*, they see a reflection of themselves, warts and all. This unique relationship between Curtis and the public, which extends to the present day, began with the character of Laurie Strode.

Despite all of Curtis' intangible qualities that made her unique as an actress, a prospective scream queen must also establish her genre credentials. She needs the ability to run for her life, be a resourceful and challenging opponent for the killer chasing her, and be able to scream her lungs out. All of this must be done while still maintaining some semblance of a beautiful appearance.

The scene where Laurie leaves the Doyle house and heads across the street to the Wallace house is, arguably, the signature scene from Jamie Lee Curtis' scream queen career. The fact that the sequence is bloodless and instead relies on mercilessly drawing out the viewer's expectations speaks volumes about *Halloween's* artistry—especially relative to Curtis' subsequent post-*Halloween* horror films—as well as Curtis' own screen presence. "When Jamie and I talked about vulnerability, I was talking about the scene where she walks across the street," says Carpenter. "The audience knows her friends are dead in the other house as she's walking over there so I thought that, if the film was working, the audience would scream 'Don't go over to that house' or 'Don't do that' and that's what happened. I had her walk really slow to really draw out the anticipation and suspense in the scene."

This scene, which would be filmed in one continuous sequence, represents the moment that Laurie Strode goes from innocent teenager to grieving heroine given that she's about to discover that her best friends have been murdered. In a way, the scene's culmination also represents the end of Laurie's youth in that her life will never be the same again. "John and I talked about Laurie and how we wanted the audience to become emotionally-invested in her and what happens to her," recalls Curtis. "That's the scene where it happens the most because when I saw the film the audience would scream at Laurie in the scene when she's walking across the street. People in the audience would yell at Laurie not to go into the house and you could tell that they were really worried about Laurie getting killed and that really amazed me. The audience had invested in Laurie and they cared what happened to me when the unreal elements became real. The audience cared about Laurie."

JAMIE LEE CURTIS: This scene is probably my favorite scene in the film because it's so simple; me just walking across the street to the other house. No screaming, no crying, nothing like that. I'm just walking slowly. From the beginning of the scene, when I open the door and walk across the street, John had the Steadicam on me and it made this booming noise for the whole scene. The camera would go back to me—boom!—and then back to the house—boom!—and then back to me and I really had to fight to concentrate and maintain the expression on my face during the filming of that scene.

Since *Halloween* was filmed out of sequence, Carpenter and Curtis established a method, a rating system from one to ten, to show how scared Laurie should be in any given scene. "We'd look at the script and I'd look at a scene and mark it a six out of ten or a seven out of ten," says Curtis. "When we were filming the scene where Laurie finds Annie and Lynda dead upstairs, John would tell me it was a nine or a nine and a half, and that helped me a lot with my performance. At this point in the filming of the movie, I was completely comfortable around Debra, John and the rest of the cast and crew. From the first day of filming to the end of the filming, I think I'd become a much better actress. I felt ike I was part of something special."

The scene where a curious and spooked Laurie walks into the Wallace house is when *Halloween* punctures any lasting image of peaceful Midwestern suburbia that might be left in the film. It's at this point that *Halloween* drops any veneer of Midwestern monotony and the film transforms into a house of horrors, a scare machine. This change occurs in the scene where Laurie walks into the upstairs bedroom at the Wallace house and is immediately confronted by the corpse of Annie who lays on the bed with the stolen tomb of Judith Myers—the sister Michael Myers brutally murdered on Halloween night 1963—overlooking her.

In the scene, a shocked Laurie bumps into the side wall, which then reveals Lynda's corpse, in the closet, as well as the corpse of Lynda's boyfriend, Bob, who also rests in the closet. Filming this scene presented a big challenge for Carpenter and Curtis in that Curtis had to accomplish a lot of things at once, and in a very limited space. In the scene, Laurie has to be simultaneously shocked and grief-stricken and, just as importantly, she must reveal the location of Bob and Lynda's corpses to the audience in order for the scene to work.

JOHN CARPENTER: We had a big problem with the filming of the scene, because I needed Jamie to move around the room and reveal the other bodies in the closet, but I also needed to show the horror Laurie feels at that moment, the numbing shock. I wasn't sure how she should get from the doorway to the other side of the room, from Point A to Point B, so Jamie and I talked about that a lot.

JAMIE LEE CURTIS: John said to me, 'I don't know what we're going to do in this scene because I need you to move from the front of the bed to the closet so we can show the other bodies.' I thought about how Laurie would react, how I would react in a situation like that, and I realized that you'd be so shocked that you wouldn't be in control of yourself. You'd be numb. I told John, 'I'll stand there and I'll be so shocked that I just stumble around the room, not even knowing where I'm going, and I'll just bump against the closet.' John was great but he'd leave you alone as an actor and let you do your thing. We talked through the scene, and found a solution that worked great.

In most horror films, and this is especially true of the legion of *Halloween* copycats, Laurie would've freaked out and gone crazy at that moment. Carpenter and Hill felt such an approach would've ignored just how a teenage girl might really react under similar circumstances. In this instance, Carpenter and Curtis decided to take the high road; Laurie internalizes her emotions in the scene, her numbing shock and disbelief, and her shock causes her to stumble around the room like a zombie. This was made even more challenging by the fact that actress Nancy Kyes wasn't present for the scene which forced Curtis to stare at an empty bed and imagine the sight of her dead best friend while also hitting her marks. For this purpose, Curtis imagined that she was looking at her mother, Janet Leigh, her own real-life best friend.

There are no screams yet; Laurie's just panting and sniffling. Laurie's first scream in the film, Curtis' first scream as an actress, occurs when Laurie bumps into the closet and sees Lynda's wide-eyed corpse. Then she screams, and the screams get louder when she sees Bob's corpse. Now the screaming has begun for Laurie in *Halloween*, and it will continue for the rest of the film, and there's a sense here that, because of the care that's put been into establishing Laurie's terror, Laurie has earned the right to scream.

Laurie's forced to process not just the loss of her best friends at this moment, but also the loss of her whole world since Annie and Lynda represented Laurie's only true link to the outside world. Laurie will never be a teenager again, regardless of her current age. Just as Michael has finally unleashed fifteen years of pent-up sexual repression on this Halloween night, Laurie's also been jolted and reawakened.

The scene where Laurie finally leaves the bedroom required some dexterity on Curtis' part so as to match cinematographer Dean Cundey's inventive lighting scheme. In the scene, Curtis backs out of the bedroom, into the darkness of the hallway, and then Michael Myers appears out of the darkness, right behind her. Michael's, The Shape's, appearance is revealed through a ray of blue light that Cundey designed just for the scene, sensing that the blue light would be an appropriate contrast between Michael Myer's white visage and Curtis' own features.

The next sequence, where Laurie is stabbed and falls down the stairwell, marked Curtis' first taste of stunt-work. She filmed the scene, which also required Curtis to wear a bloody prosthetic that was applied on her shoulder, under the guidance of stuntman James Winburn. Winburn had just arrived on the set that night to shoot the film's climactic scene where Winburn, in the form of Michael Myers, would be shot out of a balcony window (5).

Halloween's tight budget and working schedule didn't give the cast or crew time to think—or over-think—through too many details. That the film's very simplicity would turn out to be one of its most admired qualities is a testament to the synergy of the cast and crew, of which Debra Hill deserves full credit. "I made a very lean work schedule which was arranged so the actors would only show up when they were needed," recalled Hill. "None of the actors, except for Donald and Jamie, had been signed for an extended period of time. We just used them when they were needed. *Halloween* was also story-boarded, so we were very prepared prior to the first day of filming. Most of the cast and crew were friends, and most of the money went for camera equipment and lab costs. I had to call in a lot of favors on *Halloween*. It's a film we never could've made, with that budget and schedule, at any other time in our lives."

Curtis excelled under these conditions which forced Curtis to rely on her instincts and adapt to difficult circumstances. The scene where Laurie runs out of the Wallace house – having discovered her friends' dead bodies inside the master bedroom—and onto the street screaming was especially challenging as this was a Panaglide shot. The shot forced Curtis to both maintain contact with the camera and maintain her emotional level with the scene. "That's what's so different between screen acting and stage acting," says Curtis. "We shot that scene late at night, at ten or eleven at night. The crying and screaming and running were easy for me, but I had to move in unison with the camera or the scene doesn't work. I had to hit my marks in that scene, and I remember there were lots of people on the street watching me. If we'd shot that scene today, I would've asked for the street to be cleared. It was so embarrassing because I was running around and screaming on a city street in Hollywood, late at night. I felt like such a jerk."

The scene where a wounded Laurie runs out onto the street is a confirmation of the mother identity the character has assumed over Tommy Doyle and Lindsey Wallace, the two children in her care. At this point, she could easily run down the street and escape Michael Myers, especially given Michael Myers' deliberate and slow gait. She can't do this, won't do this, because she feels responsible for the children. At this point she is like a mother figure to Lindsey and Tommy in terms of being their sole guardian and protector. There are legions of stories of mothers going to superhuman lengths to protect their children from danger, whether it be pulling a car off their child, or sacrificing their lives for their children. At this point in *Halloween*, Laurie Strode is willing to go to superhuman, and supernatural lengths, to protect her children.

What Laurie doesn't know, but what is implicitly understood by both the film and the audience, is that Michael Myers has no intention of hurting Lindsey and Tommy. He's a child himself in many ways, and there's a sense that he feels a kinship to children as evidenced in an earlier scene where he comes face to face with Tommy Doyle outside Tommy's school. He lets Tommy go and studies the other kids at the school, perhaps processing his own schoolyard memories. Michael Myers is a warped, childlike monster who is, as would later be revealed in *Halloween*'s novelization, under the command of Druid spirits who control and implore, with their voices, Michael to kill. Even for Michael, killing a child is off limits, immoral. Much like Hannibal Lecter found the prospect of killing Jodie Foster's Clarice Starling character impolite and rude in Jonathan Demme's *The Silence of the Lambs* (1991), Michael Myers also seems to regard the thought of hurting children as distasteful.

In every horror film, certainly every slasher film that would follow *Halloween*, the story eventually boils down to the conflict between the film's lone survivor, typically the innocent virgin, and the film's insurmountable and relentless killer. It's a predictable dynamic, and would grow wearisome during the slasher movie wave that would peak by 1981. By 1978 however the technique was still effective and somewhat fresh. This is the Body Count Movie, a genre in which the scream queen heroine is an essential component.

The character of Laurie Strode represents the vanguard for all later scream queen heroines—or "Final Girls" as they're sometimes nicknamed—who would follow in Jamie Lee Curtis' footsteps. She is the model for all screen heroines, certainly in the horror genre, just like *Halloween* is the blueprint, the holy grail, for virtually every teen-themed horror film that's arrived since 1978. Perhaps the most interesting thing about the inevitable confrontation between the killer and the scream queen heroine—a dynamic that Curtis and *Halloween* would immortalize—is the fact that the heroine represents, by the very fact that she's still breathing, all of the other characters in a horror film who have been murdered previously. In the sense that Laurie is a walking elegy to the memory of friends Annie and Lynda, both Curtis' and *Halloween's* impact is especially remarkable.

When a teenager is killed in a horror film, or any film, it should be a sad and tragic event. Sadly, the majority of the horror films that would follow *Halloween*—including the later *Halloween* sequels—would reduce the killing of teenagers to a mere body count, a predictable and tired formality that would only serve to desensitize the audience to the sight of murdered youth, unfulfilled potential. That the image of dead teenagers, specifically the image of Annie and Lynda in *Halloween* and the grim implication in terms of their young lives being snuffed out all too soon, registers so strongly in *Halloween* is a testament to Carpenter's emphasis on atmosphere and suspense in the film, as well as Hill's focus to make the teenage characters believable and identifiable.

While Nancy Kyes and P.J. Soles deserve credit for creating believable teenage characters in *Halloween* that the viewer can identify with and recognize, it's Laurie Strode who registers the emotional impact of their deaths. Ultimately, the emotional impact of *Halloween* is a testament to Jamie Lee Curtis who invests Laurie, particularly in the film's later scenes, with the grief and disbelieving shock that any teenage girl would surely feel upon discovering that her friends have been murdered. By the end of the film, Laurie is more than a damsel in distress who must kill Michael Myers before he kills her. Laurie doesn't just represent her murdered friends, she also represents the death of a small town, Haddonfield, which will now be cloaked in the specter of death forever.

The rest of *Halloween*, the film's denouement, is entirely about Laurie and Michael, up until the very last scene when Dr. Sam Loomis finally shows up to rescue Laurie from her nightmare. In one scene, Laurie stabs Michael Myers in the neck with a knitting needle, but he won't die, a constant theme that's punctuated by the supernatural implications of the film's final shots. Another battle in the film between Laurie and Michael takes place in a cramped closet. In this scene, Laurie ends up grabbing a coat hangar, folding it into a shank and stabbing Michael Myers, who was played in the scene by Tommy Lee Wallace, in the eye.

The scene in the closet represents an extreme example of one of Carpenter's, and *Halloween*'s, main motifs which is the use of space, and how the gradual reduction of space in *Halloween* serves to almost strangle the viewer. To this end, Curtis and Laurie serve as the conduit, as the specter of Michael Myers gets closer and closer throughout the film. By the end of the film Laurie can literally touch him, and feel his cold hands. Now she's close enough to be able to hurt him too, and spill his blood. "I wanted the film to shrink as the story went along," says Carpenter. "I wanted the locations to become more and more contained, smaller, until the killer's right there in front of Laurie, and the audience, and there's nowhere to hide. He's not a dream anymore. He's all too real."

In the next scene, Laurie finds Lindsey and Tommy and sends them outside to get help. Laurie then wanders into a spare room, as The Shape slowly rises in the background. Like the scene in the Wallace house, Carpenter needed Curtis to be creative in this sequence and make the audience suspend disbelief by not asking why Laurie had chosen to stay in the house with a sleeping Michael Myers when she could've escaped with Lindsey and Tommy. "When I saw the film the first time, I wondered why she hadn't just run out of the house, but no one in the audience cared," recalls Curtis. "They were having too much fun being scared to ask questions about the holes in the plot."

Aside from the sequence where Curtis had to fall down the stairs, the most physically-demanding sequence for Curtis in *Halloween* was the filming of her final confrontation with Michael Myers when he chokes her while she simultaneously pulls off his white mask. In this sequence, where Myers' human face is finally revealed, the killer was played by Tony Moran, a twenty year-old struggling actor whose greatest claim to fame was that he was the brother of actress Erin Moran, star of the long-running television series *Happy Days*. Moran had been working as a Frankenstein impersonator on Hollywood and Vine when he got the call to audition for *Halloween*. Moran's brief encounter with Jamie Lee Curtis would earn him 250 dollars and a dubious place in both film history and Curtis' career.

Curtis and Moran did three takes of the scene. In the film, Myers' strangling of Laurie ends when Loomis arrives in the Doyle house, runs upstairs and shoots Michael Myers six times. The gunshots eventually send Michael Myers crashing through the balcony and onto the backyard grass. In this sequence, James Winburn, who'd worked with Curtis during the scene where she fell down the stairs, donned the Michael Myers persona, falling backwards out the window, onto a waiting pad.

At this point, *Halloween* finally gives the audience the meeting of Laurie and Dr. Loomis, two characters who would become iconic in the minds of horror fans and film historians. Perhaps it was a mistake on Carpenter's and Hill's part not to give Curtis and Pleasence more scenes together when writing the *Halloween* script, but given *Halloween*'s budget and tight filming schedule this wasn't possible. Their only contact in *Halloween* is when Loomis, after blowing Michael Myers over the balcony, tries to comfort a hysterical Laurie, who utters the immortal line, "It was the boogeyman…" to which Loomis calmly replies, "As a matter of fact it was." Loomis' calm reflects a grim knowledge the mad doctor has that the evil has not yet been destroyed, a belief that is confirmed when Loomis walks to the balcony and sees that Michael Myers' body is gone.

JOHN CARPENTER: Donald and I worked on this scene probably more than any other scene in the film, except for the scene where Loomis and Brackett go back to the Myers house and Loomis has a long monologue about who Michael Myers is. Donald had told me at first that he didn't understand his character and didn't understand what the movie was about so I had to explain that scene to him, and eventually he got into it. With the balcony scene, we weren't sure how Loomis should react when he sees that Michael's gone. I wanted him to be shocked, but Donald asked me if he should play the scene as if Loomis is expecting to see that Michael is gone. We did it both ways, and Donald's way was definitely the best.

JOY JAMESON, DONALD PLEASENCE'S AGENT: The only time Donald ever said anything to me about Jamie Lee Curtis was when we screened the movie later with Jamie and Moustapha Akkad and a few other people who'd worked on the film. During the screening, Donald said to me, 'I think this Jamie Lee Curtis is going to be a really big star.' Although they didn't work together much in *Halloween*, I think Donald saw something in Jamie that impressed him very much because Donald didn't throw out compliments like that easily.

KOOL MARDER: Jamie was very excited and happy to be making the film from the beginning to the end. We all felt that way, and we all helped out to make the film. Donald Pleasence drove my yellow BMW in the film, and my son was one of the trick 'or' treaters and the scene in the laundry room was filmed at my house in the Hollywood Hills. This was Jamie's first movie, and John and Debra were the perfect people for Jamie to have worked with because they built-up her confidence throughout the filming and by the end of filming you could see that Jamie had grown quite a bit as an actress.

TONY MORAN, CO-STAR: When my agent called about *Halloween*, she told me that Jamie Lee Curtis was the star of the movie and I said something like "Who the hell is Jamie Lee Curtis?" I'd never heard of her. I'd heard of Donald Pleasence. I arrived on the set in the afternoon, and the first time I met Jamie, she was sitting in the Winnebago, waiting to film a scene, and I remember that she was barely dressed at the time. When it came time to film my scene, Jamie and I went through the scene, and how I would put my hands around her throat, and how hard I would squeeze and all that. We went through that four or five times. I remember that she was very professional and very down to earth and we had fun doing that scene, although it was very weird for both of us because I was choking her. Donald Pleasence was waiting outside and he was also very focused and very professional, really intense. One of the hardest things was when Jamie would pull off my mask because that was very uncomfortable for me and John Carpenter wanted it to happen just right and he wanted the audience to see my face at an angle so that it wouldn't be exactly clear what I looked like. What I did what was that I put Vaseline over my hair so that when Jamie pulled the mask off, it just slid right off instead of sticking on my head and hurting me.

RICK WALLACE: My most vivid memory of working with Jamie on the film wasn't the final scene on the balcony, but the scene in the closet. It took many takes and because the closet was ripped apart in the scene, everything had to be put back together the way it was before for every take. Each time we'd do the scene, Jamie had to always be emotionally-ready, take after take, and she always was. She never complained, never screamed like most people would do in that situation, and she never freaked out about anything. I think Jamie grew up a lot during the filming of *Halloween*, and she was a much different person after the twenty days of filming than she was on the first day. She was much more confident by the time we'd finished. It also helped that John and Debra both served Jamie very well, even though John and Debra were very different people. John was laid-back and kind of unflappable and Debra was more of a forceful kind of person. They were like an older brother and sister to Jamie. John would talk to Jamie the same way I would talk to my daughter.

TOMMY LEE WALLACE: My most vivid memory of working with Jamie on *Halloween* isn't a scene from the movie, but a nice bit of hanging out after a shooting day on Orange Grove Avenue. Craig Stearns was my set decorator/prop man and several of us convened in Craig's orange van for an after-shoot smoke, drink and chat. That's the night I picked-up most of my impressions about Jamie as a solid, likeable human being, while we talked about life and times and things in general. By then I'd been around a few Hollywood types, especially star-brats, and she seemed refreshingly down to earth. After she left, we discovered a silver cigarette case between the seats, engraved on the inside with "Tony and Janet." Had Jamie been a creep, I guess we might've hung onto it, or sold it to a collector. God knows we weren't making much money on the show. But Jamie wasn't a creep—far from it—and I returned her cigarette case the next day.

JAMES WINBURN, STUNTMAN: I'd been doing a stunt earlier that day on the Universal lot when Debra Hill called and told me she needed someone to do a backward fall because the guy they hired fell through. I stopped off at my house in Toluca Lake, picked up my porta-pit high fall pads and drove to Hollywood. I arrived at the house at seven in the evening. I went inside the house and met with John Carpenter who explained me to what they were doing and then I worked with Jamie Lee Curtis in her scene where she flips over the stair railing to the staircase, so she wouldn't get hurt. She did a great job. Then John Carpenter asked me to watch Tony Moran so we could overlap the scene when Donald Pleasence shoots Michael backward through the double porch window doors for the fall over the patio railing to the ground. The production company only had a few shooting days left. The distribution company was breathing down the necks of John Carpenter and Debra Hill to get the film finished so they could have an edited 35 mm print so they could have a screening for the foreign market buyers for the film's release date which was going to be very soon. Jamie Lee was a tomboy in a lot of ways. After *Halloween*, I worked with her again on some television programs at Universal Studios, and she was great to work with.

Although Jamie Lee Curtis and Donald Pleasence didn't have much interaction during the filming of *Halloween*, the most contact they had was during the filming of *Halloween*'s climactic scene. In his five days of filming on *Halloween*, Pleasence—who would later compliment Curtis as being one of his most talented co-stars—had approached the film and his character as if he were the only protagonist in the film. It required a certain amount of effort on the actor's part, given that he'd never heard of Curtis before much less worked with her, to understand what Laurie Strode meant to the film, and how Laurie and Loomis would compliment each other by the end of the film. Basically, Laurie is the yin to Loomis' yang, and vice versa, and because they're both pitted against Michael Myers they're forever linked as dual-protagonists. This makes it all the more frustrating that the characters only have one scene together in *Halloween*.

All horror films, certainly those that are effective and leave a lasting impression on the audience, contain at least a grain of a supernatural element in them. Michael Myers' disappearance at the end of *Halloween*, his resurrection, is the film's supernatural suggestion, the final spook that leaves the viewer both scared and puzzled. Who is Michael Myers? Is he human? A wraith? This isn't something that Carpenter and Hill gave much thought to when planning *Halloween*; they wanted to make an effective and scary film and any gaps in logic or narrative would be damned in that pursuit.

Author Curtis Richards' 1979 Novelization of *Halloween* would provide the clearest explanation for Michael Myers' existence, stating that he was continually being resurrected by Druid spirits, an idea that Carpenter and Hill would later expand on when they conceptualized *Halloween II* in 1980. Curtis' thoughts on Michael Myers? "He's the monster, the boogeyman that escapes from Laurie's imagination," says Curtis. "You're not sure he's real until he tries to kill you and then it all becomes too real. Michael Myers is a nightmare brought to life."

This supernatural suggestion for Michael Myers' existence, for his continual resurrection, adds a whole other fantasy layer to *Halloween* that leaves the viewer confounded and haunted and full of questions, joyously so. In 2007, film-maker Rob Zombie wrote and directed a rather ill-advised and unnecessary remake to *Halloween*. In the remake, Zombie decided to forego the supernatural elements in Carpenter's film and instead demystify Michael Myers by making him "a real person" instead of the malevolent presence he exists as in Carpenter's film (6).

It was a big mistake. Zombie's film was a boring and tedious travesty precisely because there was no real fear and mystery to the Michael Myers character. In Carpenter's film, the viewer is so terrified of Michael Myers precisely because he lives behind his impenetrable white veil of evil. With no evidence of human feelings and remorse, the audience is willing to believe that Michael Myers is pure evil—even the boogeyman—whereas in the 2007 remake he appears as just another assembly-line hulking killer. The last scene in Carpenter's *Halloween* is so merciless upon the viewer precisely because it offers no relief, no reprieve, no trace of humanity, just the dark promise that the boogeyman is still out there.

It's ironic that Curtis regarded Nick Castle, the man behind Michael Myers' merciless white visage for the bulk of *Halloween*'s filming, as being "a real nice guy." Such was the camaraderie on the *Halloween* set that when Castle and Curtis were finished their scenes together, namely the scene in the Wallace house where Michael Myers stabs Laurie in the shoulder and sends her hurtling down the staircase, Curtis planted a kiss on a surprised Castle while the rest of the cast and crew erupted in laughter.

The kiss was Curtis' way of celebrating the fact that she'd survived the making of *Halloween*, and that her character, Laurie, had survived Michael Myers. It was also the beginning of a tradition for Curtis, as the actress would later kiss all of the actors who played the killers in her subsequent horror films between 1978 and 1981 (7). "Nick had been chasing me the whole film, so when the film was over, I just felt so much relief and I just kissed him in front of the crew, and everyone just laughed," says Curtis. "I decided to make it a tradition, and that if I ever did more horror films after *Halloween*, I would kiss the guys who played the killer. That's what I did."

The film ends with Michael Myers' point-of-view as he stalks around the track and eventually ends up back at the Myers house before the film fades out and the credits roll. Although this is the final scene in the film, for the *Halloween* crew there was still one more scene to be filmed, on the following day and night. This was the ambitious and complex continuous Panaglide shot that would open *Halloween* and establish the film's tone and visual approach.

Some critics and film historians would erroneously compare this stalking shot, which would ultimately run seven minutes long at the beginning of the film, to the opening shot in Bob Clark's 1975 horror film *Black Christmas* which featured a similar opening scene (8). In 1977, Carpenter and Clark had discussed a possible collaboration on a *Deliverance*-themed horror project entitled *Prey*, based on a script Carpenter had written. During their meeting, Clark had told Carpenter of his idea for a Halloween-themed sequel to *Black Christmas*, hence the false comparisons. "There was no similarity," says Carpenter. "In *Black Christmas*, the whole thing was who the killer is, his identity, but I wanted to show the killer's point-of-view, make the audience see through his eyes. Then they're shocked to find out he's a little kid."

The reality is that Carpenter intended the scene as an homage to the tour de force opening shot of Orson Welles' 1958 film noir masterpiece *Touch of Evil*, a film that, ironically, also starred Janet Leigh, in what was probably her most acclaimed film prior to *Psycho*. Carpenter and Hill both knew that this opening shot had to set the tone for the film, and the fact that they were shooting the opening scene at the end of *Halloween*'s production schedule made everyone nervous. As a result, the exhausted crew packed up their gear they'd been using from the Orange Grove location in Hollywood, where the Doyle and Wallace houses were located, and moved to Mission Street in South Pasadena where the Myers house was located.

This scene, the first scene in *Halloween,* acts as a prologue to everything that happens in the story. The scene takes place at the Myers house on Halloween night 1963. The camera focuses on the house, and then moves to the side and then slowly peeks inside as the hands of six year old Michael Myers grab a knife. His sister, Judith, who was played in the film by former *Playboy* playmate Sandy Johnson, is having sex upstairs with her boyfriend. When the boyfriend leaves, young Michael, who's seen only through his hands which belonged to Debra Hill for this scene, goes upstairs and stabs naked Judith to death in her bedroom. He goes downstairs and walks outside where his parents arrive, pull off the Halloween mask he was wearing, and reveal his angelic face.

This was all to be done in one continuous shot, although Carpenter, Cundey and camera operator Raymond Stella would make clever use of darkness to hide several subtle cuts in the scene. As Hill walked up the stairs, the cameras had to be moved and rearranged to correspond to the different lights that had been spread throughout different parts of the house. In any given take, a crew member's body part would just be an inch out of frame as the crew scrambled to make the scene work, aware that the scene's filming was destined to be a slow process.

Before this, the cast and crew, save for Pleasence, had to paint and refurbish the decrepit house to make it look like the pristine Midwestern dwelling that it would've been back in 1963. Given the effort and worry put into the scene's design, it's amazing that the scene was completed in just a few takes, and the scene itself would serve as a microcosm of the charmed *Halloween* filming experience.

JOHN CARPENTER: I was amazed that we got the shot in just a few takes, two to be exact. I thought it would be impossible; I thought we'd have a problem with every take, and that we'd have to do it over and over again and that eventually we'd have to change the whole scene because there was only enough money left to do two or three takes of that scene. The filming of that scene, and how everyone worked together to make the film, was a microcosm of *Halloween* in that everything seemed to fall into place. There were no big problems, no conflicts, nothing like that. I've never made a film since *Halloween* that went so smoothly, where everyone worked so well together.

DEAN CUNDEY: We were all young, and we were all trying to prove ourselves, and that was especially true with Jamie. We were all like that. We felt like we had to do a great job on this film or we'd never work again. Opportunities were very scarce at this moment in 1978 and this was our chance to show that we could make a film. The idea we had was to make a really classic horror film, and that really appealed to me since I'd been shooting a lot of exploitation movies. Why couldn't we make a Hitchcock type horror film about babysitters? We've all gone on to work on big budget films where you often throw money at problems but on *Halloween* we relied on a guerrilla-type imagination that I think we've all kind of forgotten as we've gone on in our careers.

JAMIE LEE CURTIS: Everyone in the cast and crew was there that night, and we all pitched it in to fix up the house and make it look good. We painted the walls, changed the wallpaper, cleaned the floors. Everyone worked together on *Halloween*, and that scene was an example of that. We were all there all day and night and I stayed until they finished the scene. That scene was an example of the great camaraderie that existed on *Halloween* and I think a lot of that was due to the fact that the cast and crew were so young. With the television I'd been doing at Universal, you'd be on the set and surrounded by a bunch of old union guys who really couldn't care less, but it was the opposite on *Halloween*. Everyone on *Halloween* had a passion for the work they were doing, and everyone on the crew had a fire in their belly, and we had fun at the same time. People had tattoos, and rode motorcycles and had really long hair but they also worked hard. It was a great environment.

DEBRA HILL: Everybody was there that last night, and it was sort of like a sad goodbye for all of us because it was like we'd established this tight little community during filming. We had to work quickly that night because there was a child monitor on set and the kid who was playing Michael couldn't work past ten, which is why I ended up playing Michael's hands in that scene. I have tiny hands so it was perfect. As for Jamie, the three of us—me, John, Jamie—had formed a tight bond and John and I both felt that Jamie's performance in the film had been amazing, and we were just hoping the film was going to turn out as good in the editing room as we thought it was during the filming.

RICK WALLACE: We were there at three in the afternoon and I remember that we left at six the next morning. We were all there, including Jamie, from beginning to end. I think we'd all felt part of something special and we all wanted to be together at the end.

By the close of May of 1978, the principal filming of *Halloween* was completed. For Jamie Lee Curtis, *Halloween*'s twenty day filming schedule had been quite a learning experience, and Curtis was a much different actress now than she was a month earlier. The close of the Spring of 1978 also meant that Curtis was once again an out-of-work actress, living in the valley with her roommate, already worrying if anymore acting roles would be soon to follow *Halloween*. In other words, she was a typical young Hollywood actress.

The fate of Jamie Lee Curtis' acting career hinged on the success of *Halloween*, especially since Curtis' television career at Universal had seemingly-reached a standstill. Having made the rounds of virtually every television series on the Universal lot, coupled with the *Operation Petticoat* experience, Curtis' career prospects were linked to *Halloween*'s. "My whole career at that point was really in John's and Debra's hands," recalls Curtis. "I didn't know if *Halloween* would affect my career, or if it would even get released, but I had faith in John and Debra and believed they would make me look good in the film. Other than that, I had no feelings, one way or the other, as to how *Halloween* would turn out."

By the end of *Halloween*'s filming, no one associated with the film—especially Curtis—could've envisioned that *Halloween* would eventually be regarded first as a classic horror film and then later as a great American film. Most certainly, no one knew that *Halloween* would mark the beginning of Jamie Lee Curtis' career as both a genre icon and a scream queen.

five

A SCREAM QUEEN IS BORN

For Jamie Lee Curtis, the making of *Halloween* had been a happy and rewarding experience which Curtis would ultimately regard, years later, as the best working experience of her life. In John Carpenter and Debra Hill, Curtis had found two people who genuinely believed in her skills as an actress. Carpenter and Hill saw the movie star in Curtis that no one else in Hollywood had seen, or would see for several more years (1).

Halloween had been a metamorphic experience for Curtis, one in which she began as an awkward, shy, self-doubting actress and left feeling that she could conquer anything. By the end of *Halloween's* filming, there was no time for Curtis to bask in the *Halloween* experience, however, much less wait for *Halloween's* eventual theatrical release which was still six months away. As the Spring of 1978 drew to a close, Jamie Lee Curtis was once again an out-of-work actress living in a modest tract house in the San Fernando Valley. Having been jettisoned from the *Operation Petticoat* television series, Curtis' career prospects were as shaky as ever. Not an ideal situation.

The life and the mind-set of an actress, especially a young actress for whom every choice and decision can have colossal repercussions, isn't dissimilar to that of a psychopath like Michael Myers. They must be cold-blooded, ruthless, and possess a very short memory. Curtis had spent much of the spring of 1978 consumed with the character of Laurie Strode, but now she had to throw the character away—almost as if Laurie Strode had never existed—and turn the page.

For Jamie Lee Curtis, the period after the filming of *Halloween* would be one of the most tumultuous times in her acting career. Quite simply, Curtis simply couldn't find anymore roles in the period after

101

Halloween's filming. This wasn't due to the fact that Curtis was being picky or was holding out for A-list movie offers. Curtis had no illusions after filming *Halloween* that she would be able to just sit around and wait for another film. There was none of that, no such ego on Curtis' part. The problem was that no one in Hollywood seemingly wanted to hire Curtis from the period ranging from the end of spring in 1978 to the fall of 1978. The arrival of Curtis' next film role would take considerably longer. "The period after I made *Halloween* was really brutal," recalls Curtis. "There was a period there of about a year where I hardly worked at all. There was nothing. It was depressing."

Was this career lull due to the stigma of being the daughter of Tony Curtis and Janet Leigh? Not likely, since Curtis and Leigh had never interfered on behalf of Jamie Lee's career, beyond the inescapable fact that Universal head Lew Wasserman was Jamie Lee's godfather. Jamie Lee Curtis was determined, from the beginning, to make it in Hollywood on her own and apart from her parents' influence which, frankly, by the late 1970's wouldn't have carried much impact anyway.

The fact that Curtis had been dismissed from *Operation Petticoat*, even though Tony Curtis had starred in the film version, further discounts this notion. For her part, Curtis just wanted to keep working, whether the material was good or bad, in film or on television. "I was ready to play anything after *Halloween*," says Curtis. "I would've played a hooker, you know, if it had been an interesting character, a good script."

In the period between June of 1978 and the end of the year, Curtis was hired for two acting roles. The first role Curtis booked, post-*Halloween*, was an episode of the television series *Charlie's Angels* entitled *Winning Is for Losers*. Curtis was the featured guest-star in the episode, which was shot in July of 1978 and would air in October, where she played a champion golfer named Linda Frey. Also in July of 1978, Curtis filmed a guest-starring role on an episode of the television series *The Love Boat*—with the multiple titles of *Till Death Do Us Part, Maybe/Chubs/Locked Away*—in which Curtis played another character named Linda.

Even back in 1978, *The Love Boat* was considered an acting graveyard, an ignominious respite for actors who were either on the way up in their careers or on the way out. Most actors who appeared on the critically-lambasted and tacky series fell into the latter category. At the ripe age of nineteen, Curtis wasn't sure which category she fell into.

Curtis filmed the episodes of *Charlie's Angels* and *The Love Boat*, both of which aired on ABC, at 20th Century Fox Studios in Los Angeles instead of Universal where Curtis had been stationed before *Halloween*. This isn't to suggest that this represented Curtis' independence from her Universal contract, far from it. She was, technically, still under contract to Universal when she filmed these episodes, and godfather Lew Wasserman wielded tremendous influence at ABC given that Universal, who had technically "loaned" Curtis out to John Carpenter and Debra Hill for *Halloween*, supplied much of the network's programming.

In 1979, Wasserman would consolidate his control over ABC even further when Universal Music Group purchased ABC Records, along with many other of the company's film and television properties. Regardless, there was no visible influence on the part of Wasserman on Curtis' career at this moment, no nepotism, although Curtis' firing from *Operation Petticoat* had already proven that notion moot. Curtis got these post-*Halloween* roles, inglorious as they were, on her own. It's also hard to imagine that Lew Wasserman would've been too obsessed over the career of one of Universal's legion of contract players, even if one of them was his goddaughter.

One of Curtis' co-stars on *The Love Boat* episode was Melissa Sue Anderson who was then starring on the wholesome family drama television series *Little House on the Prairie*. Anderson would later gain scream queen infamy of her own when she would star in the grisly 1981 slasher film *Happy Birthday to Me* under the direction of J. Lee Thompson. None of this had any relevance to Curtis at this moment in her career, least of all the thought that the next phase of her own acting career would become intertwined with, and immortalized within, the horror genre.

The greatest significance of working on *The Love Boat* episode was the fact that the episode gave Curtis the chance to act with her mother, Janet Leigh, who co-starred in the episode with Curtis. For Curtis, this was a mixed blessing. She loved the idea of working with her mother, who was as much her best friend as being her mother, but on *The Love Boat*? There wasn't much choice. Leigh hadn't appeared in a major Hollywood feature film since 1966's *Harper*, and had spent the past decade toiling on television and starring in B movies such as the 1972 mutant rabbit opus *Night of the Lepus* (2). Curtis was just trying to hang-on for dear life. Predictably, mother and daughter were cast in the episode precisely as mother and daughter.

They were two actresses—at two very different points on the age spectrum—who were both facing different forms of extinction. For Leigh, this was because Hollywood viewed her as being too old for the movies, while in Curtis' case it was the fact that no one thought of her as anything more than a television actress. Except for John Carpenter and Debra Hill that is, but who were they and who cared what they thought about Jamie Lee Curtis? Other than Carpenter, Hill, and her mother, the only person who believed in Curtis was herself although by the Fall of 1978, Curtis' confidence, which was always shaky, was especially wobbly.

The television episodes were both filmed in July of 1978, about three months before *Halloween* would gradually creep and slither out into the suburbs of America. Curtis was anxious to see *Halloween*, her first feature film, in order to gauge whether or not the film would do her career any good. Curtis was philosophical about the current state of her career. "I had a lot of fun working with my mother on *The Love Boat*, but that was more because I loved being with my mother than doing the show itself," says Curtis. "I liked *Charlie's Angels* because I was very athletic and I liked the show, but other than that, nothing really happened for my career after I made *Halloween* and I didn't know why."

JAMIE LEE CURTIS: I loved working with my mother on *The Love Boat*, reading lines with her, but I was also very nervous of us being cast together in something as part of some kind of stunt casting. I didn't like that. I was determined, after *Halloween*, that I would never appear with my mother in a horror film, for instance, because I knew a lot of people would want to exploit that idea. On *The Love Boat*, we were cast as mother and daughter, and so we were kind of a package deal, but I didn't want us to appear in something where we were cast as mother and daughter. If we were going to be cast together in a project, I wanted us to be cast as two actresses and not as part of a package deal.

JANET LEIGH: I was very nervous about working with Jamie at first because I didn't know how to approach our scenes together. Should I act like her mother, which I was on the show and in real life, or just treat her like a fellow actress? After a few takes, I could see how professional Jamie was, that she knew what she was doing, and after that I just relaxed and we just worked together like two actors, two professional actors working together.

Curtis was also aware of what she was up against. The late 1970s marked a highpoint for strong female movie roles as immortalized by the likes of Sally Field, Jane Fonda and Meryl Streep. They were the top actresses in Hollywood at this moment, and were constantly vying for the plum female film roles that were available, and for Curtis they represented where she wanted her acting career to be someday. On the other hand, they also represented how far she still had to go to be in their league (3). "The women were taking over Hollywood in the late 1970s," says Curtis. "They were my heroes, they were doing amazing work, and I felt like this nobody actress with grey teeth, a weird face and no acting talent whatsoever. I didn't see how I was ever going to get from where I was to where they were. At that time, they all seemed so far above me."

While her acting career seemed stalled, there was an interesting development in Curtis' personal life. In September of 1978, Curtis began dating Johnny Lee Schell, a rock 'n' roll guitarist who, at the age of thirty, was more than ten years older than Curtis (4). They didn't move in together, as Curtis continued to live in the modest San Fernando Valley tract house she shared with hairstylist friend Tina Cassaday. Curtis was, for the most part, staying away from the Hollywood party scene at this time, which in 1978 meant the disco clubs. She even enjoyed doing housework, although every week Curtis would leave her laundry for her mother's housekeeper to pick up.

Curtis was, much like Laurie Strode, in the process of becoming a woman. "Jamie's career was just getting started and she had a strong desire to become accomplished at the craft of acting and not just be a matinee idol," recalls Schell. "Her greatest attributes were common sense and a down-to-earth attitude. She knew she had no choice in who her parents were, and although proud of their accomplishments, Jamie never had an attitude about the Hollywood stuff. We hung around the house and did all the things normal people do, including cooking, washing-up and cleaning up the house. She and Tina shared a house in the Valley and Jamie drove an Audi station wagon that was reliable transportation, but far from flashy."

In the summer of 1978, Carpenter had shown a rough cut of *Halloween* to an executive at 20th Century Fox. Carpenter was screening the film in the hopes of landing a feature directing assignment with the studio, even though his future schedule was packed. Carpenter screened the film without music or sound effects as Carpenter, who would enlist musical consultant Dan Wyman to assist him with *Halloween*'s scoring in June of 1978, had yet to compose a score for the film. Without the music and sound effects Carpenter saw that the film had no power. "The executive hated the film," says Carpenter. "She said it was boring, that it had no life, and that it wasn't scary. I knew what was missing and that was the music, as well as sound effects. We needed the music to make the film come alive because sound is a very important part of a film, especially a horror film. If it doesn't sound scary, it doesn't work."

This was the most hectic period in Carpenter's career and life. Carpenter had started 1978 with the rapid-fire, two week filming of the made-for-television thriller *Someone's Watching Me!*, after which he moved straight into pre-production on *Halloween*. After shooting ended on *Halloween* in May, Carpenter, along with editor and friend Tommy Lee Wallace, had gone into the editing room, racing against the clock to meet *Halloween*'s proposed October release.

In August of 1978, Carpenter would head to Nashville, Tennessee to begin work on the television movie *Elvis*. Starring Kurt Russell, in what would be the beginning of a long collaboration and friendship between Carpenter and Russell, *Elvis* was a wildly-ambitious $2 million dollar project whose production would occupy Carpenter deep into the Fall of 1978. *Elvis'* grueling production schedule—combined with Carpenter's previous labors on *Someone's Watching Me!* and *Halloween* in the earlier part of 1978—had pushed the wiry, chain-smoking director to his limit (5). On top of all of this, Carpenter was planning to wed *Someone's Watching Me!* star Adrienne Barbeau, an event that would take place on New Year's Day 1979. In the midst of this flurry of activity, Carpenter was too busy to obsess over the reaction to *Halloween*, especially since *Halloween*'s ultimate verdict, in terms of commercial and critical appreciation, wouldn't arrive until long after 1978.

Before *Halloween* was screened for a paying audience, Carpenter and Hill decided to take the film to local California college campuses— places like Loyola, UCLA, USC—and screen it for film students to gauge their reaction to the film. It seemed like a good idea, given that the students were the exact demographic which *Halloween* was going to appeal to. The results were widely mixed. "When we first showed it to people, the students didn't like the film at all," recalls Dean Cundey. "After the film we'd talk to them and they'd make comments like, 'This isn't scary' or 'What's this about?,' stuff like that. It wasn't very encouraging."

The problem was that *Halloween* was an audience picture, in every sense of the term, not a film to be screened and fawned over by a bunch of bitter, over-analytical, and self-important film students. Curtis' first theatrical viewing of *Halloween* was at a sneak preview screening of the film that took place at the Pix Theater in Hollywood in late October. At the Pix Theater screening there were, Curtis recalls, only about thirty people in the audience, mostly the cast and crew, but the reaction of the crowd to the film stunned Curtis. "Towards the end of the film, the people would get up and shout at the screen, at my character," recalls Curtis. "It was a rough part of town, and it was a mostly black audience, and this black woman in the audience jumped up and screamed 'Don't go in that house,' during the scene when I walk across the street to find my friends. I remembered what John had said to me about getting the audience to identify with Laurie—to make them want to shout advice at her—and I was amazed how right he was because that's exactly how the audience reacted."

Halloween's first ever screening for a paying audience took place on October 25, 1978 in Kansas City, Missouri, a few days before the film would be screened in markets like Los Angeles and New York. Releasing the film in a small market like Kansas City was a calculated gamble on the part of Irwin Yablans who wanted to get a feel for how the film would play in front of an audience before releasing it to the rest of America. Yablans had just returned from Milan, Italy where he'd secured $800,000 in foreign sales on the basis of enthusiastic reaction to the film.

This regional strategy paid off as *Halloween* began drawing crowds almost immediately, even without any print or media advertising. "The numbers in Kansas City just kept growing exponentially and that spread to the rest of the country," recalls Yablans. "After the second week, the picture was breaking records and I knew if we were breaking records in Kansas City, the picture would do gang busters in the rest of the country. As for the reaction I got from the theaters, it was always the same. The audience would talk to the screen, and laugh at the screen. At first, I thought that might've been sarcasm, but then I realized that they were relieving tension. They were hooked."

Halloween's official theatrical debut, its defacto premiere, took place at Mann's Chinese Theater in Los Angeles where the film immediately drew huge crowds. It wasn't a *Star Wars* type of hysteria by any means, but for a genre picture the early grosses were very encouraging. The buzz and momentum generated from the film's first few screenings subsequently brought *Halloween* to Chicago and the prestigious Chicago International Film Festival. Yablans had booked *Halloween* with a local Chicago theater owner and the film would gross several hundred thousand dollars during its first run in Chicago.

Chicago represented a key moment in *Halloween*'s life-cycle as the festival was attended by most of the major film critics across America (6). Most of these snobby critics would've dismissed the film without ever seeing it, but the buzz and enthusiastic audience reaction at the festival forced these critics to take a hard look at the film. By the time *Halloween* arrived in all of the major film markets at once, the critical response that was initially dismissive had turned into a chorus of admirers: "*Halloween* is a superb exercise in the art of suspense," (David Ansen, *Newsweek*.); "One of the cinema's most perfectly engineered devices for saying Boo!" (Richard Combs, *Monthly Film Bulletin*.); "*Halloween* is an absolutely merciless thriller…I would compare it to *Psycho*. One of the year's best films," (Roger Ebert, *Chicago Sun-Times*.); "A beautifully-made thriller," (Gene Siskel, *Chicago Tribune*.)

Ultimately, *Halloween* would reap $47 million at the box office in North America, and another $8 million overseas, although actual figures are impossible to verify given the gypsy-like nature of *Halloween*'s release and the fact that many regional theater owners during this period couldn't be trusted to honestly divulge a film's grosses to the distributors and producers. Irwin Yablans had to fight, and even threaten, for every penny. Whereas today a film's grosses are tabulated through foolproof computer databases, the movie business, at the time of *Halloween*'s 1978 release, was very much a cash-and-carry, mom-and-pop kind of business model. In today's Hollywood, a film's box office performance is disseminated and tabulated in cubicles in Hollywood and New York. *Halloween* would've never stood a chance today.

This was 1978, a time when an independent film could still garner a theatrical release composed almost entirely of drive-ins and neighborhood movie houses, building an audience market by market, theater by theater. By 1978, Roger Corman was still a force in Hollywood, having cranked out a series of exploitation movies that had successfully played in enthusiastic drive-in houses throughout the decade. Ten years later, such films would solely exist in the made for video market given the prohibitive costs of film marketing and the exodus of drive-ins and neighborhood movie houses which are largely relics today.

This could've been *Halloween*'s fate, and probably would've been even back in 1978 were it not for the lucky convergence of Yablans' smart promotion, the abundance of drive-ins and neighborhood movie houses still in existence at this time, and of course the fact that *Halloween* was such a great film.

If *Halloween* had been released ten years later, it likely would've been banished to home video, but in 1978, a movie like *Halloween* could thrive. Then again it could be argued that *Halloween* was such a great film, and represented such a watershed moment in horror film history, that it probably would've survived any obstacles in its quest for public domination.

Obviously, *Halloween* was a wild commercial success, especially given that the film's final cost, including lab costs, was $325,000. *Halloween* remains one of the most profitable independent films of all time, especially given its amazing cost-to-earnings ratio, so much so that some historians have claimed *Halloween* to be the most successful independent film of all time.

This is a false myth, as the indigenously-made 1971 action-drama *Billy Jack* had grossed $70 million upon its release, although *Billy Jack*'s $800,000 budget was more than twice that of *Halloween*. In 1999, the independently-made horror film *The Blair Witch Project*, which cost $60,000 to produce, grossed almost $250 million worldwide. Of course, *Billy Jack* was eventually distributed by Warner Bros. and *The Blair Witch Project* was distributed by Artisan Entertainment whereas *Halloween* was solely distributed through Yablans' Compass International banner. In that respect, *Halloween* is the most successful independent film of all time, to the degree that this title still matters.

In terms of rentals, the amount of money returned to the producers or the studio that finances a film, *Halloween*'s take was $18.5 million. This would be a point of contention over the years since Moustapha Akkad, Carpenter, Hill and Yablans all held ownership stakes in the film. The distribution of all of this sudden wealth would take many years, and would include the threat of various lawsuits, but all parties concerned would ultimately reap millions of dollars from *Halloween* in the decades to follow (7). "The money was slow to trickle in from *Halloween*, but then one day, out of the blue, Debra and I got a check for over a million dollars so we did see money from the film but not as much as we should have," recalled Carpenter. "Debra and I were very naive about the business when we made *Halloween*, and that was a part of what made the film so great."

None of this concerned Curtis who didn't benefit at all financially from *Halloween*'s success but would reap other unexpected dividends from the film's success. Curtis was just thrilled to be the star of a film that had touched a nerve in the marketplace. Still, the success of *Halloween* was like faerie gold for Curtis in that it took many months, given the film's slow route from small neighborhood movie houses and drive-ins to the big city markets, for the film to sweep across America (8). "It wasn't like you see today where a film makes $20 million on the opening weekend and all of a sudden a star is born," says Curtis. "It wasn't like that. It wasn't like I would walk down the street and people would recognize me and ask me about *Halloween*. It started out playing in a few theaters and then it slowly moved from city to city and then slowly it just became this big thing, but my life really didn't change that much, even when the film was a hit all across America."

JOHN CARPENTER: We thought the movie had bombed at the very beginning because the early reviews were bad and there was almost no press about the film. I had basically moved on in my mind; thinking about my next projects, taking meetings on projects, not thinking about *Halloween*. It crept across the country, like *Invasion of the Body Snatchers*. Then it started playing in more and more theaters, and then I started going to festivals and that's when I could sense the excitement of the audience and how well the movie played to an audience. Then the critics started taking a second look at the film.

JAMIE LEE CURTIS: It wasn't like my life changed after *Halloween* because it took the film such a long time to make its way across America. There were no magazine articles being written about the success of the film, nothing like that. I didn't feel any different. That's why I always say that none of us knew what *Halloween* was, even at the first screenings. None of us looked at the film at first and thought it was a classic film in the genre. We were too close to the film to see it that way. No one knew.

DEBRA HILL: Seeing the film in a packed theater was a great experience because the audience really enjoyed being scared which was what John and I really set out to do with the film. We wanted *Halloween* to be a film that didn't rely on bloodshed or gore but where you felt a joy in being scared. I think the highlight was the scene where Jamie walks across the street to the other house because you could really feel that the audience was scared for Laurie. That's when I knew the film had connected with the audience.

KOOL MARDER: In all honesty, when I walked out of the first *Halloween* screening, I'd thought 'Great, this is another piece of crap that I've worked on,' and I think a lot of us felt that way at first. I'd worked on a lot of these low budget movies, and worked with Debra, and I was actually kind of mad after seeing *Halloween* because I really thought it was another bomb. I was mad that I'd wasted my time on this bomb. Early on, I think everyone thought the film was a joke, so no one knew that *Halloween* would become a classic film, no one at all.

JOHNNY LEE SCHELL, FORMER BOYFRIEND: I thought that *Halloween* was a good little B movie and that Jamie had done an excellent job in her first film. I never met John Carpenter or Debra Hill, but Jamie spoke very highly of them and I think they served Jamie very well in terms of making her film debut.

The release of *Halloween*, in late October, closely coincided with the broadcast of Curtis' most recent television appearances on *Charlie's Angels* and *The Love Boat*. Like many young stars, Curtis wasn't prepared for what would come next after her first big success, which in Curtis' case meant not much. After *Halloween* was released in late October, Curtis began knocking on doors and found that they were just as closed as they'd been before *Halloween* had been released. "When you meet with a casting director, they want to see a reel of your acting, of what you've done, and they don't care about television," recalled Curtis. "They want to see film, and now I had this film called *Halloween* to show people and it was basically 90 minutes of me running and screaming and crying. I also get to act normal in the film, and to laugh, and to show emotion, so I thought it was a good sample of my work, but no one cared. No one wanted to hire me. I couldn't get arrested again after *Halloween*."

What effect did *Halloween* have on Jamie Lee Curtis' acting career? Did it hurt or help her acting career? In retrospect, looking back from over thirty years of hindsight, the role of Laurie Strode has cemented Curtis' status as both a genre and screen icon. That's looking back more than thirty years later. From the period between late 1978 to the end of the decade, it could be argued that *Halloween* both helped and hurt Curtis' acting career, just as it could be argued, in terms of Curtis' long-term acting career, that *Halloween* would play very little or no role at all in terms of Curtis' eventual transformation into a mainstream film actress (9).

In terms of establishing Jamie Lee Curtis as a scream queen, *Halloween* was the perfect vehicle. In achieving that goal, *Halloween* was Curtis' *American Idol*, but Curtis never set out to become a scream queen, and just what was the definition of a scream queen in 1978 anyway? Perhaps the bloody sight of Sissy Spacek in *Carrie* was the most relevant image. Curtis had no intention of becoming a scream queen or becoming entrenched within the horror genre which the success of *Halloween* had suddenly resuscitated. Curtis didn't choose her eventual scream queen persona, or the horror genre, but they certainly embraced her and for the next phase of Curtis' acting career, they wouldn't let go of her.

As far as establishing Curtis as a mainstream actress, as someone who might one day play in the same league as Sally Field and Meryl Streep, *Halloween* served no purpose at all. By the end of 1978, *Halloween* was still ten years away from being considered a classic horror film, as evidenced when film critics would later contrast John Carpenter's string of post-*Halloween* disappointments by describing *Halloween* as a classic in comparison (10). *Halloween* was twenty years away from being recognized as a great American film, and thirty years from cinematic immortality, a status that the film unquestionably enjoys today.

Halloween's immortality came in December of 2006 when the National Film Registry added the film to its illustrious list of members. Such recognition is both good and bad for the film. Yes, it's wonderful that *Halloween* is now acknowledged as a great American film in addition to being regarded as an iconic horror film. If nothing else, this is evidence that *Halloween* is now considered the artistic and cultural equal of *Psycho*. This is a debatable point, but one that many critics and historians, film critic Roger Ebert being chief among them, have slowly embraced.

Certainly no other horror film since *Psycho* is held in such high regard. This is the negative part of the National Film Registry placement, and that's the fact that *Halloween* runs the risk of becoming the *It's a Wonderful Life* of its genre. Endlessly broadcast on film channels every Halloween—along with seemingly every other time of the year—and constantly overanalyzed by historians and film school theorists in dark screening rooms, *Halloween* is now recognized as such a genre staple that it's in danger of becoming shamelessly ubiquitous (11).

This is the price a film pays when it becomes a true classic. From a cultural standpoint, *Halloween* has become public domain. Not legally, as the film remains under legal copyright, but psychologically. George A. Romero's 1968 horror classic *Night of the Living Dead* fell into public domain and continues to be degraded to this day, much to the film's historical detriment. *Halloween* is public domain because, like *Psycho*, it has become a historical fact. This is probably the biggest similarity between *Halloween* and *Psycho*, from a historical perspective, in that both films have made the journey from genre classics to great American films that now rest in both film libraries and public libraries. *Halloween* is now as American as apple pie.

More than thirty years later, Curtis regards *Halloween's* classic status with gratitude and a bit of bemusement that such an unlikely low budget sleeper could've come so far. As for the comparison between *Halloween* and *Psycho*, Curtis viewed the films as being mutually exclusive from each other.

Despite *Halloween's* success, Curtis was still subconscious about being the daughter of Tony Curtis and Janet Leigh and breaking out of their shadow. "I look back years later and I see that *Halloween* really stands on its own as a masterpiece of the genre, just like *Psycho* was twenty years earlier, but that never occurred to me at the time," says Curtis. "As for me and my mother, I didn't see much similarity because our characters were so different, and Laurie doesn't get killed halfway through *Halloween*. She lives. Also, my mother had made many, many films before *Psycho* and *Halloween* was my first film. I knew there would be comparisons. After *Halloween* came out, there was a magazine article with my picture from *Halloween* and mom's picture from *Psycho*, comparing the two of us."

The Laurie Strode character was immortalized in 2007 when the character was resurrected for writer-director Rob Zombie's disappointing and miscalculated remake of *Halloween*, but the remake does Curtis' enduring legacy no favors. Filmed at many of the same California locations used in the 1978 film, including the babysitters' houses, Zombie's film, which began filming in January of 2007, put an emphasis on Michael Myers and his family, and his relationship with Laurie Strode, who was portrayed in the remake by actress Scout Taylor-Compton who was eighteen when the remake was filmed. Taylor-Compton's Laurie Strode has a Gothic-inspired look in terms of her dress and hair and is a sharp-edged counterpoint to Curtis' shy wallflower (12).

Curtis never saw the remake, at least not upon its theatrical release in August of 2007, although Carpenter, who had no official role on the remake, did give tacit approval to the production in terms of meeting with Zombie during the scripting process (13). Hill never lived to see the remake either as she would die of cancer in March of 2005. In terms of the original version of *Halloween* and the legacy of Curtis' Laurie Strode character, the remake only serves to heighten appreciation for each, along with the sad recognition of how far the standards of quality—and even the most basic sense of artistic integrity—in genre film-making have fallen since the making of the original *Halloween* back in 1978.

The concept that *Halloween* has been around for over thirty years is mind-blowing to fans and to Curtis herself. This is especially highlighted given that Curtis herself turned fifty on November 22, 2008. Curtis was nineteen when she made *Halloween*, a kid, and has now had a long and storied career full of twists and turns, ups and downs, battles won and lost. "It's amazing how much time has passed since *Halloween* and how fast the time has gone by," says Curtis. "In the late 1980s, when I was doing films like *A Fish Called Wanda*, I could look back at *Halloween* and it didn't seem that long ago because it had only been about ten years. I was nineteen when I made *Halloween*, and when ten years go by after that, it doesn't seem that long, but when twenty or thirty years go by, it's hard to believe."

The period in Curtis' career following *Halloween*'s theatrical release in October of 1978 is interesting because it was just as desperate and rough for the actress as it was in the lean months before. The *Charlie's Angels* episode aired on ABC on October 18, 1978 and the *Love Boat* episode aired on November 11, 1978, just a couple of weeks after *Halloween* had arrived in theaters. That was it for Curtis in terms of immediate acting work.

Between the end of *Halloween*'s filming—at the end of the spring of 1978—and the same point a year later in 1979, Curtis' acting output only consisted of these guest spots on *Charlie's Angels* and *The Love Boat*. It was a prolonged dark period in Curtis' acting career. "I couldn't get a job for seven months after I did *Halloween*," recalled Curtis. "*Halloween* was out—and it was doing such great business—and when *Halloween* eventually spread across the country, I thought I would get more movie roles, but nothing happened in terms of my career. People were congratulating me about the success of *Halloween* and I was eating at McDonald's."

Publicity wasn't the problem. There were, following *Halloween*'s nationwide exposure, magazine spreads on Curtis in major publications like *People* and *US*. The articles all focused on Curtis' personal life, the surprise success of *Halloween*, Curtis' dreams for the future, and on and on. Curtis' problem was that her bank account didn't match her newfound movie stardom which in itself was a non-entity, an illusion.

Like many young stars in the 1970s, an era where young actors made peanuts by today's standards, Curtis' immediate career prospects didn't match her newly-minted It Girl status. Curtis' stalled acting career belied the fact that she was headlining one of the hottest films in the nation at that moment. "Even though *Halloween* was a great film, it was a horror film and people in Hollywood looked down on horror films like they were garbage at that time," says Curtis. "People just shrugged their shoulders when I told them about *Halloween*. It would take years for *Halloween* to fully be appreciated for the great film it was. At that moment, it didn't really help my career."

Once again, John Carpenter and Debra Hill would come to the rescue. Beauty's in the eye of the beholder, and it seemed like Carpenter and Hill were the only people in Hollywood who looked at Curtis and saw the great actress she could be. After *Halloween*, she was also marketable as a scream queen, and since Carpenter and Hill were among the few film-makers making horror films at this time they were also able to see Curtis' potential marketability as a scream queen. In the rest of Hollywood, Curtis was, like every other young actress, a commodity and a piece of meat. To Carpenter and Hill, and the members of their close-knit crew, Curtis was special and talented.

In February of 1979, Carpenter and Hill, whose friendship had survived their personal breakup and the dizzying success of *Halloween* intact, were in the planning stages for their next feature collaboration, a ghostly horror-thriller entitled *The Fog*. Carpenter had just finished the grueling production of *Elvis* in December of 1978 and had just gotten married to actress Adrienne Barbeau on New Year's Day 1979 with friends Nancy Kyes and Tommy Lee Wallace in attendance. As with *Halloween*, Carpenter and Hill co-wrote the script for *The Fog* which they intended as an ensemble piece in terms of the actors' roles. Like *Halloween*, *The Fog* was going to be a family affair, with many of the same cast and crew from *Halloween* joining the project. The most notable exception was Barbeau, a then television veteran and singer for whom *The Fog* would mark, like Curtis' role in *Halloween*, Barbeau's entry into features (14).

Since Jamie Lee Curtis was now a part of this family, the Carpenter-Hill *Halloween* family, Carpenter and Hill asked Curtis if she was interested in appearing in *The Fog*. Curtis was thrilled at the idea of working with Carpenter and Hill—her "cinematic parents"—again but she also had very little choice given the current status of her acting career.

Still, Curtis felt a bit of concern; there was a voice in the back of her head that worried about typecasting. By following up her feature film breakthrough, a horror film, with another horror film, Curtis was in danger of being typecast as a horror film actress, a scream queen. By agreeing to be in *The Fog*, the trap was set. Jamie Lee Curtis was a scream queen, an identity the actress would regard as both a blessing and a curse.

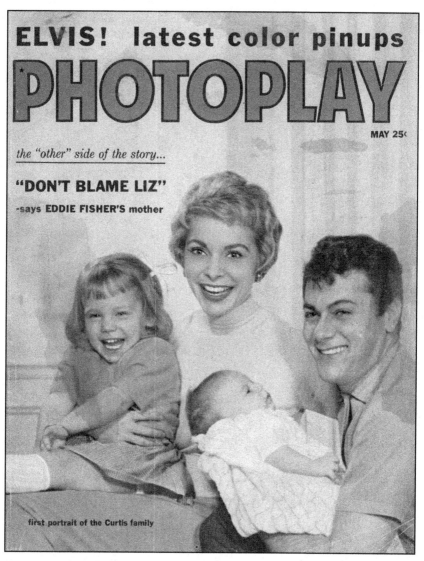

The first public image of Jamie Lee Curtis was on the cover of the
May 1959 issue of *Photoplay*. (From left to right) Kelly Curtis,
Janet Leigh, Jamie Lee Curtis, Tony Curtis.

Curtis (left) on the cover of the November 1959 issue of *Screen Stories* with sister Kelly and mother Janet Leigh.

The Curtis family on the cover of the January 1960 issue of *Photoplay*.

Father and daughter in 1960. Curtis would be estranged
from her father throughout her life.

Promotional advertisement for the television series *Operation Petticoat* (1977),
Curtis' first major role under her Universal contract.

This early publicity shot of Curtis tried to downplay her tomboyish, unconventional appearance.

Publicity shot of Curtis from *Operation Petticoat*.

Despite her famous last name, Curtis often found herself lost in the shuffle on *Operation Petticoat* amidst the series' overpopulated cast and crew. (From left to right) Dorrie Thomson, Jamie Lee Curtis, Yvonne Wilder, Melinda Naud, Bond Gideon.

Curtis was dismissed from *Operation Petticoat* after the series' first season along with most of the rest of the cast. (From left to right) Bond Gideon, Dorrie Thomson, John Astin, Yvonne Wilder, Melinda Naud, Jamie Lee Curtis.

Curtis with mother Janet Leigh in 1978.

Curtis' unconventional beauty, as evidenced in this 1978 photo, would be one of the hallmarks of her scream queen persona. Curtis would often smile with her mouth closed during the early years of her career because of her embarrassment of her teeth which were crooked and discolored.

Curtis enjoys a happy moment during the filming of *Halloween* (1978).
(Photo courtesy of Kim Gottlieb-Walker www.lenswoman.com)

John Carpenter and Debra Hill gave birth to Curtis' screen career.
(Photo courtesy of Kim Gottlieb-Walker www.lenswoman.com)

Laurie Strode is stalked by Michael Myers in *Halloween*.
(Photo courtesy of Kim Gottlieb Walker www.lenswoman.com).

Although they portrayed teenagers in *Halloween*, Curtis' co-stars Nancy Loomis (Kyes) (left) and P.J. Soles were both in their late twenties when *Halloween* was filmed in the Spring of 1978 while Curtis herself was just nineteen. (Photo courtesy of Kim Gottlieb-Walker www.lenswoman.com)

P.J. Soles (left), Nancy Loomis (Kyes) and Curtis during a break from filming on *Halloween*. (Photo courtesy of Kim Gottlieb-Walker www.lenswoman.com)

Laurie Strode tries to keep Tommy Doyle (Brian Andrews) entertained in *Halloween*. (Photo courtesy of Kim Gottlieb-Walker www.lenswoman.com)

Laurie Strode goes on the offensive. (Photo courtesy of Kim Gottlieb-Walker www.lenswoman.com)

Laurie Strode fights for her life in the closet scene from *Halloween*. (Photo courtesy of Kim Gottlieb-Walker www.lenswoman. com).

Halloween's iconic killer, Michael Myers, would become synonymous with
Curtis' scream queen persona.
(Photo courtesy of Kim Gottlieb-Walker www.lenswoman.com)

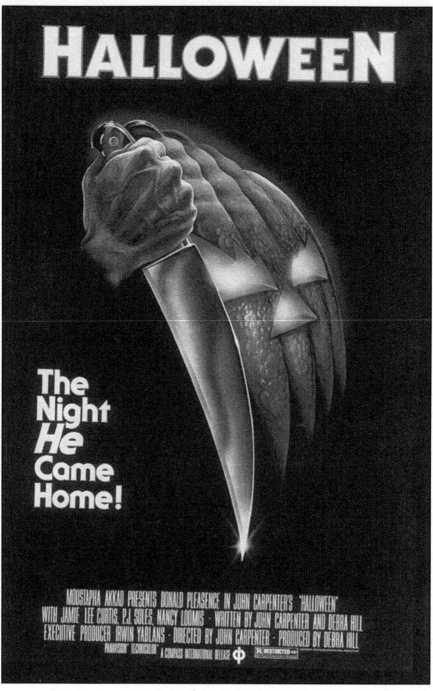

Poster from *Halloween*.

six

ENTERING *THE FOG*

The period after the theatrical release of *Halloween* was the most challenging and difficult period in Jamie Lee Curtis' young acting career, even more-so than the period following her dismissal from the *Operation Petticoat* television series. It wasn't supposed to be this way. *Halloween* had been a great commercial success, but the success of *Halloween* seemed to have no impact on Curtis' acting career, especially her fledgling film career. There were no movie offers, no meetings with top-flight Hollywood film-makers, none of that. Not only had *Halloween* not boosted Curtis' career, it could be argued that the film had, at that moment, dimmed her career prospects even further. "All people remembered about me in *Halloween* was me running around and screaming," says Curtis. "They didn't see the performance I gave in the film, and so they still didn't know whether I could act or not."

Curtis would later describe the period after *Halloween*'s release as "seven months of hell," during which the only acting roles she received were the guest parts on *Charlie's Angels* and *The Love Boat*. Dating back to the end of *Halloween*'s filming, in May of 1978, this "hellish" period— the period between *Halloween*'s release and the eventual release of Curtis' next feature film— would extend to well over a year.

For John Carpenter and Debra Hill, whose relationship by the dawn of 1979 was one of business and casual friendship, it was a whole different story. The success of *Halloween* had opened up all kinds of doors for Carpenter and Hill, a fact that Carpenter and Hill were quick to take advantage of. Following *Halloween*'s successful theatrical release in October of 1978, Carpenter and Hill signed a two-picture deal with Avco-Embassy, a genre-friendly distribution and financing company run by veteran film producer Robert Rehme. Avco-Embassy and Rehme were eager to become attached with Carpenter's and Hill's *Halloween* follow-up.

This was *The Fog*, a supernatural ghost story which Carpenter and Hill began pre-production work on in February of 1979, just a month after Carpenter's wedding—which was held on New Year's Day 1979 in Carpenter's hometown of Bowling Green, Kentucky—to actress Adrienne Barbeau who would eventually be cast in the film as well. Carpenter and Hill had co-written *The Fog* screenplay which was inspired by a spooky visit the then-couple had taken to Stonehenge, England in 1977 when Carpenter and Hill were selling *Assault on Precinct 13* at the London Film Festival.

While at Stonehenge, Carpenter spotted a fog bank that had intrigued and scared him and made him wonder "what could possibly be inside the fog?" "The visit to Stonehenge spooked me, and I thought the image of the fog was a good basis for another scary movie," recalls Carpenter who was also influenced by the 1958 British horror film *The Trollenberg Terror* which dealt with monsters hiding in clouds. "After *Halloween,* and after I'd worked so hard on *Elvis*, there was pressure on me and Debra to come up with something else very quickly, to follow-up *Halloween*. We had the idea for *The Fog*, we liked it, and decided to run with it."

The project evolved further when Carpenter and Hill attended the International Paris Festival of Science Fiction and Fantasy in March of 1979 where *Halloween* was screened and won the festival's grand prize. For Jamie Lee Curtis, the festival was a major milestone as well as Curtis won the festival's Best Actress award, her first award as an actress. In January of 1979, *Halloween* had been chosen Best Film at France's Avoriaz Festival of Science Fiction.

It was in January of 1979 that Hill began work on a first-draft screenplay of *The Fog*, which Carpenter would rewrite when they were both back in California. The pair then alternated the writing of screenplay drafts for the next month until they had a final draft script that Carpenter felt was more or less ready to shoot. "When we were in Paris one day, I told Debra that for the next film, I wanted to make an old-fashioned ghost story where the fog was a key character," recalls Carpenter. "From there we went back and forth, writing drafts of the script until I had a script that was closest to the idea I had when Debra and I were at Stonehenge and I had that scary feeling when I saw the bank of fog."

Carpenter and Hill secured a budget of $1 million from Avco-Embassy, more than three times the budget of *Halloween*. *The Fog* took place in Antonio Bay, a coastal community in Northern California, and for this purpose Carpenter and Hill drove up and down the Northern California coastline until they found a series of locations in and around the Marin County area of Northern California that seemed ideally suited to the story. More difficult for Carpenter and Hill was finding a lighthouse which would feature prominently in the story. They found this in Marin County in the form of the 109 year old Point Reyes lighthouse.

After polishing up the screenplay together, Carpenter and Hill were ready to begin filming in April of 1979, once the pair had cast the film, which is where Jamie Lee Curtis once again enters the lives of John Carpenter and Debra Hill. While writing the script for *The Fog*, Carpenter and especially Hill had written the characters in the script specifically for actors they'd worked with previously, and this was especially the case with Jamie Lee Curtis.

In addition to Avco-Embassy's support, *The Fog* would be a co-venture between Hilltopper Productions, Hill's newly-formed production company, and Entertainment Discoveries Inc. (EDI), a company run by Charles B. Bloch who was a veteran of the book publishing industry. In addition to serving as an executive producer on *The Fog*, Bloch would also oversee the novelization of Carpenter's and Hill's screenplay. Bloch's company was a wholly-owned subsidiary of Bantam Books who made a deal to publish the novelization of *The Fog* in tandem with the film's eventual theatrical release.

This cross-marketing and franchising of *The Fog*, even before the film was completed, represented quite a bold and savvy business move for Carpenter and Hill who'd learned a lot from their business experience on *Halloween* and were determined not to make the same mistakes. Of course, what no one knew at this point was that the central marketing strategy for *The Fog* would ultimately revolve around Jamie Lee Curtis.

Although Carpenter had been extremely busy since the end of production on *Halloween*, he'd been aware that Curtis had been having a hard time getting work. Curtis' personal life was also going through many changes as Curtis had parted ways with manager Chuck Binder, the man who'd brought Curtis to Universal and who had pestered Carpenter and Hill to audition Curtis for *Halloween*. Curtis had also broken-up recently with boyfriend Johnny Lee Schell. "I knew that she hadn't gotten any movie offers after *Halloween*, which surprised me because I thought she was so great in the film," says Carpenter. "When it came time to cast *The Fog*, Debra and I wrote the characters in the script specifically for Jamie, Nancy Loomis, and Charles Cyphers, and that was because we wanted to work with them again. I really wanted to work with Jamie again. We didn't write a part for her because she was out of work or because I felt sorry for her. I thought she was going to become a big star right after *Halloween*, and I wasn't sure if we'd even be able to get her. I was surprised that she hadn't gotten a lot of offers after *Halloween* because I thought she was so great."

The fact that Carpenter and Hill benefitted more from *Halloween*'s success than Curtis isn't surprising given that successful independent films, especially genre films, tend to enhance the careers of their creators far more than the actors. 1999's *The Blair Witch Project* is a good example of this, or 1980's *Friday the 13th*. The fact that *Halloween* was a critical success as well as a commercial success is evidence that Jamie Lee Curtis wasn't viewed as the star of *Halloween,* or Donald Pleasence for that matter. All of *Halloween*'s acclaim revolved around John Carpenter's artistry.

The perception was that John Carpenter was the star of *Halloween*, and it was almost as if the actors—including Jamie Lee Curtis—were seen as interchangeable parts that Carpenter had successfully manipulated. Curtis' own strong performance had been completely ignored in *Halloween*'s reviews in deference to the film's artistry. Thirty years later this has all changed, and Curtis' performance as Laurie Strode has achieved immortality, but back in 1979 Curtis' work in *Halloween* was seen as a pawn of Carpenter's and Hill's own excellent work. "*Halloween* still wasn't respectable at that point, even with some of the great reviews," recalls Curtis. "When I'd talk to all of my actor friends, and I'd mention *Halloween*, they'd look at me strange, like I should've been embarrassed about being in a horror film, as if it was trash."

Carpenter and Hill were the only ones who recognized Curtis' true value. Just as they'd given birth to Jamie Lee Curtis' film career when no one else would, Carpenter and Hill were about to give Curtis' career life once more. Carpenter and Hill were keen to replicate the enjoyable working environment on *Halloween* and thus wanted to bring as many of the cast and crew from *Halloween* onto *The Fog* as possible.

It was personal for Carpenter and Hill, as the cast and crew of *Halloween* had either been long-time friends or had become friends during the filming of *Halloween*. It was also a calculated decision. "They were like good luck charms," says Carpenter of the *Halloween* cast and crew. "If it isn't broke, you don't want to fix it. We had such a great time on *Halloween*, and everyone did such a great job, that we wanted to bring that same feeling over to *The Fog*."

Curtis was, for better or worse, part of what would be known as the Carpenter-Hill repertory company, for lack of a better word. It was a club that featured Curtis, Cyphers, Nancy Kyes, along with a legion of loyal crew members—everyone from cinematographer Dean Cundey to still photographer Kim Gottlieb-Walker—who were all keen to be reunited on *The Fog*.

Carpenter's newly-minted wife, actress Adrienne Barbeau, was cast in *The Fog*, and while *The Fog* was written as an ensemble piece, it was generally understood that Barbeau—who'd met Curtis at the end of *Halloween*'s filming as well as at a screening of *Halloween* that had taken place at the Directors Guild in Los Angeles—was going to be the lead. Barbeau and Curtis had a lot in common, and just as *Halloween* had been Curtis' feature film debut, *The Fog* would be Barbeau's entry into feature films. Like Curtis, Barbeau, who was best known for her role on the television sitcom *Maude*, was a television actress looking to make the almost impossible jump to a film career (1). Like Curtis, Carpenter was the only person who recognized such potential.

The Carpenter-Hill gang was a tight-knit unit, organized and hungry and extremely loyal. The Carpenter-Hill unit was also like an extended family unit in which the members knew everyone else's flaws and quirks and moods. For actors like Charles Cyphers and Nancy Kyes, and the others who'd worked with Carpenter and Hill previously, working with Carpenter and Hill was old hat whereas for Jamie Lee Curtis *The Fog* would only mark the second feature film she'd ever made.

Then there was the matter of whether Curtis would accept a role in *The Fog* or not, although all parties involved sensed this was just a formality. Carpenter and Hill sent *The Fog* script to Curtis who read it enthusiastically and immediately called back and said yes to being in the film. Curtis' acting fee for *The Fog* would be $20,000, more than twice what she was paid on *Halloween*. "I liked the script," says Curtis. "I thought it was very stylish and suspenseful and it wasn't overly gory.

In fact, there was almost no gore at all in the original script, which I really liked. I knew, from *Halloween*, that Debra and John would take the script and add a lot to it and make it better."

As they'd done with *Halloween*, Carpenter and Hill tried to craft the screenplay for *The Fog* in a very efficient and straightforward manner. The plot was simple, very simple, representing an old-fashioned ghost tale mixed with a modern revenge thriller. The story of *The Fog* opens with the legend of a treasure ship, the *Elizabeth Dane*, which is misled by a false beacon-light and an eerie fog that causes a shipwreck, killing all of the mariners on the ship.

The shipwreck, which took place 100 years ago, occurred off the shore of Antonio Bay, a small coastal community in Northern California. The shipwreck was deliberately caused by Antonio Bay's founders who wanted to steal the *Elizabeth Dane*'s treasure for themselves. 100 years later, in 1980, as the townspeople of Antonio Bay prepare to celebrate the town's 100th anniversary, the murdered mariners return to Antonio Bay, through the fog, to seek revenge against the descendants of their murderers, the six co-conspirators who caused their watery deaths a century earlier.

This being a modern horror film, the fog will kill anyone that gets in its way, which is where Curtis fits into the story. The name of her character in the film is Elizabeth Solley, a young, aspiring artist from a privileged background who's hitchhiking her way from California to Vancouver. She ends up spending the night in Antonio Bay, which results in her becoming embroiled in the mystery that soon envelops Antonio Bay as the fog mysteriously attacks the town and its residents. As was the case with the Laurie Strode character from *Halloween*, the character of Elizabeth Solley was also based on an old girlfriend of John Carpenter's, although this one reference hit a bit closer to home for Carpenter. "Elizabeth Solley was the love of my life," says Carpenter. "She was the girl that really broke my heart. Debra and I wrote that character just for Jamie because we felt we needed a young female lead in the film, a scream queen type role, and so I named her Elizabeth Solley after one of my old girlfriends. It worked on *Halloween* so I thought it would work again on *The Fog*."

Curtis liked the Elizabeth Solley character, if for no other reason than the fact that she was completely different than Laurie Strode. Adventurous, open, and sexual, Elizabeth Solley was nothing like Laurie Strode, and the part even allowed for Curtis to wear lipstick, makeup.

The Fog would also give Curtis the chance to experiment with a more aggressive and outgoing hairstyle under the guidance of hairstylist and former roommate Tina Cassaday who would join Curtis on *The Fog* set. "I liked the fact that Elizabeth was a lot different than Laurie," said Curtis. "She definitely wasn't a virgin, for one thing, and John had me sleeping with a guy right away in the script so this was a totally different character. I also liked the fact she was an artist, was a creative person, but at that point I would've liked anything, because I was working with Debra and John again, who I loved, and I was desperate to have a job. The biggest difference with *The Fog* was that I had a lot less dialogue, which didn't bother me because I liked being part of an ensemble. When I read the script for *Halloween*, Laurie was on every page but on *The Fog* it was spread out and I liked that."

JAMIE LEE CURTIS: In *The Fog*, the first time you see me I'm hitchhiking and then in my next scene I'm in bed with the guy who picked me up, who I just met a few hours ago, but at the same time she's not a whore. The film establishes right away that this is a completely different character than Laurie. Laurie was the kind of girl who'd never been out of her hometown, but my character in *The Fog* was much more worldly, more experienced, and she could take care of herself. I liked all of that.

It's hard to talk about Curtis' role in *The Fog*, given that *The Fog* wasn't specifically designed as a Jamie Lee Curtis scream queen vehicle. Unlike *Halloween*, the story of *The Fog* isn't told through Curtis' eyes and the viewer isn't asked to identify closely with the Elizabeth Solley character, at least no more so than the characters played by co-stars Barbeau, Cyphers, Kyes, and Tom Atkins, a newcomer to the Carpenter-Hill repertory group (2).

The fact that *The Fog* would ultimately be regarded as a Jamie Lee Curtis film—as later revealed in much of the film's eventual theatrical artwork which would feature Curtis in a screaming pose—is the most interesting part of Curtis' work in *The Fog*. When *The Fog* began filming in April of 1979, Curtis was just one part of the Carpenter ensemble, albeit with a raised profile due to *Halloween*, but by the time *The Fog* would eventually be released to theaters, in February of 1980, *The Fog* would be sold by Avco-Embassy as a Jamie Lee Curtis horror film. Somewhere between April of 1979 and February of 1980 Curtis would transform into a full-fledged scream queen, and not just any scream queen but an actress who was viewed as something of a box office draw, if only within the narrow scope of the horror genre.

All of this was still almost a year away for Curtis who approached the filming of *The Fog* as if it might be the last feature film opportunity she might ever get. Adding to the pressure of her work on *The Fog* was the fact that Curtis would be working with her mother, screen legend Janet Leigh. Carpenter and Hill had met Leigh at a screening of *Halloween*, and just as Carpenter and Hill had written roles in *The Fog* for all of their friends, they decided to include Leigh as well, if she was interested.

For his part, Carpenter was thrilled at the prospect of working with Leigh, not to mention having mother and daughter in the same film. The commercial appeal of this pairing certainly wasn't lost on Carpenter and Hill either. "I met Janet at one of the screenings of *Halloween* and I was thrilled when she told me how much she liked the film, and we sort of hit it off after that," recalls Carpenter. "She told me that *Halloween* was the kind of film Hitchcock would've liked, which was very flattering, and so when Debra and I were writing *The Fog*, we decided to write a part for Janet."

JANET LEIGH: When I saw *Halloween*, I was very impressed and I felt that John shared a lot of the same qualities as Alfred Hitchcock. Hitchcock was the kind of director who created the movie all in his mind before he shoots a single frame, and John Carpenter was the same way. I also noticed that John would always look for ways to shoot a scene where he wouldn't have to constantly intercut between one thing and another. That's how Hitchcock used to work. Having said that, John wasn't one of those young directors who was obsessed with copying shots of other film-makers or trying to make films that were just like Hitchcock's films. He was very unique.

Curtis was thrilled at the prospect of working with her mother, but scared as well. Appearing on an episode of *The Love Boat* was one thing, but appearing in a feature film together was a whole different story. Curtis was very skittish about appearing with Leigh in a film, especially a horror film. She'd been hurt, after the release of *Halloween*, by the media's relentless comparisons between her and her mother and the constant parallels that had been drawn in terms of their respective roles in *Halloween* and *Psycho*.

Because of this, as well as her own lingering self-consciousness about living in the shadow of her famous parents, Curtis was especially adamant that her and Leigh should never appear in a horror film together. "My mother and I spent years trying to find a project that we could star in together, so I was very protective about that, and I didn't want that to be exploited," says Curtis. "I absolutely didn't think it was a good idea for me and my Mom to appear in a horror film together, if for no other reason than how the media would exploit that."

The character that Carpenter and Hill created for Leigh in *The Fog*, Kathy Williams, is a matriarchal type of figure in the film, much like Leigh would be on the set and amongst the local townspeople of Point Reyes station and Inverness where most of *The Fog's* exteriors would be filmed. In the film, Kathy Williams is the chairwoman of the town's anniversary celebration while also worrying about the fate of her sailor husband who's murdered in one of the film's early scenes. It wasn't a complicated or particularly interesting role for Leigh to play, but Leigh was excited about making a feature film, and working with Curtis and her friends, and everyone on the set was excited to have her there (3).

Even though Curtis had a tremendous amount of respect and trust in Carpenter and Hill, and in their integrity as filmmakers, she was still reluctant to join her mother in *The Fog* while Leigh was much more excited about the prospect of being in the film. Leigh hadn't been in a feature film, a major feature film, since 1966's *Harper*, and was keen to get back on the big screen and possibly reignite a film career that had gone cold.

Ultimately, Carpenter and Hill found the perfect compromise, as they tailored *The Fog* script so that Curtis and Leigh would virtually never appear on screen together in the finished film. Ironically, most of Leigh's scenes in *The Fog* are with Nancy Kyes who played Sandy Fadel, Kathy Williams' assistant. Just as Kyes had been linked with Curtis in *Halloween*, she was now being paired with Curtis' mother. Indeed Curtis and Leigh would only share one scene in the finished film which would take place inside a Church during the film's climax where Curtis and Leigh are joined by several other characters. "The script for *The Fog* wasn't about me and my mother so that made me feel a lot better," said Curtis. "We weren't a team in the film, which is what I wanted to avoid because the biggest issue I had was that I didn't want me and my mother to be viewed as a package deal."

TOM ATKINS, CO-STAR: I believe I first met Jamie at a screening of *Halloween* that was held at the Directors Guild in Los Angeles. She was charming, sweet, and I thought she did a hell of a job in the film. I also thought John made a terrific movie. I was impressed by Jamie's performance in *Halloween*, and I was looking forward to working with her.

ADRIENNE BARBEAU, CO-STAR: Jamie and I were always around each other when we were making *The Fog*. The entire cast and crew was like a big group of friends that got together to make a movie. That was the way John liked it, and I could see why because it made everyone feel like they were a part of the movie. Even though Jamie and I didn't have any scenes together in the film, I felt like we were all together. Janet fit in really great. Everyone loved having her around. She would get up in the morning and she'd amaze us all by jumping rope, and Janet and Jamie loved being around each other. You could see how close they were. We were all friends.

JOHN CARPENTER, CO-WRITER/DIRECTOR: Debra and I really wanted to work with Jamie again after *Halloween*, and when we met Janet at the screening of *Halloween*, a lightbulb went off in my head and I thought that it would be so great to write a part for Janet in *The Fog*. I grew up loving movies like *Touch of Evil*, and of course *Psycho* and I'd always admired her as an actress and dreamed of working with someone like her when I was a kid. Working with her on *The Fog* was a dream come true, and I think she had a lot of fun too.

DEAN CUNDEY, CINEMATOGRAPHER: We were all excited about working with Janet on *The Fog* because she was the best-known actress we'd ever worked with. Although her role in the film was basically an extended cameo, we all liked having her around. She was a very prestigious Hollywood figure and her presence made everyone happy. In terms of working with Jamie again on *The Fog*, it was nice to see that Jamie hadn't changed at all from *Halloween*. There was a real naturalness to Jamie, and there was a family feeling on the set, and Jamie never acted like an employee of the Hollywood machine. I remember that Jamie approached *The Fog* with the same focus and intensity she'd brought to *Halloween*.

JAMIE LEE CURTIS: My mother has always been my best friend, and she was always there for me, especially early in my acting career. When I lost my virginity, I called her and we talked about it, and when I'd be sick she'd hold my head while I was throwing up. When I lost my job on the TV series, and lost other acting jobs, she was the person I went to because I wasn't close to my father. When I was young, I made mistakes, like a lot of young actors, and my mother was always there for me, more as a friend than a parent. In terms of us acting together in a movie, it was something I was very reluctant to do because I didn't want my mother and I to be viewed as a package deal. I didn't want to get hired for a movie on the condition that my mother would be hired, or vice versa. I didn't want us to become the mother and daughter acting team or anything like that. That's why Mom and I liked doing *The Fog* so much, because John specifically didn't cast us as mother and daughter.

KIM GOTTLIEB-WALKER, STILL PHOTOGRAPHER: My most vivid memory of working with Jamie and Janet on *The Fog* was how pleased they were to be working on a film together. They had great playfulness when they were together and they both had a great sense of humor.

DEBRA HILL, CO-WRITER/PRODUCER: We worked backwards when we were writing the script for *The Fog* because usually you write a script with characters and then cast actors for the roles, but on *The Fog* we picked the actors we wanted to work with and then wrote characters for them. Because we knew Jamie, and Nancy, and Charles Cyphers from *Halloween*, we tailored the characters around them. With Jamie, we felt that she'd want to play someone a lot different than the shy Laurie Strode character so that's how we created that character. John and Adrienne had worked together on *Someone's Watching Me!*, and had gotten married, and so he tailored her character to fit her personality. When we met Janet after *Halloween* came out, we asked her if she'd like to be in our next movie, and when she said yes we created a character just for her.

JANET LEIGH: People forget that I made films in virtually every genre there is: comedy, horror, drama, westerns, musicals, period movies, you name it. I hadn't made a real movie in several years before *The Fog*, and I was really drawn to Debra and John because they seemed like they were really exciting young talents. I told Debra and John that if they had a part for a middle aged lady I was up for it, and they did. I also liked the character they gave me. She was a warm, loving woman, and you feel sorry for her, and she was also a bit scatterbrained. I enjoyed the whole filming. Jamie and I didn't have hardly any scenes together but we were on the location together and it was a lot of fun to be on the set of a movie together, as two actors. People used to ask me what kind of role I'd like to play with Jamie and I always said that my favorite role was just being her mother.

JOHNNY LEE SCHELL: When I was with Jamie, Janet Leigh treated me as one of the family and was everything you'd want a star to be. Jamie and her mother were very close and Jamie was most often compared to her mother's physical appearance, although Jamie is much taller. I think Hollywood was quick to judge Jamie because of her heritage, but her perseverance made that irrelevant.

TOMMY LEE WALLACE, CO-EDITOR/PRODUCTION DESIGNER: Nancy and I didn't hang-out with Jamie and Janet much during filming and Janet, though professionally cordial to all, didn't seem much interested in hanging out and making friends. I don't think the separation between Jamie and Janet in the film was strange. The movie wasn't written about their relationship; it was simply a bit of stunt-casting. The mother-daughter tie-in was mostly Debra's idea, I think, and looked upon as more of an insider's novelty than as anything relevant to the movie experience itself. I think mother and daughter were both amused and delighted to have the chance to work together.

The teaming of Curtis and Leigh in *The Fog* is interesting in retrospect given that Curtis, who turned fifty-one years old in November of 2009, is today virtually the same age that her mother was when they made *The Fog* together (4). Curtis' own daughter Annie, who was born in December of 1986, is a couple of years older than Curtis, who was twenty when she made *The Fog*, was at the time of *The Fog*'s filming.

A lifetime goes by quickly, and in terms of the relationship between Curtis and Leigh it's clear to see, in the hindsight of the thirty years that have passed since *The Fog* was made, that the daughter has transformed into the mother.

Curtis' first scene in The Fog, and Elizabeth Solley's introduction in the film, occurs when she's hitchhiking on the side of the road and is picked up by a local fisherman named Nick Castle, played by Tom Atkins. While driving along in Castle's truck, the characters are haunted by a ghostly presence that eventually causes the windows in Castle's truck to explode. Atkins and Curtis filmed this scene on a stage. "My most vivid memory of working with Jamie on *The Fog* was of Jamie and me sitting in a beat-up old pickup truck on a stage somewhere, with Tommy Lee Wallace outside rocking the truck with a two-by-four," recalls Atkins. "Jamie and I were in the truck howling with laughter between takes of trying to act terrified as the windows blew out."

Castle then takes Elizabeth back to his house where they sleep together, although the actual sex act occurs off-screen except for one passionate kiss. The scene represented Curtis' first as an actress that had any kind of sexual overtones, although *The Fog* required no nudity on Curtis' part (5). Curtis wasn't comfortable with the thought of taking her clothes off in any film and Carpenter and Hill certainly weren't going to ask her to do it this time. This was non-negotiable.

Atkins, who remembers Curtis as being "a real professional who always knew her lines," felt a bit awkward given that he's almost twenty-five years Curtis' senior. Atkins' career, prior to *The Fog*, included a string of minor film and television roles. Unlike Curtis, Atkins had done a lot of stage work, a setting the actor enjoyed very much. Atkins and Curtis have a lot in common, especially in retrospect. Just as *Halloween* had launched Curtis' career as a scream queen, *The Fog*, which would cement Curtis' status as a scream queen, would mark the beginning of a long career for Atkins as a genre actor, or a scream king. "I had no idea what I was getting into," recalls Atkins with whom Curtis shares most of her scenes in *The Fog* (6). "I never thought *The Fog* would be the beginning of a whole string of horror films for me, but then after *The Fog*, I was hired for a string of them—*Creepshow*, *Halloween III*, *Night of the Creeps*—and people just started seeing me as that guy."

Like Curtis, Atkins was about to become part of John Carpenter's unofficial repertory company. Atkins had met Carpenter through his own close friendship with Barbeau, and Atkins had even attended an early screening of *Halloween*. Atkins' most vivid memory of working with Curtis on *The Fog*, aside from Curtis' professionalism, was the actor's observation of Curtis' close bond with Carpenter and Hill. "It was like a little cult in the way all of us worked together as one," recalls Atkins. "Jamie and John had a very good working relationship, and Jamie knew exactly what John wanted and John knew how to talk to Jamie and how to get the best out of her, and from everyone. Everyone was very down to earth. When Jamie and I did the scene in the bed, we had fun with the scene and I don't think the age thing ever came into play, on screen or off. We had a lot of fun working together."

As a future "Scream King" himself, Atkins has a unique perspective on Curtis' career. In the mid-1980s, after appearing in a string of horror films that had turned the once journeyman actor into a minor genre celebrity, Atkins proclaimed that he wanted to be a "modern day Vincent Price." It was a self-fulfilling prophecy the actor would later try to avoid. "I met Vincent Price a long time ago at a pastry shop in Los Angeles, when he was at the end of his career and I was closer to the beginning of mine," recalls Atkins. "I wanted to be like Vincent Price. I ran into Jamie a couple of years after we made *The Fog* when I was doing some stage stuff on *Halloween III: Season of the Witch*. She'd already done a couple other "fright films," but she was in between jobs and she didn't want to do another "Fright" film, but she just wanted another job. Scream Queen and Scream King are titles imposed by other people, not us."

One of the biggest challenges for Curtis, and the entire cast and crew on *The Fog*, was working with the fog machines which were very unpredictable and unreliable. This was 1979, years before digital effects would make the use of fog machines almost seem prehistoric, and creating the fog effects for the film were a constant problem for Carpenter. This is ironic, in retrospect, given that the ill-fated 2005 remake of *The Fog*, which had a budget of $18 million, would use digital effects for its fog images, save for a few exterior shots which were taken from live fog banks.

Back in 1979, in the era of "hard effects," Carpenter had no such options, and the results were often arbitrary and chaotic, emblematic of a production that ended up being a lot more complex and difficult than it had originally seemed on paper. "The cast and crew were great on *The Fog* but the film itself was just a real grind, a constant struggle," recalls Carpenter. "Nothing was easy, nothing worked like I thought it would when Debra and I planned the film out in our heads. I felt like we were being punished, in some ways, for the wonderful experience of *Halloween*. I guess you pay a price for that when you have such a great experience like *Halloween*, and *The Fog* was payback."

As with *Halloween*, the discussions between Carpenter and Curtis on *The Fog*—in terms of Curtis' character—centered on Elizabeth Solley's vulnerability. "What I loved so much about working with John is that he was the first director who saw past my looks, my exterior, and saw the real person I was," says Curtis. "He wanted me to be vulnerable, which is how I really felt at the time. I don't know how he saw that in me because no one else would've looked at me at that time and saw me as a virginal sixteen year old babysitter or an artist in *The Fog*. In *The Fog*, all of the characters are vulnerable, not just me, because of this ghostly menace that's attacking the town. With *The Fog*, John let me show a different aspect of myself. I would've done anything for John, played any type of character he wanted me to play."

Unlike *Halloween*, whose filming had been quite bruising and physical for Curtis, the experience of making *The Fog* was pain-free for the actress. The most difficult scene for Curtis in *The Fog*, and the most awkward, would occur when Curtis had to work with the fog machines. This would be for a scene where Curtis finds herself trapped in the middle of town. Curtis is in Nick Castle's truck, trying to start the truck and take off before the ghastly and glowing mariners, and their deadly hooks, descend on her.

The scene required fog to blow into the middle of town from all directions, indicating the oncoming presence of the ghostly mariners closing in on Curtis. Carpenter and crew had five fog machines ready for the scene, which was filmed on location in downtown Point Reyes, with the intention of filling up an entire block with the fog.

The problem was that the effect required still air and there was a strong wind blowing in unpredictable directions which caused the fog to blow away from where Carpenter wanted it to be. Realizing that conditions at the location would never be suitable to get exactly what he wanted in terms of making the fog effect work, Carpenter resorted to desperate measures. In the scene, Curtis is in the truck when the fog bank approaches the truck from all directions, trapping her. The script called for Curtis to stop the truck, act terrified, and back the truck away from the fog. Curtis did a rehearsal of the scene, without the fog, and it had worked perfectly, but when the fog machines were brought in, the wind took hold and blew the fog all around the street. Carpenter then asked Curtis to drive forward in the take of the scene, Carpenter's intention being to reverse the film in post-production to give the illusion that Curtis was backing away from the fog in the scene.

JAMIE LEE CURTIS: That scene was the ultimate example of low-budget film-making. When we first tried the scene, the fog machines pumped so much fog into the street that it looked like a wall of fog, but then the wind came and blew all of the fog away. John couldn't control the fog, so we talked about it and John asked me to drive straight, and that he'd reverse the shot to make it look like I was going backwards. I had to act backwards in that scene, so I couldn't blink, or do anything. I ended up driving straight into the fog, and it appears in the film like I'm backing the car away from the street, and then I stopped and they poured fog over the car.

Although *The Fog* had three times the budget of *Halloween*, the challenges of making the film were tenfold. The problematic fog effects were emblematic of a production whose filming had become more difficult and ungainly that Carpenter ever envisioned. Although *The Fog* only had a modest $1 million budget, the production itself belied this in terms of the film's overpopulated cast list as well as the need for numerous special effects, most notably in terms of the fog effects and the glowing specter of the vengeful mariners. Everything about *The Fog* seemed much, much bigger than *Halloween* and this was especially true in terms of the film's casting.

Whereas Carpenter and Hill only had the money to hire one name actor for *Halloween,* in the form of Donald Pleasence, *The Fog* featured— in addition to Leigh—two distinguished actors in its cast in the form of Hal Holbrook and John Houseman, although Houseman only worked for one day and Holbrook worked for five days on the film. Curtis and Leigh even had trailers on the set in the form of "Honeywagon" trailers that included a bed, kitchen and restroom. Despite this, mother and daughter often stayed in one trailer together during *The Fog*'s filming.

Point Reyes Station, which had a population of 300 at the time of *The Fog's* filming, was a charming, almost jewel-like little coastal town perched between a cluster of rolling hills and nearby Tomales Bay which is located near the town of Inverness where most of the cast and crew stayed during filming. Barbeau and Carpenter later bought a house in Inverness that was destroyed by a fire in 1995 (7). Throughout filming, a strong wind from the nearby Pacific Ocean chilled the cast and crew, not to mention the teams of locals who would gather around to watch the filming. "It was so cold on the streets that we would run for shelter when we weren't filming," recalled Curtis who, much like was the case with *Halloween*, smoked cigarettes constantly on the set, a habit that drew her even closer to the chain-smoking Carpenter (8). "It was freezing. I could barely speak without my teeth chattering."

The locals were thrilled to have a film being shot in their small town. In one scene, when the creeping fog attacks the town's generators, the local residents agreed to shut off all of the lights for a two-block stretch in order to simulate a mini blackout in Antonio Bay. Despite the bitter conditions, Curtis, who was still only two years into her acting career, thoroughly enjoyed making *The Fog*, and most of the credit for that goes to Carpenter and Hill. The communal and warm spirit on *The Fog*, which had also existed on *Halloween*, had tightened the bond between the trio who were now close friends.

seven

JAMIE LEE CURTIS' *THE FOG*

Although *The Fog* wasn't at all intended to be a Jamie Lee Curtis starring vehicle, the film would represent Curtis' growing influence as a cinematic scream queen. Between the period of the start of *The Fog*'s filming, in April of 1979, to *The Fog*'s eventual theatrical release in February of 1980, Curtis would transform from an actress into a bankable scream queen. Since *The Fog* would ultimately be marketed as a Jamie Lee Curtis horror film, as the reuniting of the successful elements from *Halloween*, the film's eventual commercial success can be tied to Curtis' presence.

None of this is to diminish the fine work of Adrienne Barbeau who would, after all, receive higher billing than Curtis in *The Fog*. Although *The Fog* was intended as a largely ensemble film, if there was a lead role in the film it was certainly that of Barbeau's Stevie Wayne character, and Barbeau's robust performance certainly justifies her top billing. Stevie Wayne is a local disc jockey in Antonio Bay, at a remote radio station located inside a lighthouse. Like Tom Atkins, *The Fog* represented for Barbeau, who'd previously worked with future husband Carpenter on the made-for-television movie *Someone's Watching Me!*, the beginning of a second career—not just as a film actress but also as a genre icon.

After *The Fog*, Barbeau would re-team with then-husband Carpenter in the 1981 action-fantasy *Escape from New York*, which would be followed by a string of later genre films, including *Creepshow*, *Swamp Thing*, and *Two Evil Eyes*. Prior to *The Fog*, and the subsequent genre career that would follow because of it, Barbeau had been a singer and had enjoyed a long stage career. Like Curtis, *The Fog* would indelibly link Barbeau to the horror genre. For Curtis, this was because of the screaming image of herself that would be omnipresent in almost all of the *The Fog*'s promotional artwork, and for Barbeau it was because she was married to John Carpenter. Barbeau and Curtis had a lot in common, and the biggest thing they had in common was their identification with John Carpenter.

Like Curtis, Barbeau is the first to admit that she never would've had a film career without the influence and support of Carpenter. This wasn't due to a lack of talent, which Barbeau clearly possessed, but rather an example of the stigma that was attached to being a television actress in the 1970s in terms of making the transition into feature films. Barbeau and Curtis both started out in television, although Barbeau's over thirteen years older than Curtis and had infinitely more television credits than Curtis had by the time they worked together on *The Fog*. Despite the fact that Barbeau had much more acting experience than Curtis by the time they worked together on *The Fog*, the similarities between the two actresses, and their career trajectories, are quite striking and telling.

Barbeau had been, much like Curtis had been before she was hired for *Halloween*, labeled a television actress prior to her feature film debut, a result of her work on the popular television sitcom *Maude* where Barbeau played Bea Arthur's daughter. Barbeau found the challenge of moving from television to features just as daunting as Curtis had back in the spring of 1978. Enter the John Carpenter connection in both of Barbeau's and Curtis' lives. Just as Carpenter, with the support of Debra Hill, was the only one who was able to appreciate Curtis' potential as a film star during the making of *Halloween*, he would undergo the same process with Barbeau on *The Fog*. The difference was that Barbeau and Carpenter were husband and wife (1).

Just as Carpenter had given birth to Curtis' film career, and in many ways her very identity as a woman, he had done the same with Barbeau on *The Fog*. The major difference between the Barbeau-Carpenter relationship and the Carpenter-Curtis relationship, besides the fact that Barbeau and Carpenter had gotten married before *The Fog* had begun filming, was that with Curtis, Debra Hill had acted as a mother figure in the birth of Curtis' film career whereas Carpenter had discovered Barbeau alone. The fact that Barbeau, like Curtis, continues to be a busy actress to this day is a testament to her pop culture identity that would be born with *The Fog*. *The Fog* would be to Barbeau's career what *Halloween* was to Curtis': a launching pad to a movie career, something better. An escape from television.

Although *The Fog* would eventually be marketed and sold as a John Carpenter-Jamie Lee Curtis re-teaming, the film clearly accomplished for Barbeau her goal of jump-starting a successful film career, and it would be the same for co-star Tom Atkins. They would both benefit from *The Fog* greatly, but for Jamie Lee Curtis, *The Fog* would have an even greater effect in terms of immortalizing her as a scream queen. Yes, *Halloween* was a blockbuster, but no one was sure how much of that, if anything, was a result of Curtis' presence. *The Fog's* eventual commercial success would plant the seeds that Curtis indeed had legs as a scream queen, and would serve as proof that *Halloween* fans would flock to see her in other genre films. *The Fog*, combined with the recent success of *Halloween*, would establish Jamie Lee Curtis as cinema's reigning scream queen even though *The Fog* was never intended to be a Jamie Lee Curtis vehicle. The trap was about to be set.

Whereas Jamie Lee Curtis and Janet Leigh share one scene together in *The Fog*, located near the end of the film, Barbeau and Curtis have no scenes together in the entire film. This distance didn't extend outside of filming as both actresses got along fine on the set of *The Fog*, and Barbeau especially enjoyed spending time with Leigh whose classy presence had a calming influence over *The Fog's* cast and crew. Leigh's stately presence helped prevent the hippie culture that had ruled on *Halloween*, although there would be no time for laying down on *The Fog*. For all of the *Halloween* veterans who'd joined *The Fog*, it soon became obvious that *The Fog* was no *Halloween* (2).

Although Barbeau and Curtis share no scenes in *The Fog*, there's a similarity in terms of the distant relationship between their characters in *The Fog* and the relationship between Sam Loomis and Laurie Strode in *Halloween*. Like Loomis and Strode in *Halloween*, Elizabeth Solley and Stevie Wayne are virtually unaware of each other but are both trying to unlock the mystery of the 100 year old curse that has befallen the sleepy town of Antonio Bay. Stevie Wayne does this from her lighthouse radio station and Elizabeth Solley does this, with the help of Tom Atkins' Nick Castle character, on the streets of Antonio Bay where she finds herself continually under attack by the fog. In this regard, Elizabeth Solley is closest to Laurie Strode, the scream queen, while Stevie Wayne is more like Sam Loomis, especially in the way she counsels the townspeople from the lighthouse.

Because so many of the cast and crew of *The Fog* had worked on *Halloween* comparisons between the two films were inevitable, even while *The Fog* was filming. The comparisons were heightened by the fact that, as with *Halloween*, Carpenter and cinematographer Dean Cundey shot *The Fog* in wide-screen Panavision in order to give the film a grander feel and de-emphasize the project's low budget trimmings. There was optimism among the cast and crew, but not the growing confidence around the project that fueled *Halloween* and made everyone around that film feel like they were part of something special.

The same camaraderie that existed on *Halloween*, and which helped bring so much magic to that experience, was also present on *The Fog*, but the cast and crew of *The Fog* sensed that the film wasn't working, wasn't flowing the way *Halloween* did. Carpenter, who would later become one of *The Fog*'s toughest critics, was oblivious to this at the time. "When we were making *The Fog*, I thought we were making a great film, and I think Debra felt the same way," recalls Carpenter. "I was very excited about the film. It wasn't until later, when we got to the editing room, that we realized the film was in deep trouble because it just wasn't scary. That was the miscalculation on *The Fog*. We thought we were making a scary movie but it didn't work. It wasn't scary."

The Fog's lack of thrills was evident to Carpenter when he turned the finished film over to Tommy Lee Wallace to cut and edit into shape, just like they'd done so successfully on *Halloween* where, according to Carpenter, the film had "cut like butter." It was a different story on *The Fog*. There was no flow to the film, no momentum, no driving force that carried the film from beginning to end into a cohesive whole. The first cut of the film Carpenter and Wallace assembled, the cut that was screened for Avco-Embassy's Robert Rehme, only ran 80 minutes long (3). Not a good sign. "I was very busy working on other projects so I wasn't in the editing room all the time and when I looked in one time I could see that things weren't very good," says Carpenter. "When I watched the film the first time, I was really shocked. It just wasn't very good. It wasn't scary. It sucked."

Avco-Embassy president Robert Rehme agreed, after screening a cut of the film, and agreed to give Carpenter and Hill an additional $100,000 to do badly-needed re-shoots. These re-shoots, which an exhausted Carpenter undertook in October of 1979, almost entirely consisted of shock images, namely scenes where the characters in the film are attacked by the ghostly sailors. Carpenter was making the film gory, at least in tone if not visually since the actual finished film contains, like *Halloween*, hardly any on-screen blood. "We tried to be very subtle with *The Fog* and the problem was that there was no action, no violence, and the story just kind of hung on the screen," says Carpenter. "It wasn't exciting, so I went back with Jamie and the other actors and we inserted a bunch of shock sequences to make the film play better, to make it more exciting."

Carpenter's re-shoots on *The Fog* marked the beginning of Curtis' evolution in the film from supporting player to the film's main star, although Curtis' performance also had something to do with this, namely her ability to scream. Carpenter's and Hill's original script didn't call for Curtis to scream, but featured Curtis more as a reactive supporting character who responds, like the other characters do, to the supernatural terror that descends upon Antonio Bay. All of that changed in Carpenter's re-shoots which were geared upon featuring Curtis in jeopardy, like she'd been in *Halloween*. It worked on *Halloween*, and it would work on *The Fog*, just not nearly as well.

There were also more commercial reasons. Rehme sensed, quite correctly, that the trend in horror films was towards more gore, more visceral shocks. Rehme insisted Carpenter do this, not that Carpenter and Hill—who were well aware of the marketplace's shift to more gore and violence—needed any explanations. Curtis would be the lynchpin of this new approach to the film, towards Carpenter's second try at making the film work. "The problem was that nothing much happened in the film in terms of action," says Carpenter. "A big part of that, the studio felt, was that there weren't enough shocks. I knew we had to start over but I wasn't sure where we'd get those scenes from. First, I decided to make the kills in the film more graphic, because in the original version they'd mostly happened off-screen, and then I decided to give Jamie more scenes where she's in the action, being terrified. The studio liked that."

The re-shoots included a scene set in a morgue where a corpse on a slab reanimates and walks towards Curtis who has her back turned. Another scene features Atkins and Curtis onboard the *Sea Grass*, the ship that's attacked at the beginning of the film, where a lifeless hand explodes out of a wall and lands on Curtis' shoulder, causing Curtis to scream. Carpenter also heightened the violence quota, filming the stab wounds and throat-slashing images caused by the ghostly sailors and their choice of weapon, their merciless rusty hooks. Whereas in the original version all of these things had been implied, they were now being realized in a visceral way. Carpenter's old fashioned ghost story had become modernized.

Carpenter was, and is, a realist. He knew, as did Curtis, Hill and the rest of *The Fog*'s cast and crew, that such measures were of a stop-gap nature and weren't going to transform *The Fog* into anything more than it was, and is: a stylish, fun, mildly effective, but largely middling slice of horror-fantasy. For Carpenter, finishing *The Fog* had been a matter of survival, and the director gave serious thought to quitting directing altogether because of the grueling experience. For Carpenter, Curtis, Hill and all of the *Halloween* veterans who'd joined *The Fog*, there was an unspoken realization that the making of *The Fog* had been much more problematic than *Halloween*. *Halloween* was smooth whereas *The Fog* had been bumpy and uneven, and had required superhuman effort on Carpenter's part just to be made workable.

After completing the re-shoots on *The Fog*, Curtis would once again take stock of her acting career, much like she'd done following her desolate period after the filming of *Halloween*. Although she had a lot of fun making *The Fog*, when principal filming wrapped in May of 1979, Curtis was just as doubtful about the film's prospects—and her own performance—as she'd been prior to *Halloween*'s release. "The difference with *The Fog* was that I knew people were going to see the movie because of Debra and John and all of the people involved with the movie," says Curtis. "I didn't know *Halloween* would be released, but I never thought people would want to see *The Fog* to watch me, even though I'd been in *Halloween*. I looked at John and Debra as the stars of *Halloween*, not myself, so I didn't see myself as a box office draw in horror films but I guess other people did. Because my role in *The Fog* wasn't very large, I didn't consider *The Fog* to be my film."

Happily, and surprisingly, Curtis wouldn't have to wait long at all for her next movie role. Even though *The Fog* was still months away from its February 1980 theatrical release, there was a buzz about Curtis in terms of her commercial appeal as a horror movie actress, a scream queen. This had taken place even before *The Fog*'s October 1979 re-shoots. Perhaps the first evidence of Curtis' growing stardom was in the first job she got following the completion of *The Fog*'s principal photography in May of 1979.

This was a guest celebrity appearance on *Circus of the Stars*, a network television variety series of specials in which celebrities were asked to perform circus feats. In June of 1979, Curtis appeared on the third installment of the series that aired on CBS. Janet Leigh had appeared on the series' first installment back in 1977 (4). For all of its tacky packaging, the *Circus of the Stars* appearance—where Curtis was joined by such celebrities as Cathy Lee Crosby, Sammy Davis Jr., Jamie Farr and Valerie Perrine—represented Curtis' first network television variety special appearance. In the bigger scope of Curtis' acting career, the *Circus of the Stars* appearance perhaps represented that Curtis had entered the mainstream public consciousness.

Obviously, this wasn't because of *The Fog*, which was still months away from release and in need of serious alterations and repair. This was, as is everything associated with Jamie Lee Curtis' career, a result of *Halloween*. Even by June of 1979, when *Circus of the Stars #3* aired, *Halloween* was still playing in theaters to enthusiastic crowds, furthering the notion that Curtis was a bankable scream queen. *The Fog*'s eventual release would only cement and validate the idea that Jamie Lee Curtis' attachment to a horror film project was a guarantee of success.

In July of 1979, Curtis received her first film offer outside of the Carpenter-Hill umbrella when she was hired to star in a horror film project entitled *Prom Night*. In August of 1979, Curtis would fly to Toronto, Canada to shoot the teen horror film, a slasher film, which would be financed with Canadian tax shelter dollars and which was constructed as a virtual *Halloween* knock-off. In November of 1979, Curtis would fly to Montreal, Canada, to film *Terror Train*, another horror film that would be pitched as "*Halloween* on a train." Things were happening in Curtis' career very quickly.

The Fog hadn't even been released yet, and Curtis found herself in demand. It was a big confidence boost for Curtis, even if the only offers she was getting were for horror and slasher films. "I was so flattered to be offered those movie roles, without even having to audition, that I think I would've done them regardless of what they were about," says Curtis who was unapologetic about her growing scream queen status. "If you were a young actress in the late seventies and early eighties, they offered you those types of movies, the slasher movies. That's just the way it was. I didn't take it personally. It was a job, it was business, and they were paying me lots of money. It was a learning experience."

Then there was the matter of the seven year television contract that Curtis had at Universal. The contract didn't expire until 1984, assuming Curtis was interested in doing more episodic television. She wasn't, and the contract itself didn't bind her from seeking other roles. If making *The Fog* accomplished anything for Curtis, besides cementing her image as a scream queen, it had emboldened her desire to be a movie star. She was now enthralled with the movie-making process and was even becoming a student of the camera, studying Carpenter's and Cundey's work on *The Fog* and *Halloween*, even fantasizing about directing her own feature film one day.

Curtis wanted to make more films. The experience of making *The Fog* and *Halloween* had fueled her hunger for movie stardom and heightened her view that television work, certainly the television work she'd done outside of *The Fog* and *Halloween*, was redundant and stale. Still, Curtis was skittish about how *The Fog* would be received, and especially nervous about *Prom Night* which would complete filming in the middle of September of 1979. Curtis was also keenly aware that not all of her future film collaborations would be as happy as the ones with Carpenter and Hill. In the Carpenter-Hill universe Curtis was looked at as being special and wonderful whereas to the rest of Hollywood Curtis was viewed as just another young actress. Carpenter and Hill had seen qualities in Curtis that no one else would recognize for several years to come.

Neither Carpenter or Curtis had any idea that *The Fog* would mark their second and last collaboration as director and actress, not including a later voice cameo that Curtis would perform for Carpenter in 1981's *Escape from New York*. *The Fog* would represent the last time they would ever work so closely together again, but they had no idea at the time. "I was spoiled as a young actress when I got to work with Debra and John because they were such good people," says Curtis. "I owed them my career, and working on *Halloween* and *The Fog* were the happiest experiences in my career. You hope that your other experiences will be just as good, but they're not. When I made the other horror films it wasn't the same thing, and I was always comparing everyone with John."

In September of 1979, Curtis would return to the Universal lot to film her last television appearance under her original seven year contract, a contract she had no use for anymore. Curtis had just returned from Toronto, Canada where she'd shot the horror film *Prom Night* and had yet to start work on *The Fog* re-shoots so it was a very hectic period for Curtis. Curtis' last appearance under her Universal contract was an episode of the cheesy science-fiction adventure series *Buck Rogers in the 25th Century*, a low-rent entry in the post-*Star Wars* grab-bag sweepstakes that had also included *Battlestar Galactica* and *Logan's Run*. Curtis was cast in an episode entitled *Unchained Woman*, playing the main guest role part of Jen Burton, the girlfriend of a space fugitive who finds herself trapped in prison for her boyfriend's crimes (5).

In the episode, which was directed by television veteran Dick Lowry, Curtis is rescued and freed from prison by the iconic Buck Rogers, played by Gil Gerard, who wants her to spill the beans on her boyfriend's criminal activities. The most interesting thing about the episode, in terms of Curtis' career, is Curtis' high voltage, sexy appearance. Donning lip-gloss, a Farrah Fawcett hairdo, and a tight outfit that emphasizes Curtis' voluptuous frame, the episode showcases a sexier Jamie Lee Curtis than had ever been seen on film and television before. The other most lasting image from the episode is that of Buck Rogers saving Jen from being eaten by a sand-squid. The episode was broadcast on NBC on November 1, 1979 three months before *The Fog's* eventual theatrical release. This was none too soon for Curtis and her mother who were both anxious to see the finished film, just as Curtis was anxious to be done with episodic television work forever (6).

When Curtis and Leigh screened *The Fog* for the first time, they enjoyed the film but that was primarily due to the thrill of seeing both of them in a movie together, even if they were barely on screen together. Later, Curtis would reflect a more lukewarm feeling towards the film, despite the fact she enjoyed making the film and was very grateful to Carpenter and Hill for giving her the opportunity. "I thought it was a fun movie, but it wasn't as good as *Halloween*, obviously," recalls Curtis. "It's hard when you make a film, your first film, and it's such a great film, like *Halloween* was, and then you make another film, with the same people, and everyone does the best job they can but it just doesn't turn out the same. I think we all felt a lot of pressure to follow *Halloween* up with something that was as good or close to it and that's hard to do because *Halloween* was a once-in-a-lifetime thing. I think we all realized that when we finished *The Fog*."

The Fog was released in North America on February 8, 1980 and the film would eventually gross a robust $21.3 million during its theatrical run. It was a great commercial success for Carpenter and Avco-

Embassy given the post-production struggles and the film's modest $1 million budget. *The Fog's* box office total was a little less than half that of *Halloween*, and it was clear to everyone that the enthusiasm and hysteria surrounding *Halloween* had extended to *The Fog* in terms of audience interest. At the same time the film was released into theaters, Bantam Books released the novelization, penned by Dennis Etchison, of the film which would eventually sell into multiple printings. The reviews for the film were lukewarm, mirroring Carpenter's own middling reaction to the film: "The problem is with the fog. It must have seemed like an inspired idea to make a horror movie in which clouds of fog would be the menace, but the idea just doesn't work. The movie's made with style and energy, but it needs a better villain," (Roger Ebert, *Chicago Sun-Times.*); "Silly but beguiling horror film with shock effects typical of its director," (*Halliwell's Film Guide.*); "An uneasy venture down a blind alley," (Tom Milne, *Monthly Film Bulletin.*)

The problem with *The Fog* was that the film was flawed in its basic construction. The basic story lacks focus, is overpopulated, and fails to offer any sort of compelling villain that the audience can clearly identify with. There's too many explanations and too much back-story that only makes the story convoluted. *Halloween* was simple, and simplicity was what made that film's basic story so effective. In *Halloween*, the villain, Michael Myers, is established in a very simple way that's conveyed to the audience in sharp focus, embodied in Donald Pleasence's creepy monologue where he describes Myers in crisp, horrifying detail. *The Fog* is never able to clearly define its villain, much less establish a basic legend or origin that makes as much sense as *Halloween's* wonderfully direct and simple prologue. Basically, the main difference between *The Fog* and *Halloween* is that *Halloween* had a compelling and frightening villain and *The Fog* doesn't.

The message in *Halloween* was direct and sharp whereas the explanations in *The Fog* are convoluted and seem desperate. Another problem is that *The Fog* doesn't play by any rules in that the fog in the film's title is so unpredictable it seems to target everyone, whether they be the town's ancestors or not. The fog is too random and unpredictable to function as an effective story device. The more the film tries to explain itself, through the film's rather talky legend, the more lingering disappointment the viewer feels. In *Halloween*, the threat of Michael Myers was direct and visceral, but in *The Fog*, the ghostly sailors attack with such randomness, and their motives are so murky and undefined, that it's hard to figure out exactly who they are, what they are, and what they want to accomplish. The audience can clearly identify with the evil in *Halloween*, which was grounded in everyday life, but not with the fog.

Another problem with *The Fog*, and this relates to Jamie Lee Curtis, is that the film doesn't really belong to any character. If there is a lead in the film, it would have to be Barbeau's Stevie Wayne character. Barbeau certainly creates a memorable character in the film, but the fact is that none of the characters register strongly in the film, certainly not as interesting three-dimensional characters. The fact that Curtis registers at all inside the rather thin and underwritten character of Elizabeth Solley is a testament to Curtis' undeniable charisma and screen presence. These qualities would result in *The Fog* being marketed around Curtis' persona, despite her supporting role status in the film.

In many ways *The Fog* would serve as a microcosm of Carpenter's career in terms of his emphasis on scaring the audience amidst the absence of deep and layered characterizations. "My main goal with my films is to scare the audience, shock them, make them jump, and I don't apologize for that," says Carpenter. "I don't make character-based films, films that deal with issues, because when you're making a horror film, if you don't scare the audience there's no movie."

None of this is to suggest that *The Fog* is a terrible film, far from it. It's an agreeable, stylish, sporadically entertaining horror film, entirely digestible, but in comparison to the great *Halloween* it's a disappointment if for no other reason than *Halloween* worked splendidly while *The Fog* struggles to register, despite Carpenter's most determined efforts. In comparison to the garbage that would follow *Halloween* through 1981, *The Fog* appears in much more glowing terms, but compared to *Halloween* itself it was a disappointment. *The Fog* was a massive struggle for Carpenter and Hill, especially the grueling post-production re-shoots that made the film salvageable, and Carpenter would later lament that these struggles almost felt like punishment for all of the good luck that had surrounded *Halloween*.

It's interesting to note that neither Carpenter or Hill were thrilled when Avco-Embassy built much of *The Fog*'s marketing strategy around Curtis, implying that *The Fog* was a Jamie Lee Curtis film. This was especially true of a poster Avco-Embassy released that featured a screaming Curtis being assaulted by the ghostly sailors. Carpenter and Hill felt that this would give the audience the false impression that Curtis was featured throughout the entire film, along the same lines as *Halloween*, and thus was false advertising. "The poster made it seem like it was Jamie's movie and that she was playing the same role she did in *Halloween*, but one of the main reasons Jamie did the film was to play someone who was completely different from Laurie Strode," recalled Hill. "Avco-Embassy wanted to play-up the *Halloween* connection as much as possible so they focused on Jamie and John."

Carpenter's and Hill's own ambivalence over *The Fog* would be symbolized when, years later, they would serve as producers on the development of the ill-fated $18 million remake of *The Fog* that was released in October of 2005 to dismal reviews and mediocre box office. Ironically, filming on the remake began in the coastal area of British Columbia, Canada on March 14, 2005, just one week after Hill herself passed away after a long battle with cancer. The remake featured actress Maggie Grace, best known from the television series *Lost*, in Curtis' role, although Grace's character was renamed Elizabeth Williams in the remake. Whereas Elizabeth Solley was a hitchhiker in the 1980 film, Elizabeth Williams is an Antonio Bay native who's the daughter of Kathy Williams, played in the remake by actress Sara Botsford.

Curtis would later say in interviews that she hated her own performance in *The Fog*, a harsh statement for the actress to make given how little Curtis is given to do, in terms of her acting range, in the film. It's impossible to judge Jamie Lee Curtis as an actress or gauge her future potential based on the brief and thin characterization she's given in *The Fog*. She's effective in the film, and Curtis' charisma and personality shine through as always, but it's impossible to criticize her performance in *The Fog* because she's just not given much to do in the film, the same of which can be said of every other actor in the film except maybe for Adrienne Barbeau.

The fact is that Curtis was her own harshest critic during the early years of her film career and hated virtually all of her early performances. This suggests that the self-consciousness and self-doubt Curtis harbored from Choate and her teenage years hadn't been worn off by her newfound, albeit not earth shattering, movie stardom. "I hated my performance in *The Fog*," said Curtis. "I just hated it. I thought it was terrible. The thing is, I tend to put myself down all the time."

JAMIE LEE CURTIS: I think the reason *The Fog* didn't work, the reason it wasn't as good as *Halloween,* was that the horror in the film wasn't grounded in reality. In *Halloween,* you had a bunch of teenagers in a small American town, and everyone in the audience could identify with that world. *The Fog* wasn't believable enough, but I still thought it was an entertaining movie. What that film did for me, as an actress, was to allow me to shed the whole shy persona I had in *Halloween* and show people that I could play a character who's more worldly, more sexy, someone who can take care of herself.

JOHN CARPENTER: I tend to love all of my films, even the ones that were box office failures, but *The Fog* is one of those film that I don't think about very much, except to remember how hard we had to work in post-production to even make it presentable. It's just not one of my favorite films, and I think Debra felt the same way and that's one of the reasons we agreed to do a remake of it. I didn't mind seeing a remake being made because I think you should do remakes of movies that aren't great, and hopefully make them better. *The Fog* wasn't a great film, far from it, and I was looking forward to someone else taking the idea and maybe doing a better job with it. Still, the film was very successful and still has an audience today. It's become a minor horror classic and I'm proud of that.

Curtis' lack of self confidence in herself at the time of *The* Fog's release made her as doubtful about *The Fog*'s chances as she had been about *Halloween.* The difference this time was that *The Fog* didn't revolve around her, or at least that's what she'd thought when filming was completed. Robert Rehme, who was still the president of Avco-Embassy when *The Fog* was released in February of 1980, had supreme confidence in Curtis, especially in terms of her drawing power. A lot of the credit for this also goes to Carpenter whose numerous re-shoots featured Curtis prominently, including several scenes where Curtis is screaming.

After viewing the re-shot version of *The Fog,* Rehme felt much better about *The Fog* and was convinced that Curtis was the film's major asset, primarily in terms of her scream queen appeal. "There's a scene in the film where a dead hand falls out and touches her shoulder and she just screams her head off and I saw that as the defining image in terms of selling the film," recalls Rehme. "I felt Jamie Lee Curtis would have a big appeal to horror fans and that the film should be marketed as a Jamie Lee Curtis film, as well as a John Carpenter film because they'd been so successful with *Halloween* and we wanted *The Fog* to be our *Halloween*."

Avco-Embassy had marketed *The Fog* entirely upon Carpenter and Curtis, emphasizing their success with *Halloween* and promising that history would repeat itself. After Carpenter and Hill, who merely viewed Curtis as a friend and a talented young actress, Rehme was the first person to recognize Curtis' scream queen persona and its marketing potential. Yes, *The Fog* was a John Carpenter film, a fact that the film's publicity materials made perfectly clear, but Jamie Lee Curtis was just as much the main attraction as the director of *Halloween* was.

Ironically, the screaming image of Curtis used in the film's promotional artwork wasn't a scene in the film. On the film's poster artwork that Avco-Embassy made specifically for the purpose of highlighting Curtis, Curtis's character, Elizabeth Solley, is pictured standing in front of a door while the ghostly hand of a vengeful sailor crashes through the door and reaches out for her. The image never actually appears in the film, but was an inspired creation of Avco-Embassy's publicity department. The only similar image in the film is when Curtis is in a church at the end of the film—the only scene in the film where Curtis appears with her mother—and a ghostly hand crashes through a window and grabs her, causing Curtis to scream. Avco-Embassy had its "hook" with which to sell *The Fog*.

Technically, Adrienne Barbeau received top billing in *The Fog*, in terms of her name appearing before Curtis' on the list of credits, and Barbeau certainly received a lot of publicity from the film. Despite Avco-Embassy's emphasis on Carpenter and Curtis, it wasn't as if Barbeau's role in the film was overlooked, as evidenced by the long genre career that Barbeau would enjoy as a result of the film and her relationship with Carpenter. "Without *The Fog*, I probably wouldn't have had a film career, so I'm very grateful for that film," says Barbeau. "It was a great experience, and the film also led to a long career for me in the horror genre."

Regardless, the perception was that Jamie Lee Curtis was the star of *The Fog*, and a main reason for the film's box office success. After the film's theatrical release, Rehme signed Curtis to a three picture deal at Avco-Embassy, in the hopes that the company would develop more genre vehicles for Curtis to star in.

Ultimately, no films would result from the deal for Curtis, although Avco-Embassy would acquire and release two of Curtis' upcoming horror releases, *Prom Night* and *Roadgames*. In 1980, Rehme tried to package Curtis with Robin Williams—who was then starring in the television series *Mork & Mindy*—in a science-fiction romance film project entitled *Out of Sight,* but the project never got off the ground. Basically, Avco-Embassy would end up releasing two more Jamie Lee Curtis horror films without having to pay her anything extra for them.

Perhaps the biggest significance of *The Fog* for Curtis, aside from the film's branding of her as a scream queen, was her relationship with Carpenter and Hill. *The Fog* wasn't the end of their association together but it marked the end of their collaboration, primarily between Carpenter and Curtis. In 1981, Carpenter and Hill would act as producers on *Halloween II*, starring Curtis, in which Hill was a constant presence on-set while Carpenter would be busy with pre-production work on *The Thing. The Fog* would be the last film the trio would all work on together, hand-in-hand. They were still friends, and always would be, but the professional relationship between Curtis, Carpenter and Hill would never be the same again after *The Fog.*

This wasn't by design. By 1980, Carpenter and Hill had a western script they wanted to make entitled *El Diablo*, a script that Carpenter and Tommy Lee Wallace had conceived during *The Fog*'s long gestation, and had mentioned a possible role for Curtis. This project, like so many others, would languish for years before being resurrected in 1990 as a made-for-cable movie. By that time, all parties involved had long moved away from each other.

After the release of *The Fog*, Carpenter and Hill moved right into pre-production on *Escape from New York* which they'd begin shooting in August of 1980. With a budget of $7 million, *Escape from New York* was an epic project for the duo—along with the rest of the Carpenter-Hill unit who would also join the project—and was the most expensive film Avco-Embassy had ever financed up to that point. It would also mark the completion of Carpenter's two picture deal with the company. Carpenter and Hill, who would end their collaborative partnership shortly after *Escape from New York*, were moving in different directions and Curtis was ready to do the same.

If Carpenter and Hill represented parental figures for Curtis in terms of her acting career, Curtis was now ready to leave home and spread her wings, even if this meant starring in a string of slasher films. This would turn out to be the case, between 1980 and 1981, but at least they would be her films. Just as Carpenter wanted to graduate to big studio genre films, the kinds his USC colleagues were getting to make, and Hill was anxious to produce different kinds of films in various genres, Curtis was looking to prove that she could carry a movie on her own and disprove the idea that she was nothing more than a Carpenter-Hill creation. Mostly, Jamie Lee Curtis just wanted to keep working.

Jamie Lee Curtis was about to leap out on her own into the great Hollywood unknown without the supervision of Carpenter and Hill. By the time of *The Fog*'s theatrical release, in February of 1980, Curtis had already completed work on two other horror films, *Prom Night* and *Terror Train*, both of which would be released later that year. 1980 would be the year that Jamie Lee Curtis became the undisputed queen of horror, whether she liked it or not. 1980 would be the year of the scream queen.

eight

GRADUATION DAY

By July of 1979, Jamie Lee Curtis had completed principal photography on *The Fog*, her second feature film, completely unaware that she would later have to return, in October, to do numerous reshoots for the film. In June, Curtis had made her first network television variety special appearance when she appeared on CBS's *Circus of the Stars* (1). By this time, *The Fog* was still months away from its eventual February 1980 theatrical release and Curtis was anxious to find her next film project. She was desperate not to see a repeat of the bleak career period that followed *Halloween*, nor did she want to rely on friends like John Carpenter and Debra Hill for her next job. She wanted to get a film role by herself, preferably a job that had little or no connection to *Halloween*.

In retrospect, this period in Curtis' film career is very significant in that *The Fog* would represent the second and final teaming between Carpenter and Curtis as actress and director. Curtis, who was very much Carpenter's and Hill's "film child," was now on her own, although this wasn't apparent to Curtis, Carpenter, and Hill at this moment. Like a teenager who's anxious to leave home, Curtis was looking for some independence, to go out into the world—a world outside of the Carpenter-Hill umbrella—on her own.

This is where *Prom Night* entered Curtis' life, and for Curtis the project would represent a degree of independence, both as an actress and as a young woman. Independence from the Carpenter-Hill unit? In the sense that *Prom Night* was a project that Curtis got on her own, the answer is yes. The three friends never had any discussions about Curtis "moving on," but it seemed obvious, after *The Fog*, that all three friends were ready to do just that.

The trio would eventually reunite in 1981 for *Halloween II*, but in a much less personal capacity than had existed on *The Fog* and *Halloween* (2). By 1981, the differences between the three friends would be palpable whereas by 1979 the divide amongst the trio, in terms of each of them wanting to move in different creative directions, was less visible. If Curtis was anxious to break free of the Carpenter-Hill connection it was to show Hollywood that she didn't need them, and wasn't merely a Carpenter-Hill creation. In this respect, *Prom Night* was a very important film and represented a crucial time in Curtis' acting career.

Prom Night was a project that Curtis actually sought out herself, and there were actually several *Halloween* connections, although they were hidden under the surface. Curtis knew that the success of *Halloween* had turned her into a scream queen, and that the release of *The Fog* could cement that image. Curtis would've been blind to not have recognized that other film producers would be anxious to cast her in their own horror films and capitalize on the success of *Halloween*. This description would fit *Prom Night* to a tee.

Curtis knew this, accepted who she was becoming, and didn't really care, as long as she didn't do anything that directly disrespected her work with Carpenter and Hill. Curtis was very philosophical and entirely realistic about her immediate career prospects. "I was a young actress, I was being offered movie roles during this period, and there weren't many young girls getting offered movies at that time so I felt very lucky, even though the material wasn't great," recalls Curtis. "I was a young actress and I was in an era where they were making a lot of slasher movies, and those were the kinds of movies they offered. If you were a young actress you got offered a lot of crud."

Prom Night was the brain-child of film-maker Paul Lynch, a British emigre to Canada whose debut feature was the 1973 country-western drama *The Hard Part Begins*. The film, which had a budget of only $95,000, received mild reviews but did little business and by the mid-1970s, Lynch—much like fellow Canadian film-maker William Fruet, who would also make the transition from serious dramas to exploitation and horror films—was desperate to come up with a commercially-viable film project. To this end, Lynch followed up *The Hard Part Begins* with the 1978 wrestling drama *Blood & Guts*, but the film did little business. "If you were a Canadian film-maker back in those days it was hard to make a living," says Lynch. "A lot of us were making good movies in the early 1970s, but we were starving to death."

By 1979, Lynch decided it was time to generate his own horror project, inspired by the commercial success of *Halloween* which was still doing strong business in drive-ins and second-run movie houses. Lynch's motives weren't purely cynical or derivative; Lynch was a rabid Alfred Hitchcock devotee, having been particularly fond of *Psycho*. Lynch was keen to make a horror film that elicited some of the same beats, albeit in the prism of the teen-slasher genre that was in the process of becoming so ubiquitous in the marketplace.

In the spring of 1979, Lynch met with *Halloween* producer Irwin Yablans and pitched Yablans a horror project entitled *Don't See The Doctor*, the concept of which revolved around a murderous gynecologist. Yablans, who had now become the port of call in Hollywood for horror and slasher projects, wisely rejected the concept. Nonetheless Yablans liked Lynch's drive and passion and suggested to Lynch that he try and develop a horror project that revolved around a holiday-theme, something in the vein of *Halloween*.

Lynch, who'd been dividing his time between Los Angeles and Toronto, Canada, quickly found his inspiration when he was driving back to his Sunset Boulevard hotel from Yablans' office and saw an advertisement on top of the hotel that read "For Your Prom Night, After Six Tuxedo Rentals." A horror movie was born. "I thought the prom night concept was a great idea because it's something every kid goes through, except for me because I'd dropped out of high school and never had my own prom," says Lynch. "I made a poster myself and then decided to pitch the idea to producers, and this time I was confident that I would succeed."

A week later, Lynch went back to Yablans with his proposal for his prom-themed horror film only to discover that Yablans was in New York on business and wouldn't be back in Los Angeles for another week. Lynch had no script, and no real outline for any characters or story, just some poster artwork featuring a knife in a heart with blood spewing out of the heart and the title *Prom Night* emblazoned over the image.

Lynch didn't want to sit and wait. That Friday, Lynch attended a film festival party in Los Angeles where he met Toronto-based film producer Peter Simpson. Like Lynch, the burly, sharp-tongued Simpson was also looking to move into more commercial prospects. Simpson listened to Lynch's pitch and liked what he heard, bemused by Lynch's enthusiasm and the brazen artwork Lynch had created. A partnership was formed.

Besides Yablans, Peter Simpson represents the second most direct *Halloween* connection to *Prom Night*, although Simpson's connection was much more tenuous. Simpson had recently produced a family-adventure film called *The Sea Gypsies* which was released in 1978. The film was notable because it co-starred Nancy Kyes who'd shot the film before she made *Halloween*.

Yablans' non-involvement with *Prom Night* did play a key role in Jamie Lee Curtis becoming involved with the project. Since Yablans had become, after the success of *Halloween*, the man to see for slasher film projects, word about *Prom Night* spread quickly around Hollywood. Curtis heard about the project and, reckoning that she was the current It Girl of the horror scene, wanted to star in the film. "It took *The Fog* a long time to get released, so I was anxious to find another movie, any movie," says Curtis. "I was basically looking for anyone who wanted me, and I knew that would be another horror movie. If I'd been a producer at that time, I wouldn't have looked at me for anything other than horror because that's all I'd done."

Prom Night would be produced by Simpson through his Simcom Ltd. company, with much of the film's $1.6 million budget to be raised through public offerings and tax shelter investments. *Prom Night* would become known as the vanguard of the Canadian tax shelter films that would define the Canadian film industry throughout the 1970s and early 1980s. The tax shelter era was a product of the Canadian government's efforts to boost Canadian film production by offering generous tax deductions, never imagining that this would lead to a flood of exploitation and horror films.

This program, known as the Capital Cost Allowance (CCA), offered producers generous tax credits and loopholes, and provided strong incentive for investors to park their money in Canadian films. The program also required producers to hire Canadian talent as the tax credit system operated on an escalating scale based on the number of Canadians that were in the cast and crew of any film. Basically, the size of the tax credit correlated to the number of Canadians used in a film. The more Canadians, the more money.

Prom Night, which would turn out to be the most commercially-successful indigenously-produced Canadian film during this period, would eventually come to represent another sub-genre of the tax shelter period: the "slash for cash" era. *Prom Night* would mark the beginning of a series of Canadian-made, *Halloween*-inspired horror-slasher films that would dominate the Canadian film industry between 1979 and 1982. In retrospect, *Prom Night* would not only cement Jamie Lee Curtis' status as cinema's reigning scream queen, but also as the queen of the slashers and the queen of the tax shelter horror films.

Curtis knew nothing about Canada—much less the fledgling Canadian film industry and its socialist paradigm—when she heard about *Prom Night*, although Tony Curtis had recently shot two films in Canada (3). Jamie Lee Curtis had never been to Canada, but had heard good things about the country and began to enthusiastically pursue the *Prom Night* project. "I wanted it bad," says Curtis. "I just felt—after doing *Halloween* and *The Fog*—that if there was a horror project out there, that I should be the first choice to do it. If I was a scream queen, and that's how people looked at me at that time, I wanted to take advantage of it."

Before Lynch and Simpson could meet with Curtis, they needed a script. To this end, Simpson recruited a writer named Robert Guza, Jr. who came up with a story for *Prom Night* and also wrote a first draft screenplay which was later rewritten by William Gray, a former music critic turned screenwriter who had worked as an editor on Lynch's *The Hard Part Begins* and had co-written the screenplay for *Blood & Guts*. "Robert actually wrote much of the script for the film, even though he only got a story credit," says Gray. "He wrote a first draft script that was the basis for the film and I rewrote his script and turned it into a final draft."

Prom Night's shooting script, which represented Gray's polishing and rewriting of Guza's first draft, eventually came in at a whopping 122 pages. The script was full of extended exposition, endless dialogue sequences, but little in the way of on-screen action or violence. This was a result of a dearth of inspiration amongst the film-makers. Aside from *Halloween*, and 1976's *Carrie*, there weren't a lot of direct inspirations in terms of trying to adapt the horror-slasher formula. It was the summer of 1979, almost a year before *Friday the 13th* and the rest of the post-*Halloween* slasher crowd would swamp the marketplace. As a result, both *Carrie* and *Halloween*—especially *Halloween*—would be prominent in terms of *Prom Night*'s execution and planning.

The plot of *Prom Night* was simple, very simple. The story opens with a ten year old girl named Robin Hammond who, after being tormented by four other youngsters during a hide and seek game they call "Kill," accidentally falls through the window of an abandoned building and is killed instantly. After watching the girl fall to her death from the second story window (Gray's script was more graphic and had the girl being decapitated by a pane of glass), the four remaining children, the four co-conspirators, make a pledge never to talk about the accident again or the roles they played in young Robin Hammond's death.

Cut to six years later where the four children are now high school seniors getting ready for their high school prom. Someone who witnessed Robin Hammond's death six years earlier decides to get revenge by plotting to murder the four co-conspirators during their prom night celebration. The lead character in the story is Kim Hammond, the part that Curtis would be cast in, the older sister of the dead child. In the story's denouement, Kim's brother, Alex Hammond, is revealed to be the masked killer who both witnessed his sister's death and then took revenge on prom night.

It was all pretty basic, textbook horror-slasher stuff and in retrospect seems surprisingly formulaic given the lack of points of reference that *Prom Night* had to go on by the summer of 1979. There also didn't seem to be any obvious borrowing from *Halloween*, aside from the concept of a masked killer attacking teenagers which was an approach that certainly hadn't been originated by *Halloween*. This would all change in post-production when Simpson, without Curtis' knowledge and without much of Lynch's input, would include story elements that were transparently derivative of *Halloween*.

Curtis found the original 122 page shooting script kind of boring, very talky, but relatively harmless. In other words, she had few objections. "The script I read for *Prom Night* was completely different from the film that was released," recalls Curtis. "The script I read was nothing like *Halloween* and nothing like the final version of the film. I wouldn't have done the film if I thought they were going to copy *Halloween*."

JAMIE LEE CURTIS: It was a role that was offered to me; the first role that I was ever offered. *The Fog* I considered a gift; *Halloween*, I never understood why I got that, until later. When you doubt yourself as I did, you never understand why people hire you. I practically would have paid to make that movie. I had only made two movies up to that time, they offered me three times the money I was paid on *The Fog*, and it was the first role that was actually offered to me.

WILLIAM GRAY, WRITER: I hadn't seen *Halloween* when I was hired to rewrite Robert Guza's first draft script, and I didn't see *Halloween* until we were in Toronto shooting *Prom Night*. I think we copied a lot of things on *Prom Night*, and *Carrie* was a big inspiration, and I'd seen that film and tried to incorporate elements of that film into our script. As for Jamie, I didn't know her at all before I met her in Toronto, and I guess I thought of her as a television actress, and the daughter of Tony Curtis and Janet Leigh, although I was aware that *Halloween* had been a big hit.

PAUL LYNCH, DIRECTOR: Everyone thinks we set out to copy *Halloween* on *Prom Night*, and I loved *Halloween*, but *Psycho* was much more of an inspiration for me when I was planning *Prom Night*. I based *Prom Night* more on Hitchcock and also Brian De Palma more than John Carpenter. I wanted to focus on Jamie's character and the rest of the teens and make them interesting people, and draw the suspense out of their characters, like Hitchcock did with *Psycho*. I thought Jamie, in addition to being a great asset to a horror film, would be the perfect actress to carry the kind of suspense film I wanted to make.

It would seem that casting Jamie Lee Curtis in *Prom Night* would be an easy decision given her success in *Halloween*, and her growing reputation within the genre, but the decision wasn't as cut and dried as it appeared, especially for producer Peter Simpson. Lynch was much more enthusiastic about Curtis' involvement than Simpson, who was actually kind of ambivalent about casting Curtis in the film. "I didn't get the whole Jamie Lee Curtis thing back then, and that was my mistake because Paul knew she was a star," recalled Simpson who died of lung cancer in 2007. "I thought we could cast any girl in the film, anyone who was good, and I was wrong because I don't think we would've had a movie without Jamie Lee Curtis."

Simpson, who had a production office in Century City, California, actually had his heart set on actress Eve Plumb, best known as one of the stars of the *Brady Bunch* television series. After *The Brady Bunch* had ended in 1974, Plumb continued working non-stop in television, establishing herself as a teen movie-of-the-week queen, in addition to making a slew of episodic television appearances throughout the 1970s. Despite her legion of television credits, Plumb had never made a feature film and, like every young actress, was keen to make the transition (4). Simpson, who'd been actively developing some other projects with Plumb in mind, thought that Plumb would be a good fit for *Prom Night*.

All of that changed when Curtis showed aggressive interest in the project. Curtis met with Lynch and Simpson at Simpson's office in July of 1979. "I would've done anything to get the part in *Prom Night*, at that time, because I still didn't have much confidence in myself and I was scared no one would hire me, even after doing *Halloween* and *The Fog*," says Curtis. "With *Prom Night*, I would've killed to have made that movie, because they just offered it to me, and I didn't even have to audition for the film which blew me away. It was the first time someone had actually offered me a film role so it was very flattering and made me feel good about myself."

Actually, Curtis did have to perform an audition for Lynch and Simpson but the audition involved dancing and not acting. During pre-production the film-makers couldn't decide whether the music in *Prom Night*, which would be a big part of the film, should have a disco flavor or be more rock-oriented. It was 1979, and while there were some grave signs that disco might be on the way out, no one was completely sure. Ultimately, the film-makers chose disco, inspired by the fact that *Saturday Night Fever*, released in 1977, had been one of the biggest hits of recent years. Curtis, who ended up being paid $60,000 for her work in *Prom Night*, also knew disco well, having modeled a line of disco fashions for a magazine spread several months earlier (5).

JAMIE LEE CURTIS: They offered me the part and then asked me if I'd like to spend six weeks in Toronto and for someone who was as insecure as I was, the idea of making a movie, any movie, was so exciting that I think I just let out a sigh. I thought my character in the film wasn't very sophisticated or interesting but I didn't care because I was so happy to have a job that was paying so well. I was so excited that I called my mother and she couldn't believe how much I was offered for the movie because that was a lot of money back then. Looking back, I think the producers saw me as an asset for selling their horror movie which was more than I thought of myself at that point.

PAUL LYNCH: Actually, Jamie did audition for Peter and I but it was a disco-dancing audition and not an acting audition. I knew she was a good actress, after seeing *Halloween*, but I really wanted to see if she was a good dancer because we were doing a prom-themed movie and I wanted to do a big dance sequence. Peter and I took Jamie to a dance studio down on La Cienega in Los Angeles and we asked her to do some dancing and she just danced her head off. She was a great dancer, unbelievable, and that's what finally convinced us that she was perfect for the film.

PETER SIMPSON, PRODUCER: The first time I met Jamie was when she walked into my office in Century City, and she wasn't what I was expecting, to say the least. I was expecting this quiet, shy, kind of virginal-seeming girl but Jamie was very confident and brash. She walked into my office and just put her legs on my desk, very forward, not what I was expecting, and she also had a bit of a dirty mouth. I was looking for an actress who was kind of the ultimate virgin, the ultimate good girl, the perfect innocent, and Jamie was anything but an innocent young girl. I didn't think she was quite right for the part until I saw her work on the set.

The rest of the roles in *Prom Night* were cast simultaneously in Los Angeles and Toronto. Besides Curtis, all of the remaining cast members in *Prom Night* would possess Canadian birth certificates, a requirement of the tax credit system. Basically, you could hire one American star—which in this case was Jamie Lee Curtis—for the purpose of selling the film, but the rest of the cast and crew had to be Canadian if investors and producers wanted to enjoy the maximum benefits of the tax credits and loopholes that were being passed around like candy during this period.

The most experienced actor that was cast in *Prom Night* was Canadian-born Leslie Nielsen who had enjoyed a modestly-successful acting career in Hollywood, mostly in television. After filming *Prom Night*, Nielsen would complete work on the comedy-spoof film *Airplane* which would kick-start Nielsen's transition into that of a comedic actor which would later catapult Nielsen to movie stardom in the late-1980s with the successful *Naked Gun* films. Nielsen was cast as Raymond Hammond, the father of Curtis' Kim Hammond character in Prom *Night*.

The most interesting part of Nielsen's casting in *Prom Night*, from the perspective of Curtis' career, is that Nielsen would ultimately receive top billing over Curtis in the film. This is strange given that Curtis was being paid more and most certainly represented a much more valuable asset to the film-makers, in terms of selling *Prom Night*, than the veteran actor Nielsen did. Such was the idiocy of the Canadian film industry, an industry that lacked any type of commercial sense and which stubbornly refused, and continues to refuse, to accept the concept of a star system. Nielsen's seniority, and Canadian birth certificate, would be given preference over Curtis' undeniable genre appeal.

Besides Nielsen, the most experienced actors in the *Prom Night* cast were Eddie Benton, who was cast as Wendy, Curtis' romantic rival in the film, and Antoinette Bower, who was cast as Vi Hammond, Kim's mother in the film. Bower was a veteran actress who'd had a long career in Canada and Hollywood, mostly in episodic television, while Benton, who would later change her professional name to Anne-Marie Martin, was a year older than Curtis, an acting contemporary of Curtis', and had a long list of credits in episodic television.

Gray and Lynch had known Eddie Benton, the name that Curtis recalls knowing Benton by during this period, since May of 1973 when they met the then-fifteen year old aspiring Canadian actress on the set of Lynch's *The Hard Part Begins* in Toronto where Benton was from. "She was friends with a girl in the film, and Anne-Marie, as we knew her, showed up and asked me for a part in the film, but I found her a bit unlikable at the time and I didn't give her a part in the film," recalls Lynch. "We knew each other for years and had kind of a love-hate relationship. Shortly after *The Hard Part Begins*, Anne-Marie went down to Los Angeles with actor Art Hindle and that's when I saw her again. In terms of casting her in *Prom Night*, Wendy was Jamie's rival in the film, and I needed someone who could be really obnoxious and mean and I thought of Anne-Marie."

Benton and Curtis, who would become friends on the set of *Prom Night*, hadn't met before but had a lot in common. Not only were they virtually the same age, but both started out in television, and while Curtis' film career had begun with horror films like *Halloween* and *The Fog*, Benton had, prior to being cast in *Prom Night*, completed a science-fiction film entitled *The Shape of Things to Come*. Budgeted at $3.2 million, twice the budget of *Prom Night*, *The Shape of Things to Come* would be released in May of 1979, just a couple of months prior to the start of filming on *Prom Night*. Benton's mother, Sylvia Martin, was also an actress and would be given a small part in *Prom Night* on the suggestion of William Gray who had remained friends with Benton since their first meeting during the filming of *The Hard Part Begins*.

The most significant casting in *Prom Night*, from Curtis' perspective, was probably that of actor Casey Stevens who was cast in the role of Nick McBride, Kim Hammond's boyfriend in the film; the prom king to Kim Hammond's prom queen. As the male lead opposite Curtis in the film, Stevens would ultimately receive third billing in the film, behind Curtis and Nielsen. Sadly, Stevens' pairing with Curtis would be the highlight of his all-too-brief acting career.

Stevens had been raised on a farm in the Eastern Townships of Quebec, a million miles from the Hollywood fishbowl that had surrounded Curtis. Stevens, who was adopted, was an avid movie lover who dreamed of becoming an actor. In 1977, Stevens headed to Montreal where he toiled as an extra on film locations before landing his first professional role: a small part in the Montreal-shot film *In Praise of Older Women*, which was released in 1978. In 1977, the spiritually-minded Stevens also hitchhiked to India where he spent several months studying meditation and yoga from Hindu monks.

In 1978, the French-Canadian Stevens, who had curly brown hair and striking blue eyes, went to Los Angeles to continue his acting quest, with no success. By 1979, Stevens was living in Toronto, Ontario where he supported himself by working at technical and trade conventions, as well as a local Toronto deli where the outgoing Stevens would stage impromptu performances with his many friends.

Stevens landed the role in *Prom Night* in mid-1979 when *Prom Night*'s Toronto casting director, Karen Hazzard, saw Steven's face while combing through scores of headshots. "Casey was thrilled to have gotten the role in *Prom Night* which Casey thought was going to launch his acting career," recalls Marty Galin, a close friend of Stevens. "Casey knew that Jamie Lee Curtis was in the film, and I remember Casey regarding her as being a big Hollywood star. I don't recall if we'd seen *Halloween* before that or not, but Casey had been told that *Prom Night* was going to be a copy of *Halloween*."

As with Curtis, Stevens was hired for *Prom Night* on the condition that he could dance, which he assured the production he could even though in reality he'd never danced before. It wasn't the first time the determined Stevens had told a white lie to get a role. In 1978, Stevens had been cast in an unreleased motorcycle film called *Running Free* on the assurance that he could ride a motorbike, which he couldn't. The carefree and fearless Stevens had passed the test with the motorbikes, learning to ride like a pro, and he was confident that learning to dance with Jamie Lee Curtis wouldn't be anymore of a challenge.

Stevens signed-up for disco-dancing lessons with a Toronto dance teacher, just several weeks before *Prom Night*'s August start date. Soon Stevens found himself doing "flips and far-out moves" and in a state of disbelief that he was about to star in a major motion picture opposite Curtis. "He was a nice kid, but he was very bland as an actor and I don't remember why we cast him in that role," recalls Lynch. "I never thought he was a very good match for Jamie."

Stevens was largely hired because he had a Canadian birth certificate, his most important qualification for getting the chance to star in a film alongside Jamie Lee Curtis. This would be the case for the rest of the film's casting which was done in Toronto. The rest of the *Prom Night* cast was filled with a group of green and inexperienced young Canadian actors, including David Mucci, Pita Oliver, Mary Beth Rubens, Sheldon Rybowski, Joy Thompson, and Michael Tough who was cast as Curtis' brother in the film, Alex Hammond, who also turns out to be the film's killer. Many of these young actors were still in high school in 1979 and for most of them *Prom Night* would mark their feature film debuts.

The crew was also almost entirely Canadian, and also very inexperienced. *Prom Night* had no problem meeting its Canadian content quota required tor the tax incentives. For all of the dentists and lawyers in Canada who had a few extra few thousand dollars they wanted to shield from the tax man, known in Canada as Revenue Canada, *Prom Night* certainly seemed like a good, sound investment. With Jamie Lee Curtis, the only American-born actor in the cast, as its star, *Prom Night* was a can't miss prospect.

Prom Night not only represented a degree of professional independence for Curtis, given that it was the first feature film she'd ever been officially offered outside of her relationship with John Carpenter and Debra HIll, but it also represented many firsts for Curtis as an actress. *Prom Night* was the first film she ever shot outside of Hollywood, in Canada no less, a country she was completely unfamiliar with. "When they offered me the part, they just said to me 'How would you like to spend a few weeks in Toronto?' and that was very appealing to me," says Curtis. "I just wilted when I heard that because I was so flattered that someone wanted me, and I was excited that I was going to be traveling and filming in a different location."

More significantly, *Prom Night* was the first film that Curtis would shoot without the protective influence of Carpenter and Hill, along with the tight-knit legion of cast and crew that Curtis had grown so attached to as an actress during the filming of *The Fog* and *Halloween*. With Paul Lynch directing, and Robert New serving as cinematographer on *Prom Night*, this represented the first time Curtis had ever worked with a new production unit. "*Halloween* was such a great experience and as a young actress you think it's always going to be like that but it's not," says Curtis. "I was spoiled on *Halloween*."

That's not a slight on *Prom Night* or the film's cast and crew, but more of a recognition that Curtis was now, like every other actress, a commodity to be bought and sold. There was a real caring and protectiveness for Curtis on *Halloween* and *The Fog* where Curtis was viewed as beautiful and special. Without the bonds of the Carpenter-Hill unit, Curtis was now, like every other actress, just another young starlet. "I didn't know John Carpenter but I'm guessing that the biggest difference Jamie found between the two of us was that I don't like to work with actors that much," says Lynch. "I liked to leave the actors alone, and that's the approach I took with Jamie because I could see she was such a natural."

Curtis arrived in Toronto, Canada at the end of July in 1979 in preparation for *Prom Night*'s August 7, 1979 starting date. *Prom Night*'s filming schedule would eventually extend from August 7 to September 13 of 1979. Curtis' arrival in Toronto wasn't met with the attention or fanfare one would expect given Curtis' pedigree and her rising star status.

While Curtis' co-star, Leslie Nielsen, was put up in Toronto's luxurious Sutton Place Hotel, Curtis was deposited in a much more modest dwelling, since demolished, that was located on Yonge St., a rather colorful area in Downtown Toronto that's famous for massage parlors, sex shops and strip clubs. William Gray and Robert Guza, *Prom Night*'s two writers, stayed in adjacent rooms.

The hotel wasn't a dive by any stretch of the imagination, but if Curtis needed an ego-check, the humble accommodations certainly fit the bill. Here was Curtis, a visiting Hollywood star with an illustrious pedigree, and she was being welcomed to Toronto as if she were just another faceless actress. The situation was undeniably small-time, and a clear signal that Nielsen was viewed as being more valuable to the production than scream queen Curtis, a notion that would be proven false upon *Prom Night*'s theatrical release in 1980. For her part, Curtis had more important things to worry about, namely trying to perfect her dance moves.

Prior to the start of *Prom Night*'s filming, Curtis would spend ten days practicing dance moves in preparation for an extended dance sequence that would appear later in the film. Paul Lynch's sister, Pamela Malcolm, was a dance choreographer who'd been working in New York, and Lynch decided to bring his sister to Toronto for *Prom Night*'s filming in order to choreograph the film's big disco dance number. Malcolm's biggest job would be to work with Jamie Lee Curtis and Casey Stevens and teach them how to dance. "Jamie was actually very much a natural dancer to begin with," recalls Malcolm. "Casey really struggled with the dance moves, and it was much more difficult for him to learn the dancing and so Jamie had to help him out a lot with the dancing."

Although Curtis was a good dancer, having undergone some dance training previously, she arrived at *Prom Night*'s filming with a nagging back injury that was the result of some poor gymnastics training. Casey Stevens, on the other hand, was strictly uncoordinated in terms of trying to dance, in addition to being constantly worried about his contact lenses falling out. Malcolm worked with Curtis and Stevens for six hours a day to get them in shape for the film's big dance sequence. "Jamie was tenacious and was a good dancer because of dance training, but she also had a bad back because of some improper gymnastics training," recalls Malcolm. "Casey was just the nicest, sweetest guy but he had two left feet, and he was always worried about his contact lenses falling out, and he just couldn't see his feet, no matter how hard he tried. The challenge was to work around Jamie's bad back and Casey's two left feet."

Prom Night was filmed entirely in Toronto, Canada, primarily around the Don Mills Collegiate High School in Toronto where *Prom Night*'s fictional Ohio high school, Hamilton High, was located. Another prominent location in the film would be the Scarborough Bluffs, located near the edge of an ocean-side cliff, that was used to represent the school's exterior. It was at the high school that the cast and crew had their first real introduction to Jamie Lee Curtis, although some, like Stevens, had met her prior to the start of filming. It was an odd dynamic: a Hollywood actress working with Canadian unknowns, amateurs. Curtis' presence on the set made quite an impression, for more reasons than one.

Curtis' first screen appearance in *Prom Night*, which was actually shot later in the filming schedule, occurs at a cemetery where Kim Hammond and the rest of the Hammond family stare at the grave of Kim's dead sister, Robin Hammond, on the sixth anniversary of Robin's accidental killing. It's a brief scene but Curtis trembles with emotion and projects the grief and sorrow of the entire Hammond family without having to say a word. Without any dialogue, Curtis effortlessly establishes the character of Kim Hammond, in addition to selling the film's somewhat shaky and unconvincing premise.

If Jamie Lee Curtis was ever going to get a chance to test her appeal as a scream queen, and her ability to carry a horror film solely because of her sheer will, it was going to be with *Prom Night*. With *Prom Night*, there was no relying on Carpenter and Hill for guidance and support. Curtis was on her own.

This scene, Kim Hammond's first appearance in the film, was shot at St. James' Cemetery in Toronto, towards the end of filming. The weather was drizzly and overcast, a mood that extended throughout much of the shoot. By this point, the cast and crew of *Prom Night* had seen enough of Curtis to know they were around a special presence, a real movie star. The legend of Jamie Lee Curtis, both the actress and scream queen, had followed Curtis from Los Angeles and arrived in Toronto onto the set of *Prom Night*. Regardless of Leslie Nielsen's top billing in the film, there was no doubt who the real star of *Prom Night* was and it was Jamie Lee Curtis. No other horror film in Curtis' scream queen career would rely on Curtis' invaluable presence as much as *Prom Night* would.

MARTY GALIN, FRIEND OF CASEY STEVENS: Casey said that his relationship with Jamie Lee Curtis had some rough edges at first, but that they became closer and closer as the film went on. Casey was a very attractive person, and when he put on his contact lenses they made his blue eyes just sparkle. I think Casey saw in Jamie a type of person he'd never met before and I think Casey introduced Jamie to a world, in Toronto, that she'd never seen before.

WILLIAM GRAY: I was in the room right next door to Jamie's at the hotel on Yonge St. and we became pretty good friends. I'd never seen *Halloween* before we worked on *Prom Night*, believe it or not, and so Jamie and I went to a local theater where *Halloween* was still playing and we watched the movie together. Me and Jamie Lee Curtis watching *Halloween* in a movie theater! I loved the movie, and that's when I realized, "Oh, we're ripping off *Halloween*" and then we walked out of the theater and these fans walked up to Jamie, not believing they were standing in front of the star of *Halloween*. I just found Jamie to be a really great person, and what I loved the most about Jamie was the way she talked about her mother, Janet Leigh. She was talking about her mother, and how important she was to her, and you could see how much she loved her mother. She never talked about her father.

PAUL LYNCH: What was immediately obvious about Jamie was that she was a fabulous actress, and I think the entire cast and crew were immediately impressed by her professionalism and her ability to get into her character. Jamie would work on the script and improve her dialogue during scenes. One time, we were shooting a scene where Jamie and Leslie Nielsen were in a classroom and Leslie walked out and said to me, "This Jamie Lee Curtis is amazing. She's rewriting the script, she's so professional, I can't believe what a good actress she is." He was right.

PAMELA MALCOLM, DANCE CHOREOGRAPHER: Jamie was a young and tenacious girl, very hard-working, and when she arrived in Toronto she wanted to call the shots, and she acted like she was in charge. She was the total opposite of Casey Stevens, who was very humble and shy. Casey and Jamie got along well, and were affable together, but they had no chemistry together. I think Casey put up with Jamie's behavior because he was such a nice guy whereas another guy might've smacked her. Early on, I wanted to have lunch with Casey and Jamie but Jamie blew us off, and she would always want to be on our own, like she was this big Hollywood star who wanted to avoid the rest of us. I think this was because Jamie was very young, and still growing up, because she wouldn't have gotten away with that type of behavior if she was in her thirties or forties. In terms of the work, Jamie always worked very hard, especially when it came to dancing.

DAVID MUCCI, CO-STAR: I was eighteen years old when we did *Prom Night*, and I'd heard about *Halloween*, and that Jamie was a star, but the biggest thing to me was that Jamie was the daughter of Tony Curtis and Janet Leigh. That was exciting and impressive, to be acting with someone like that. Jamie was very nice and generous. I first met Jamie when we were having lunch, and Paul Lynch was there, and Jamie started looking at me and she was holding up her hands in the shape of a camera lens and then she moved her hands in front of my face. She was looking at me with her hands, and I realized that she was trying to direct me, trying to see how we would look on screen together.

ROBERT NEW, CINEMATOGRAPHER: Paul and I talked about *Halloween* which was going to be our blueprint for *Prom Night*. *Halloween* was dark, spooky, and it kept you off-base, on edge, and that's the feeling we wanted to create with *Prom Night*. Paul and I watched *Halloween* and we focused on Jamie and talked about how we would photograph Jamie in the film, how to make the best use of her. The first thing we noticed was that Jamie was a good-looking girl and very pretty. We decided we would start out with the image of this all-American girl, with a nice domestic setting, and then make the tone of the film darker as we went along. Jamie was ready from the word go, very eager and enthusiastic, a really nice person and a real professional. I thought of Jamie as the star of *Halloween*, as opposed to John Carpenter, and not the child of Hollywood royalty although you certainly couldn't ignore who her parents were.

LESLIE NIELSEN, CO-STAR: The thing I remember most about Jamie was her intelligence as an actress. From the first time I met her, I was impressed with how professional and prepared she was as an actress, more so than any of the other young actors I'd ever worked with.

MARY BETH RUBENS, CO-STAR: I met Jamie for the first time in the makeup room, and the first thing I noticed was what a powerful presence she was. She just had a very strong presence, and part of that was her Hollywood pedigree, because of her famous parents, but most of it was because of Jamie's star quality. She had an aura. I wouldn't say I was intimidated by her, because she was very nice, but she was a formidable presence. It wasn't a Hollywood attitude; it was her power. I think Jamie was in rough shape when she arrived to do *Prom Night*, physically and psychologically, and I think *Prom Night* represented a transitional period in her life. I also noticed that she had very bad teeth which surprised me given her pedigree and who she was. She was almost twenty-one, and I think she was uncertain about her future. Other than that, she was very down to earth, very professional, and extremely focused. She was a star.

SHELDON RYBOWSKI, CO-STAR: The legend of Jamie Lee Curtis was definitely present around the set when we shot *Prom Night*. I was in high school at the time and when I told my friends I was doing a horror movie with Jamie Lee Curtis they all freaked out because they'd all seen *Halloween* and loved it so much. As for Jamie, she was very approachable and down to earth.

PETER SIMPSON: I think I misread Jamie when I first met her in Los Angeles because when she arrived in Toronto she was a total professional. I didn't realize what an asset she was until she showed up on set and I saw the star presence she had, especially in terms of the horror films. Paul saw that, and I didn't, and Paul deserves credit for that because he saw Jamie's star quality and I was the guy who wanted to cast the girl from *The Brady Bunch*.

JOY THOMPSON, CO-STAR: I met Jamie for the first time in the school gymnasium, and I was kind of nervous about approaching her but then she just walked right over to me and put her around me and said "You're perfect" and that's the way she was throughout the filming. She was very down to earth, and even though the rest of us, the Canadian actors, were very inexperienced, she treated us with respect, as fellow actors.

MICHAEL TOUGH, CO-STAR: My first meeting with Jamie Lee Curtis was both awkward and memorable. Jamie Lee put her arm around me and said, "Come on, baby brother, let's get to know each other." The next thing I knew we were bra shopping in the Eaton's department store in the Don Mills Plaza. An interesting choice of field trips to take a hormone-charged teenaged male! I recall that Jamie was very friendly, very approachable. I think the cast came together quickly as a group of late-teen to early twenties actors truly enjoying a new and exciting opportunity.

GEORGE TOULIATOS, CO-STAR: The producer said right upfront "This is going to be our version of *Halloween*" so it was quite obvious what we were doing and it was obvious that Jamie Lee Curtis was the main reason that the film was being made. I wasn't really that intimidated by her at all, because I really wasn't a big fan of her father, Tony Curtis. I mean, it wasn't like she was the daughter of Ralph Richardson.

STEVE WRIGHT, ASSISTANT DIRECTOR: I would say that Jamie arrived with a bit of a Hollywood attitude, which isn't to say she was rude, because she wasn't, but that she was used to doing things in a certain way. Jamie's first scene in the film was a scene at a cemetery, staring at the grave of her dead sister, and I shot most of that scene because Paul Lynch was busy with something. I remember I looked at Jamie and asked "Do you think we got it?" and she said, "Yes, we got it, let's move on" and I said, "Well, I think we should wait for Paul Lynch to decide because he's the director of the movie" and she said "Let's go, I don't want to do this anymore." Later on, I found out that Jamie was scared of cemeteries, and that's why she was so uptight, because for the rest of the shoot she was fine. Ironic that the star of so many horror movies would have a phobia of cemeteries.

Curtis' uneasiness at being around a cemetery, which was the setting for her character's first scene in *Prom Night*, was a microcosm of the difficult transition period Curtis was experiencing at the time of *Prom Night*'s filming, both as an actress and a young woman. Despite the success she was enjoying in her acting career, Curtis was still very uncertain about her skills as an actress, about her own physical appearance, and still very subconscious about her Hollywood pedigree.

Prom Night is a document of this stormy transition period in Curtis' career and life. This is visible in Curtis' look in the film which features a much more sexier and sophisticated dress and hairstyle. *Prom Night* is set around the time of high school graduation, which is ironic given how tumultuous and uncomfortable Curtis found her time at

Choate to be. Although Curtis was now twenty and on the verge of her milestone twenty-first birthday, the high school scenes in *Prom Night* brought back a lot of feelings and memories for Curtis. The making of *Prom Night* would represent, career-wise, Jamie Lee Curtis' own graduation, both as an actress and as a scream queen.

nine

THE MAKING OF *PROM NIGHT*

Prom Night's most visible cinematic influences were 1976's *Carrie*, without the pig blood or the telekinetic protagonist, and Jamie Lee Curtis' own *Halloween* in terms of the film's omnipresent and stalking killer. The former influence was embodied in the characters played by Eddie Benton and David Mucci. Benton's character in *Prom Night*, Wendy, is Kim Hammond's rival for the affections of Casey Stevens' Nick McBride character in the film, and she enlists Mucci's Lou Farmer character to help her try and sabotage Kim's prom night. Basically, Benton and Mucci fill the same roles that Nancy Allen and John Travolta played in 1976's *Carrie* with Curtis representing the victimized Sissy Spacek protagonist, save for the ability to make objects move.

The influence of *Halloween* was of course embodied in Jamie Lee Curtis' mere presence and this relationship would ultimately catapult *Prom Night* to box office success upon the film's theatrical release in 1980. The most interesting part of this dynamic is the relationship between Kim and Wendy in the film, as well as Benton's and Curtis' own relationship. Although they played hated rivals in the film, Benton and Curtis actually struck up an immediate friendship on the set of *Prom Night* that would extend long after filming.

In one of the film's funniest scenes, Curtis is standing in an empty school gym and practicing her dance moves when an angry Wendy confronts her and informs Curtis, referring to the upcoming prom, that "It's not who you go with, honey, it's who takes you home." Curtis' response is brilliant as she just nods her head at Wendy, as if to suggest that she welcomes a confrontation with Wendy. As with virtually everything in *Prom Night*, Curtis gives this scene more dramatic power and emotional weight than the material warranted or which was present in the script.

Benton, who was also known as Anne-Marie Martin to some of her colleagues and friends at this time, and Curtis were very much acting contemporaries as both were young women in their early careers who were trying to advance in Hollywood. Both Benton and Curtis had gotten their starts in episodic television—Benton with an episode of *Wonder Woman* in 1976 and Curtis with a 1977 episode of *Quincy M.E.*—and both actresses had found the transition from episodic television to feature films difficult.

In this regard, Curtis had pulled ahead of Benton by the time of *Prom Night*'s filming, by virtue of *Halloween* and Curtis' resulting scream queen persona which Benton would later emulate with a role in the 1981 horror film *The Boogens*. Following the filming of *Prom Night*, Benton would also follow in Curtis' footsteps by filming an episode of *Buck Rogers in the 25th Century* entitled *Twiki is Missing* which would air on January 31, 1980, almost three months after the broadcast of Curtis' *Unchained Woman* episode. The filming of the *Buck Rogers* episode would be Benton's last acting appearance under the name Eddie Benton, the name that Curtis and most of *Prom Night*'s cast and crew knew her by during filming, before she would change her professional name to Anne-Marie Martin for good (1).

Eddie Benton and Jamie Lee Curtis were true acting colleagues with much in common, although Benton's own Toronto upbringing and Curtis' Hollywood upbringing couldn't have been more different. Because they had a lot in common, in terms of the fact that they'd followed parallel career paths, it's probably not a surprise that the two women would've struck up a quick friendship during the filming of *Prom Night*. The fact that Benton and Curtis were the only two Los Angeles-based actors in the *Prom Night* cast, in the midst of a group of young Canadian unknowns, also brought them together in the sense that Benton was the only member of the *Prom Night* cast that Curtis could relate to.

WILLIAM GRAY: I'd known Anne-Marie ever since I'd worked on *The Hard Part Begins* as an editor and I'd seen her hanging around the set. She went down to Los Angeles and we kind of followed each other for the next couple of years, and we stayed friends for years. She was just a really great person and when I met Jamie Lee Curtis, I thought she was a really great person and I think they were very much alike, both great people. Anne-Marie met Jamie for the first time in Toronto, when I met Jamie, and they just hit it off at first sight. They were also both very beautiful women.

PAUL LYNCH: I'd known Anne-Marie before we did *Prom Night* together. I met her when I was shooting *The Hard Part Begins* back in 1973, and Anne-Marie showed up on the set because she had a friend in the movie. She was just a kid, still in high school, and she wanted a part in the movie, but I didn't give her one because I found her a bit obnoxious, even though I love her and think she's beautiful. We had a love-hate relationship. She changed her name to Eddie Benton because there was another actress with a similar name, but I always knew her as Anne-Marie. She went down to Hollywood with an actor named Art Hindle a couple of years later and we'd bump into each other from time to time. When it came time to cast the part of Wendy in *Prom Night*, I knew I needed someone who could be really arrogant and obnoxious and I thought of Anne-Marie. There's a scene in *Prom Night* where Anne-Marie's in her bedroom and laying on her bed in her underwear, and I found out that Anne-Marie spent 200 dollars on underwear for the scene. I just laughed when I heard that and thought "That's my Anne-Marie." Anne-Marie and Jamie were a good match in the film.

DAVID MUCCI: Both Eddie and Jamie took their parts in the film very, very seriously. Although Eddie and I had most of our scenes together in the film, she barely spoke to me during filming. She was very professional, but she kept to herself and wasn't that friendly to me during filming and we barely spoke. Jamie was very friendly and helpful, like in the cafeteria scene where I grab her and then I get into a fight. It was a complicated scene because the cafeteria was full of kids and there was a kid with tray of food right behind me, and then I had to do the fight. If I knocked over a tray, and the scene was wrecked, it would've been hard to start over so there was a lot of pressure for Jamie and I to get the scene done in one take and we did it. I think Eddie and Jamie bonded for the simple fact that they were both L.A. actors and the rest of us were Canadians. Also, most of us, the Canadian actors, were basically day-players on the film so we weren't on the set all the time.

ROBERT NEW: Jamie Lee brought a lot of attitude and a lot of honesty to her performance in the film. She enjoyed making the film and she had fun with the scene where Anne-Marie was getting in her face and saying mean things to Jamie. I think Anne-Marie and Jamie had a bit of friendly rivalry during filming and they had fun with that.

MARY BETH RUBENS: I think Jamie and Eddie became friends on the set for the simple reason that they were both L.A. actors and the rest of us, the Canadian actors, weren't, and so Eddie was the only one that Jamie could relate to. Even though Eddie was originally from Toronto, she'd been working in LA a long time before *Prom Night* and she could understand what Jamie was going through at that time.

Curtis got along fine with the Canadian actors, but it was an awkward dynamic given that Curtis, who wore a pink satin crew jacket from *The Fog* while on the set, was the only American-born actor in the cast and given the vast difference in experience levels. Although Antoinette Bower and Leslie Nielsen, who played Curtis' parents in the film, were grizzled veterans of both Canadian and Hollywood productions, most of the young Canadian actors—most of whom were paid between $6,000 and $8,000 for their work in *Prom Night*—had never made a film before *Prom Night* much less worked with a Hollywood "professional" like Jamie Lee Curtis. They were basically amateurs in terms of film acting, something that's very apparent in the finished film.

The pressure of starring in a film was especially felt by Curtis' co-star, Casey Stevens, who was, according to the memories of the cast and crew, a really nice guy who was somewhat awestruck by the film-making process. Despite his enthusiasm and strong work-ethic, Stevens struggled to hold his own during his scenes with Curtis and often felt overmatched in her presence. "Casey was very shy, very soft, and you'd never imagine him and Jamie being together in a million years," recalls co-star Mary Beth Rubens. "Casey had blue eyes and curly brown hair, and he was a nice guy, but as an actor he was stiff and was too laid-back to keep up with Jamie."

In the film, Curtis and Stevens share a tender scene overlooking a cliff where they lock eyes and then Stevens nervously tries to shed his guilt over his role in Robin Hammond's death. The setting is outside of the school, but the actual scene was shot at Scarborough Bluffs, which was a great distance from the Don Mills Collegiate location where much of *Prom Night* was filmed. In the scene, Kim and Nick are talking about their relationship, with Nick being torn between his love for Kim and his guilt over the fact that he was one of the four kids responsible for Robin Hammond's accidental death six years earlier.

The scene on the cliff showcased Curtis' ability to reveal strong emotions in a scene, and also highlighted the contrast between her forceful presence and Stevens' own carefree, laidback personality. "I watched Casey and Jamie do the scene on the cliff and I could see Jamie grinding away at the scene," recalls Mary Beth Rubens. "Casey was just kind of standing there and reacting to what she was doing and so the cinematographer decided to take the camera and just focus on Casey's blue eyes. As an actress, Jamie had an incredible ability to be in-the-moment and to stay in character and you could see it in that scene."

Eddie Benton wasn't the only member of the *Prom Night* production that Curtis became close to during the making of the film. During filming, Curtis became involved with a member of the lighting crew who looked like "a young Brad Pitt" according to assistant director Steve Wright. "I heard about that when I was talking to a crew member one day about Jamie and I said something like, 'Isn't Jamie just so wonderful?' and the crew member looked at me and said, 'You'd better keep your mouth shut because she's having an affair with this guy' which surprised me," recalls Lynch. "I had no idea. It certainly didn't affect her work on the film because she was a total professional throughout but I was caught by surprise."

It's certainly not unusual on the set of a film, where cast and crew form a nuclear family dynamic during the course of several intense weeks of filming, for an actress to start dating a member of the crew. The filming of *Prom Night* represented a crossroads in Curtis' career and her personal life, and although Curtis' relationship with the crew member was the first such relationship she'd formed on the set of a film, it wouldn't be the last.

Curtis' relationship with Casey Stevens during the filming of *Prom Night* was much more of a surprise, given their respective backgrounds and personalities. Curtis and Stevens began casually dating as filming on *Prom Night* progressed, something the rest of the cast and crew were completely oblivious to. "Casey was the kind of person who fell in love a lot and I think he fell in love with Jamie on *Prom Night*," says Marty Galin. "They started dating on the film, and they went to clubs and restaurants together and Casey took her around Toronto, to places she'd never been before."

Although Curtis is, regardless of Leslie Nielsen's top billing, unquestionably the star of *Prom Night*, the fact is that Curtis doesn't have that many scenes in the film. Eddie Benton has more screen time than Curtis does in the film. Benton's scenes in the film, where she's planning to sabotage Kim's prom, are used as filler, as padding for *Prom Night*'s entire middle section. Curtis' scenes are more sporadic and concentrated towards the end of the film where Kim heads to the prom and is eventually confronted by the masked killer who turns out to be her brother, Alex.

For a horror film, and certainly one that would later become a staple of the horror-slasher genre, *Prom Night* is pretty boring and uneventful, certainly in terms of action and violence. The film opens with the accidental death of Robin Hammond, which is then followed by an hour of exposition and filler. It's not until the third act when some more action occurs in the form of the masked killer who terrorizes the school prom. The eventual violence in the film is, with the exception of one decapitation scene, relatively minor and tame by the gruesome standards of the horror genre between 1978 and 1981.

Prom Night's lackluster pacing was the result of a combination of Lynch's earnest desire to take a subtle approach to the horror genre, and the fact that William Gray's bulging final draft script was much more of a psychological-drama than a straight-out slasher film. "The reason there wasn't much action in the film was because I was trying to build the characters and establish a lot of tension," says Lynch who kept a *Psycho* shot-book on set for inspiration (2). "I wanted to draw out the suspense like Hitchcock did in *Psycho* and surprise the audience at the end when they find out who the killer is."

When the story finally moves to the prom night sequences at the high school, the film finally generates some action as the masked killer begins to execute his plan for killing the four students responsible for young Robin Hammond's death. The first kill in the film occurs with Mary Beth Rubens' Kelly character who is slashed across the throat with a glass shard.

The scene is interesting in the sense that it puts a bit of a twist on the whole "sex equals death" formula that many critics had discerned from *Halloween's* structure. Rubens' character is murdered after she refused the sexual advances of her boyfriend, Drew, who then abandons her in the school change-room and leaves her to die. The irony of the scene, and its moral implications, wasn't lost on Curtis either. "The girl gets killed because she doesn't have sex with her boyfriend in the film," said Curtis. "She says no, which is what good girls are supposed to do, and she gets killed for it which was kind of ironic. To me it's no big deal. Teenagers are going to fuck, and that's it. I was a good girl too and when I turned eighteen, I got a lot better."

There's not much violence in *Prom Night*, partly because *Prom Night* was shot before *Friday the 13th* and the endless glut of other slasher films that would begin landing in theaters in 1980. There was no point of reference, in terms of blood and violence, except for recent horror hits like *Carrie* and *Halloween*, *Prom Night's* two most direct inspirations. Both of those films also had long stretches of dramatic build-up and suspense punctuated with action-packed and violent third acts.

Looking at *Prom Night*, it's easy to see that the film tries to follow this same strategy, in terms of establishing a tedium that will later be punctuated by terror. The major difference is that *Carrie* and *Halloween* were both full of artistic flourishes while *Prom Night's* artistry is much more difficult to appreciate. "The look of the film was supposed to represent the All-American dream gone horribly wrong, with Jamie representing the All-American girl," recalls cinematographer Robert New. "We open the film with pretty shots, pretty images, almost like an all-American fairytale with kids getting ready for the prom and then it all goes wrong. Then we have different camera angles, stalking angles, very dark and uneasy, and we increased the use of shadows in the photography as the film went along."

Aside from the murder of Kelly in the film, there are four other murders in the film, most of which are relatively bloodless. Jude Cunningham, played by Joy Thompson, is killed in a van outside the high school along with her boyfriend, Slick, played by Sheldon Rybowski. Wendy Richards, Kim Hammond's hated rival, is killed inside the high school, and later, Wendy's partner in crime, Lou Farmer, is decapitated on the dance floor, his head resting on the dance floor amidst a growing pool of blood in the film's sole gory highlight. "One of the things they tried to do in the film, and I don't think it was successful, was to introduce different suspects for the killer in the film," recalls co-star David Mucci. "The audience was supposed to think my character might've been a suspect, along with some other characters, but it wasn't executed very well in the film."

To be fair, part of the reason for *Prom Night*'s long stretches of idleness and tedium was because of Lynch's desire to create a psychological drama that was more like *Psycho* than *Halloween*, an approach that Lynch reinforced by constantly referring to his beloved *Psycho* shot-book for inspiration throughout *Prom Night*'s filming. "The reason there's not much action or violence in the film, between the first scene and the murders at the end of the film, is that I was trying to make a film like *Psycho*," explains Lynch. "I wanted to build-up the psychological drama and suspense and then have an exciting finish when we reveal the killer. I wanted to put Jamie at the center of this, just like her mother had been in *Psycho*, except there was no way we were going to kill Jamie in our film."

Just as Curtis had channeled her own painful high school memories for her portrayal of Laurie Strode in *Halloween*, Curtis brought the same experiences and memories to the Kim Hammond character in *Prom Night*. Given that Curtis' high school experience had been so difficult, and that Curtis herself doesn't recall even going to her own high school prom much less being a prom queen, filming *Prom Night*'s high school scenes was undoubtedly a challenge for Curtis whose own high school identity was alien from Kim Hammond's. "I certainly did not have a joyous high school experience," recalled Curtis. "I don't think I went to my prom. I don't remember. That's how bad it was. I was very shy and quiet."

Perhaps the most poignant element of *Prom Night* is that the film serves as a time capsule, much like *Halloween* did, in terms of portraying teenagers in the late-1970s through their clothes, their music, and their tribal customs. Curtis' own unhappy high school experience, and her distaste for growing up as a teenager in the 1970s, had engendered in Curtis a fatalistic outlook and an obsession with death that had convinced Curtis she wouldn't live until the age of thirty. In 1979, Curtis had thought this prophecy might be coming true when she was incorrectly diagnosed as having Multiple Sclerosis (MS) after Curtis had complained of double vision and unexplained neurological problems. Luckily, this diagnosis was bogus, as would turn out to be Curtis' vision of an early death for herself.

In some ways *Prom Night* represented a chance for Curtis to create a new high school experience, putting aside the element of the masked killer in *Prom Night*, that she had never enjoyed and this is especially true in terms of prom night and the dancing that's a rite of passage for graduating high school students. Whereas Curtis herself had been largely ostracized throughout her high school years, which would manifest in Curtis' bleak outlook towards the future, Kim Hammond is one of the most popular girls in high school, and is going to the prom with one of the most popular boys in school in the form of Casey Stevens' Nick McBride character. In many ways this was the kind of teenage experience that Curtis herself could only have dreamed of back at Choate, with the exception of being stalked by an axe-wielding killer.

Perhaps Curtis' most memorable scene in *Prom Night* is when Kim and Nick, Hamilton High's Prom King and Prom Queen, have their big dance scene in the school gymnasium. The outrageous dance sequence, which lasts about three minutes in the film and features an array of disco moves and poses, required a lot of practice on the part of Curtis and Stevens who had worked hard, both before and during the film's production, to get the dance moves just right in concert with dance choreographer Pamela Malcolm, Paul Lynch's sister.

WILLIAM GRAY: Jamie was very much a natural dancer and the scene wasn't that difficult for her whereas Casey really struggled with the dancing and had to work a lot harder than Jamie did to get the moves right. The scene was embarrassing. We copied everything on *Prom Night*, and with that scene we were copying *Saturday Night Fever*. The biggest debate we had when we were planning the film was whether to use disco music or rock music. We went with disco because of the success of *Saturday Night Fever*.

PAUL LYNCH: In the script it said there was a wild disco sequence so we had to create a sequence out of that. Peter Simpson and I felt like we needed a big dance scene in the film and that's why I had my sister, who was a dance choreographer, work on dancing with Jamie and Casey Stevens for ten days before we started shooting. I wanted a dance sequence that would at least hold a candle to something like *Saturday Night Fever*, if not being quite as good. I thought the scene turned out good, and most of that was due to Jamie who was a very good dancer. Casey had to work a lot harder to get the dance moves down.

PAMELA MALCOLM: We had fun with the scene, but it was the end of filming and it was really hot and humid in the gymnasium. Paul could barely stand up during the filming of the scene because it was so hot and Jamie really carried the scene because Casey had two left feet. We also had to work around Jamie's back at all times, and eventually we got through the scene. Poor Casey was such a nice guy, and I think he'd had his fill of Jamie by the end of filming. Casey trained for hours and hours in the dance studio but he couldn't do lifts, and some other ambitious dance sequences that I'd planned for the scene. A few years after we made *Prom Night*, Paul told me that Casey was sick with AIDS and then I heard that he died, and that made me very sad.

DAVID MUCCI: The dance scene was really crazy and fun. Casey had a stunt double who was standing off in the corner with a wig and everything, but Casey was really determined to try and do the dance scene himself. They used a double for Casey in some of the takes, if you watch the film closely.

ROBERT NEW: Casey and Jamie worked for two weeks on the dancing. Jamie was really into the dancing and really burned it up on the dance floor whereas Casey wasn't that much into it. Jamie pulled Casey around the dance floor and carried him through the scene. They got along fine, although I think Casey was a bit in awe of Jamie. In terms of shooting the dance number, we had the scene well-covered and shot from an angle. The biggest challenge was with the dance floor itself because it was an under-lit plastic floor and if you stomped on the floor, the cameras would shake so we used a Steadicam for much of the dance scene. We shot the scene off the floor, with the camera off the floor, and we used a Dolly on the dance floor when Casey and Jamie were twirling around the dance floor.

MARY BETH RUBENS: Jamie had legs that went on forever, and an incredible amount of energy. She was tireless and she just kept going and going, and she was a great dancer.

SHELDON RYBOWSKI: Before they filmed the scene, Jamie walked out and surveyed the stage and planned out all the moves she was going to do. She was very prepared. My one scene with Jamie in the film was when I arrived at the prom with Joy Thompson, and I handed Casey Stevens a joint and then I kissed Jamie on the cheek. I was supposed to shake Jamie's hand or something, but I kissed her on the cheek instead and she was shocked. She went "Oh," but she was really cool about it, and then we had to do more takes and for continuity purposes I had to kiss her cheek over and over again.

JOY THOMPSON: I remember that Casey Stevens had a hard time doing the dancing while Jamie found it quite easy. As for the dancing, that was the type of thing kids were doing back in 1979 so when we were watching them do the scene it wasn't that funny.

STEVE WRIGHT: We had two cameras for that dance sequence, and there was also dry ice and the floor was covered with oil and I remember that Jamie actually slipped and hit the floor hard during one take.

The climactic scene in *Prom Night* occurs when Kim and Nick are confronted by the masked killer on the stage. The axe-wielding killer grapples with Nick who eventually pushes him away after which Kim grabs the axe and smacks the killer in the head. The killer was played by stuntman Terry Martin, although actor Michael Tough donned the killer's black mask at certain times during filming. "The axe fight scene took place at the end of our filming schedule and everyone was very hot and frustrated," recalls Robert New. "Before we shot the scene, Paul stood up and lectured the cast and crew to pull it together because it was a dangerous scene and someone could get hurt, and Paul wanted everyone to band together and pull the scene out. I remember that Casey had a stunt double for the scene and that Jamie was very adept at doing the action and physical stuff."

Both this scene, and the film's final scene which takes place outside the gymnasium, were shot on the last two days of filming. It was a very grueling finish to what had been a relatively peaceful and routine shoot, and this was primarily because Toronto was going through a record heat-wave during the end of *Prom Night*'s filming schedule. "We shot that scene on a Saturday, all day and all night, and then we finished the movie on Sunday and the heat was unbelievable," recalls Lynch. "It was the worst heat-wave Toronto had ever seen those last two days and everyone was very tired and uncomfortable. We just wanted to finish it."

The final scene in the film, which also represents Curtis' dramatic highlight in the film, happens outside the gymnasium. It's in this scene that *Prom Night*'s wounded and dying killer stumbles outside and then falls to the ground. Curtis runs out, leans down to the killer who she immediately recognizes as her brother, Alex. She pulls off Alex's black mask, and then her face trembles like crazy with emotion and grief as she watches her brother die, recognizing also that Alex murdered her friends who were responsible, six years earlier, for the death of Alex and Kim's sister, Robin.

It was a very emotional scene and so Lynch and cinematographer Robert New decided to focus the camera tight on Curtis' eyes as she convulses and trembles with emotion. In the shooting script, Kim says nothing, but when Curtis and Lynch were discussing the scene, Lynch decided that Curtis should say something to her dying brother. "I felt like Jamie should say something, anything, to end the movie, some line of dialogue that people would remember, but we couldn't think of anything good," recalls Lynch. "As it turns out, Jamie didn't need to say anything because her reaction was so poignant and powerful. When the music hits at the end of the film, it just makes it a great scene."

PAUL LYNCH: It was a very powerful scene, and I was almost staggered by it when I saw it. When the music hits and you see Jamie's face, it's just very emotional, and I felt I had created something very beautiful. I believe at that moment that Jamie's character has lost her mind, and that her life will never be the same after that night. Jamie deserves half the credit for that scene, and the movie, because she had the ability to project so much emotion. I let Jamie make her own choices in that scene, as with the rest of the film, and she was brilliant.

ROBERT NEW: Jamie emotionally transformed that scene into a very touching scene and it was very powerful to watch. She went to a place in that scene that Paul didn't expect and it left Paul and the rest of us a bit awestruck actually.

MARY BETH RUBENS: Jamie had bottomless depth as an actress, and a strong connection to human feelings. She also has an ability to make you feel what she's going through and that's because she has such a strong presence. In that scene, when the camera hit her face, you could see her whole body vibrate.

MICHAEL TOUGH: This was a very hard scene for me. I'd never done a dramatic and emotional scene like this before and I spent hours trying to get ready. I remember Jamie being very supportive during my pacing time just off set. She kept encouraging me and reminding me to not get too worked-up off camera. Save some of it. I remember crying during the actual scene and I remember being exhausted after we did that scene. That was one of those moments in an actor's career where you understand why you love what you do. I truly was passionate about acting back then. It wasn't until a couple of years later that I was a jaded and cynical old pro!

STEVE WRIGHT: Jamie was going to say something in that scene, but then she changed her mind and told us she wasn't going to say anything, as was in the script. When we filmed the scene, she leaned down to her brother and she said something. She changed her mind, and the boom guy and the sound guys were really angry because they had to record this and Jamie said she wasn't going to say anything. That's why you don't hear her say anything in the film.

Prom Night wrapped filming on September 13, 1979 and then Curtis, who'd pretty much kept to herself throughout filming, was gone, back to Los Angeles where she would soon begin work on *The Fog* re-shoots as well as filming her guest appearance on *Buck Rogers in the 25th Century*. In November, Curtis would return to Canada, to Montreal, for the filming of her next horror film, *Terror Train*. None of the cast and crew of *Prom Night*—save for Eddie Benton who Curtis recalls last seeing about ten years ago—would ever see Curtis again (3). "No, Jamie got on a plane right after we finished filming and I've never seen or spoken to her since," says Lynch. "The only time I've seen her is in watching all of the great work she's done over the past three decades since we did *Prom Night*. I feel very lucky to have worked with her on the film."

Prom night represents a fateful time in everyone's life because it represents the end of youth, and the end of friendships that have grown over many years. After this point, life is completely different and friends lose touch, or drift away, or change completely. It's the same with people who work on a film, the cast and crew who form bonds—however short-lived—that last a lifetime on celluloid but are in reality very tenuous. For Curtis, the making of *Prom Night* had been a blip, a detour, a vacation, and something she wanted to quickly move past. It wasn't the same for the cast and crew, most of whom would regard their association with Curtis in *Prom Night* as a career highlight.

The most poignant example of this is Casey Stevens who'll forever be remembered as Prom King to Curtis' Prom Queen, as Curtis' high school boyfriend. Curtis' and Stevens' lives would move in sharply different directions after they parted ways in September of 1979, following the end of *Prom Night*'s filming. While Curtis was destined for acclaim and stardom in the years to follow, *Prom Night* would represent Stevens' lone moment in the spotlight. "The success of *Prom Night* had no residual effect on Casey's acting career," recalls friend Marty Galin. "Casey was convinced that *Prom Night* would launch him to stardom, and he threw a big party at his apartment when the film was completed, but nothing happened after that."

Following *Prom Night*'s filming, Stevens closed out 1979 with appearances on episodes of the Canadian television series' *King of Kensington* and *The Littlest Hobo*. Following *Prom Night*, Stevens had been set to star in an untitled film project as a dope smuggler who sneaks a ton of marijuana into America, but the project never came to pass. Stevens' final professional acting role was a small part in the made-for-television film *Escape from Iran: The Canadian Caper* which was broadcast in 1981, although Stevens was also an un-credited extra on the 1981 film *Threshold*.

In 1981, Stevens made another trip to Los Angeles where he found no success in terms of career prospects but did end up getting married and divorced in quick succession. Stevens then returned to Toronto where he settled into a career as an airline steward at Air Canada. By 1983, Stevens had turned the page on his acting career, and had also found religion, becoming a born again-Christian and volunteer missionary in Toronto. Stevens never forgot about Curtis. "Casey tried to get a hold of Jamie, but she'd moved on and I don't think he ever saw or spoke to her again," recalls Marty Galin. "By 1983 and 1984, Casey had given up the quest for fame, had become religious, and Jamie had obviously changed a lot too in terms of her career."

Stevens, who was a heterosexual, died of an AIDS-related illness in 1987. Prior to his death, Stevens was in the midst of using his sizable *Prom Night* earnings to try and refurbish a rundown hotel near his Quebec hometown. "We never really found out how Casey got AIDS, but I never saw Casey do drugs at all," recalls Galin. "Casey fell in love a lot, and he had lots of encounters, and he was heterosexual, and loved women, but he was also adventurous, and the 1980s were a dangerous time for that because of AIDS. Casey's friends felt very lonely for him at the end because Casey's mother, a wonderful woman, died shortly after Casey died. Casey's funeral was in Quebec and there was a memorial in Toronto with Casey's many friends. Casey was a carefree, adventurous, laidback guy who loved life, loved going to art galleries, loved having parties at his apartment, and made friends very easily, all over the world."

For Curtis, *Prom Night* represented a pleasant little vacation to Canada, a nice paycheck, and a bit of independence as Curtis rapidly approached her twenty-first birthday. Curtis thought nothing more of *Prom Night* when she returned to Los Angeles, other than that she regarded the film as harmless, unsophisticated genre fare. *Prom Night* wouldn't arrive in theaters for nearly ten months due to a prolonged post-production period that would result in extensive re-shoots that would change the film completely, much to Curtis' later chagrin.

Shortly after the end of *Prom Night*'s principal photography in mid-September, producer Peter Simpson realized he had a film that didn't really work, certainly not well enough to get the lucrative American distribution deal he coveted. The film wasn't exciting enough, and there wasn't enough action, certainly not in comparison to *Carrie* and *Halloween*, *Prom Night*'s two most obvious inspirations. "The film was too slow, and the build-up wasn't exciting enough, but I felt it had potential," recalled Simpson. "I knew if we retooled the film, and added some scenes, that I could get a good deal, so that's what we did."

Simpson went back and re-shot several scenes that changed the tone of the film quite considerably, namely in terms of enhancing the film's similarities to *Halloween*. The heart of the re-shoots, which were filmed by Simpson and written by John Hunter, a veteran Canadian screenwriter who'd collaborated with Gray and Lynch on *Blood & Guts*, concerned the subplot of an escaped child killer named Leonard Murch who is established as a key possible suspect in Robin Hammond's tragic death.

This is a complete red herring since the audience knows full well that Robin Hammond was accidentally killed by the four kids in their "Kill" game six years earlier, but Simpson had his escaped psychopath, his Michael Myers. Simpson felt this was an especially important element given that the film's eventual killer, Michael Tough's Alex Hammond character, wasn't, in Simpson's opinion, strong enough to sustain the film alone. "The red herrings were kind of silly but they made the film more exciting," said Simpson. "The problem on *Prom Night*, looking back, was that we didn't have a strong enough killer, like Michael Myers in *Halloween* or Jason in the *Friday the 13th* movies. All we had in our film was some geeky teenager in a ski mask."

Simpson also added a psychiatrist character, in the vein of Dr. Sam Loomis, and various stalking camera angles to heighten the film's creepiness and pacing (4). All of this was, of course, shamelessly derivative, not to mention being just plain silly. The re-shoots were a testament to the cynical and derivative tone of the project, not to mention the Canadian film industry itself of which the 1980 release of *Prom Night* would usher in a disheveled and murky phase in Canadian cinema comprised almost entirely of exploitation and horror films. "It was all crap," recalls co-star Joy Thompson. "There were some good movies made during that period, but they were outnumbered by the garbage. As a Canadian actor during that period it was an ugly period because on the one hand there was a lot of work to be had but on the other hand it was all crap. As a Canadian actor, you just took the money and ran."

Simpson screened his revised cut of *Prom Night* in the Spring of 1980 for Avco-Embassy's Robert Rehme who agreed to buy the film for distribution. Avco-Embassy had established an "Exploitation Department" solely for the purpose of distributing horror films and Avco-Embassy felt that *Prom Night* would be a good fit in the marketplace. Rehme also believed that Jamie Lee Curtis was a star and that any horror film with Curtis attached would be a big hit, a fact that had been proven-out by *Halloween* and would be cemented by *The Fog*'s successful release in February of 1980.

Basically, Jamie Lee Curtis was the sole reason *Prom Night* was bought by Avco-Embassy—who'd also signed Curtis to a three-picture deal on the basis of *The Fog* and *Halloween*—and the main reason the film had even existed. To the extent that *Prom Night* is even slightly palatable as a horror film, the credit goes to Jamie Lee Curtis, a fact that the filmmakers attest to. "At least half of the credit for *Prom Night* goes to Jamie Lee Curtis because she's such a great actress and she just owned the film with her presence," says Lynch. "I don't think the film would've worked without her."

In a way, *Prom Night*, for all of its flaws, was the ultimate proof that Jamie Lee Curtis was now a bona-fide movie star, even if it was something as disreputable as scream queen movie stardom. If Curtis could survive a film like *Prom Night*, and even make such a film respectable and commercially-viable, she could survive anything. If Jamie Lee Curtis could carry a film like *Prom Night*—even despite the fact she had very few scenes in the film—and make the film a hit based solely on her presence, what could she do with better material?

Curtis herself screened *Prom Night* in Los Angeles, just prior to the film's American theatrical release in July of 1980. Curtis was subsequently furious when she saw the crass similarities between *Prom Night* and *Halloween* that had developed during *Prom Night*'s re-shoots which Lynch was largely removed from. Curtis was shocked to see the changes in the film that weren't at all present in the script that she'd initially agreed to make. "All that psychopathic killer stuff was not in the original script, not in the script I agreed to do," said Curtis. "They added that after they cut the movie. I'm very angry about that because I feel I wouldn't have made the movie had it been a remake of *Halloween*, which is exactly what they were trying to do."

Prom Night is Curtis' least favorite of her post-*Halloween* horror efforts during her scream queen reign between 1978 and 1981. Expanding to her entire career, Curtis lists the 1999 science-fiction thriller *Virus*—a film that Curtis refers to as "a piece of shit"—as the worst film of her entire acting career. Regardless, Curtis hated *Prom Night*. "I didn't like the film, and I didn't like my performance in that film, but I never liked my performances in any of those films," says Curtis. "I didn't like it but it was the only one of the horror films I did after *Halloween* and *The Fog* that was a hit, which didn't make sense to me."

Prom Night was a hit, a modest hit, but a hit nonetheless when the film made its American theatrical debut on July 18, 1980. Released with just over 250 prints, *Prom Night*, which wasn't released in Canada until September 12, 1980, grossed almost $15 million at the North American box office. Only *The Fog*, which was released in February of 1980, and *Friday the 13th*—which was released in May of 1980 and which would nearly equal *Halloween*'s success—grossed more in terms of independent horror releases that year. In terms of Canadian horror films, or the "Slash for Cash" category, *Prom Night* was the undisputed king of the period, its most direct competitor being 1981's *Happy Birthday to Me* which would gross $11 million upon its theatrical release.

It's kind of ironic, given Curtis' harsh feelings towards the film, that Curtis received her first professional acting award nomination for *Prom Night*. Curtis received a nomination for Best Performance by a Foreign Actress at the 1981 Genie Awards, Canada's modest version of the Oscars. Curtis didn't attend the awards ceremony in Toronto where Curtis' next horror film, *Terror Train*, would also receive several Genie nominations.

The Genie nomination was ridiculous of course, and the nomination was more of a reflection of the back-slapping and bureaucracy rife in the Canadian film industry, both then and now. Curtis had nothing to be ashamed of in terms of her performance in *Prom Night* but it certainly wasn't worthy of any type of award nomination given Curtis' sparse dialogue in the film and Curtis' limited number of scenes. There would be many accolades and awards in Curtis' bright acting future but Curtis' work in *Prom Night* didn't warrant such recognition. Curtis was undoubtedly relieved when the Best Actress Genie went to Susan Sarandon for her excellent performance in *Atlantic City*.

As was the case with *Halloween* and *The Fog*, *Prom Night* was also destined to receive the remake treatment although the modernized version of *Prom Night*, released in 2008, was a name-only remake that had no relation to Curtis' Kim Hammond character or any of the other story elements from the 1980 film. The 2008 film, which was directed by Nelson McCormick and written by J.S. Cardone, concerned a psychotic high school teacher who's obsessed with a female student, played by blonde actress Brittany Snow, and subsequently murders everyone who stands in the way of his deranged pursuit.

Like Scout Taylor-Compton from the *Halloween* remake, and Maggie Grace from *The Fog* remake, Snow is a pale substitute for Jamie Lee Curtis, the gold standard for all scream queens. Although critically-reviled, 2008's *Prom Night*, which had a budget of $18 million, was a modest teen hit, grossing more than $40 million domestically, a testament to the name value of the 1980 film and, by definition, the endurance of Curtis' scream queen icon status.

In terms of Curtis' film career, the modest success of *Prom Night*, combined with the successes of *Halloween* and *The Fog*, clearly established that Jamie Lee Curtis was a box office draw, if only inside the horror and slasher genres. Critical reaction was a whole other story. The reviews for *Prom Night*, which noted the film's transparent copying of *Halloween*, were universally negative, echoing Curtis' dim view of the film. "The sorriest ripoff of the year," (Tom Allen, *The Village Voice*.); "Utterly inept," (Roger Ebert, *Chicago Sun-Times*.); "Because it's so easy to figure out the killer's identity by simply keeping track of who is off screen a lot, much of the movie is just vamping for time," (Vincent Canby, *The New York Times*.)

She'd asked for it. Curtis had pursued *Prom Night*, and the film had been a financial success and an artistic embarrassment. Good thing that Curtis never looked at Hollywood through an artistic prism, certainly not during her scream queen period. "I was happy that *Prom Night* was successful because that meant I would get more movies, and that's all that mattered to me at that point in my career," says Curtis. "My attitude was that I wasn't the one who wrote and directed these films, and so I just tried to do the best job I could and I just hoped that I would get better opportunities in the future."

After the end of filming on *Prom Night* in September of 1979, Curtis had flown back to Los Angeles along with *Prom Night* writer William Gray, who was on the same flight, and new best friend Eddie Benton who would be renamed Anne-Marie Martin by the time of *Prom Night*'s release (5). "We flew back together, and I think Anne-Marie was on the plane too because Jamie and Anne-Marie had become good friends," recalls Gray. "When we flew into Los Angeles, Janet Leigh was waiting at the airport and I loved being able to meet her because I was a fan and because of the way Jamie had talked about her mother. She was a very nice woman. I stayed in touch with Jamie for a little while afterwards, and we hung out together, mostly because I was friends with Anne-Marie."

In October of 1979, Curtis completed her re-shoots on *The Fog* for John Carpenter and then focused on her next horror film project, *Terror Train*, which would begin filming in Montreal, Canada at the end of November, almost right on the date of Curtis' twenty-first birthday. Curtis had already signed on for *Terror Train* when she arrived in Toronto to shoot *Prom Night*, a fact that *Prom Night*'s cast and crew were well aware of. Curtis describes the period between August of 1979 and October of 1980—the period spanning the filming and theatrical releases of both *Prom Night* and *Terror Train*—as her "crud period." "When I did the slasher films after *Halloween*, I came up with a nickname for myself and it was the Queen of Crud," recalls Curtis. "That's how I saw myself at that moment."

The Queen of Crud moniker that Curtis bestowed upon herself reflects the fragile self-esteem and self-consciousness that still plagued the actress in terms of both her physical appearance and her worth as an actress. In terms of her beauty, Curtis still didn't think she was beautiful, especially since her teeth were still crooked and grey, a problem that wouldn't be fixed until after Curtis' twenty-first birthday, in 1980, when Curtis would have her teeth capped and straightened.

The trademark Jamie Lee Curtis smirk that appeared in *Halloween*, the defense mechanism Curtis created to hide her teeth, had been very apparent on *Prom Night* as well. "You could see on the set that she didn't like to smile at all and we all knew about her teeth," recalls Joy Thompson. "I think it actually helped her as an actress because it made her seem more vulnerable, more of a real person."

In terms of her acting career, Curtis was, at this time, very pragmatic about her immediate prospects, almost resigned to the fact that projects like *Prom Night*, projects that were derivative copycats of the *Halloween* formula, were going to play a prominent role in her immediate acting future. Curtis took it all in stride; she was happy that *Prom Night* had been a financial success and happy that the film's success might establish her as a bankable actress, if only in the horror and slasher genre. Curtis looked at this period in her career, the period between 1979 and 1980, as her Hollywood form of a college education. "For someone my age, those were the only kind of movies being made," recalled Curtis. "Those films were like college for me. They taught me how to act."

Curtis was twenty years old when she finished work on *Prom Night* in mid-September, just a couple of months short of her twenty-first birthday, an event she would celebrate on the set of her next film, *Terror Train*. It's an age where most kids are winding through college and making plans for what they want to do with the rest of their lives. Curtis herself might've been finishing up a law degree if she'd stayed at the University of the Pacific, but Curtis had chosen acting and now, about three years in, she had no regrets. She was a movie star, she had a rising career, and she was becoming famous, all in the context of being a scream queen, a title with which Jamie Lee Curtis was becoming synonymous.

ten

HALLOWEEN ON A TRAIN

In November of 1979, Jamie Lee Curtis would continue her exploration of Canada when she flew to the city of Montreal, Quebec, Canada to begin filming *Terror Train*, her next horror film. This was a quick turnaround for Curtis who'd recently finished *Prom Night*, and then returned to Los Angeles to film the *Buck Rogers* episode and the re-shoots on *The Fog*. It was a busy time, but Curtis was unfazed. She was full of energy and anxious to continue her film career.

Curtis had also begun to embrace her rising status as a cinematic scream queen after some initial reluctance. "I auditioned for lots of other movies after *Halloween* and the only offers I got were for horror movies like *Prom Night* and *Terror Train*," recalls Curtis. "I was nineteen, twenty years old at this time and I didn't feel like I was in a position to turn down work, and nor did I think I should turn down any work. It was all great experience for me."

Curtis had no resistance to *Terror Train*, not from the moment she was first made aware of the project. As with *Prom Night*, Curtis had sought out *Terror Train*, and aggressively pursued the starring role in the film. Curtis had already signed on to star in *Terror Train*, a project that would also be known as *Train to Terror* up until the start of pre-production, prior to the start of filming on *Prom Night* in Toronto. This was something the cast and crew of *Prom Night* had also been well aware of. Even at this early point in her career, Curtis had learned the important rule of finding the next acting job before the current one had been completed. "She talked about *Terror Train* when we were shooting *Prom Night*," recalls *Prom Night* co-star Sheldon Rybowski. "She said she was going off next to do this horror movie that was set on a train and she was really excited about it."

Jamie Lee Curtis was once again at a major turning point in her career and life, a definite transition period. She was about to turn twenty-one, an iconic period in any young woman's life. For Jamie Lee Curtis, the actress and scream queen, this moment in time would represent the jump from teenage actress to young adult star. Although she'd played a high school senior in *Prom Night*, it was obvious that Curtis was outgrowing her teenage scream queen identity, both emotionally and physically. Her cheekbones were more solid, her beauty, as unconventional as it was, was becoming more defined and set. She was a woman.

Curtis was growing into her own skin as an actress. Laurie Strode was gone. When Curtis read the script for what would become *Terror Train*, she was relieved to see that the character she would be playing, a character named Alana Maxwell, was a pre-med student. "When I read the script, I saw that it was basically the same as *Prom Night* and all of the other horror films that were being made, and that my character was basically the same," recalled Curtis. "What I liked about the script was that Alana was a bit stronger, a bit more defined and sophisticated than the other girls I'd played. I wanted to work on the character, make her more developed, and that's what I decided to do."

Like *Prom Night*, *Terror Train* was very obviously inspired by the success, if not the artistry, of *Halloween*. Until the profitable release of *Friday the 13th* in mid-1980, which would inspire its own legion of rip-offs, virtually every horror film that was developed during this period used *Halloween* as a template. Curtis didn't see *Terror Train* as a blatant *Halloween* ripoff, at least not based on her first reading of the script. "It kept me turning the pages, kept me guessing as to what was going to happen," recalled Curtis who also found the train setting somewhat fresh. This was, after all, late 1979, and *The Fog* and *Prom Night* were both still months away from release. 1980 would be the crescendo of Jamie Lee Curtis' scream queen career with the release of *The Fog*, *Prom Night* and finally *Terror Train*.

The inspiration for *Terror Train* was very deliberate, almost hilariously so. The genesis of *Terror Train* was the brain-child of Daniel Grodnik, a young writer-producer who'd screened *Halloween* and the 1976 comedy-thriller *Silver Streak* during a weekend and had a brainstorm. Grodnik envisioned a concept for a horror film that was "*Halloween* on a train." Grodnik told the idea to his wife who thought it was silly, commenting that she thought the concept sounded terrible. Grodnik was undeterred and decided, half-jokingly, to call the project *Terrible Train*, knowing full well that his modest kernel of inspiration still needed a lot of development.

It was the Spring of 1979 and the success of *Halloween* was still looming over Hollywood, particularly amongst low budget producers looking to quickly cash in with their own *Halloween* ripoffs. "*Halloween* made quite an impact on me, obviously, and Jamie Lee's performance in the film had a lot to do with that," recalls Grodnik. "I wanted to do my own *Halloween* movie and when I saw *Silver Streak* I found my setting in a train. The concept was '*Halloween* on a train' the whole way and throughout the whole production process we never hid the fact that we were trying to make our own version of *Halloween* that was set on a train."

Grodnik took his concept to Sandy Howard of Sandy Howard Productions who was already in the midst of trying to capitalize on the fresh horror boom before he heard Grodnik's "*Halloween* on a train" pitch. Howard was preoccupied with the development and financing of a horror film entitled *Death Ship*. In April of 1979, Howard was about to travel to the Cannes Film Festival to promote *Death Ship*, a film that would be produced by Montreal-based film producer Harold Greenberg, when the notorious Howard heard Grodnik's pitch. He loved it. "He loved it, he really got it," recalls Grodnik. "What happened was that I was in Sandy's office pitching *Terror Train*, and I went into a back office and scribbled about twelve pages of story. I had a deal with Sandy Howard by the afternoon."

In May of 1979, Howard traveled to Cannes to sell *Death Ship* where he also set about raising money for *Terror Train*. Howard eventually raised much of *Terror Train*'s financing through pre-sales which is the funding of a film's production costs through the granting of a license for a film's rights by a producer to a distributor in a particular territory before the film is actually completed. Howard, who was a master of exploitation and gimmickry, had turned this business practice into an art form. *Terror Train* was born. Almost.

The life-cycle of *Terror Train*, both the period before and during the film's production, would be the most labyrinthine of all of Curtis' horror films, in more ways than one. Like *Prom Night*, *Terror Train* would benefit greatly from Canadian film tax credits, as well as the ubiquitous tax shelter dollars. Unlike *Prom Night, Terror Train* was to be an American-Canadian co-production, one of the very first that had ever been attempted.

With Canadian dollars flying around, Howard had been very eager to capitalize on this ideal business situation and had formed a co-production partnership with Montreal-based producer Harold Greenberg—Howard's collaborator on *Death Ship*—to produce *Terror Train* through Greenberg's company, Astral Films. Combined with the pre-sales dollars and *Terror Train* represented quite a profitable enterprise even before a single foot of film had been shot and before Jamie Lee Curtis had even officially signed onto the project.

The Canadian tax credit deal, at least the deal that *Terror Train* would exist under, operated on a four-to-one ratio meaning that for every one dollar that was invested in a Canadian film the producer would receive four dollars back in tax benefits. There were some catches. As with *Prom Night*, virtually all of the cast and crew positions in *Terror Train* would have to be filled by Canadians in order to qualify for the tax credit.

Additionally, the film would have to be completed by the end of the 1979 calendar year to receive the tax benefits which would result in a horribly-rushed production and filming schedule. "That's when I found out from Sandy that I wouldn't be credited either as a writer or producer on the project," recalls Grodnik. "Because of the tax situation, they had to have a Canadian write the script, direct the movie, and be the producer of record. I was disappointed but then Sandy asked me, 'Do you want this movie to get made or not?' I certainly did."

To write the script for the film, Howard hired Canadian-born writer Thomas Y. Drake who turned Grodnik's and Howard's largely illegible synopsis into a lean and workable 104 page script. It was during the scripting process that the project gradually evolved from *Terrible Train* to *Switchback* to *Train to Terror* until all parties would finally settle on *Terror Train*, just prior to the start of production. In terms of a director, Howard took a chance and chose Roger Spottiswoode, a 34 year-old editor and aspiring director who'd racked up some impressive credits working with legendary maverick director Sam Peckinpah and editing such classic Peckinpah films as *Straw Dogs, The Getaway*, and *Pat Garrett and Billy the Kid*. Spottiswoode was young, hungry, a magician in the editing room, and he also had Canadian heritage.

This is interesting film lore in regards to the colorful goings-on in the Canadian tax shelter horror era, but what does it have to do with Jamie Lee Curtis and her scream queen image? Everything. All of the elements of *Terror Train*—from the story's inception, to the project's financing and packaging—were contingent on Jamie Lee Curtis' involvement. Grodnik, Howard, and Howard's right hand man—*Terror Train*'s executive producer, Lamar Card—had predicated everything on the belief, the hope, that Jamie Lee Curtis would become attached to the project.

LAMAR CARD, EXECUTIVE PRODUCER: Jamie was the only actress that we thought of and I don't know if we could've made the movie without her. If you were doing a horror movie, she was the only one to get and she brought a star caliber to the project because of *Halloween*. *Terror Train* was a different kind of horror film because Sandy wanted to make a real prestige type of horror film, assembling top notch elements, and I think that impressed Jamie. It wasn't difficult to get her; she had no real objections to the script or the people involved and we were thrilled to have her because she legitimized the project.

JAMIE LEE CURTIS: I liked the concept for *Terror Train*, and I liked how the script was kind of a whodunit and kept you guessing. I was also impressed with all of the talented people who were going to be involved with the project. Like *Prom Night*, it was a role that was offered to me, no questions asked, which was very flattering to me because during that period I was up for a lot of non-horror roles that I wasn't getting. The only thing I didn't like was the *Terror Train* title which seemed kind of cheap and gimmicky to me. I liked the title *Switchback* much better.

DANIEL GRODNIK, CO-PRODUCER/WRITER: Even though *The Fog* and *Prom Night* had yet to be released when we were starting to put *Terror Train* together, it didn't matter because *Halloween* had made such a great impact that Jamie Lee Curtis was a horror star. I knew Debra Hill and as Sandy and I were putting this project together I called up Debra and told her that I was doing a *Halloween* type of horror film and that we were going to go after Jamie Lee Curtis. I didn't want to copy *Halloween* without telling Debra, and I thought Debra might've been upset but she wished us good luck with the film and good luck in getting Jamie for the film. Jamie substantiated every horror film she appeared in just with her presence and that's what she brought to our film. She substantiated *Terror Train*.

The budget for *Terror Train* was $2.7 million, about $1 million greater than the budget of *Prom Night* which Curtis hadn't even finished when *Terror Train* was in pre-production. The sizable budget—sizable for the horror genre at this time—was the biggest of Curtis' career thus far. In fact, *Terror Train's* budget would be larger than any other slasher film made during the period between 1978-1981. 1981's *Happy Birthday to Me* and Curtis' own *Halloween II*, which would also be released in 1981, both had budgets of $2.5 million. That being said, no one associated with *Terror Train*, and this is especially true of director Roger Spottiswoode for whom the making of *Terror Train* would be a backbreaking experience, would recall *Terror Train* as representing the *Gone with the Wind* of either the slasher genre or of Jamie Lee Curtis' scream queen career.

Terror Train would be the most expensive horror film that Curtis made between 1978 and 1981 and the increased budget, though still modest by Hollywood standards, was reflected in the number of *Terror Train's* marquee production elements. For Curtis, this was most notable in the casting of veteran actor Ben Johnson who'd won a Best Supporting Actor Oscar for 1971's *The Last Picture Show*. The venerable Johnson, who died in 1996, had spent more than thirty years toiling in countless westerns—having appeared in many of John Ford's films—and had attained mid-level film stardom after his Oscar victory. Like Donald Pleasence, Johnson was a name, just as Jamie Lee Curtis was, by the fall of 1979, a name, and no longer just because of her famous parents.

The genial, old-fashioned Johnson agreed to star in *Terror Train* largely because of his affection for Spottiswoode with whom Johnson had worked with and gotten to know when Spottiswoode had edited *The Getaway*. Johnson knew that *Terror Train* represented Spottiswoode's big chance to establish himself as a feature film director and the genial character actor signed on mainly for that purpose, with the understanding that Spottiswoode would excise the "nasty words" in the *Terror Train* script that Johnson found distasteful (1).

Curtis' two other main co-stars in *Terror Train* were magician David Copperfield and actor Hart Bochner. By the fall of 1979, Copperfield, who'd previously won acclaim for his lead role in a Chicago-based production of *The Magic Man*, had just completed the second in what would be a long-running series of his network televison magic specials. Copperfield's involvement with *Terror Train*, as with many of *Terror Train*'s elements, was a result of luck and timing. Sandy Howard was a big fan of magic tricks, was aware of Copperfield's rising career, and after reading Thomas Drake's script which included a magician character, Howard approached Copperfield to be in the film. Copperfield, who was interested in exploring a possible acting career, agreed to be in the film which would represent Copperfield's first and last feature film appearance.

Hart Bochner had something in common with Jamie Lee Curtis in that Bochner was also part of Hollywood royalty, although to a much lesser degree than Curtis. Bochner was the son of veteran character actor Lloyd Bochner and like Curtis, Bochner's own acting career was just a few years old. Prior to working on *Terror Train*, Bochner, who was born in Canada but raised in Los Angeles, had appeared in the films *Breaking Away* and *Islands in the Stream*. He was considered a rising young star, although his Canadian birth certificate was a key factor in his casting (2). The rest of the cast, pursuant to the tax credit ratio that was vital to *Terror Train*'s financing, would be filled out, as was the case with *Prom Night*, with young Canadian kids once the production took shape in Montreal in late November of 1979.

With Curtis, Copperfield, and Johnson, *Terror Train* had three mid-level stars, an unheard of pedigree for any slasher film of that era. *Terror Train*'s impressive production pedigree didn't end there, not by a longshot. Howard and Spottiswoode had also managed to secure famed cinematographer John Alcott, of Stanley Kubrick fame, to shoot *Terror Train*. Alcott would also bring camera operator James Devis and gaffer Lou Bogue, both of whom were also veterans of working with Kubrick. Needless to say, having Stanley Kubrick's "A" camera team attached to *Terror Train* was quite a coup for any slasher film made during this period and certainly for Curtis' own scream queen career.

This was the ultimate example of luck and timing as John Alcott had just come off working with Stanley Kubrick on *The Shining* for nine months where the energetic Alcott, who'd won an Oscar for his work with Kubrick on 1975's *Barry Lyndon,* grew tired of Kubrick's production schedule that had called for only one camera set-up a day for nine months. "I didn't think we had a chance at getting John Alcott, but he'd just come off *The Shining,* and he was exhausted," recalls Spottiswoode. "I told him we were going to be doing about thirty set-ups a day on *Terror Train,* which was crazy, and he was intrigued. He thought it would be fun."

Terror Train's impressive production and technical credits highlight the fact that *Terror Train* represents a real anomaly, both in terms of Curtis' scream queen career and for the horror-slasher era of this period. *Terror Train* offers an interesting paradox. On the one hand, the characters and story in the script represent the basest elements of the slasher movie formula while on the other hand the film's technical credits would be top-notch.

Unlike all of the trash that was about to flood the marketplace between 1980 and 1981—as represented by such titles as *The Burning, Happy Birthday to Me, Mother's Day, My Bloody Valentine, New Year's Evil—Terror Train* had some genuine artistic pretensions. Yes, maybe *Terror Train* was going to be trash but it was going to be well-made trash. If *Terror Train* was going to be cut from the same cloth as all of the other *Halloween*-inspired slasher films, in terms of character and story, at least the cloth would have a nice weave.

The plot of *Terror Train* was primitive and simple and would follow the slasher formula to a tee, although it could be argued that *Terror Train* would establish its own slasher film template that many future horror films would copy. The story follows the members of a college fraternity, pre-med students, who've chartered an excursion train for a New Year's Eve masquerade party celebration before facing the next phase of their lives. Unbeknownst to the college kids, there's a psychopathic killer on board who sets out to gruesomely murder them one by one. An added twist in the plot, an inspiration of Drake's, is that the killer assumes the costume of each victim he kills thereby adding a whodunit angle to the story.

Besides the elements of the psychopathic killer and the group of young victims, elements that were universal to all of the horror-slasher films released between 1980 and 1981, there didn't seem to be any obvious borrowing or inspiration from *Halloween* present in this basic synopsis. As the script for *Terror Train*—which would be rewritten many times before and during the film's production—evolved, the project became less of "*Halloween* on a train" and more of a template for its own slasher sub-genre: the geek horror film.

This is where Curtis' character in *Terror Train*, Alana Maxwell, fits in. *Terror Train* opens with a prologue where a shy young pledge named Kenny Hampson, who also happens to be an amateur magician, is lured by the members of the Sigma Phi fraternity into a darkened bedroom where he's promised a tryst with Curtis' Alana Maxwell character. What he finds instead is a female cadaver, the sight of which drives the kid insane. The script leaves no doubt that poor Kenny Hampson is the film's subsequent killer, the geek, the tormented nerd or victim who will rise up to claim bloody revenge against his tormentors in the story (3).

Kenny Hampson is the geek in the story, in more ways than one, the innocent and vulnerable freak who's the victim of some kind of horrible, twisted prank that results in the geek being either disfigured, driven insane, or both. The genre, of which *Terror Train* would serve—along with, to a lesser degree, *Prom Night*—as one of the vanguards, also usually includes a crude legend and some symbolic location where the monstrous geek dwells and waits to take revenge against his tormentors, or anyone else who gets in the way.

Although the makers of *Terror Train* had assembled the technical elements to match the artistry and style of *Halloween*, the project was already, during the film's brief pre-production process, heading down the low road. This represents the difference between artistry and inspiration. Who's to say that *Halloween* wouldn't have turned into a geek horror film in lesser hands and who's to say that Carpenter, Curtis, and Hill wouldn't have indeed made such a film if *Halloween* had been shot in 1979 or 1980 instead of 1978? *Halloween* established the gold standard for horror films and as a result any subsequent horror film made during this period could only be considered a reaction to *Halloween*, a facsimile, a *Halloween* model.

Curtis knew all of this, especially after the experience of making *Prom Night*, and knew why the producers of *Terror Train* wanted her just as she knew why the producers of *Prom Night* had wanted her. She was the face of *Halloween*, and if a film producer was going to do their own *Halloween* type of horror film, who better to get than Jamie Lee Curtis? Curtis was a willing co-conspirator. If this was the genre she was going to be trapped in, she wanted to make the most of it. "I started to worry about typecasting as a scream queen around the time I made *Terror Train*," recalls Curtis. "It was my fourth horror film in two years and I wondered if I was pushing my luck a bit. I decided *Terror Train* would be the last one of these kinds of horror movies because I wanted to do other things."

Sandy Howard knew that Curtis, and her association with *Halloween*, was *Terror Train*'s biggest asset, and would be the film's main selling point. Then again, at this point, in late 1979, Curtis only had one film to her credit, and that was *Halloween*. *The Fog* and *Prom Night* were still months away from theatrical release and so even though *Terror Train* would represent Curtis' fourth horror film in less than two years, Curtis still had to prove herself. This is why Howard felt that the inclusion of Ben Johnson and his veteran presence would be a nice compliment to Curtis. If Curtis brought audience identification and scream queen iconography to a horror project, the venerable Johnson brought class and integrity, not to mention a gold statue.

Terror Train would begin filming in Montreal on November 21, 1979, just a day before Curtis' iconic twenty-first birthday. Originally, *Terror Train* was going to be shot in Vancouver, but the production was moved to Montreal for logistical and practical reasons, not to mention the fact that Montreal was the home base for Canadian producer Harold Greenberg and his Astral Films company. *Terror Train* represented one of the very first American-Canadian film productions, and the city of Montreal was very immature and undeveloped in terms of film production. There were no production houses, few acting pools, sparse crews, and inexperienced stuntmen. The last element would prove to be very fateful during *Terror Train*'s production.

Astral Films was in dire financial straits by the time of *Terror Train*'s filming in late 1979. The company was still a few years away from the blockbuster success of the 1982 teen sex comedy blockbuster *Porky's* which would, along with its two later sequels, catapult the company's fortunes. Greenberg, who died in 1996, later morphed his company into the communications giant Astral Media which has subsequently divested its film properties, including the rights to *Terror Train*. Back in 1979, Greenberg was genuinely hoping that *Terror Train* and the presence of Jamie Lee Curtis would result in his first commercial blockbuster.

Although *Terror Train* represented the second consecutive film that Curtis would shoot in Canada, the two productions were different in many ways. The budget on *Terror Train* was almost twice that of *Prom Night*, and the number of skilled professionals associated with *Terror Train* dwarfed that of *Prom Night*. Perhaps the biggest difference was the technical challenges that *Terror Train* would present for John Alcott, Curtis, Spottiswoode, and the entire cast and crew. All of this had to do with the train in the film's title, and the fact that *Terror Train* would be shot not on a set or a sound-stage but on a real train.

For this part, production designer Glenn Bydwell, a Montreal architect, had made contact with the legendary Steam Town Foundation in Vermont who eventually supplied *Terror Train*, at a cost of $100,000, with a 1948 locomotive along with five train cars that would be used for the bulk of filming. Bydwell then scurried around Montreal, sifting through antique shops and junkyards to find accessories with which to decorate the train's interiors. The train had arrived in Montreal in early November and was assembled by Bydwell and his team just a few days before the start of filming and Curtis' own much-anticipated arrival.

As was the case with *Prom Night*, Curtis was surrounded during the filming of *Terror Train* by a group of inexperienced young Canadian actors. Most of the actors were from Montreal or Toronto, and for virtually all of them, *Terror Train* would mark their film debuts. The list of young Canadian hopefuls, and would-be victims, included Joy Boushel, Howard Busgang, Sandee Currie, Derek MacKinnon, Anthony Sherwood, Greg Swanson and Timothy Webber. As had been the case with *Prom Night*, the difference in experience between Curtis and her Canadian counterparts would prove to be quite pronounced and telling. The big difference was that this time Curtis was joined by Ben Johnson's veteran presence, not to mention Hart Bochner who, much like Eddie Benton from *Prom Night*, would serve as a fellow young Hollywood actor that Curtis could identify with. As with Benton and Curtis, Bochner and Curtis would become friends during filming, although Curtis would also become quite close with several of her Canadian co-stars as well.

The most interesting casting here was that of Derek MacKinnon who was cast as Kenny Hampson, the deranged and vengeful killer who Curtis eventually faces off with at the end of the film. For MacKinnon, the part was much more complex than playing Jamie Lee Curtis' would-be killer as MacKinnon's character is disguised for much of the story as the blonde and sexy female assistant to David Copperfield's magician character. Unlike the other Canadian novices that would join Curtis in the cast, MacKinnon wasn't even an aspiring actor when he received this plum acting assignment.

Derek MacKinnon was, appropriate for the character he plays in the film, a cross-dressing performer in Montreal who was part of a cross-dressing revue entitled *Alisha & Company* that had been performing in bars and clubs around Quebec in 1979. MacKinnon, who played Alisha in the act, heard about *Terror Train* through an acquaintance and reluctantly went to a Montreal audition, knowing nothing about film-making, horror films, much less Jamie Lee Curtis. "I'd heard of Jamie Lee Curtis, I think, but I didn't know anything about the movies when I auditioned for *Terror Train*," recalls MacKinnon. "I think they were desperate to get someone for this part, someone who could play a transsexual, and I was fairly well known for my drag act in Montreal and so my name was mentioned."

MacKinnon had been performing in the northernmost part of Quebec when he heard about the *Terror Train* part and sheepishly took a bush plane back to the city to meet with casting director Ingrid Fischer (4). "What was funny about the auditions for *Terror Train* was that none of us, none of the local actors, knew what the film was about or even that Jamie Lee Curtis was in the movie," recalls MacKinnon. "You just read what they gave you, and it wasn't until later that we found out what this movie was, and found out that Jamie Lee Curtis was starring in the movie. I went in with a real attitude, like I didn't care, which was honest because I wasn't an actor. Friends thought I was crazy, and they'd say to me, 'This is the chance of a lifetime, a big movie,' but I didn't care and I was shocked when I got the call to do the film."

As was the case with *Prom Night*, virtually any young Canadian actor with a pulse had a real shot at landing a part in *Terror Train* and working with cinema's greatest scream queen, Jamie Lee Curtis. While the *Terror Train* production office certainly looked for the best actors they could find, they were bound by the quota rules of the tax credit deal. "Before I was given the part I met with Roger Spottiswoode and Roger wanted to see me get angry because I was playing the killer in the film and so he started calling me names," recalls MacKinnon. "He'd heard I was a cross-dressing performer and he called me a fag and a sissy and I got angry, and I stood up and headed for the door, and Roger said, 'Yeah, you're just a fag and a sissy who likes to dress up like a girl, and I turned around and I gave Roger an evil glare and said, 'What did you call me?' and Roger smiled and said, 'That's what I'm looking for, that's the killer.' This was my first movie. I didn't know what to think."

The Canadian supporting actors weren't even given the full script for *Terror Train*, much less knowing that they were going to be working on a horror film, when they were first gathered in Montreal. There was no mention of Jamie Lee Curtis until just a week or two before Curtis would arrive in Montreal in the third week of November. "They brought us all together except that there were two actors for each role in the film—two Mitchys, two Mos, two of every character in the story—and they had a competition for each role between the two actors," recalls MacKinnon who was paid $40,000 for his first and last starring movie role. "They'd keep one actor and get rid of the other one. It was like *Survivor*. I don't think any of the actors who were rejected ever did anything. After the cast was assembled we were told about Jamie Lee Curtis and *Terror Train* and what this whole thing was going to be about."

Terror Train's chaotic and haphazard pre-production was emblematic of the cynical, not-ready-for-primetime nature of the Canadian film industry at this time. *Terror Train* was burdened by Montreal's inexperience as a film production hub, the Canadian content requirements of the tax credit deal, which necessitated the use of inexperienced Canadian performers, and a December 31, 1979 finish deadline that would loom over the production like a guillotine. "The film had to be in the can by the end of December or we wouldn't have gotten the tax credit because our deal was going to expire," recalls Grodnik. "It was an incredibly fast production. From the moment I pitched the 'Halloween on a train' story to Sandy to the end of filming was about six months."

Jamie Lee Curtis arrived in Montreal a couple of days before *Terror Train's* first day of filming on November 21, 1979. Unlike was the case with the more modestly-budgeted *Prom Night*, Curtis' arrival in Montreal was met with the enthusiasm befitting a young star born into Hollywood royalty. This was evident not just in Curtis' paycheck for *Terror Train*—her biggest yet at $80,000—but also the fact that Curtis was put into a top-floor suite at Montreal's luxurious *Hotel Manoir Le Moyne*. Curtis' suite was adjacent to David Copperfield, who'd begun dating co-star Sandee Currie, and Derek MacKinnon who would be the witness to many strange occurrences, both on-screen and off-screen, during *Terror Train*'s colorful and frenzied production.

MacKinnon was placed next to Copperfield and Curtis at the hotel because Spottiswoode wanted the three actors to generate chemistry together, especially given their characters' bizarre relationships in the film. The other more important reason was that the production office wanted to keep MacKinnon's involvement in the film a secret. Because MacKinnon was a fairly well-known local transsexual performer, and *Terror Train*'s denouement hinged on the surprise of Kenny Hampson's transsexual disguise, MacKinnon was kept hidden throughout filming. "They'd take me in cars to and from the hotel, like I was a big movie star," recalls MacKinnon. "When I wasn't working on the set, Roger, who I think wanted to kill me, had me take boxing lessons at a local arena because he wanted me to develop an angry and aggressive personality for the film."

For Curtis, the diverse, French-speaking city of Montreal was quite a culture shock, but Curtis, ever the professional, wasn't intending to use the making of *Terror Train* as a vacation. Even if she were, *Terror Train*'s rushed production schedule would allow little time for sightseeing. The first night Curtis arrived at the Montreal hotel, Curtis began internalizing and studying the *Terror Train* script with the intention of making her character, Alana Maxwell, as strong as she could possibly be within the constraints of the horror-slasher genre.

Upon Curtis' arrival, Curtis and MacKinnon had dinner with Copperfield who'd just flown in from Los Angeles and was a bit nervous about making his feature acting debut. "We were staying in close quarters, and we were going to be working together a lot in the film so we thought it would be a good idea for us to get to know each other," recalls MacKinnon. "It was nice, and we got along well enough, but I felt uncomfortable because I wasn't a part of that Hollywood world. David and Jamie kind of spoke to each other in a Hollywood language, almost like I wasn't even there. From that point on, the three of us became very close, and I saw them as real people."

The next day, Curtis joined the rest of the cast in Roger Spottiswoode's hotel suite for what would be several days of rehearsals. To this end, Spottiswoode was joined by Caryl Wickman, an accomplished editor and Spottiswoode's then-girlfriend who had, much like Spottiswoode, gained a reputation in Hollywood as an editing wizard who had the ability to fix and tweak movies that weren't clicking. Early in pre-production there had even been talk that *Terror Train* would be Wickman's feature directing debut but she deferred to Spottiswoode for whom she would provide invaluable assistance during *Terror Train*'s production both as an uncredited scriptwriter and as a defacto acting teacher (5).

While Curtis and Bochner, both young Hollywood pros, were ready to go, Spottiswoode recognized that the Canadian kids in the cast were green and inexperienced and would need lots more preparation. To this end, Curtis was also an asset. "Jamie was always very generous and kind with me and the Canadian kids because although some of them had a bit of experience, many were first-timers," recalls Spottiswoode. "Caryl worked with the kids, especially the ones who'd never made a film before, and she helped the extras too. She did exercises with the actors and got them prepped a few days before we might need them. She ran a sort of kindergarten acting class during production because so many of the kids had no experience at all."

In addition to the rehearsal sessions in Spottiswoode's suite, Spottiswoode and Wickman suggested that Curtis and the rest of the actors create character biographies, brief histories for their characters. "I asked Jamie and the other actors to imagine and write out a more complete biography for their character than was in the script because the script didn't have much characterization," says Spottiswoode. "After they'd written the stuff out we discussed these characters during the brief rehearsal period and it helped them and me to see the characters as being distinct and different."

For her part, Curtis envisioned that her character in the film, Alana Maxwell, was a girl from a modest upbringing who was struggling to pay her way through medical school. Curtis envisioned Alana as a strong-willed young woman from a troubled childhood who possessed an inner strength that would help her cope with any adversity she might face, whether it be trying to graduate or escaping from a masked killer. "I think the biographies helped us know our characters and know the other characters," recalls MacKinnon. "We didn't have much time to think about them so they weren't that detailed. I wrote that my character had killed his mother when he backed his car out of the driveway so some of it didn't make much sense."

GLENN BYDWELL, PRODUCTION DESIGNER: Jamie was a funny, curious girl who had a real life-force about her. She was a real team-player and everyone on the film, especially Jamie and the other actors, quickly formed a team when we started filming. There was a good vibe on the film because we were all young kids and we were all kind of growing up together on this film and that was especially true of Jamie and the other actors in the film.

LAMAR CARD: Jamie was a real professional and you could see that the first time you met her. She had a real star quality about her and she was a very serious actress and she had an uncanny ability to get into character. She took her character, and the film, very seriously, more than the rest of us did, and she was very supportive, especially with the younger actors.

DON CARMODY, LINE PRODUCER/PRODUCTION EXECUTIVE: She was barely a star when we made *Terror Train*. She'd only been seen in *Halloween*. *The Fog* and *Prom Night* hadn't come out yet. I remember her being somewhat suspicious of who we were and wondering if we were real film-makers or not, but basically she was friendly and professional. She seemed very young to me at the time, although our ages weren't that far apart.

JAMIE LEE CURTIS: I liked working with Roger because he was very open to my suggestions about my character. We talked about Alana and we went over the qualities that made her special. By the time I made *Terror Train*, I'd really learned the elements that went into creating a believable heroine, a scream queen. The most important quality, which I learned from John Carpenter on *Halloween*, is vulnerability, so that the audience can identify with her, and roots for her to survive. A heroine also has to have an inner strength to fight the evil, or terror, that's chasing her. With Alana I created a history for her, created a life for her, so I could sympathize with her, almost as if she were a friend of mine.

PENNY HADFIELD, COSTUME DESIGNER: I did the costumes for the film and I asked Jamie what costume she wanted to wear in the film—since the characters in the film are having a masquerade party on the train—and Jamie immediately said, "I want to be a pirate" so we gave her a pirate costume. She wore tall black boots, black velour pants and a white blouse with an open neck and puffy sleeves. For the opening scenes in the film, the frat house scenes, Jamie and the others wore clothes that looked appropriate for the socioeconomic bracket their characters were in. Jamie was very easygoing and cooperative to work with. I ran into her years later at a screening and reminded her who I was and what she'd worn in *Terror Train* and she said something to the effect that it wasn't a very complimentary costume she'd worn in the film: to wear white on top and black on the bottom sort of cut her in half. I didn't think she had to worry about that because she looked so cute in the costume and she was very slender.

DEREK MACKINNON, CO-STAR: Jamie tried really hard to fit in with the rest of us, but she was very subconscious about how people looked at her and about her family name. There were times where she looked at us, the Canadian actors, and she'd say, "I wish I could just be like you; I wish I could just be an unknown actor instead of being who I am." Even though she was becoming a star herself, she still thought people were only interested in her because of her last name.

RAY SAGER, ASSISTANT DIRECTOR: I was a bit star-struck when I first met Jamie. I'd acted in some horror movies myself, and I was a big horror fan, and I was a big fan of *Halloween* which I'd seen recently in Chicago. I was blown away by *Halloween*, and by Jamie's performance, and I told this to Jamie when I met her in Montreal, because I was really thrilled to be working with her. I think I scared her a bit at first.

ROGER SPOTTISWOODE, DIRECTOR: What I remember most about meeting Jamie and working with her was how great she was to work with and how incredibly professional and experienced she was for her age. She knew what she could do well, she knew what her strengths were as an actress, and looking back I can say that she was most generous about my own lack of experience. *Terror Train* was my first film and I knew almost nothing, although my experience as an editor helped a bit.

TIMOTHY WEBBER, CO-STAR: I'd met with Caryl and Roger at the hotel in Montreal for the audition and when I was going down in the elevator I was with Ingrid Fischer, the casting woman, and she told me I had the part. That's when I found out that Jamie Lee was involved in the film and I was told that I would be playing Jamie Lee's boyfriend in the film. At that point, I'd read the script except for the ending which was kept secret from us until the end of filming. I met Jamie for the first time at the cast rehearsal which took place for a few days in Roger's suite. She was a known actor, and I was playing her boyfriend, and I thought she was a real sweetheart. Jamie had a leg up on the rest of us because she was an experienced professional and the rest of us were newbies. From the start of filming, the four of us—me, Jamie, Hart Bochner, Sandee Currie—became fast friends and it was kind of like we were on a cruise ship together when we were making this film. We were like a bunch of kids on a cruise throughout the filming.

The Jamie Lee Curtis that had arrived in Montreal was a different Jamie Lee Curtis than had appeared even as recently as a couple of months earlier when Curtis had filmed *Prom Night* in Toronto. No longer viewed as a teenage actress, either by herself or her peers, Curtis was at the dawn of adulthood, embodied in the form of her twenty-first birthday. The tomboy that was first introduced in *Halloween* had disappeared and Curtis was now evolving, cautiously and slowly, into a sexy adult actress—complete with a more aggressive hairstyle and a heavier use of makeup—who was growing more and more comfortable in her own skin than ever before.

The filming of *Terror Train* would extend to just a few days before Christmas, a week before New Year's Eve 1979. For Curtis the looming end of the 1970s would represent a time where Curtis had to take stock of her career as well as her future dreams and goals. How many more years could she continue playing scream queen heroine roles? Although her character in *Terror Train* was slightly older and more sophisticated than Curtis' character in *Prom Night*, the writing was on the wall. There were only so many *Prom Nights* and *Terror Trains* Curtis could make before she would become as endangered as a teenage horror movie victim.

She would either have to grow as an actress, and show Hollywood that she could do other things as opposed to just run and scream, or watch her career die a slow death. Being the Queen of Crud, cinema's ruling scream queen, was nice, and Curtis' fragile self-confidence enjoyed the attention, but what about the future? If Curtis was going to keep the scream queen crown, and stay in the horror genre, what kind of roles would she be playing five, ten years down the line? Would the films and the parts get better and more sophisticated or would she still be recycling the *Halloween* formula by the time she was thirty?

It was a difficult dilemma for Curtis, namely the prospect of turning down film roles for the purpose of reinventing her acting career. She remembered the bleak career drought that had followed the making of *Halloween* and didn't want to repeat the experience. The offers of *Prom Night* and now *Terror Train* had boosted not just her bank account but also her fragile self-confidence that would still be visible during the filming of *Terror Train.* "I'd kind of made a decision that after I made *Terror Train* I was going to make a determined effort to find a non-horror part after that," says Curtis. "It was hard because I was very conscious of not turning down parts. At the beginning, I just looked at it as work but the more and more I became identified as a scream queen, the more I was worried of being typecast, of being trapped in the horror genre forever."

Jamie Lee Curtis was ready to drive a stake through the 1970s for the purpose of re-inventing herself as an actress.

eleven

THE MAKING OF *TERROR TRAIN*

Jamie Lee Curtis began work on *Terror Train* on November 21, 1979, inside the mammoth All-Pak warehouse in the Montreal suburb of St. Pierre where the bulk of the film would be shot. The warehouse housed the train cars that production designer Glenn Bydwell and his crew had assembled together for the film. Curtis and the rest of the cast and crew settled in for what would be a hectic month-long shoot that would end just before Christmas and would represent the most technically-challenging of any of the horror films that Curtis made between 1978 and 1981.

The biggest technical challenge for the cast and crew was working on the train itself which would be difficult to control throughout filming. Additionally, the narrow confines of the train would make the lighting and staging of scenes very difficult, and there was no money left in the budget to buy sets. As a solution, cinematographer John Alcott completely reconfigured and rewired the main locomotive's archaic 1940s lighting system, lighting the train with hundreds of tiny bulbs whose wires would be connected to a large central panel that would be controlled by over 300 dimmers.

It was all very technical, but Curtis was impressed with the detail and technical precision that was going into the making of this horror film. Curtis had a deep understanding of the camera and camera technique, an appreciation she'd developed from working with John Carpenter and Dean Cundey on *The Fog* and *Halloween*, and had learned how to make the best use of the camera in terms of her acting. Curtis' ability to own the camera, to make the camera work for her, was one of her most hidden qualities as a scream queen, and this skill would be put to the test during the filming of *Terror Train*.

John Alcott and Roger Spottiswoode weren't Carpenter and Cundey, and no film-making duo would ever have as much chemistry with Curtis, but Curtis immediately felt she was in the hands of skilled, talented film-makers, something that hadn't been as apparent when Curtis had shot *Prom Night* in Toronto. "It just seemed like a classy picture on all levels," recalls Curtis. "Roger was a good director, and great at cutting scenes together, and good at communicating with actors. John Alcott was just a genius and the way he controlled the lights was amazing because he would look at the grid, see what light was needed, and talk through the radio in this funny English voice and the lights would appear on cue. I knew, if nothing else, that it was going to be a beautifully-shot picture, just because John Alcott was there."

Simulating the movement and rocking motions of the speeding train was just as challenging for the cast and crew. This problem was solved by having a crew-member named Jerome South rock the train with a big iron bar. "We were very nervous about how to get the train's rocking motion and so we simply jammed a big iron bar between the springs of the car we were filming in," recalls line producer and production executive Don Carmody. "There was a big black guy on the crew who would lift it up and down. It worked fine and we never had anymore problems."

The necessity to complete *Terror Train* before the end of 1979, because of the tax credit deal, forced Spottiswoode to shoot *Terror Train* on a hellish schedule and to cram two months worth of filming into thirty days. Making this more difficult was the fact that the cast and crew were limited to shooting between six in the evening to three in the morning. This unusual work schedule was necessary in order to avoid the outside noise that was present all around the warehouse during the day and which would've made daytime filming almost impossible. Accordingly, Curtis and the rest of the cast and crew would work from six in the evening to three in the morning for virtually the entire shoot which meant that there would be little time for partying or socializing, or so it would seem.

Adding to the challenge was the fact that Montreal's weather had been very chaotic and unreliable. Although the vast majority of *Terror Train*'s filming would take place inside the warehouse, on the train, the rare instances of exterior filming were greeted by several inches of unexpected snow which would cause the camera to continually freeze. This happened during the filming of the scene where the characters are outside the fraternity, along with the scene where Curtis and the other members of the fraternity board their chartered train. "The snow appeared out of nowhere and it was so cold that we'd start filming and the camera would just freeze," recalls Spottiswoode. "It was a very difficult shoot from beginning to end."

Because of *Terror Train*'s time pressures, given the conditions of the tax credit deal, Spottiswoode created a wildly-ambitious production schedule that would call for thirty camera setups per day. Spottiswoode also had to rehearse and stage the scenes on the train set, although Caryl Wickman, who would function as both an uncredited producer and uncredited writer on *Terror Train*, was a big help in this area. "I had a shot-list each day and I would give it to John Alcott and we'd use half of our time for lighting and the other half for rehearsing and shooting," recalls Spottiswoode. "If I had 38 set ups one day, it meant eleven hours divided by sixteen because John would have eight minutes to light the scene and I'd have eight minutes to shoot. For a long scene, we'd do maybe three takes."

Terror Train's frantic shooting schedule combined with the claustrophobic and cramped conditions on the train set caused Curtis and the rest of the cast to come together and bond very quickly. After a few days, Curtis' Hollywood aura, and any perceptions she might've had before she arrived in Montreal, had worn off and Curtis and the Canadian actors quickly gelled. As was the case on *Prom Night*, where Curtis made fast friends with co-star Eddie Benton A.K.A. Anne-Marie Martin, Curtis formed an instant friendship with one of her *Terror Train* co-stars.

This was Sandee Currie, a young actress from London, Ontario who was making her film debut on *Terror Train*. Currie, who'd began seeing David Copperfield, played Mitchy, Alana's best friend in the film. As was the case with Curtis and Eddie Benton on *Prom Night*, Currie and Curtis hit it off right away, always joking around, and constantly hanging around together during filming. "They were very close during filming," recalls co-star Derek MacKinnon. "Jamie helped Sandee out a lot with her scenes because Sandee was very nervous and inexperienced and they had a similar sense of humor. They were inseparable on the set."

Unlike her relationship with Eddie Benton, Currie and Curtis didn't seem to have much in common. Although Benton, like Currie, had grown up in Canada, Benton was very much a grizzled Hollywood veteran when she and Curtis had met on the set of *Prom Night*. In contrast, Currie was virtually a complete neophyte, full of dreams and hopes for her acting future. Like many young actresses, especially young Canadian actresses during the tax shelter slasher era, Currie was enthusiastic, young, and just happy to have a job, and genuinely believed that *Terror Train* would be the beginning of a long and illustrious acting career (1). "Jamie and Sandee were very tight during filming," recalls co-star Timothy Webber. "Sandee was very outgoing, a gorgeous girl, and Jamie was also gorgeous, and there was lots of girl-shit going on between them and Hart Bochner and I were like brothers during the shoot. We were all very tight during filming."

There's a heartfelt and tender scene in the film, very poignant in retrospect given what became of Currie, where Alana and Mitchy are freshening up in the washroom and talking about the future. In the scene, Alana's worried about paying for medical school, and worried that she and Mitchy will, as so often happens to friends after college, lose touch and drift apart. The scene ends with Mitchy reassuring Alana and then the two friends exchange a heartfelt hug. "Yeah, Jamie really helped Sandee with that scene," recalls assistant director Ray Sager. "Sandee was very nervous and Jamie just kind of pulled both of them through it. Jamie could do that."

In the film, Alana and Mitchy are two of the six members of the Sigma Phi fraternity who were responsible, some more than others, for the cruel sex prank that drove pledge Kenny Hampson mad. Besides Alana and Mitchy, the group of six includes Doc (Hart Bochner), Ed (Howard Busgang), Jackson (Anthony Sherwood) and Alana's boyfriend, Mo (Timothy Webber). As the film moves to the train setting, a disguised Kenny has snuck onto the train and is planning to take revenge by killing the group one by one. Since there's a costume party on the train, the killer gradually assumes the costume of each victim which makes his identity a changing mystery.

It's pretty basic slasher film stuff, although the switching identities angle is quite inventive, especially since the audience knows that Kenny Hampson is the killer. Eventually it's revealed that Kenny has disguised himself as the pretty blonde assistant to David Copperfield's magician character whom Kenny later murders. The violence is also pretty typical of the period with the various characters being slashed, stabbed, strangled. Currie's Mitchy character is strangled and has her throat cut. The goriest kill in the film is when Bochner's Doc character, the main target of Kenny's revenge, is slashed across the throat and then decapitated. For Curtis and the rest of the *Terror Train* cast, life off-screen pretty much resembled the world on-screen, save for the masked killer and the rising body count. They were—Curtis and the Canadian actors—a group of young actors who were just happy to be working on a movie, just happy to be alive, with nary a worry about the future or the dawn of a new decade. Because Curtis and the other actors were primarily working from six in the evening to three in the morning, there wasn't much to do in Montreal after filming since most of the bars and restaurants were closed. It was tough, but Curtis and the rest of the cast and crew would still find plenty of opportunities to have fun during filming.

Once a week during *Terror Train*'s month of filming, Curtis and the rest of the cast would travel to a local Montreal club called *Rejean's* to do interviews and publicity for *Terror Train* in front of the local Montreal press. Other than that, Curtis and the rest of the cast and crew would have all-night parties back at the hotel, most of which were organized by assistant director Ray Sager who would regularly host parties in his hotel suite almost every night. "There wasn't anywhere to go when we stopped work at three in the morning so I had the parties in my suite," recalls Sager. "Everyone from the film, including Jamie, would show up at the parties, except for David Copperfield. He didn't show up until the end of the filming when he made an appearance. Because I'm a magician myself, I made him do a magic trick to get in."

Of course the biggest party for Curtis was to be for her twenty-first birthday which fell, ironically enough, on the second day of *Terror Train*'s filming. Despite *Terror Train*'s intensive work schedule, a makeshift birthday celebration for Curtis was held at the hotel where the *Terror Train* producers presented Curtis with an expensive pen-case. There was also much buzz and speculation on the set that Janet Leigh was going to arrive in Montreal to celebrate Curtis' iconic twenty-first birthday. "I couldn't stay at Jamie's birthday party because I was too busy working on my character but I remember meeting Janet Leigh and she was very nice," recalls MacKinnon. "You could tell that

Jamie and her mother were very close, although Jamie didn't like to talk about her parents at all. That was a subject you knew not to bring up around Jamie."

Curtis insists that her mother never appeared in Montreal for her twenty-first birthday celebration, or during any other period in *Terror Train*'s filming, although Curtis and Leigh talked on the phone regularly during filming. Regardless, one person who definitely wasn't in Montreal for Curtis' twenty-first birthday was her father, Tony Curtis, although he did send his daughter a bouquet of flowers and a rather memorable birthday present. Coincidentally, Tony Curtis had been in Montreal a year earlier when he'd shot the film *It Rained All Night the Day I Left*. "We had a birthday party for Jamie at the hotel and it was a lot of fun and Tony Curtis sent a birthday present for Jamie," recalls Timothy Webber. "When Jamie opened up her present it turned out to be stock from MGM. We all laughed. You could tell they weren't close."

Curtis did have a special visitor during the filming of *Terror Train* and this was her current boyfriend, and later fiance, Ray Hutcherson. Hutcherson, who'd just recently met Curtis, was a fledgling screenwriter whose lone produced writing credit had been, and would remain as, a 1978 episode of the American television series *Baretta*. Like previous boyfriend, guitarist Johnny Lee Schell, Hutcherson was a decade older than Curtis, a recurring pattern in many of Curtis' relationships. Curtis' relationship with Hutcherson had an interesting dynamic that revolved around Curtis' scream queen career. While Curtis took a very pragmatic and somewhat unaffected view towards her horror films, Hutcherson, who would later be married to actress Nora Dunn, flatly objected to the subject matter and violent themes of the horror films that were making Curtis a star (2). "He feels my work endorses that, makes it okay," said Curtis in 1980. "To a point, I agree with him. But it's my job. It's not the type of film I'd go and see. But there are people who enjoy this sort of film. I'm not in a position where I could turn down a film because I don't believe in what it says. I never felt exploited in the horror films. I never had to flash my tits or swear in any of these movies, and most of the characters I played were resourceful, strong women."

As had been the case on *Prom Night*, Curtis' star presence—as newly-minted and unproven as it was—and dogged professionalism made quite an impression on the entire cast and crew of *Terror Train*. Even the grizzled Ben Johnson was won over by Curtis, and would later comment that Curtis was "a little sweetheart to work with." This could be described, in the context of Curtis' scream queen career, as the "Jamie Lee effect" in terms of how Curtis' colleagues were often blown away by the powerful combination of Curtis' Hollywood pedigree, her unconventional beauty and star quality, as well as Curtis' own disarming and forceful personality that would manifest itself through Curtis' often colorful choice of words when interacting with colleagues. She made quite an impression on people.

With her twenty-first birthday, a new relationship, and an acting career that was approaching a major crossroads, Curtis' life was growing increasingly complicated but Curtis never let outside forces interfere with her acting. "Jamie was very disciplined on the set and the work dynamic on the set was very good," recalls Spottiswoode. "John Alcott was a very tough disciplinarian and he wouldn't tolerate anyone being unprofessional. If an actress stayed out late, John would look at her in the morning and say, 'Darling, what time were you out until? I'll fix it now but not again.' Jamie wasn't one of those who stayed out late and partied. She respected John and knew he would make her look great if she did her part."

DON CARMODY: There was one scene that Jamie did in the film where she's being chased by the killer and she's fighting him off and Jamie's shirt was supposed to be ripped. It was just supposed to be ripped, but the guy who played the killer ripped Jamie's entire shirt off, as well as part of Jamie's bra! Obviously, we had to redo that scene over again. It didn't faze Jamie that much although it was a very embarrassing situation. She was a total professional.

JAMIE LEE CURTIS: I never really understood why I was a scream queen, why I was the face of the genre during this era, because most of the other scream queens, like my mother, were very beautiful and I didn't think I was beautiful. When I got to the end of that era I finally started to understand why the audience identified with me in these movies and that was because people saw me as a real person. The audience would look at me and they would see themselves. I think I was also good at acting terrified because I was really scared of horror movies and I think I did more running and screaming in *Terror Train* than any other horror film I ever made.

PENNY HADFIELD: I think when we started filming we mostly knew Jamie as part of Hollywood royalty, and it was the same with Hart Bochner because his father was Lloyd Bochner who was also a well-known actor. It was a very tough filming schedule on *Terror Train* and there were long nights and everyone became very tired, but it was also a very well-made film. John Alcott would insist that all of the stand-ins for Jamie and the other actors in the film have the same costumes so he could get the lighting just right. He was a real perfectionist. It was cold in the warehouse and it was hard to move around in the train. Ben Johnson was a real "oldie goldie," a very gracious man, a real pro who was in poor health when we shot the film. Jamie and the other young actors really looked up to him.

DEREK MACKINNON: I remember when we were at a nightclub and everyone was drinking but Jamie would be scared to take a drink. She'd look around to see if people were watching her, if there were people taking pictures of her, because she was very worried about her image. She said to me, 'If I take a drink, people will say that I'm an alcoholic' and so she was very guarded about stuff like that. Ben Johnson, on the other hand, was very laid-back. He'd bring me into his trailer, pull a bottle of vodka out of the freezer, and he'd tell me, 'Derek, you're a talented actor but you're taking this too seriously. You can't take it too seriously. It's just a movie.' Jamie took her work, and her image, very seriously.

RAY SAGER: Jamie was a very controlled person. Jamie liked to have fun but she would never let herself go. We had parties in my suite almost every night and Jamie would come to the parties and she'd have a drink but never more than one drink. She'd show up, have a drink, talk a bit, and then she'd leave. She would never go wild. She was also very subconscious about her fame and her family name. You always avoided the subject of her parents when you were around her, especially her father. Mostly, Jamie just wanted to be kind of anonymous; to be treated as just another actor.

ROGER SPOTTISWOODE: Jamie had a wisdom and experience far beyond what you would expect for someone her age. Ben Johnson would always quote John Ford and he'd always tell me how John Ford did things ("You don't need words, Ben, no words...just play the part").

When I first met Ben he took me aside and gently told me that he thought there were too many words in the script and that Ford always said that you didn't need words. Jamie was different. Jamie didn't need to quote John Ford. She had a tremendous grip on character, and she had complete belief that if she became the character the lens would see into her and portray the character, so she didn't need to "act" and just had to "become." She had a tremendous sense of where the camera was and what it would see and she would adjust accordingly. She made few requests, and carried herself with tremendous grace and modesty. She was also enormous fun to work with.

TIMOTHY WEBBER: The four of us—me, Jamie, Sandee, Hart—became very tight during filming. It was also nice to have Ben Johnson around because he was such a great actor and a veteran influence for the rest of us, and a lot of fun to be around. He was a really prestigious actor who commanded a lot of respect from all of us, just as Jamie did. It was a very constrained set on the train, freezing cold, and there weren't any breakaway walls so you could barely move. This made it difficult for Roger to work with the actors and so Caryl Wickman worked with us a lot and we all, including Jamie, loved working with Caryl who became a close friend of mine right up until her death. After *Terror Train*, Hart Bochner stayed in Montreal and we spent Christmas together, and Jamie and I kept in touch by writing letters for a couple of years after we made the film, obviously way before there was E-Mail. We'd write letters and talk about life and Jamie would tell me about her career and about wanting to escape the horror genre. I think Jamie had decided that *Terror Train* would be her last horror film.

All things considered, given the rushed production schedule, the filming of *Terror Train* ran fairly efficiently and smoothly. There were however a few calamities that took place during filming and these involved a couple of stunts that went horribly awry. This was a product of the lack of experienced crew-members that existed in Montreal at this time, especially professional stuntmen. Although there were no credited stuntmen in the finished film, several local stuntmen worked on the film with often hilarious results. "We had stuntmen on the film but they weren't real stuntmen," recalls assistant director Ray Sager. "They said they were stuntmen, but when it came time to do the trick, they screwed up."

The first accident on the set occurred during the filming of the scene where the character of Jackson, played by Anthony Sherwood, has his face smashed into a mirror by a masked Kenny Hampson. A Montreal stuntman named Gaetan LaFrance was commissioned for the stunt which required him to put on the lizard costume that the Jackson character was wearing and then smash the mirror with his face. LaFrance wore a protective sleeve over his head for the stunt and then put on the lizard costume and proceeded to bang his head against the mirror, over and over again.

The mirror wouldn't break, not even a bit, and so then a frustrated LaFrance proceeded to hurl his face repeatedly into the mirror, to no avail, failing to note that the mirror was made of tempered glass and was virtually impenetrable. Meanwhile, Curtis and several other members of the cast and crew were standing back and watching this in disbelief. "He just threw himself into the mirror over and over again and it wouldn't break," recalls Sager. "The rest of us were watching and trying to hold our laughter. It was so stupid. When he took off the sleeve, you could see boils all over his head. Then he yelled, 'My name is Gaetan LaFrance and I'm a professional stuntman and I've never been so humiliated in my life' and then he just took off."

The other major calamity that took place during *Terror Train*'s filming affected Curtis directly. This was during the filming of the scene where Curtis is hiding behind a cage while a masked Kenny Hampson hovers around the cage with a large wrench in his hands. In the scene, Curtis grabs an available letter spike and drives it through the cage and into Kenny's eye. Interestingly, this was virtually the only sequence where Derek MacKinnon didn't portray Kenny Hampson in a scene. Unlike *Prom Night*, where stuntman Terry Martin had played the masked killer for the bulk of that film, MacKinnon played Kenny Hampson throughout the film, even donning all of Kenny's changing masks.

In this scene, a stuntman was used because of the danger inherent in Curtis pushing the spike into the killer's eye. Both Curtis and Spottiswoode thought that the letter spike had been properly scored by the prop crew, but the spike was actually real and when Curtis shot the scene, the stuntman was poked in the eye and injured. Although Spottiswoode recalls the episode as "a minor accident," MacKinnon recalls Curtis walking off the set in anger. "The stuntman's eye was hurt and

Jamie was really angry about that and she walked off the set," recalls MacKinnon. "I think that was the only time I ever saw her really angry during the shoot."

MacKinnon himself didn't survive his encounters with Curtis unscathed, especially during the sequences in the film where Kenny is chasing Alana throughout the train. "She accidentally stabbed me in the back when we did one scene," recalls MacKinnon. "When we did the scene at the cage, I was in that scene with the wrench, which weighed fourteen pounds, and when I broke the light with the wrench the glass landed on me and the sparks made the glass expand and later on they were pulling chunks of glass out of my back."

During the filming of another chase sequence, Curtis accidentally banged her head on a door, but Curtis was a trooper and no stranger to physical contact and a few bruises. Curtis was, according to cast and crew, more worried about her blouse and making sure it stayed on throughout the filming. "There was something going on with Jamie's blouse because she wouldn't let anyone touch her blouse," recalls Sager. "I don't know if it didn't fit her properly or she just didn't want anyone to see her breasts but she was very guarded about that blouse."

Curtis' blouse was accidentally torn during the filming of one scene, and towards the end of filming, MacKinnon was ordered not to put his hands on Curtis' blouse lest anymore cleavage be accidentally revealed. "When we did the scenes at the end I was told not to grab Jamie's blouse because Jamie didn't want people to see her breasts in the film and what size they were," recalls MacKinnon. "I was told she was planning to have plastic surgery after the movie and she didn't want anyone to notice the size of her breasts in the movie because she didn't want anyone to notice the difference in size after she had surgery. I could see the difference later on when I saw her in movies like *Death of a Centerfold* and *Perfect*. They looked a lot bigger."

Curtis has flatly denied this, denied that she ever had any form of breast augmentation, although Curtis has subsequently acknowledged undergoing various plastic surgery procedures in her later career and life. A close inspection of Curtis' breasts in the period between 1978 and 1979 reveals that they look perfectly normal in terms of shape and size, although they would certainly appear more robust in the period ranging from 1981 and on. True or not, the growing speculation around Curtis' appearance during this period perhaps reflects the beginning of another pivot, another transition, in the scream queen's career, from the Queen of Crud to The Body.

Terror Train's climactic scene occurs between Alana and Kenny in one of the abandoned train cars. In the scene, Kenny, in the guise of a conductor's uniform, reveals his true identity to a horrified Alana. Then Kenny pulls Alana close for an extremely deranged and twisted kiss. The kiss then triggers in Kenny painful flashback memories of the fraternity prank which allows Ben Johnson's Carne character, the train's conductor, to move behind Kenny with a shovel. He then whacks Kenny out of the train and sends Kenny crashing into an icy lake to his presumed death.

The most interesting part of the filming of this scene was the kiss. The kiss wasn't in the script, and was added on the insistence of Curtis who felt it would add power to the scene and to the end of the film. "I just thought that if she kissed him that it would bring a lot of tenderness to the scene and to the film," recalls Curtis. "The kiss was totally my idea. All during filming, I was looking for ways to make my character more interesting but there weren't many opportunities because most of the film was about the action and the killer."

The idea of kissing Jamie Lee Curtis was a big surprise for the transsexual Derek MacKinnon who had no idea his stint playing the deranged Kenny Hampson would include this added fringe benefit. MacKinnon would actually kiss Curtis twice, the second time being at the end of filming when Curtis would carry out her ritual—a ritual that Curtis began with Nick Castle at the end of filming on *Halloween*—of planting a kiss upon the guy who was playing her screen nemesis. "Jamie was very uncomfortable about doing that scene, with kissing me, and it was very awkward but she insisted on it, and insisted on adding tenderness to the scene," recalls MacKinnon. "She was a great kisser, and I thought we did a really strong scene, and then at the end of the filming she just kissed me out of the blue, right in front of the crew, and that kiss was even better than the one we filmed."

Terror Train's transsexual theme is interesting because Curtis herself was going through a period in her career where tabloids had begun spreading the false and outrageous rumor that Curtis herself was a hermaphrodite who was born with both female and male genitalia. This is a hateful and ridiculous rumor—obviously born out of Curtis' own androgynous, tomboyish appearance and sexuality that's especially present during the climactic scenes between Alana and Kenny—that has nonetheless become an urban legend over the years, fueled also by Curtis' later inability to bear children. "The tabloids wrote things like that about her and it was unbelievable to see her go through something like that," recalls MacKinnon. "Everyone who was around her could see what a beautiful woman she was."

Like the final scene of *Prom Night,* where Curtis' face was eerily twisted in a state of warped convulsion, Curtis' reaction to Kenny's kiss is just as horrific and raw, with her lips contorted and quivering in response to the perverse act. Curtis' masculine, raw sexuality is on full display during these final scenes. With her hair frazzled, her face covered with terror, her makeup dripping all over her face, Curtis appears like a caged, seething animal who's no longer preoccupied with grief over her murdered friends, nor any possible thoughts of revenge, but is instead focused on basic survival. These images represent Jamie Lee Curtis, in terms of her scream queen persona, in her most basic and savage form.

Although the final confrontation between Alana and Kenny represents the end of the film, it wasn't the end of *Terror Train's* filming. On the last day of filming, a skeleton crew traveled to New Hampshire to film the icy exterior sequence where Kenny hurtles out of the train and then falls into an icy ravine which is seemingly his final resting place. Art director Guy Comtois played the killer as he's floating lifelessly in the icy water because the stuntman who was supposed to do the scene became scared of the freezing water and kept trying to swim instead of playing dead.

Curtis' last day of work on *Terror Train* was the filming of *Terror Train's* origin sequence, the prank sequence that drives Kenny crazy, which was shot on December 22, 1979, *Terror Train's* second to last day of production. This is the opening scene in the film, where young pledge Kenny Hampson is duped by Hart Bochner and the rest of the nasty frat members into thinking he's going to have sex with Curtis in the upstairs bedroom of the frat house. This scene, Curtis' last filmed scene, was shot inside a real frat house located across the street from Montreal's McGill University where the film opens.

By this time, Spottiswoode had grown impatient with the inexperienced Derek MacKinnon who in turn thought Spottiswoode was trying to make his life hell. "He wasn't an actor; he was a transvestite from the streets of Montreal, and he wasn't familiar with the concepts of a contract and showing up for work on time," recalls Spottiswoode who allowed Caryl Wickman to work closely with Curtis and MacKinnon for this scene. "In a strange way though he did a pretty good job. He was familiar with that world of cheap theater and was strangely effective."

Before the scene in the frat house was shot, Curtis went upstairs to the bedroom to prepare for the scene. MacKinnon was downstairs, preparing for the scene with Wickman who'd grown close to MacKinnon along with Curtis and the rest of the cast who found Wickman's presence invaluable (3). "Roger wanted me to go upstairs naked for the scene and I was very nervous about that until Caryl talked him out of it," recalls MacKinnon. "Another strange thing that happened was that Hart Bochner and the rest of the cast, including David Copperfield who'd actually flown back in from Los Angeles just for the end of filming, were all sitting downstairs on a couch when I went upstairs to do the scene with Jamie. Hart told me to 'break a leg' before I walked upstairs to face Jamie. I was very nervous about the whole thing, and so was Jamie."

In the bedroom scene, Kenny walks into the darkened room where he hears Curtis' sexy voice imploring him to move over to the bed and to "kiss me." When Kenny moves to the bed, he doesn't find Alana's warm body in the bed but rather a decomposed cadaver that the cruel frat pranksters stole from a University lab.   Kenny then freaks out and has a nervous breakdown while Curtis, who co-star Howard Busgang recalls being "very nervous" prior to the filming of the scene, watches in stunned horror.

The cadaver was played by a young Montreal actress named Nadia Rona who went through five hours of makeup for her scene with Curtis who stood behind the bed and offered Rona encouragement (4). "They put me on a table and then Jamie and the guy walked into the bedroom," recalls Rona. "Jamie was very friendly and pleasant, and Roger was also very nice and supportive. We would shoot the scene over and over again and each time the guy, Derek, would keep falling on top of me. That was the worst part for me because he wasn't very coordinated and he kept doing the scene wrong. Jamie was always behind me and kept asking me if I was okay, almost like she felt protective of me. I could tell she was a very dedicated actress. It took many hours to film the scene, and everyone was tired, and when we finished, we all had a glass of wine."

This was the last scene Curtis shot in the film, and as was the case at the end of *Prom Night*'s filming, Curtis flew back to Los Angeles immediately afterwards, anxious to celebrate Christmas and New Year's Eve back at home. Like *Prom Night*, the friendships that Curtis had formed on *Terror Train* with her inexperienced Canadian counterparts would quickly become a distant memory, although Curtis did maintain a correspondence with co-star Timothy Webber for a couple of years after *Terror Train*'s filming. "When the film came out in 1980, there was a premiere in Montreal and Hart Bochner showed up along with his father but Jamie didn't show up," recalls MacKinnon. "I later traveled and did press for the film for a year but I never saw Jamie again."

Curtis did remain friends with Bochner and the two would later co-star on a failed televison pilot called *Callahan*, a *Raiders of the Lost Ark* spoof that would air in 1982 (5). As for the Canadian actors, several of them—most notably Anthony Sherwood and Timothy Webber—have had long and productive careers in Canadian film and television but *Terror Train* would be their one and only brush with Jamie Lee Curtis. Although Curtis and Webber kept in touch via letters, Curtis says she never actually saw any of her Canadian colleagues again. This includes Sandee Currie, who Curtis had befriended during filming. For Currie, the role of Curtis' best friend—both on-screen and off-screen—would sadly represent the most notable role in her all-too-brief acting career and life.

Like many young Canadian actors of the period, Currie's acting career slowly deteriorated and faded away following her work in *Terror Train*. Currie appeared in a handful of film and television roles, all filmed in Canada, that were scattered throughout the 1980s but found the stardom that her role in *Terror Train* seemed to promise elusive. "Sandee and I were both living in Montreal when we did *Terror Train* and I saw Sandee a year later when she made a big-budget Canadian comedy film called *Gas* which was shot in Montreal," recalls Webber. "Then I heard she moved to Toronto, but I don't think I ever saw her again. She was a lovely girl."

Ironically, Sandee Currie's last acting role was in the 1989 film *Street Justice* which was also produced by Sandy Howard. Like Casey Stevens, Currie's dreams of a big acting career were quickly crushed by the harsh and inexorable reality of trying to survive as a Canadian actor in the post- slash-for-cash, post-tax shelter era. Like many such actresses that came out of this cynical period in Canadian film history, Currie knocked on all of the doors in her pursuit of stardom but they just didn't open for her.

In the early 1990s, Currie moved to Los Angeles where she worked at a law firm while pursuing an acting and singing career in her spare time. In 1996, an otherwise healthy Currie was beset by a strange illness called Toxic Shock Syndrome that caused her organs to fail and shut down. Currie then became brain dead after which her family pulled the plug. Sandee (Sandra) Currie died on November 3, 1996. Like Curtis' doomed prom date, Casey Stevens, there's a sad irony in Currie's passing in that the film industry that Currie had so much wanted to impress didn't even know she'd passed away (6).

The specter of death surrounds *Terror Train* more than any other horror film in Jamie Lee Curtis' scream queen career. More cast and crew from *Terror Train* have died than from any of Curtis' other films. Besides Currie, the long list includes Ben Johnson, Greg Swanson, writer Thomas Y. Drake, uncredited writer and producer Caryl Wickman (Wickman died of cancer in 1987), producer Sandy Howard, producer Harold Greenberg, art director Guy Comtois, hairstylist Huguette Roy, and cinematographer John Alcott who died in 1986. "Huguette Roy jumped out of a window," recalls MacKinnon. "It's like the movie is cursed because everyone's dead from that movie. It's unbelievable."

Terror Train represented a first in Jamie Lee Curtis' scream queen career in that it would be the first film of hers to be released by a major studio, which in the case of *Terror Train* would be 20th Century Fox who would eventually acquire *Terror Train* under a negative pick-up deal. By the early 1980s, every studio in Hollywood was setting up their own would-be horror franchises. It was sort of like what happened in Hollywood during the independent film revolution of the mid-1990s where all of the studios established their own independent film divisions. Fox's motivations were much less artistic in regards to *Terror Train*. "We tried to make '*Halloween* on a train' and Fox thought *Terror Train* could make just as much money as *Halloween* had," recalls co-producer and co-writer Daniel Grodnik. "They were very enthusiastic about the film."

Actually, what made Fox so enthusiastic about *Terror Train* was Jamie Lee Curtis. Contrary to popular belief, *Terror Train*'s producers had no agreement of any kind with Fox prior to filming, and it wasn't until a cut of the finished film was shown to Fox executives that Sandy Howard and his partners were able to secure a deal. Without Jamie Lee Curtis, the $2.7 million venture likely would've gone down the drain, although without Curtis' initial attachment, *Terror Train* probably never would've been made.

Under the terms of Fox's negative pickup deal with *Terror Train*'s producers, whereby the studio essentially bought the film for distribution, *Terror Train* made a nice profit for its financiers prior to ever being released. "The entire film was completed prior to us showing it to Fox for domestic release and Jamie played a bit part in getting the deal with Fox," recalls Grodnik. "Looking back, I think it was Jamie as well as John Alcott's brilliant photography that closed the deal."

With Fox's involvement, and the studio's marketing muscle, Curtis had her first big Hollywood studio film, but Fox's involvement with *Terror Train* would turn out to be a mixed bag. Although Fox would ultimately spend several million dollars promoting *Terror Train* upon the film's October 1980 theatrical release, the studio's marketing of *Terror Train* would be bungled, disjointed, and completely out-of-touch with the marketplace. "They bungled the movie," recalls executive producer Lamar Card. "They were a big studio who were just getting into the horror business and they didn't know how to sell the movie."

Instead of promoting *Terror Train* as a Jamie Lee Curtis film, thus heightening the appeal of the film to *Halloween* fans, Fox would curiously choose to downplay Curtis' attachment to the film. This is most visible by the fact that Ben Johnson would receive, much like what happened with Curtis and Leslie Nielsen on *Prom Night*, top billing in the film over Curtis, both in the film's credits and in the studio's publicity literature. This was despite Curtis' obvious box office appeal which had been emboldened by *The Fog*'s successful release in February of 1980. "Fox spent millions on *Terror Train*," recalls Daniel Grodnik. "I couldn't believe it when I opened *Variety* one day and saw a double-page ad for the film, but they really didn't know how to market the film."

Fox was a stately Hollywood studio who, unlike an edgy independent company like Avco-Embassy, had no understanding of the horror genre or what would appeal to horror audiences. To a studio like Fox, an actor like Ben Johnson, and his Academy Award, represented respectability and this was also still a time where leading men were almost always given top billing over their female co-stars. Even by 1980, it was rare that an actress received top billing over her male counterpart, and so even though Curtis was infinitely more important to *Terror Train*'s bottom line than Johnson was, Johnson would get top billing. By giving Johnson top billing over Curtis, Fox thought they were following the successful formula of *Halloween* where Donald Pleasence had received top billing over a then-unknown Curtis. It worked on *Halloween*, so why wouldn't it work with *Terror Train*? Such ignorance and misunderstanding of the horror marketplace was commonplace for the Hollywood studios who began releasing their own horror films between 1980 and 1981. Fox had *Terror Train*, Columbia Pictures had *Happy Birthday to Me* (1981), MGM had *He Knows You're Alone* (1980), Paramount had both *Friday the 13th* (1980) and *My Bloody Valentine* (1981). Of all of these films, *Friday the 13th* would be the lone big hit.

Fox's bungling of *Terror Train*, and their failure to exploit Curtis as an asset in terms of the film's marketing, was most evident in the artwork that Fox released prior to *Terror Train*'s North American theatrical release in October of 1980. The art featured the killer wearing a Groucho Marx mask, one of the many disguises Kenny Hampson assumes in the film, and wielding a knife. It was a silly image, not frightening at all, almost hilarious, and undoubtedly left audiences confused as to whether *Terror Train* was a horror film or a horror spoof. This image certainly didn't embody the "*Halloween* on a train" concept from which the project had been first conceived.

After originally scheduling *Terror Train* for a Halloween 1980 theatrical release, Fox's then Vice-President of Advertising and Publicity, Robert Cort, decided to move-up *Terror Train*'s release to October 3, 1980 out of fear that the newly-minted slasher film market was already wilting. It was no big deal because if *Terror Train* did strong business, the film would surely drive right through the lucrative Halloween date with the momentum of a speeding locomotive. Fox was very enthusiastic about the film, and even anticipated that *Terror Train* would gross $40-50 million domestically, roughly equal to the numbers that *Halloween* had totaled.

It didn't happen. *Terror Train* only grossed $8 million upon its release in October of 1980, which is ironically about half of what *Prom Night* took in when that film had been released in July of 1980. Of the horror-slasher films released in 1980, *Terror Train* lagged behind not just *Prom Night* ($14.8 million) but also *The Fog* ($21.3) and the year's juggernaut, *Friday the 13th* ($39.7 million). It wasn't a terrible performance, and the film would later reap millions through cable and video rentals, but *Terror Train* was definitely not a hit.

In Hollywood parlance, *Terror Train* didn't "make it" and the film's disappointing performance gave Fox all the impetus it needed to withdraw from the Dead Teenager business as quickly as it had gotten involved. By late 1980, it was already becoming obvious, with the exception of *Friday the 13th*, that the newly-minted horror boom was already fading. Predictably, the reviews of *Terror Train* were uniformly negative with a few pauses of grudging admiration for the film's technical competence and for Curtis' undeniable star power. "Miss Curtis looks like a real person, and this is to her advantage. But one does wish she didn't keep getting so lost on the train. It is uncanny. One moment the corridors are full of roistering fraternity brothers and their dates, and the next moment everyone has disappeared. Then Miss Curtis stands alone, looking stricken. Next time, she should take a bus," (John Corry, *The New York Times.*); "Curtis is to the current horror film glut what Christopher Lee was to the last one or Boris Karloff was in the 1930s. She was the star of *Halloween*; she also starred in Carpenter's disappointing *The Fog* and the utterly-inept *Prom Night*, and now here she is again. At this point in her career, if she should get a straight role in a conventional movie, she might start screaming and running away from the camera just on reflex," (Roger Ebert, *Chicago Sun-Times.*); "Shocks and blood in the Carpenter tradition, adequately mounted," (*Halliwell's Film Guide.*)

The film's disappointing performance also quashed thoughts Sandy Howard had of turning *Terror Train* into a long- running horror movie franchise. In fact, there was an alternate ending for *Terror Train* that had been filmed where Kenny Hampson's hand crashes out of the ice at the end of the film. Howard wanted to do *Terror Train 2* but the film's poor box office showing, as well as Curtis' indication that she had no interest in signing up for a sequel, killed such plans. Ironically, many people—from fans to even some of the people who made the film—labor under the illusion that *Terror Train* was a success, given the popularity the film has enjoyed in its afterlife. *Terror Train* would eventually become a popular genre staple thanks to the cable and video market. Three decades later, the film stands as both a shining example of Jamie Lee Curtis' scream queen persona—because of the amount of running and screaming Curtis does in the film—as well as a vanguard of the Canadian tax shelter horror genre. As with *Prom Night*, *Terror Train* lives on today as both a time capsule of its era—in terms of the clothing and music of the period—and of Jamie Lee Curtis' scream queen career. Years later, Sandy Howard—who died in 2008—contacted Harold Greenberg's Astral Films about doing a sequel or remake to *Terror Train* only to find out that the rights had already been sold. As with *Halloween*, *The Fog*, and *Prom Night*, *Terror Train* has also received the remake treatment in the form of *Train* which was written and directed by Gideon Raff. *Train* is a loose updating of *Terror Train* that featured actress Thora Birch in the female lead. *Train* was released by Lionsgate Entertainment in 2009.

Curtis herself did little to promote *Terror Train* when it was released, aside from a handful of interviews, and nor did Fox make any such demands of her. Since *The Fog*, *Prom Night* and *Terror Train* were all released within a span of eight months (*The Fog* in February, *Prom Night* in July, *Terror Train* in October) in 1980, Curtis would often find herself talking about all three films, and would sometimes forget which film was which.

Curtis was ambivalent about *Terror Train*'s disappointing performance, and a bit miffed as to why *Prom Night*, which Curtis didn't like nearly as much as *Terror Train*, performed much better. Perhaps subconsciously, Curtis was happy about *Terror Train*'s failure, secretly hoping that the film's poor performance might hasten the end of her horror career. "I thought *Terror Train* would be a big hit because it was such a beautifully-shot and well-made film, but I guess it just missed," says Curtis. "I don't know why *Prom Night* did so much better because I thought *Terror Train* was definitely a better film."

JAMIE LEE CURTIS: I think *Terror Train* had all of the elements to be a really good horror film except maybe the most important part which was a good script. Roger was a great director, and the actors were good, and John Alcott shot it beautifully, but the story was weak and there wasn't enough attention spent on the script. It wasn't a success, and you never know why these things work or not. I didn't like the title; I thought it was silly and I think the audience might've felt that way too, but mostly it was the script. I still liked the film.

Although *Terror Train* wasn't the end of Jamie Lee Curtis' scream queen career, it marked a turning point in her career. With the arrival of 1980, Curtis was now determined to find non-horror roles that would allow her to make the transition from scream queen to serious actress. That's why the relative failure of *Terror Train* didn't bother her very much; Curtis had no interest in making anymore *Prom Nights* or *Terror Trains*. Although *Prom Night* had been a modest hit, Jamie Lee Curtis was now twenty-one years old and was clearly past the point of being able to play teenagers anymore.

In that respect, the failure of *Terror Train* might've been a blessing in that *Terror Train*'s commercial failure may have expedited Curtis' desire, and her sense of urgency, to transition to non-horror films. The one horror project looming in Curtis' future at the beginning of 1980 was the proposed sequel to *Halloween*, *Halloween II*, which was in development. Curtis felt obligated, out of loyalty to John Carpenter and Debra Hill, to star in any sequel to *Halloween* that would be made, but that would be it. Besides the future sequel to *Halloween*, Curtis was determined not to make anymore slasher films, anymore *Halloween* ripoffs, and she would stay true to this bargain. "I was almost looking forward to the time when the horror movies wouldn't be as popular and I wouldn't be in as much demand," recalls Curtis. "I was getting tired; I was ready to do something new."

Not only did Curtis not want to act in anymore horror films, she also didn't watch them, period. Although Curtis had always hated watching horror films, she would, during her scream queen career, be forced to attend screenings of horror films out of contractual and personal obligations. No more. On New Year's Day 1980, Curtis made a resolution never to watch another horror film. An unpleasant experience watching Ridley Scott's 1979 horror/science-fiction classic *Alien* pushed Curtis over the edge. "Something awful, really awful," recalled Curtis. "I didn't like *Alien*. I just couldn't take watching it, and I pledged not to watch anymore horror films again after seeing that film."

Curtis was also interesting in branching out into other areas of the movie business, namely in terms of directing and producing. This was something that friend Debra Hill, a role-model of Curtis', had also encouraged Curtis—whose colleagues had always been impressed by Curtis' understanding of the camera and grasp of the film-making process—to explore. In the fall of 1980, Curtis enrolled in a cinematography class at UCLA which Curtis recalls joining at three different points until acting work forced Curtis to regrettably dropout. Sadly, Curtis' increasingly-busy acting career would put whatever film-making ambitions she had permanently on the back-burner.

As *Terror Train* was being prepared for release, Curtis had already begun the process of taking baby steps towards non-scream queen roles. Prior to *Terror Train's* release in October of 1980, Curtis had returned from Australia where she'd filmed the psychological suspense-thriller *Roadgames* for Australian director Richard Franklin, a Hitchcock devotee and film craftsman who, in the tradition of his idol, favored an emphasis on classic suspense techniques and a restrained use of violence. There were some horror and scream queen elements in *Roadgames*, including a stalking killer, but *Roadgames* would turn out to be a complete departure from all of Curtis' previous genre films. For one thing, *Roadgames* would be the first genre film in which Jamie Lee Curtis wouldn't be required to scream.

Jamie Lee Curtis' last episodic television appearance under her Universal contract was in the 1979 episode of the television series *Buck Rogers in the 25th Century* entitled "Unchained Woman." The episode aired on NBC on November 1, 1979.

Jamie Lee Curtis and Tom Atkins in a scene from *The Fog* (1980).
(Photo courtesy of Kim Gottlieb Walker www.lenswoman.com)

Curtis' character in *The Fog*, Elizabeth Solley, is an aspiring artist who ends up
spending the night with Tom Atkins' character, Nick Castle. Atkins is almost
twenty-five years older than Curtis. (Photo courtesy of Kim Gottlieb-Walker
www.lenswoman.com)

Curtis and producer /co-writer Debra Hill on the set of *The Fog*. Curtis and Hill would remain friends until Hill's death in 2005. (Photo courtesy of Kim Gottlieb-Walker www.lenswoman.com)

The Fog marked the first time that Curtis and her mother, Janet Leigh, appeared together in a feature film, but they would only share one scene together. (Photo courtesy of Kim Gottlieb-Walker www.lenswoman.com)

Curtis and Leigh in a scene with co-star Hal Holbrook. (Photo courtesy of Kim Gottlieb-Walker www.lenswoman.com)

Elizabeth Solley finds herself under attack. (Photo courtesy of Kim Gottlieb-Walker www.lenswoman.com)

Curtis with her mother, co-star Adrienne Barbeau, and director/
co-writer John Carpenter on the set of *The Fog*. (Photo courtesy of
Kim Gottlieb-Walker www.lenswoman.com)

Poster from *The Fog*. *The Fog*
was marketed as a Jamie Lee
Curtis film, even though Curtis
only had a supporting role in the
film. (Photo courtesy of Matt
Hankinson)

Spanish poster from *The Fog* also played-up Curtis' genre appeal.
(Photo courtesy of Matt Hankinson)

Prior to beginning work on *Prom Night* (1980) in 1979, Curtis modeled various disco fashions.

Curtis was hired for *Prom Night* partly because of her dancing ability.

Slim, sleek and smooth, this cascade ruffle wrap dress creates a fine aura of the great feminine mystique in its innocent blue essence. It has an appeal to guarantee the wearer star treatment at any location — whether theater, party or disco. This fashion is a knock out of a scene stealer and is a sure way to create disco dynamite. $20.

For your nearest PHASE II and INIFINITY fashion outlet and more fashion photos turn to page 72.

Advertisement shows Curtis wearing a cascade ruffle wrap dress that promises to "create a fine aura of the great feminine mystique in its innocent blue essence."

1980 photo of Curtis shows the beginning of Curtis' emergence as an unlikely sex symbol.

Curtis in a scene from *Prom Night*. (From left to right) Curtis, David Mucci, Joy Thompson, Pita Oliver. (Photo courtesy of Peter Simpson)

Curtis with co-stars Leslie Nielsen (left) and Michael Tough during the filming of
Prom Night. (Photo courtesy of Peter Simpson)

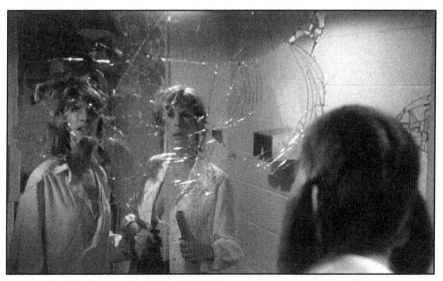

Kim Hammond (Curtis) is spooked in a scene from *Prom Night*. (Photo courtesy
of Peter Simpson)

Curtis worked with *Prom Night* co-star Casey Stevens for many hours to perfect their dance moves in the film, and Curtis and Stevens also dated during filming. Friends of Stevens say he fell in love with Curtis during the filming of *Prom Night*. (Photo courtesy of Peter Simpson)

Curtis became friends with co-star Eddie Benton (AKA Anne-Marie Martin) during the filming of *Prom Night*. (Photo courtesy of Peter Simpson)

Casey Stevens
Starring in Prom Night
To be released early
1980

**Trainco
Talent
(416) 977-0292**

1980 agency photo of Casey Stevens. Stevens' acting career stalled after *Prom Night* and Stevens eventually left acting and became an airline steward. Stevens and Curtis never saw each other again after the filming of *Prom Night*. Stevens died of AIDS in 1987.

Curtis and Stevens dance in *Prom Night*. The gym scenes in *Prom Night* were filmed during a record heat-wave in Toronto. (Photo courtesy of Peter Simpson)

The dance number in *Prom Night* was choreographed by director Paul Lynch's sister, Pamela Malcolm. (Photo courtesy of Peter Simpson)

Although Curtis was a natural dancer, Casey Stevens had great difficulty with the dancing scenes in the film. (Photo courtesy of Peter Simpson).

The dance sequence in *Prom Night* was inspired by the film *Saturday Night Fever* (1977) much like the project itself was modeled after *Halloween*. (Photo courtesy of Peter Simpson)

Curtis turned twenty-one during the filming of *Terror Train* (1980) in November of 1979. (Photo courtesy of Lamar Card/Card Motion Pictures)

During the filming of *Terror Train*, Curtis became very close with co-stars
Sandee Currie, Hart Bochner and Timothy Webber. (From left to right)
Sandee Currie, Hart Bochner, Timothy Webber, Jamie Lee Curtis.
(Photo courtesy of Lamar Card/Card Motion Pictures)

Alana Maxwell (Curtis) screams her head off in a scene from *Terror Train*.
(Photo courtesy of Lamar Card/Card Motion Pictures)

Alana is comforted by train conductor Carne (Ben Johnson).
(Photo courtesy of Lamar Card/Card Motion Pictures).

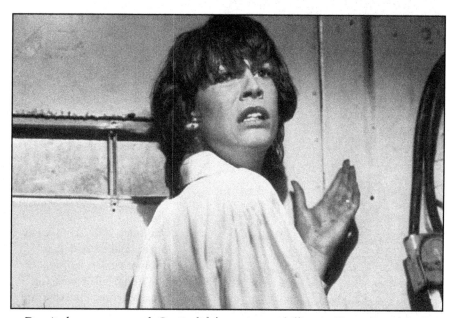

Despite her genre appeal, Curtis didn't receive top billing in *Terror Train* which was given to Oscar winner Ben Johnson. (Photo courtesy of Lamar Card/Card Motion Pictures)

Alana is confronted by the murderous Kenny Hampson (Derek MacKinnon). (Photo courtesy of Lamar Card/Card Motion Pictures)

Although 20th Century Fox spent millions of dollars promoting *Terror Train*, the studio failed to exploit Curtis' genre popularity and the film was a box office disappointment. (Photo courtesy of Lamar Card/Card Motion Pictures)

twelve

A KANGAROO SCREAM QUEEN

Roadgames, which Jamie Lee Curtis would begin filming in Australia in June of 1980, represents the first major turning point in Jamie Lee Curtis' acting career, and the beginning of the end of her scream queen horror career. *Roadgames* wouldn't be a total genre departure for Curtis; once again her life would be put in jeopardy by a crazed killer, but *Roadgames* was different. It was a suspense-thriller and Curtis would see enough in the *Roadgames* script to make her believe that the project would be a good first step in removing the Queen of Crud title from her image.

Curtis' first contact with the *Roadgames* project came during the filming of *The Fog* in April of 1979, and the appearance of an ambitious and bright Australian film-maker named Richard Franklin. Franklin had actually visited *The Fog*'s California set to talk to John Carpenter not Curtis. Carpenter and Franklin had gone to USC together with Franklin, who attended USC between 1967 and 1969, being two years ahead of Carpenter who would leave the school in 1971.

Carpenter and Franklin were casual friends and Franklin had visited the set of *The Fog* mainly to get reacquainted with his old school friend. Franklin also wanted to meet Janet Leigh whom Franklin had admired greatly ever since a twelve year old Franklin had first viewed *Psycho* back in his hometown of Melbourne, Australia. "I loved *Psycho* and Hitchcock, but I also loved American cinema in general," recalled Franklin. "I also loved John Ford's films as much, if not more, than I loved Hitchcock's films, although Hitchcock's style had the biggest influence on my own film- making style."

Franklin's powerful memory of seeing *Psycho* for the first time was the inspiration for Franklin's life-long obsession with Hitchcock's work

269

as well as for Franklin's own desire to be a film-maker. After spending his younger teenage years in an Australian Rhythm and Blues musical group called *The Pink Finks*, Franklin re-dedicated himself to his love of film-making and entered USC film school in 1967. "They were only screening European films at USC; that was the big thing at that time, and that shocked me," recalled Franklin. "One time in class we were screening *A Hard Day's Night* and I asked the lecturer when we were going to study American films, especially Hitchcock, and the lecturer looked at me and said, 'Oh, I've heard about you; you're the one who's interested in tired old hacks like Ford and Hitchcock.' I was shocked when I heard that."

Franklin, who'd begun making amateur 8MM home movies around the same time he first saw *Psycho* at the age of twelve, was a student of Hitchcock's in more ways than one. Franklin, who was thirty years old when he first met Jamie Lee Curtis and Janet Leigh on the set of *The Fog*, was an obsessive Hitchcock fanatic who had studied every frame and shot of the grand master's work. For Franklin, who died of prostate cancer in 2007, the stylistic influence of Hitchcock would shade the rest of his career and life.

Franklin had no real idea at this point who Jamie Lee Curtis was upon their first meeting, other than she'd starred in *Halloween* which didn't register that much for Franklin who had just directed a psychological-thriller film entitled *Patrick* which received a sparse release in North America. "I visited *The Fog* to see John because his career seemed like it was really taking off and I was anxious to get my own career going as well," recalled Franklin. "I met Jamie and Janet and they were very nice, and I remember wondering what John saw in Jamie to cast her in his movies. It seemed to me that John had seen a certain Hawksian quality in Jamie; that she was a very unconventional heroine. Of course, Janet Leigh was a great Hawksian heroine herself."

The relationship between Carpenter and Franklin, in terms of their film-making approaches and the influence of Alfred Hitchcock, is interesting. By 1979, Hitchcock had been semi-retired for several years, was gravely ill, and would eventually pass away on April 29, 1980, leaving many film critics and historians to ponder which, if any, upcoming film-makers might follow in Hitchcock's footsteps and carry on Hitchcock's cinematic legacy.

The most obvious torchbearer was Brian De Palma who, by 1979, had already spent a decade memorializing Hitchcock in a string of Hitchcockian pastiche suspense-thrillers such as *Sisters* and *Obsession*. Carpenter had drawn comparisons to Hitchcock because of *Halloween*, but Carpenter—who would later seem somewhat uncomfortable and burdened by *Halloween's* critical success—had always wanted to focus on the horror and science-fiction genres and wasn't long for the suspense-thriller genre. That left Richard Franklin who, unlike De Palma, had a direct connection with Hitchcock himself.

While at USC, Franklin had organized an ambitious retrospective of Hitchcock's work which led to a fateful meeting with the legendary master of suspense. In 1968, while mounting his Hitchcock USC retrospective, Franklin—who'd always dreamed of screening *Vertigo* for his class in all of its technicolor glory—was planning to screen 1948's *Rope* when he learned that the film had been withdrawn from distribution, and that Franklin would have to contact Hitchcock's office at Universal Studios and get permission in order to screen the film.

Franklin sent a written request to Alfred Hitchcock Productions and was stunned shortly afterwards when he was called out of class to a telephone call from Alfred Hitchcock himself. This first introduction led to Franklin inviting Hitchcock to Franklin's class where Hitchcock later presided over a three hour discussion of his career with Franklin serving as moderator. A casual friendship was formed and, in the fall of 1968, Hitchcock would invite Franklin to be an official observer during the filming of *Topaz* (1969). In 1975, Franklin—who would make his own feature directing debut with the bawdy 1975 Australian comedy-western *The True Story of Eskimo Nell*—would also be invited to observe the filming of *Family Plot* (1976), Hitchcock's final film.

The genesis of *Roadgames'* script began after the release of Franklin's *Patrick* in 1978. *Patrick's* writer, screenwriter Everett De Roche, was working on a television series called *The Truckies* for the Australian Broadcasting Corporation (ABC), Australia's national government television station, and had penned an episode for the series that was entitled *Roadgames*. Like the *Truckies* series itself, the proposed *Roadgames* episode followed a cross-section of strange people who move up and down the vast Australian roads and subsequently form a quirky little community.

Franklin had first suggested the story to De Roche and upon the show's broadcast suggested to De Roche that the *Roadgames* concept might be the basis for an interesting feature film project. "There was a bit of an element of *Canterbury Tales* in *Roadgames* and we were also influenced by *Sweeney Todd* and the story of the Demon Barber," recalls De Roche. "A *Sweeney Todd* musical had just been produced by Richard's friend, Stephen Sondheim, and Richard and I would listen to the music constantly as we traveled around Australia, through the Nullarbor Plain, which is Australia's longest road and one of the longest stretches of road in the world, looking for possible filming locations for *Roadgames*. We were interested with the idea of human meat; that someone might travel in a van across the Nullarbor with a fridge full of meat that might not really be meat—it might be human. It sounded funny and scary."

De Roche and Franklin began hammering out *Roadgames'* script in the summer of 1979 when Franklin was serving as co-producer on the film *The Blue Lagoon* which was being directed by Randal Kleiser, another friend of Franklin's from USC. Franklin's other USC contemporaries had included such future Hollywood giants as George Lucas and Robert Zemeckis. Franklin brought De Roche over to Fiji, where *The Blue Lagoon* was being filmed, and they worked on the script for *Roadgames* during *The Blue Lagoon*'s filming. "We kept talking about raw meat and *Sweeney Todd* and the idea of a killer who would travel up and down the roads killing people," recalls De Roche. "They were weird conversations we had. We'd talk about cutting a woman's arms and legs off and putting them in plastic bags and hiding the bags all over the place."

Ultimately, Franklin ended up giving De Roche a copy of the script for Hitchcock's classic 1954 suspense-thriller *Rear Window* and instructed the writer to create "*Rear Window* on the Australian highway" since *Rear Window*, with its blend of black comedy and nail-biting suspense, had exactly the kind of tone that Franklin wanted to impose on *Roadgames*. "I thought that the open highways of Australia would make a great setting for a thriller in the vein of *Rear Window*," recalled Franklin. "It's a very creepy and interesting and weird setting and I wanted to bring humor into the story by focusing on the strange characters that drive up and down those roads in real life. *Rear Window*, like most of Hitchcock's films, was a very funny film and I wanted *Roadgames* to also have that mixture of comedy and suspense."

Roadgames was financed by both the Australian government, through the government's various film funding corporations, and by Avco-Embassy who would provide funding through a pre-sales agreement. Additionally, the Australian financiers would enlist completion guarantor Sue Milliken from Film Finances Inc. (the American division of Film Finances had also bonded *Terror Train*) to oversee the production and ensure that *Roadgames* would be completed on budget and on schedule. The arrangement, however necessary and understandable from the point of view of the cost-conscious Australian financiers, would drive Franklin nuts. "I always felt like there was someone looking over my shoulder," recalled Franklin. "There were a lot of things I planned to do in the film that I couldn't do because I had to maintain the rigid filming schedule and basically just finish at all costs."

The budget for *Roadgames* was $1.8 million which was peanuts by Hollywood standards, but which would make *Roadgames* the most expensive film to be shot in Australia up until 1980, and the second most expensive film, behind *Terror Train*, that Curtis had shot in her career up to this point.

The financing arrangement would turn out to be a mixed blessing as the different priorities of Avco-Embassy, *Roadgames'* American distributor, and the Australian financiers—as well as Australia's Actors' Equity union—would conflict throughout *Roadgames'* production.

The first major hurdle that Franklin faced during pre-production on *Roadgames* was casting. Franklin and De Roche had originally written *Roadgames* as a vehicle for Sean Connery, but Connery's asking price—which would've been more than the film's entire budget—made him out of reach. Avco-Embassy wanted a name actor for the male lead while the unions in Australia wanted an Australian actor. "Avco told me to find a good actor with some international standing and there were none of those in Australia at that point in time," recalled Franklin. "There were lots of good actors in Australia back then but none of them had international standing. The Australian financiers didn't care; they just wanted to make Hollywood happy and for the film to be successful. It was the unions who caused most of the trouble."

Eventually, Franklin and Bernard Schwartz, who was *Roadgames'* American producer, settled on Stacy Keach, a powerful dramatic actor from the stage, for the film's male lead. Keach was best known for his strong performance in John Huston's brilliant 1972 boxing drama

Fat City. Keach, who would learn to operate a sixteen-gear truck for his role in *Roadgames*, hadn't attained full-fledged film stardom following his triumph in *Fat City*—largely due to unfortunate circumstances beyond his control—but he was certainly a recognizable actor with some international standing (1). In May of 1980, prior to filming *Roadgames*, Keach would appear at the Cannes Film Festival to promote the film *The Long Riders* which Keach had starred in for director Walter Hill (2). Franklin had no objections to Keach's casting and neither did Avco-Embassy or the Australian financiers.

The most contentious moment of *Roadgames'* colorful production history would concern Jamie Lee Curtis' casting in the film. Although Franklin had met Curtis on the set of *The Fog* in 1979, Franklin wasn't even thinking about Curtis when he was in pre-production on *Roadgames*. After Keach was cast as *Roadgames'* male lead, Franklin felt that he was free to cast an Australian actress for the female lead to balance out the film and placate Actors' Equity. In this regard, Franklin chose Lisa Peers, an Australian actress who was two years older than Curtis and whose previous experience had been on Australian episodic television.

This brought outraged yelps from genre-savvy Avco-Embassy who suggested Curtis' name to Franklin who was rather ambivalent about the subject. The female lead in *Roadgames* was a relatively minor part in relation to Keach's role in the film which occupied the heart of the story. "I cast Lisa Peers in Australia, but when I spoke to Avco, they wanted a name and they told me to try Jamie Lee Curtis," recalled Franklin. "I had an in with Jamie because of my relationship with John and because I'd met Jamie on *The Fog*. John gave me Jamie's number, and I called her and told her about the project and her character and she said yes fairly quickly."

Curtis' casting in *Roadgames* was entirely a last minute process. It was May of 1980, about a month before *Roadgames* would start filming, and Curtis had, ironically, just returned from Cannes where she'd made an appearance to promote *The Fog*. Curtis was basking in *The Fog*'s success, and was also looking forward to—largely for the purpose of putting the films behind her—the upcoming releases of *Prom Night* and *Terror Train* later in the year. After all of that, Curtis was looking for her next acting job which she hoped would be located outside of the slasher film genre.

Curtis met with Franklin, Everett De Roche, and Bernard Schwartz in Los Angeles to discuss the project. It was a comical meeting given that Curtis' father, Tony Curtis, and Bernard Schwartz shared the same birth name given that Tony Curtis' birth-name is Bernard Schwartz. While Franklin was in Los Angeles, Curtis screened *Patrick*, Franklin's 1978 thriller about a coma patient who uses telekinetic powers to terrorize the people around him, in order to gauge Franklin's work. Curtis was impressed with the film, even though the Australian film had been poorly-dubbed for its American release.

Curtis was impressed with Franklin's gentle demeanor and his film-making pedigree, especially the fact that Franklin had studied, in a roundabout way, with the great Hitchcock. Franklin's friendship with Carpenter earned Curtis' personal trust, as if Franklin were a charter member of the "Carpenter-Hill unit" even though Franklin had scarcely crossed paths with Debra Hill (3). "Alfred Hitchcock is one of the old directors that I would've most liked to have worked with and I liked the fact that Richard used Hitchcockian techniques in his films," recalled Curtis. "But Richard wasn't just a copycat who took shots from Hitchcock's films. He wasn't just Hitchcockian, he was Franklinian too. He was a good director."

JAMIE LEE CURTIS: I screened *Patrick* in Hollywood to see Richard's work and I was really impressed with the film, and with Richard as a director, even though the dubbing of American voices was terrible. I trusted Richard; after seeing *Patrick*, I knew that *Roadgames* would be a smart thriller and not a horror film. That was in the script too; it was really clever and funny and smart. I liked Richard's idea of doing a movie that was like *Rear Window* on a highway, and I knew that Richard had studied with Hitchcock—and was friends with John Carpenter—and so I thought he would do a good job.

EVERETT DE ROCHE, WRITER: I remember Jamie as being delightfully earthy and fun to be around and very irreverent about her Hollywood upbringing. I didn't know anything about her except she was the daughter of Tony Curtis and Janet Leigh which had me in awe. I met Jamie in Los Angeles, and she was with me and Richard and we were going to a restaurant when Jamie met producer Bernard Schwartz. When Richard introduced Jamie to Bernard, Jamie quickly replied,

"Didn't you used to be my father?" because Bernard Schwartz is Tony Curtis' birth-name. It was really funny.

JON DOWDING, ART DIRECTOR/PRODUCTION DESIGNER: Richard arranged a screening of *Halloween* for myself and cinematographer Vincent Monton before Jamie arrived in Australia. Richard wanted all of us, including himself, to get a sense of what Jamie was like as an actress and also to see the techniques that had made *Halloween* so successful because the plan was to reference a lot of films in *Roadgames*, especially the Hitchcock films. I thought *Halloween* was a well-constructed film, and I was struck by how young Jamie looked in the film—and the command she had as an actress—and also by what a great screamer she was.

RICHARD FRANKLIN, CO-PRODUCER/DIRECTOR: I found Jamie to be very charming and likable, but I didn't really look at her as a real star at this point in her career. She was in *Halloween*, and that was a big hit, but I thought John Carpenter was the real star of *Halloween* and not Jamie. To me, Jamie was just a talented young actress, not a big star, and so we never changed the script for Jamie, or made the part bigger which I think was a mistake. I've always said that I wished I'd given Jamie a bigger part in the film.

LISA PEERS, ACTRESS: I was cast by Richard Franklin in *Roadgames* in Australia after Stacy Keach was cast in the film, and I was really excited about working with Stacy Keach in my first film, and in my first American film. I'd never heard about Jamie Lee Curtis at that point. I'd gotten a green card and after I made *Roadgames* I was planning to go to Hollywood to try my luck. Then I met with the producers, and I actually brought my dog to the meeting. A few days later, my agent calls me and tells me they've replaced me with Jamie Lee Curtis. My agent told me it might've been because the producers didn't like my dog, but I knew that wasn't it. They wanted American actors in the film, even though the movie was going to be set in Australia. I was devastated. Nothing against Jamie Lee Curtis, but it really hurt me and changed everything in terms of my career because even though *Roadgames* didn't end up being a big hit film, I think it would've changed my career.

Franklin's ignorance to Curtis' stardom, to the Jamie Lee Curtis legend, is a bit baffling. Although Curtis only had two feature films in release—in terms of *Halloween* and the recently-released *The Fog*—by the time of the start of *Roadgames'* filming in June of 1980, wasn't she already a star? Hollywood certainly seemed to think so, which was why Curtis had been asked to be a presenter at the 52nd Annual Academy Awards ceremony that was held at Los Angeles' Dorothy Chandler Pavilion on April 14, 1980. Curtis presented, alongside actor George Hamilton of *Love at First Bite* fame, the Oscar for Best Cinematography which was won by Vittorio Storaro for his work on *Apocalypse Now* (1979).

Prior to making *Roadgames*, Curtis had never worked on a film whose shoot was longer than a month whereas *Roadgames'* production schedule would eventually extend to a whopping 68 days. Even though Curtis would have few scenes in *Roadgames*, she would be required to be on set virtually every day for a production that would become increasingly draining and exhausting during the course of filming. "I felt really bad because I didn't feel we were using Jamie in the film as much as we should," recalled Franklin. "When we got to Melbourne, Jamie spent most of her time in the hotel just waiting to be needed. In retrospect, I wish we'd beefed up Jamie's part and given her more to do."

Roadgames would be filmed all over Australia, primarily in and around the massive Nullarbor Plain—a desert wasteland that stretches about 1200 km from east to west between South Australia and Western Australia—and in Melbourne where Curtis and the rest of the cast and crew would also do a lot of interior studio filming. In all, the production would spend two weeks filming along the vast Nullarbor Plain while the bulk of the rest of filming would be done in Melbourne. Actually, when filming on *Roadgames* began on the Nullarbor Plain, in the first week of June of 1980, Curtis herself was nowhere to be found.

Curtis was in Sydney, Australia promoting *The Fog* at the Sydney Film Festival during the first week of *Roadgames'* filming on the Nullarbor Plain. Curtis was treated like a big star at the prestigious festival and was flanked by American film journalists, including writers from the *Los Angeles Times* and *Variety*, who would end up following Curtis all the way to the barren and desolate set of *Roadgames*. If Richard Franklin hadn't been entirely convinced that Curtis was a movie star, Curtis' star-studded arrival was a wake-up call. Likewise for Curtis, the Australian setting was a big culture shock for the Hollywood-born actress, to say the least.

Curtis arrived on the Nullarbor Plain about a week into *Roadgames'* filming which wasn't a big deal since *Roadgames'* filming would span over two months, and Curtis's character in the film, Pamela "Hitch" Rushworth, doesn't have any dialogue in the story until almost 35 minutes into the film. "When people see the movie, they always ask why Jamie doesn't have more to do in the film and I reply that I wish we had done more with her, but at the time I didn't recognize that she was a star," recalled Franklin. "My biggest regret on *Roadgames* was that I didn't recognize Jamie's obvious star quality earlier and given her a bigger part in the film. I think that was because Jamie was only twenty-one when we made *Roadgames*. I was kind of old-fashioned and I didn't look at actors who were as young as Jamie was as being stars."

For Curtis, the last remnants of Hollywood glamour were soon stripped away when Curtis—upon her arrival on the Nullarbor Plain in the second week of June of 1980—checked into the gas station motel truck-stop that housed *Roadgames'* cast and crew. The Spartan living conditions were completely alien to anything that Curtis had ever experienced before. Besides the motel, which contained a small restaurant along with the gas station, there was nothing but desert for at least 100 miles. "It was a combination road-stop motel, fuel stop, truck rest area, and grocery stop for the few locals who drove hundreds of miles to pick-up supplies," recalls production manager Greg Ricketson. "An added factor was that the only available water was 'hard" bore water. You needed special soap and shampoo to get a lather and you had to work hard for that and you certainly couldn't drink the water. Most of us simply gave up trying to wash our hair. It wasn't an illustrious space for Jamie when she arrived."

These close living quarters which housed the majority of *Roadgames'* cast and crew, including Curtis and Keach, allowed Curtis to quickly bond with her Australian counterparts, as well as with the vast country itself where Curtis would be living for more than two months. "The place where Jamie and the rest of us stayed was like out of a Robert Rodriguez-Quentin Tarantino movie in terms of the setting," recalls art director and production designer Jon Dowding. "There was nothing but desert surrounding the motel for 100 miles, but in back of the motel there was this two-lane blacktop and in back of that there was this big junkyard of broken-down vehicles, strewn out for miles and miles, that had died before they could make it to the highway."

JAMIE LEE CURTIS: *Roadgames* was unlike any of the films I'd made previously. Not only were we filming in Australia, but we were going to be filming for two months and none of my previous films had gone longer than a month. Stacy Keach and I were the only Americans working on *Roadgames* and when I arrived in Australia to make the film, I was immediately surrounded by all of these Australian men, and Australian men are the most macho men around. I don't think women had been allowed inside Australian public bars until the 1970s. They like their women soft, and that's not me. The first night on location I played pool with some of the guys from the crew and beat them.

JON DOWDING: When Jamie arrived in Australia, I think most of us still identified Jamie as the daughter of Tony Curtis and Janet Leigh, and we were very much in awe of her Hollywood pedigree, more than anything. When she arrived on the Plain, she went in for costuming and she seemed very down to earth. She was tall and willowy and extraordinarily beautiful.

RICHARD FRANKLIN: Jamie arrived on the Plain, which is in the middle of nowhere, and I couldn't believe that she'd brought the media with her. It was totally unexpected. Jamie was very eager when she arrived, bright-eyed and bushy-tailed, and very enthusiastic about working on the film. I found Jamie to be unpretentious, unassuming, but a little insecure being so far from home, although she became much more comfortable in the environment as we moved along. Yes, I think some of the male attitudes were a little politically backward, and probably still are, but we were in the Outback. I think she was excited to be away from home, away from Hollywood, and working on a film that wasn't a slasher movie.

STACY KEACH, CO-STAR: The only thing I'd known about Jamie before we met on *Roadgames* was that she'd been called the queen of scream, a title that Jamie absolutely hated. When I met Jamie for the first time, at the motel, I thought she was incredibly beautiful and I quickly discovered that she had a great sense of humor and I was surprised by what a dedicated and serious actress she was.

SUE MILLIKEN, PRODUCTION EXECUTIVE: I was the completion guarantor's representative on *Roadgames*, for the completion bond company Film Finances. That meant I was a production executive with the responsibility of ensuring the film kept to its budget. I remember Jamie very well from the film. She was very young, very nice and grounded. She was a bit nervous about being in a strange country with a lot of people she didn't know. But she did her job well and was extremely nice to work with and to have around. I admired her and I've watched her career with interest and respect ever since.

GRANT PAGE, CO-STAR/STUNT COORDINATOR: We didn't know Jamie from *Halloween*. We knew her as the daughter of Tony Curtis and Janet Leigh, because Jamie had only made one or two films at that point. We were kind of in awe of working with the daughter of Tony Curtis and Janet Leigh. I first met Jamie at the gas station motel and the first thing I noticed about Jamie was that she had an Australian personality and work ethic in the sense that she was dramatically honest and she brought that to her acting, and it was effortless and easy for her. When we would talk, she'd talk about Los Angeles and her career, and then she'd open up to me about her darkest family secrets because we had a trusting relationship that was full of honesty.

GREG RICKETSON, PRODUCTION MANAGER: I met Jamie at a place in at the motel called "the bar" the night before the first day of shooting in the desert and I was bowled over. I was twenty-five and making my way up the production ladder, and she was a twenty-one year old star who was very sassy, attractive, open, gregarious, friendly and totally accepting of the shitty place we were going to be working in for the next several weeks. She had no airs, no complaints about the shitty (but best room in the motel) room she'd moved into hours earlier.

One of the biggest challenges for Curtis and Franklin during *Roadgames'* filming was in dealing with the local unions, primarily Australia's Actors' Equity union. Actors' Equity were angry at Franklin for casting Curtis and Keach in *Roadgames* instead of hiring Australian actors, oblivious to the fact that Franklin's hand had been forced by *Roadgames'* American financier, Avco-Embassy. "Avco never told me I couldn't cast Australians in the leads, but they told me I needed actors who had international standing," recalled Franklin. "There weren't any such actors in Australia at that time, and so we cast Jamie and Stacy. Because Stacy had been cast before Jamie, Jamie took a lot of unfair criticism from the unions who were angry that we had two Americans in the leads."

Since Keach, who did receive some criticism from the Australian media, had already been cast in Los Angeles, Curtis took the brunt of the criticism and hostility from the local film community who accused Franklin of being a "sell out" and blamed Curtis, who was seen as the embodiment of Hollywood imperialism, for killing the film industry for Australian actors. The union wasn't entirely being unreasonable; they understood the casting of a recognizable American actor like Keach in the film in terms of securing financing and selling the film. The understanding was that an Australian actress would be cast in the female lead, and in this respect, Curtis' casting over local actress Lisa Peers was considered a slap in the face (4).

JAMIE LEE CURTIS: We were really the first Americans to do a film there, in terms of American actors doing a movie with American financing in Australia, and so the local media thought the Australian film industry was selling-out to Hollywood. Richard got abuse, I got abuse, Stacy took some abuse. My part had been given to an Australian actress, but when Avco-Embassy got involved they wanted an American actress. It wasn't easy.

EVERETT DE ROCHE: I heard secondhand, because I wasn't there for most of the filming, that some idiot walked up to Jamie shortly after her arrival in Oz and said something like "So what the fuck are you doing putting Aussie actors out of work?" which was a terrible thing to say because Jamie was such a great girl. The comment reportedly had Jamie in tears, even though she's a tough gal, and Richard and I were both furious about that and the whole bureaucracy that was rampant in the Australian film industry. Jamie proved what a great actress and a person she is by not letting any of that bother her and giving a great performance in the film.

RICHARD FRANKLIN: I'd cast Lisa Peers, but Avco-Embassy insisted on a name and they wanted Jamie Lee Curtis, who I'd met briefly on *The Fog*. I wouldn't have had a problem using Jamie or Lisa in the film but it wasn't my decision as Avco had final say in terms of casting. The unions didn't understand the influence of the distributor and so they blamed Jamie which was unfortunate because I know Jamie became very upset.

GRANT PAGE: I don't remember there being any kind of hostility towards Jamie when she arrived on the set and started working on the film. It was just the one union that was angry. The cast and crew on *Roadgames* loved Jamie. We loved her from the first moment we met her, and we all bonded immediately. Jamie and I developed an especially trusting relationship with each other during filming and we had tremendous honesty with each other, and Jamie would really open up to me about her personal life, her family, her career in Hollywood, everything. Her tremendous honesty was the thing that most struck me about Jamie because I think that was what made her a great actress as well.

LISA PEERS: When I found out I'd lost the part in the film to Jamie Lee Curtis I complained to the union because I was really devastated and upset about it. I feel bad about any controversy that Jamie had to deal with because I wasn't angry at her; she's a great actress. I thought it was silly to have a film that's set in Australia and to cast an American actor, Stacy Keach, as a truck driver and then cast an American actress as a hitchhiker in Australia. It didn't make sense. They should've cast an Australian actress in the female lead because that's what the story called for.

GREG RICKETSON: I think the whole controversy had to do with Actors' Equity protecting the interests of its members in an immature and rapidly-developing and subsidized industry. *Roadgames* was the biggest project made in Australia at that time, and the argument was that it wouldn't be made unless Richard had Jamie Lee Curtis who was hot, as well as Stacy Keach. Jamie's fault? Of course not. If Jamie was in the eye of a storm, she didn't create it, and was never resented for it. It was all part of the development of a new industry. Everyone on *Roadgames* loved Jamie Lee for the natural and friendly and collegiate girl she was. The political storm around her had no impact whatsoever.

None of this hostility towards Curtis came from the cast or crew of *Roadgames* who were immediately smitten with Curtis due to her enthusiasm, sense of humor and tireless work ethic. This was especially true of Stacy Keach, Curtis' co- star in *Roadgames*. For *Roadgames* to work, Curtis and Keach had to have strong chemistry with each other, to roll off each other's lines, to counterpunch with each other in the vein of Humphrey Bogart and Lauren Bacall in Howard Hawks' 1944 film *To Have and Have Not*. "To be a Hawksian actress, like Bacall was in Howard Hawks' *To Have and Have Not*, Jamie had to be feisty, insolent, saucy and Jamie had all of those qualities," recalled Franklin. "I was surprised Jamie and Stacy were such a good fit. I think they worked at it a lot."

Roadgames tells the story of Pat Quid, played by Keach, an eccentric and obsessive truck driver hauling cargo all over Australia, which inevitably leads him up and down the maddening Nullarbor Plain. As the film opens, Quid, who applies nicknames to the strange motorists (his "Roadgames" which includes such nicknames as Captain Careful and Frita Frugal) he encounters on the roads, becomes transfixed by a man in a green van he nicknames "Smith or Jones."

Quid, whose only companion is a half-dog, half-dingo named Boswell, suspects Smith or Jones, who's played by stuntman Grant Page in the film, as being responsible for the murders of several women. A cat and mouse game ensues between the two men, extending from the Nullarbor Plain to Perth where Quid is headed to deliver his truck-full of frozen meat. In true Hitchcock tradition, Keach ends up being wrongly implicated in the murders along the course of his journey.

Quid's obsessive relationship with Smith or Jones is clearly inspired by Jimmy Stewart's voyeuristic nightmare in 1954's *Rear Window* with Smith or Jones acting as Quid's Raymond Burr, the elusive killer. The implication that Quid's meat might be human flesh is a clear nod to Hitchcock's macabre black humor that made such a big impression on Franklin, especially in *Psycho* which Hitchcock himself always thought of as a comedy. "Australians have that same kind of dark humor as well, so I wasn't just borrowing from Hitchcock in terms of the humor in *Roadgames*," said Franklin. "*Roadgames* is a distinctly Australian film and even though our inspiration was to do *Rear Window* on the highway, Australia is a major part of the film, both in terms of the place and the people."

It would be unfair to suggest that *Roadgames* is purely a Hitchcock pastiche, and that Franklin is nothing more than a skilled copycat, or that Curtis' casting represented some kind of in-joke gimmick. The most direct Hitchcockian influence in *Roadgames*, in terms of style, is a restrained use of violence, as well as a reliance on the bread and butter Hitchcock technique of fooling with the audience's expectations through the use of sly and subtle misdirection. This is what Franklin—the film-maker and film student—took from Hitchcock, not a shot-by-shot blue-print of Hitchcock's films from which to borrow from, although Franklin himself had virtually memorized every shot in every film that Hitchcock ever made.

The killer's pursuit of his victims in *Roadgames*, namely the female drifters and hitchhikers whose bodies he discards along the Australian outback without a trace, has shades of Jack the Ripper who was immortalized by Hitchcock in his 1926 film *The Lodger*, Hitchcock's first thriller and the film that Hitchcock considered to be his first true film. *The Lodger* was made less than 40 years after the actual Jack the Ripper Whitechapel murders from 1888, which gives that film a creepy subtext, and the film's influence is certainly present in *Roadgames* with the Australian desert doubling for Whitechapel and the female victims doubling for the prostitutes that Jack the Ripper had preyed upon.

Roadgames' most obvious wink to Alfred Hitchcock concerns Curtis' character, Pamela Rushworth, an American hitchhiker who Quid simply calls "Hitch." Hitchcock had passed away just before the start of *Roadgames'* filming and Franklin actually wrote to Hitchcock's widow, Alma Reville, to offer his condolences and to ask for Reville's blessing to use the character name Hitch for Curtis' character. "It was an excuse for me to contact her and pay my respects, and she was really nice about it and gave her warm blessing," recalled Franklin. "She thought it was ironic that I was doing a thriller with Janet Leigh's daughter."

Curtis' Hitch character is the daughter of an American diplomat and Hitch's pedigree is evident in her trendy appearance and worldly aura. Curtis' Hitch is a quick- witted, sassy girl looking for adventure while Quid is a closet-intellectual with a dry sense of humor. Hitch serves as *Roadgames'* red herring; she's caught in the middle between Quid and Smith or Jones and when Smith or Jones kidnaps Hitch later in the film it provides the thrust for Quid to finally vanquish Smith or Jones once and for all. "Without Jamie in the film, it would've been pretty much a silent movie because Quid wouldn't have had anyone to talk to except for his dog," said Franklin. "When Jamie and Stacy are talking in the film they're really explaining the story to the audience."

That's not to say that Curtis has a thankless role in the film. She's very charming, and Curtis and Keach work up some nice heat during their scenes together, but Curtis' purpose in *Roadgames* isn't to be the focus of the story but rather to facilitate the Quid character. This is Quid's story, told from Quid's point-of-view. In this respect, Curtis represents Franklin's variation of Hitchcock's MacGuffin story device, the ticking time bomb under the desk that casts a specter over everything; the object that the film's hero, Quid, must eventually recover before his battle is won.

Curtis' appearance in *Roadgames* also provides the impetus for much of the film's use of misdirection largely because of Curtis' limited screen time and the fact that her character doesn't fit with the genre conventions of Curtis' previous films. For Franklin, this was the main benefit that Curtis' scream queen image brought to *Roadgames*. "If they've seen Jamie in *Halloween*, they would see her in *Roadgames* and expect her to be the hero of the story and that's not what happens," recalled Franklin. "I wanted to mess with Jamie's image, and a big part of that is the fact that she's not in the film that much unlike in *Halloween* where the whole story was told through her eyes. There's more suspense that way because you don't know what's going to happen to Jamie, and because Jamie's not the lead in the film, the audience even expects that her character could be killed."

The idea of treating Jamie Lee Curtis as a potential throwaway murder victim in *Roadgames*—as essentially bait for the film's villain, Smith or Jones—is one of the film's most unexpected developments. In all of her previous horror films, Curtis had been the protagonist, the decider of her own destiny in terms of attacking her nemesis, but in *Roadgames*, Curtis is completely at the mercy of both her ruthless captor and her potential savior in the form of Keach's Quid.

Franklin's unorthodox use of Jamie Lee Curtis in *Roadgames*—from Curtis' delayed first appearance in the film to her sudden disappearance from the film to the portraying of Curtis as a helpless and reactive victim—represents Franklin's most clever use of misdirection in *Roadgames*. The result is that the audience's expectations are altered and shattered. It's as if *Roadgames* is asking the audience, especially the horror audience that had so closely identified with Curtis in *Halloween*, to question the one inescapable and immovable fact of Jamie Lee Curtis' genre career which is that Jamie Lee Curtis, the scream queen, is indestructible and can never be defeated.

thirteen

THE MAKING OF *ROADGAMES*

Jamie Lee Curtis' character in *Roadgames*, Pamela "Hitch" Rush-worth, is very much in the tradition of the unconventional Howard Hawks—or "Hawksian"—heroine. This isn't so much because of the character, and the way the character was written in *Roadgames'* script, but rather because of Curtis' own image and personality. Curtis' own unconventional beauty—specifically in terms of her angular features and androgynous look—and feistiness provides a nice compliment to Quid's gruff exterior in the film. "She's very stubborn and insolent, like the great Hawksian women," said Richard Franklin. "She's beautiful but rough around the edges at the same time, and Jamie brought a lot more edge to the character than I thought she had when we first met."

The relationship between Hitch and Quid in *Roadgames* also closely mirrors the relationship between Grace Kelly and James Stewart in *Rear Window*. Like Kelly and Stewart, the relationship between Hitch and Quid serves to provide the viewer with speculation as to the killer's motives. As Hitch and Quid talk out loud, and offer theories as to Smith or Jones' murderous activities, their questions mirror those of the audience. Hitch and Quid share the same voyeuristic fantasy, as well as the same maddeningly-obscured view of their villainous quarry, as Kelly and Stewart had in *Rear Window* when Kelly and Stewart would stare at Raymond Burr's suspicious Lars Thorwald character through the window of Stewart's apartment.

The dynamic of the Hitch-Quid relationship also takes on much the same dynamic as that of Humphrey Bogart and Katharine Hepburn in 1951's *The African Queen* in addition to the relationship between Bogart and Lauren Bacall in Howard Hawks' *To Have and Have Not* (1944). This is visible in *Roadgames* in the predictable way that Hitch and Quid argue at first, and exchange sarcastic comments about each other that disguise an obvious attraction between them, before the walls finally break down and these two people from different worlds slowly develop an affection and trust for each other. This bond is emboldened later in the film when Hitch is kidnaped by Smith or Jones and Quid is left as the only person who can save Hitch from sure death.

Hitch and Quid certainly have chemistry in the film, but their chemistry is more gently-romantic and sweetly-paternal than sexual, primarily due to the fact that Quid is about twice Hitch's age. The relationship between Hitch and Quid is tinged with bittersweet regret on the part of Quid who seems to lament, given the obvious sparks between himself and Hitch, that he weren't ten or fifteen years younger and could take better advantage of the situation without the harsh moral implications that are present in a relationship between an older man and a young girl.

Curtis' ability to invest Hitch with some degree of youthful innocence, along with the strength and vulnerability that is the hallmark of Curtis' scream queen persona, is the real reason why Franklin cast Curtis in the role of Hitch. "Jamie had that uncanny ability to make you care about what happens to her character," recalled Franklin. "I realized that was the secret to her success as a scream queen. The audience could relate to her and they cared whether she lived or died."

Although Avco-Embassy had insisted that Franklin cast name actors—actors of "international standing"—for *Roadgames'* two leads, Curtis wasn't the only choice available to Franklin for the role of Hitch. Jodie Foster and Brooke Shields were two other candidates mentioned for the role of Hitch during *Roadgames'* pre-production, both of whom were probably hotter names than Curtis was by 1980. They also would've cost a lot more than Curtis who was paid $50,000 for her work in *Roadgames*.

Jodie Foster and Brooke Shields, aside from their respective asking prices, were way too young to be considered as potential partners— certainly in the way that Bacall and Bogart were partners in a film like *To Have and Have Not*—for Stacy Keach (1). Franklin needed an actress who had name value, yes, but also an actress who could be a convincing ingenue; a girl stuck between innocence and womanhood. "Hitch was an ingenue part and there weren't many actresses around at that time, besides Jamie, who were experienced and established but who were also still ingenue types," recalled Franklin. "Jamie was someone who was somewhere between being a teen star and being a romantic heroine, which is what the part needed. The fact that Jamie had made several films before *Roadgames*, one of which—*Halloween*—was the most successful independent film ever made, was the icing on the cake."

JAMIE LEE CURTIS: I'd always wanted to make a film like *To Have and Have Not*, to be able to have dialogue like that, and I thought *Roadgames* was pretty close to that, at least for me. I loved the interaction between me and Stacy in the film. I'm a hitchhiker, he picks me up, and we start talking, and I think this was the first film where I had conversations with another character in a movie. We talk about all of the murders, and the missing women in the area, and we talk about theories about why the killer is doing this. It was interesting, and I thought the characters were very likable, and I liked that none of the stuff in the film was graphic. It was more like Bogart and Bacall on the road than *Halloween* on the road.

RICHARD FRANKLIN: Avco insisted on casting both leads with recognizable actors of international standing, and it's hard to find a young ingenue who's well-known, and I definitely saw Hitch as an ingenue part. We could've cast girls like Jodie Foster and Brooke Shields but it wouldn't have worked because they were too young to be viewed as a potential partner for Quid, in the way that Lauren Bacall was a partner to Humphrey Bogart in *To Have and Have Not*. That would've been creepy. Jamie was perfect because she was right in the middle of making the transition from young actress/child star to a young woman and possible romantic heroine. Jamie was sexy enough—and certainly a good enough actress—to be a heroine, while still being young enough, and innocent enough, so the audience wouldn't be too uncomfortable with Hitch's and Quid's relationship.

Quid is more of a father figure, or maybe a flirtatious uncle, to Hitch in *Roadgames* than a potential romantic partner. It was the same between Curtis and Stacy Keach who became fast friends on the set of *Roadgames*. Forming close bonds with co-stars was becoming a pattern for Curtis as she'd previously developed close friendships with Eddie Benton A.K.A. Anne-Martin on *Prom Night* and Sandee Currie on *Terror Train*. This was completely different.

Curtis was twenty-one and Keach had just turned 39 when *Road-games* began filming, and the veteran actor was joined on *Roadgames* by then-fiancee Jill Donahue whom Keach would marry in 1981. Donahue, who would become Keach's third wife, would accompany Keach throughout *Roadgames'* filming and the trio—Donahue, Curtis, Keach—would be inseparable throughout much of the shoot (2). Unlike Eddie Benton and Sandee Currie, who were very much Curtis' contemporaries, Curtis looked at Keach as a veteran influence from whom she could learn a lot from, not just in terms of acting but in terms of the life of a professional actor and the dedication required in such a difficult and stressful occupation. If anyone was looking for a father figure it was Jamie Lee Curtis. Despite the fact she had a loving relationship with stepfather Robert Brandt, and always regarded him as a father figure, Curtis' strained relationship with Tony Curtis was a painful subject for her and would be for a long time. On the set of *Roadgames*, much like *Prom Night* and *Terror Train*, Curtis' lingering feelings of abandonment and resentment towards her father were exacerbated by the fact that everyone looked at her as the daughter of Tony Curtis and Janet Leigh, and not just as Jamie Lee Curtis the actress, which is the only way Curtis wanted people to view her.

To the degree that Stacy Keach served as a male role model for Curtis during the filming of *Roadgames*, a mentor figure that she could rely on, it had a positive influence on Curtis who would later regard *Roadgames* as the most satisfying of her post-*Halloween* scream queen filming experiences. "The relationship between Jamie and Stacy was very much a gently- paternal kind of relationship," recalls art director and production designer Jon Dowding. "It was very sweet and innocent and they had a lot of fun together."

Stacy Keach, with whom Curtis had developed a crush on after seeing the film *Fat City* when she was fourteen, was an actor's actor and had spent the previous three years traveling the world in theatrical productions, his first love, as well as appearing in various film projects. "I learned a lot from Jill and Stacy in terms of how to travel as an actor and how to live on location and make it like a home," recalled Curtis. "When Jill and Stacy arrived, Jill put flowers in their room, and they had candles, rugs, ashtrays, pictures, everything. When I was with them, it felt like we were in a home."

One time, during filming along the Nullarbor Plain, Curtis and

Keach went off and played around in one of the nearby sand dunes. When they returned to the filming location, the shocked crew informed them that the sand dunes were populated by scorpions, deadly snakes, and spiders, any of which could've killed them with a single bite.

After two weeks of filming along the massive Nullarbor Plain, the cast and crew of *Roadgames* moved to Melbourne where the bulk of the rest of the film's two-month filming schedule would take place. This is especially true of the scenes between Curtis and Keach inside the truck's cockpit, all of which would be filmed inside a Melbourne studio. Other than that, Curtis would, much like her Hitch character does for the majority of the film, spend the rest of the filming in limbo, virtually out of sight.

When *Roadgames* leaves the Nullarbor Plain location, Curtis' Hitch is basically invisible for the rest of the film, a red herring that exists only in Quid's, and the audience's, mind. This happens during a truck-stop scene in the film where a curious Hitch peeks into Smith or Jones' green van, looking for clues of Smith or Jones' bloody handiwork. Smith or Jones then leaps out of a sleeping bag and abducts Hitch. While this is happening Quid is in the truck-stop's bathroom, watching a closed bathroom stall where he thinks he has Smith or Jones cornered. When Quid goes back outside, he discovers that Smith or Jones has taken Hitch.

The scene where Curtis is abducted by Smith or Jones in the back of the coffin-shaped green van is the only time in the film where scream queen Curtis even gets close to screaming. When Smith or Jones jumps out of the sleeping bag and envelops Curtis, she shrieks, sighs, but doesn't ever let out a scream. "Jamie screamed when we did the scene, when I jump out of the sleeping bag, because I really shocked her," recalls co-star Grant Page. "She had a great sense of humor, and wasn't afraid of doing anything, but she didn't like to be shocked like that."

Unfortunately, in terms of Curtis' role in *Roadgames*, when Smith of Jones abducts Hitch, he also removes Curtis from much of the rest of the film. After Hitch is out of the picture, *Roadgames* focuses on the one-on-one conflict between Smith or Jones and Quid of which the unseen Hitch is made to represent the prize of their battle, the object that Smith or Jones uses as bait to drive Quid crazy.

When the cast and crew moved to Melbourne, Curtis spent the bulk of her time filming the interior truck scenes with her and Keach, and pretty much laying in wait in her Melbourne hotel room. "It was a bit awkward when we went to Melbourne because Jamie really spent most of the time just cooling her heels at the hotel," recalled Franklin. "After the film leaves the Nullarbor, Jamie's character disappears, and doesn't appear until the end of the film, so Jamie didn't have anything to do."

Keach and his fiancee, Jill Donahue, had an apartment in Melbourne, and Curtis would spend a lot of time hanging out with the couple, often joined by co-star and stuntman Grant Page. "Stacy, who was a very smart man, and I would always play chess in Stacy's and Jill's apartment, and Jamie and Jill would just sit together and laugh at us," recalls Grant Page. "While Stacy and I were playing chess, Jamie and Jill would have these long talks about the state of the world and all kinds of deep subjects. We all got along really well and we trusted each other and we believed we were making a good film."

One time, while staying at the hotel in Melbourne, Curtis was invited down to the hotel bar to play some pool with some men, perfect strangers, who had gathered around and wanted to meet Curtis. "She told us that she'd been invited by these guys to go play pool and she just went by herself, no questions asked," recalls Page. "That was Jamie. She loved life, and she wasn't intimidated by anything or anyone. As it turned out, I think she was a pretty good pool player and held her own with the men."

JAMIE LEE CURTIS: I learned a lot from Stacy, both in terms of acting and the life of an actor. He was great on the set and very helpful to me, always there for me. We spent a lot of time just talking about acting and one time Stacy asked me about my character and asked me, "What animal is your character, Jamie?" I didn't know what he meant, but then he said, "I'm an ape, because I'm always on the move, swinging from the cab in the truck." Hearing that really opened my mind, and made me think about Hitch in a whole new way, and gave me a new way to look at a character. For the rest of filming, I pretended that Hitch was a cat. Cats are very mysterious creatures. They have attitude, they have a certain majestic aura about them, and they're very wary of people. That's how I played Hitch.

JON DOWDING: Jamie was very much one of the gang during filming, very much a part of the crew. We would talk over a cigarette and she'd talk about her career and life in Los Angeles and how she was looking forward to leaving the scream queen roles and doing more different film projects. She was looking to the future and she had a lot of hopes for the future and her career. Jamie and Stacy had a great relationship. It was a very gentle, paternal kind of relationship they had during filming.

RICHARD FRANKLIN: When we got to Melbourne, Jamie really spent most of the time just cooling her heels at the Melbourne hotel, and I felt bad about that. Jamie's character serves to provide the basis for Quid to overcome his insecurities and the chip on his shoulder by rescuing the damsel in distress from the killer. Jamie and Stacy had very good chemistry together which we later saw as being kind of similar to that of Bogart and Bacall. Actually, it was the Australian distributor who later branded Stacy and Jamie as "Keach and Curtis," almost as if they were the new Bogart and Bacall. I think that might've been pushing it a bit, but they had great chemistry, both on and off-screen.

STACY KEACH: I loved working with Jamie on the film. We had so much fun together, and we both loved being in Australia for this period of time. The thing I most remember about Jamie is her great sense of humor, and what a sharp wit she had. Richard Franklin also had a very black sense of humor so the three of us made a great team. Working with Jamie was like being with someone who was on the verge of becoming a great actress, because this film was really a turning point in her career in terms of moving from the queen of scream into more challenging roles. You could see on this film that she was growing up, changing, and she was just great to work with.

GRANT PAGE: Jamie never lost her sense of humor throughout the filming of *Roadgames* even though filming became difficult and quite exhausting towards the end. When Jamie went off by herself to play pool with some guys, that's who she was. She was a vibrant young woman who was just having fun with life. Jamie was never intimidated by anything, and she was a very serious actress who could get into character in a second. I think Jamie and Stacy were method acting in terms of their friendship and social life during filming. Jamie and Stacy had a good friendship, they connected on the film, and it was like a form of method acting between them.

GREG RICKETSON: One of my main tasks as production manager on *Roadgames* was to secure an appropriate "facility" for Jamie to use throughout filming. I explained to her that it was going to be very modest, and to talk to me if she had any problems, and I nervously accepted her assurance that it would be okay. The modest facility was a tiny caravan towed on the back of a car. It had no washing or toilet facilities, was genuinely small, and Jamie would have to share "bathroom facilities" with Stacy. These were called "portaloos" and they're small fibreglass cubicles with a toilet, a tiny hand basin, and a tank below the toilet for collection in which you had to place bright blue toxic chemicals to assist the breakdown of waste. Anyway, the next morning, at five in the morning, I was towing the "Jamie Lee Curtis/Stacy Keach" mobile toilet to location, and halfway there I heard an enormous wrenching and cracking sound. I brake, and look out the window to see the "portaloo" in full flight, overtaking me, in the air, a flume of blue toxic liquid trailing behind. Having broken its bolts from the trailer, it travels probably 200 feet in the air, and slowly crash-lands on the highway and slides to the roadside. I continued to the location, and awaited Jamie's arrival for her makeup call, and I was genuinely terrified, embarrassed, suicidal. Then Jamie Lee Curtis shows up, took one look at her "caravan," wasn't hugely impressed, but shrugged the shoulders and said it was okay, and when told about there being no "toilet" facility, she said "Is that what that thing was beside the road?" and said it was okay. She was a great girl, good-humored, easy to get on with, and trusting in us that we'd done all we could to make her feel comfortable. My memory is that Jamie Lee Curtis remained pretty well the same easy, approachable person throughout the shoot in Australia. There were indeed a few moments of tension—some of them with director Richard Franklin, and I think some to do with Jamie's boyfriend—but I certainly don't remember anything but a thoroughly wonderful girl who was great to work with.

Curtis had a special visitor during her time in Melbourne in the form of current boyfriend, and soon to be fiance Ray Hutcherson whom Curtis had been seeing for about seven months by the time *Roadgames* had started filming. Curtis and Hutcherson, who'd always railed against Curtis' slasher films, had recently taken up residence in a modest two-bedroom tract house in Studio City, California that

Curtis was renting. "When he arrived in Melbourne, Jamie kept their relationship to herself, and we didn't see much of them together," recalls Page. "Jamie was very honest, and would open up to me about everything in her life, but she kept her boyfriend private."

Curtis' relationship with Hutcherson, which would nearly result in marriage in 1981, was the first serious relationship in Curtis' life. Being involved in such a committed relationship was a welcome change of pace for Curtis who, even at the tender age of twenty-one, had grown tired with the dreary Hollywood singles scene. "I always thought of myself as sexy and single but it wasn't much fun," recalled Curtis. "I used to wear a ring when I would go to bars so I wouldn't get bothered by guys all the time. Being single wasn't easy."

Curtis had a lot of free time when *Roadgames* was in Melbourne, certainly too much free time for someone who had as much to offer a film like *Roadgames* as Curtis did. As with *The Fog*, it's hard to talk about Curtis' role in *Roadgames*—in the context of *Roadgames* being considered a "Jamie Lee Curtis film"—given how relatively-minor Curtis' part in the film is. While Curtis' role in *The Fog* would subsequently expand and grow, thanks mostly to the later re-shoots that were performed on that film, Curtis' role in *Roadgames* never expanded from its size in Everett De Roche's original script.

Some film critics, and even Franklin himself, would later describe Curtis' role in *Roadgames* as a "glorified cameo" which is ridiculous given that Curtis certainly has, for example, a substantial amount of dialogue in the film in her scenes with Keach. Still, Curtis is invisible for three- quarters of *Roadgames* and not even Curtis' powerful screen presence can diminish that sad fact. "My biggest regret of working with Jamie on *Roadgames* was me always wishing that I'd given her a bigger part," recalled Franklin. "In retrospect, I clearly didn't make the best use of Jamie in the film."

Curtis doesn't make her first live appearance in *Roadgames* until about 35 minutes into the film, and a double was used to represent Hitch's form in some earlier scenes. The next twenty minutes of the film are spent with Hitch and Quid and their discussion of, and pursuit of, Smith or Jones. Then Hitch is kidnapped, and then both Curtis and Hitch disappear until the end of the film when Curtis makes her reappearance.

None of this took away from Curtis' enjoyment of working on

Roadgames, a film that represented for Curtis a welcome change of pace from the slasher films of which her recent career had been entirely devoted to. Likewise, the Australian setting, eons from the bustle of Hollywood, was a welcome respite for Curtis who used the downtime in Melbourne to not only bond with the cast and crew but also to weigh her career options. "*Roadgames* was the first step in my non-horror film career," recalls Curtis. "It was an important film for me, even though it wasn't a big success. It proved to me that I could make a good film that didn't rely on gore and that I didn't have to always be the scream queen."

For his part, Richard Franklin found Curtis' counsel helpful during filming. Much like Franklin had screened *Halloween* with his crew prior to Curtis' arrival in order to study that film's technique and Curtis' acting style, Franklin would occasionally pick Curtis' brain during the filming of *Roadgames* as to the secrets of making a successful thriller. "Jamie had a very good knowledge of the camera and technique and we would talk about *Halloween* and the techniques that John Carpenter had used in that film," recalled Franklin. "The biggest thing Jamie talked about was the use of shock and surprise, and so we added a shot where a tired Quid thinks he sees a giant kangaroo in his headlights which is really just a harmless marsupial hopping away from him. It was silly, but it had a jolt, which was what *Halloween* was all about, the jolts."

Curtis and Franklin also talked about Carpenter's great use of Panavision in *Halloween* in terms of adding space to the scenes in that film and giving Carpenter the freedom to build terror out of all four corners of the screen, which was one of *Halloween*'s core techniques. *Roadgames* was also shot in Panavision, although this was more of a given, considering the dimensions of the endless Australian landscape. "The main reason I shot *Roadgames* in Panavision was because it matched the shape of the truck's windscreen, although I was well aware of the success Carpenter had with it in *Halloween*," said Franklin. "Our film revolves around a central figure, Quid, and I wanted the audience to become involved with his voyeuristic journey as he looks out from this truck."

Aside from doing studio work in Melbourne, for the scenes where Hitch and Quid are riding in Quid's truck, Curtis' only other filming in *Roadgames* concerned *Roadgames*' denouement which would be filmed on the streets of Perth. Franklin, in his energetic naivete, had largely shot *Roadgames* in sequence which meant that most of the film's night shooting, about twenty days worth, was back-loaded to the end of the production schedule. The result was an exhausted and frayed crew, and this would make the end of filming on *Roadgames* somewhat of an agonizing slog.

To make matters worse, Franklin was under extreme time pressures from his Australian financiers who'd recruited a completion guarantor, an entity that's contracted to ensure that a film is completed on schedule and within its budgetary and contractual specifications, to basically watch over Franklin and make his life a living hell. "I had a very ambitious ending planned for *Roadgames* with a lot of moving parts and I had to scrap that because the financiers were breathing down my throat," recalled Franklin. "Eventually, we paired it down to the basics of Quid catching up to Smith or Jones, and rescuing Jamie from the back of the green van."

Pressure from the investors and the film's completion guarantor forced Franklin to severely alter *Roadgames'* climax which would be filmed in a maze of narrow back alleys in the city of Perth. This is where a crazed Quid finally chases down Smith or Jones' green van, where Curtis is presumably still being held captive, and eventually corners the psychopath in one of the alleys, crushing the green van with the truck.

Franklin had planned and story-boarded a wildly-ambitious chase sequence but the investors, fearing that the film wouldn't be completed on budget and on schedule, nixed Franklin's plans and a compromise was reached. The final chase sequence between Quid and Smith or Jones that Franklin eventually filmed was exciting and visually-sharp, just paired down and shortened. "What was really frustrating was that we ended up finishing the picture ahead of schedule and with a bit of money to spare," said Franklin. "I was in a constant battle with the completion guarantor and the investors who just wanted the film to get finished, no matter what."

The most dangerous part of the finale is the sequence where Quid's truck lands on top of Smith or Jones' green van which miraculously stays upright while Curtis' Hitch character is still inside. Quid runs out of the truck and pulls Hitch out of the van to safety. Curtis herself was never in the van during this scene. "We filled the van with drums so it wouldn't be crushed by the twenty-five ton truck," recalls co-star and stunt-coordinator Grant Page. "Jamie was never in the van for that scene. It would've been too dangerous for her. The only time she was ever in that van was the scene where I jumped out of the sleeping bag and grabbed her."

In the next sequence, Quid overpowers Smith or Jones who turns onto a street where they're both confronted by a horde of police officers who still believe Quid is the killer they're searching for. It's not until the cops free Curtis—and she fingers Smith or Jones as her kidnapper—that Quid is freed from his Wrongfully Accused status, a story device that represented another of *Roadgames'* most obvious Hitchockian inspirations.

Unlike in *Halloween* and *Prom Night* where Curtis was directly responsible and pro-active in dispatching and killing her nemesis, her boogeyman, Curtis has to rely on a man, in the form of Keach's Pat Quid character, to save her in *Roadgames*. It was the same situation in *Terror Train* where a terrified Curtis had to be rescued by Ben Johnson's Carne character who whacked the killer out of the train with a shovel while a stunned Curtis watched in horror.

In *Roadgames* and *Terror Train*, the characters of Hitch and Alana Maxwell aren't capable of destroying the killer themselves. They need help. They both need men to save them. That's not a sign of weakness, or sexism on the part of these two films, but rather an example of heightened realism in these films in terms of establishing the limits of Curtis' own emotional and physical endurance as a scream queen. The message is that, yes, Curtis is a scream queen, and she is resourceful and tough, but she's not Wonder Woman in terms of possessing superhuman strength or supernatural powers.

Curtis' sole purpose in *Roadgames* is to be the film's red herring, Richard Franklin's version of the Hitchcockian MacGuffin. This is evident in the way that Curtis' Hitch character, through her disappearance, serves to drive the plot and motivate Quid's actions, even though Hitch's own identity is largely unimportant to the story (3). This is how Franklin viewed the Hitch character, something the director would later regret. "The part of Hitch never changed from the original script, or when Jamie joined the project, and obviously I wish we'd done more with Jamie," recalled Franklin. "I always said that if I'd known Jamie was going to become a superstar, I would've written a bigger part, but maybe she already was a star and I just didn't recognize it."

The irony that *Roadgames* was the first movie in which Jamie Lee Curtis wasn't required to scream wasn't lost on Curtis. It was a small victory, certainly, but Curtis was well aware that her transition from Queen of Crud to respected film actress would be taken in baby steps, not leaps and bounds. "No, I didn't scream at all in *Roadgames,* which wasn't something I thought about until I saw the finished film," recalls Curtis. "It was the first movie I made where I didn't have to scream, and I was happy about that because I never thought of *Roadgames* as a horror movie. It was a suspense-thriller. It was classy."

The biggest compromise forced on Franklin with *Roadgames*, and the film's closest brush with the horror genre, concerned the film's final scene. In the finished film's final scene, Quid's meat quarry has arrived in Perth and a cleaning lady is seen scrubbing the back of Quid's truck. She pulls on a string leading from the ceiling and then she looks up and watches a severed head plop into her cleaning bucket. This image wasn't very subtle, certainly not in keeping with the rest of Franklin's restrained approach to the story, but it wasn't Franklin's call.

De Roche and Franklin originally wanted the existence of the head to be implied and never shown, but genre-savvy Avco-Embassy—who not only had cast approval but also had final cut approval of the film (except for the Australian release where Franklin would have final say) —had other ideas. Avco-Embassy sensed that *Roadgames* didn't have enough gore to be marketable and insisted that the shot of the rather unconvincing-looking head be included. "They wanted to be able to market the film as a horror film so that's why the shot of the head was added even though *Roadgames* clearly wasn't a horror film," said Franklin. "That was the climate. The investors wanted a shock ending, and they wanted to keep the door open for a sequel."

The appearance of the head gave Avco-Embassy the hook they felt they needed on which to market *Roadgames* as a horror film, as "*Halloween* on a road," which is what the company intended all along. "I don't think they knew what to do with the film because the film didn't really fit into any of the defined categories," said Franklin. "The movie was about a serial killer, but there was almost no blood or gore in the film except for the added ending, so it really wasn't a horror film. It was a suspense-thriller, an old fashioned type thriller in the tradition of Hitchcock, and that totally went against the grain of the marketplace which was then being crowded with slasher movies."

In retrospect, even if Avco-Embassy had taken the high road and marketed *Roadgames* as a classy suspense-thriller, it probably wouldn't have mattered anyway. Like its quirky Australian setting and eclectic cast of characters, *Roadgames* was an anomaly, a cinematic orphan that would require many years of patient viewing and critical reassessments before it would find an appreciative audience. "They marketed it as a horror film, which I thought was a big mistake," recalls Keach who, prior to working on *Roadgames*, had worked with *Exorcist* writer William Peter Blatty on the comedy-thriller *The Ninth Configuration*, another red-headed stepchild of a genre film that had been unsuccessfully released in February of 1980. "No one knew what to do with the film. If people were expecting a horror film, they were going to be disappointed."

As with all of Curtis' previous genre films, Curtis received second billing to Stacy Keach, her male co-star, in *Roadgames*, and deservedly so given the actors' respective screen-time in the film. Interestingly, Avco didn't feature Curtis or Keach prominently in any of the film's promotional materials. This was especially evident in the film's poster artwork which featured the picture of a woman—the film's first victim, who's killed in a motel room at the beginning of the film—being strangled to death.

Roadgames was released in Los Angeles in February of 1981 where it did no business whatsoever, absolutely nothing. The film was released in North America as *Road Games*, with a space between *Road* and *Games* whereas the title appears on- screen as *Roadgames*. The film was released in New York a year later where it performed no better. *Roadgames* took in less than half a million dollars at the North American box office, making it easily the least commercially successful of Jamie Lee Curtis' genre films. This is ironic since Curtis considers *Roadgames* to be, besides *Halloween*, the best film she made during her scream queen career. "I couldn't believe that *Prom Night*, which I hated, was a hit while *Roadgames* did nothing, absolutely nothing," says Curtis. "I liked the film a lot but there just wasn't an audience for the kind of intelligent, stylish thriller that we made."

For Lisa Peers, the Australian actress Curtis replaced in the role of Hitch, *Roadgames*' commercial failure was of little consolation. "Even though *Roadgames* wasn't a hit, it would've been my big break, the film that was going to establish me as an international actress," recalls Peers. "It was the film that was going to take me to America, so losing the job was really devastating to me. I couldn't even watch the movie when it came out because it was too painful. The only good part of the whole ordeal was that the producers honored their obligation to me and paid me for the film, but I would've much rather acted in the film. Nothing against Jamie Lee Curtis, but I was very hurt by this."

If *Roadgames* had been marketed as a Jamie Lee Curtis film, would that have helped the film's box office performance? Probably not. The problem with *Roadgames* is that, despite its admirable intentions and stylistic flourishes, it lacks excitement and impact. While it may be facile and simplistic to describe the film as boring and overlong, the film's long stretches of inactivity and idleness—intended to create a sense of atmosphere, detail and mood—serves the purpose of dissipating, not increasing, the fear and suspense that Franklin is trying to establish in the film.

All of these techniques worked really well in *Rear Window*, but *Roadgames* is no *Rear Window*, or "*Rear Window* on the road" for that matter. That's not a criticism of the film, or a fatal flaw, but more of a recognition that *Roadgames* is a meticulous, quirky, stylish work of craftsmanship that provides small, tranquil rewards to the patient viewer. As with most of the films in Richard Franklin's career, *Roadgames'* admirable ambitions and careful direction don't entirely translate to any sort of overpowering entertainment or genuine thrills. The reviews for the film were similarly low-key and modestly-respectful. "This 18-wheel psycho-killer thriller simply runs out of gas," (Paul M. Sammon, *Cinefantastique.*); "Tolerable but overlong road thriller," (*Halliwell's Film Guide.*)

Like all of the films from Curtis' scream queen career, *Roadgames* would enjoy a somewhat enthusiastic cinematic afterlife over the years. This later cult status for *Roadgames* would be emboldened by praise from such unlikely admirers as film-maker Quentin Tarantino who would later praise Richard Franklin, who died of prostate cancer in 2007, as one of his favorite directors. *Roadgames* has found a second audience through cable and video, and a warm reappraisal of the film from critics, fans, and film historians—both in terms of the film and in the context of Franklin's overall career—has elevated *Roadgames* to the status of minor classic.

In terms of Jamie Lee Curtis' scream queen career it's interesting that *Roadgames* is considered, along with Steven Spielberg's *Duel* (1971) and the 1979 Australian road thriller *Mad Max*, as one of the vanguards of the "vehicular thriller" sub-genre, the only such entry in Curtis' genre career. Later films in the genre would include *The Hitcher* (1986) and *Breakdown* (1997).

Although *Roadgames* would be Curtis' first and last trip to Australia, it wouldn't be her last encounter with Richard Franklin, the man who Curtis considers to be the best post- Carpenter film-maker she worked with during her scream queen career. In the fall of 1981, Franklin was recruited by Universal Pictures to direct *Psycho II*, the long-awaited sequel to Alfred Hitchcock's iconic masterpiece *Psycho*. Franklin, who had set up shop in Los Angeles by this time, met with Curtis about playing the film's lead heroine, essentially re-imagining her mother's role from the 1960 film.

Curtis would consider the idea, intrigued also by the suggestion that Janet Leigh would also be attached to the sequel, but ultimately both Curtis and Franklin decided that Curtis' casting would be a bad idea, both for Curtis and the film. "Jamie and I talked about it and we realized that having her in the film would've taken away the suspense in the film given what happened to her mother in the first film," recalled Franklin who would later arrange a private screening of *Psycho II* for Curtis and Leigh just prior to the sequel's release in June of 1983. It was the last time Curtis and Franklin ever saw each other. "We also thought it would be exploitative, and although we really wanted to work together again, it was just a bad idea."

Franklin eventually cast then-ingenue Meg Tilly in the $5 million-budgeted sequel which became a modest hit, and would be the most commercially-successful film of Franklin's entire career. *Psycho II* would be the highpoint in Franklin's Hollywood career which was hamstrung by bad luck and unfortunate circumstances. After *Psycho II*, Franklin directed the brilliant 1984 children's fantasy-thriller *Cloak & Dagger*, but the film was a commercial failure (4). Franklin was later attached to such lofty Hollywood projects as *The Lost Boys* and *Witness*, but both projects fell through for Franklin. "Richard was just too nice to make it in Hollywood," says Grant Page. "He wasn't ruthless enough to do what you have to do to be successful there, and he also had a lot of bad luck."

After an unhappy experience directing 1991's *F/X 2: The Deadly Art of Illusion*, a gadget-heavy sequel to 1986's suspense-heavy *F/X* which would've been much more in Franklin's stylistic wheelhouse than the noisy sequel, Franklin left Hollywood and returned to Australia where he would spend the twilight of his career and life. Franklin died on July 11, 2007 of prostate cancer in Melbourne, Australia at the age of 58. He'll be remembered as a skilled craftsman who also happened to be Jamie Lee Curtis' favorite director from her scream queen career, other than John Carpenter. More than that, history has been quite kind to Franklin and his films in terms of the generous critical reappraisals that many of Franklin's films—from *Roadgames* to *Cloak & Dagger*—have received over the years.

For Curtis, *Roadgames'* commercial failure—and the general indifference that greeted the film's release—was disappointing but the experience of living and working in Australia for two months had been invaluable. The experience of making *Roadgames* had recharged Curtis' batteries and made her focus even more clearly upon her future career goals. The most obvious of these goals was to leave her scream queen persona once and for all.

The last roadblock to the end of Jamie Lee Curtis' scream queen career was the moral and personal obligation—both to the audience and to John Carpenter and Debra Hill—that Curtis felt to reprise her Laurie Strode character in *Halloween II*, the sequel to *Halloween* which, by the time Curtis returned home to Los Angeles from Australia in August of 1980, was still in the planning stages. "I believe in loyalty," said Curtis. "I owe Debra and John. They gave me a career. *Halloween II* is the end of a circle which started with *Halloween*."

Curtis was looking forward to getting it over with in terms of fulfilling her final obligation to the scream queen persona that had made her a movie star but which was also putting her in a box from which there might be no escape. It had been, by the dawn of 1981, almost three years since Curtis had shot *Halloween*, but it must've seemed like twenty years for Curtis who'd subsequently made four more films, done some forgettable television, been involved in several relationships, changed her appearance constantly, and basically transformed from a teenage girl into a woman in front of the public.

The most lasting images of this era in Curtis' acting career—her scream queen era between 1978 and 1981—were of Curtis screaming her lungs out, running from a would-be killer, acting terrified, trembling with emotion. By 1981, Jamie Lee Curtis had seen enough, and was ready to move on and become an adult actress. *Halloween II*, which would begin filming in April of 1981, would be significant for Curtis in many ways, both professional and personal, and would mark the end of Jamie Lee Curtis' scream queen career.

fourteen

THE LAST HORROR FILM

In August of 1980, Jamie Lee Curtis returned to Los Angeles from Australia where she'd spent more than two months filming *Roadgames*. The time in Australia was valuable for Curtis who, given her few scenes in *Roadgames*, had lots of time to take stock of her career and her personal life. In October of 1980, *Terror Train* was released and was a critical and commercial disappointment. *Terror Train's* failure was a mixed blessing for Curtis who didn't like to fail at anything, especially in terms of her acting career, but was also looking forward to embarking on her non-horror acting career.

To the extent that the failures of *Terror Train* and then later *Roadgames* in early 1981 would hasten Curtis' transition from scream queen to serious actress, so be it. On November 22, 1980, Curtis turned twenty-two years old, completely unaware that 1981 was going to be the most chaotic and turbulent time in both her acting career and her personal life. The looming end of Curtis' scream queen career would just be the tip of the iceberg.

In terms of branching out from her scream queen persona, Curtis knew what she was up against in terms of trying to show Hollywood that she was capable of being a good actress in roles that didn't require her to scream or be chased down dark corridors by masked killers. Curtis looked at her acting idol Meryl Streep as a role model, a beacon of light for the type of career she hoped to one day attain. The difference was that Streep had never been a scream queen, and had an acting pedigree—and the awards to go with it—that Curtis would never be able to compete with.

On December 13, 1980, Curtis appeared as a guest host on NBC's comedy sketch television series *Saturday Night Live*. This was during the dark period of the show when *Saturday Night Live* was in a critical and ratings abyss following the glory days of John Belushi, Chevy Chase and Bill Murray. Curtis' own wicked sense of humor was something that might've been alien to audiences who'd only seen Curtis in horror roles but was certainly no secret to her filming colleagues who'd all regarded Curtis' sense of humor as one of her most attractive qualities (1). Curtis didn't appear on *Saturday Night Live* to promote anything, not really. *Prom Night* and *Terror Train* were both out of release, while *Roadgames'* theatrical release was in terminal limbo from Avco-Embassy and in fact the film wouldn't be released in New York, where *Saturday Night Live* was filmed, until about a year later. Curtis went on *Saturday Night Live* to show America that she could be funny, and that she had other dimensions in her acting repertoire.

Basically, the *Saturday Night Live* appearance was designed to re-introduce Jamie Lee Curtis to the American public, and given that Curtis had no intention of being a scream queen anymore, this was certainly necessary. Of course, Curtis' scream queen career was going to be a major point of reference in terms of the show's arc, and this was okay to Curtis. Curtis had always been her own toughest critic and was looking forward to making fun of herself in front of America, or at least the few million people who were still watching *Saturday Night Live* at this rock-bottom moment in the show's history.

After Curtis was introduced on the show by the announcer, Curtis walked out onto the stage where she was greeted by loud applause and cheers. Curtis then went on to perform a brief monologue in front of the audience. Although Curtis had a biting sense of humor, live television is a shock to any young performer's system, and doing comedy on live television is completely different than cracking foul-mouthed jokes on a movie set. Curtis' opening monologue was short and sweet and entirely related to her scream queen persona:

JAMIE LEE CURTIS: Thank you! Far out! Far out! I've gotta tell you all it's absolutely great to be here, and I finally have something to do on a Saturday Night! You know, I gotta tell you, one thing I always seem to notice is that audiences expect certain things from certain performers. They always want Steve Martin to say, "I'm a wild and crazy guy!" Right? And you can never hear Springsteen sing without hearing "Born to Run." Right? If you ever see Rodney Dangerfield, you always have to hear him say, "I tell you. I get no respect!" Well, I know a lot of people out there have seen me in *Halloween* and *The Fog* and (audience applause)...Thank you! And, they're all expecting me to do one thing. Well...this is for you...

At this point, Curtis—who would later guest-host *Saturday Night Live* for a second time in 1984—let out a piercing scream to more loud cheers from the audience. It wasn't exactly a Sally Field "You really, really like me" moment, but Curtis was happy to accept the positive reinforcement. In terms of Curtis' performance on the show, Curtis' only major sketch on the 1980 episode was a sketch called *Attack of the Terrible Snapping Creatures.* In the sketch, two roommates named Gail (played by Gail Matthius) and Laurie, obviously played by Curtis as a nod to her *Halloween* character, discover an outbreak of clothes-pins in their new apartment.

The show wasn't much, and certainly no one was ready to brand Jamie Lee Curtis as the next Goldie Hawn after her appearance on *Saturday Night Live*, but to the degree that Curtis' appearance on *Saturday Night Live* allowed her to show another side of herself, it was a positive experience. It certainly couldn't have hurt. By the end of 1980, Curtis was wondering where her next acting role was going to come from, biding her time before the inevitable *Halloween II* would finally be ready to start filming. 1981 would represent a flashpoint in Curtis' acting career, her personal life, her scream queen career, and the horror genre itself. In terms of her acting career, 1981 would mark the end of Curtis' scream queen career with the making and release of *Halloween II.* In terms of the horror genre, 1981 would mark ground zero of the horror-slasher film explosion. 1981 would see the arrival of more genre films, especially slasher films, than any other period in film history. In terms of Curtis' personal life, 1981 would be the year that twenty-two year old Curtis was to be married, and the year that Curtis would endure some of the deepest personal problems of her career. By the dawn of 1981, Curtis had become engaged to screenwriter boyfriend Ray Hutcherson and the two were living together at Curtis' quaint little two- bedroom house in Studio City, California. Curtis and Hutcherson were planning to be married in June of 1981.

Curtis' house in Studio City was the portrait of Suburbia USA, complete with a maple tree in the backyard along with a hammock. Curtis had a dog named Clark as well as two cats named Emilia and

Yuri whom Curtis had named after two of the characters from the 1977 film *The Turning Point*. Curtis, a self-described "cleanliness freak," did her own housework and enjoyed living a quiet domestic life outside of the Hollywood glare. It was a disarmingly calm setting for Curtis whose life was about to enter its stormiest period. "I'm boring," said Curtis. "I do the dishes. I wash my clothing. I read. I watch TV. I'm real boring."

Curtis went whole-hog into the role of bride-to-be for her planned June wedding to Hutcherson. Curtis started reading *Brides* Magazine and would even conceptualize a design for her wedding dress that was going to be a white kimono combined with a colored sash. The honeymoon was going to be in Greece. None of these plans would ever come to pass. Curtis' relationship with Hutcherson, much like Curtis' scream queen career, wouldn't survive the making of *Halloween II*.

For Jamie Lee Curtis, one of the main benefits of being a scream queen—and of having made five genre films in less than three years—was a degree of financial independence. By 1981, Curtis wasn't in a position, unlike was the case two years earlier, where she had to grab the first film role that was offered to her. Still, rejection is never easy and although Curtis went out on numerous movie auditions in early 1981, she didn't get any jobs.

This was a moment, in early 1981, where Curtis' resolve to leave the horror genre was severely tested given the scarce non-horror career prospects she was confronted with at that time. To this end, Curtis decided to take the bold step of creating her own acting roles by forming her own film production company. In 1981, Curtis established Generation Productions along with her mother, Janet Leigh. The third member of the fledgling company was Curtis' older sister, Kelly Lee Curtis, who'd been apprenticing as a would-be stockbroker with stepfather Robert Brandt (2).

The John Carpenter-Debra Hill influence is also visible here as Debra Hill had formed her own production company, and was already developing several non-horror film properties. By 1981, Hill was in the midst of developing a feature film version of the popular board game *Clue* that would eventually be released in 1985. Carpenter and then-wife Adrienne Barbeau had also formed their own production company, Hye Whitebread Productions, for the purpose of developing their own feature film projects. Curtis was inspired by this. "Debra was a real role model for me," recalls Curtis. "I really admired the way that she took control of her career, and made things happen for herself. She inspired me to want to get into producing, to take charge of my career."

Curtis formed Generation Productions for the purpose of creating roles for herself. Curtis also wanted to develop a quality film vehicle that she and her mother could appear in together. Although mother and daughter had worked together on an episode of *The Love Boat*, and had both appeared separately in *The Fog*, neither of those projects had satisfied Curtis' desire to work with her mother on a more substantial film project. Sadly, this would never come to pass.

Curtis was also anxious to work with then-fiancé Ray Hutcherson on a film project. Hutcherson had written a script that revolved around the Peace Corps that Curtis would attach herself to both as a star and as a potential producer. Primarily, Curtis started the production company in order to create roles for herself instead of waiting for others to give them to her.

Interestingly, Hutcherson had written a western-themed script entitled *Ride the Diving Horse* that Roger Spottiswoode, Curtis' director on *Terror Train*, spent some time developing as a possible film project. In 1980, Hutcherson and Spottiswoode—along with Glenn Bydwell, *Terror Train*'s production designer—had traveled to West Virginia, Hutcherson's stomping grounds, to scout potential locations for the proposed film project. "Roger and I met Jamie and Ray in Los Angeles and then we went to West Virginia, where Ray was from, to look at locations," recalls Bydwell. "Ray was a good guy, and he was a very serious writer with a European sensibility, an art house sensibility, and *Ride the Diving Horse* was like that. It was the kind of project that was more in tune with the 1970s than the 1980s. It was a good script, and we were all keen on making it, but the project eventually drifted away."

Unfortunately, none of these projects got off the ground, and neither did Curtis' production company which quickly vanished without a trace. Looking back, Curtis was still too early in her career, and lacked the capital or influence—and the respect of Hollywood financiers in terms of Curtis' own box office credibility—to make Generation Productions a viable entity while Janet Leigh's presence, beloved and respected as she was, no longer wielded any real influence in Hollywood.

Ironically, the only product, the only tangible legacy—aside from stacks of business cards—to come out of the whole Generation Productions experiment was a horror story that Curtis herself had written. Actually, it was a twenty page treatment Curtis wrote for a prospective horror film project, entitled *The Myth*, which Curtis hoped to either produce or to sell to a big Hollywood production company.

Secretly, Curtis felt that *The Myth* might be the perfect film with which to make her feature directing debut although she was, and is, very much a realist. She knew, even back in 1981, that a project like *The Myth*, or any film project, could take years or decades to get a green-light. Regardless, Curtis was very enthusiastic about the project in early 1981 and proud that she'd created something, anything, out of her own imagination. "It's my idea and my horror film," she said. "I wrote a horror film. In fact, I wrote a wonderful horror film. It's absolutely fabulous."

The Myth, the story that existed in Curtis' twenty page treatment, was about a series of natural disasters that happen all at once. The rest of the story details are somewhat sketchy. "It was more of a disaster film than a horror film," recalled Curtis. "It was fun. It was something I wanted to do for Generation, although it was something that could've been made as a Roger Corman movie as well. Something that's fun, something I wrote."

Curtis, who'd also attended the cinematography class at UCLA until acting work made study impossible, envisioned *The Myth* as a project she would produce for the company, but the concept never made it past the treatment stage. Film-making just wasn't in the cards for Jamie Lee Curtis, which is sad given just how much somebody in her position would've had to offer as a film-maker, particularly as a genre film-maker, if that had been the route Curtis had chosen.

Like *Psycho* star Anthony Perkins, who later became a film-maker himself, Curtis had studied John Carpenter and his methods the same way Perkins, who would prove himself a fairly adroit film-maker, had studied Hitchcock. Like Perkins, Curtis—having made five genre films of wildly-varying quality in less than three years—certainly would've had her own creative ideas, her own vision, for what she would've liked to have seen in a horror film, based on her own experiences, her point-of-view as a scream queen. The fact that audiences will never get to see this, to see what Curtis' vision as a film-maker would've been, represents a real missed opportunity, both in terms of Curtis' career and for horror fans (3).

Although Curtis looked at 1981—and in particular her obligation to make *Halloween II*—as the year she would make a clean break from the horror genre and her scream queen persona, the tentacles of the horror genre ran deep inside of her. 1981 was ground zero for the horror-slasher genre, not just because of the number of genre films that would be released in 1981 but also because 1981 was the year that Hollywood embraced the horror-slasher genre and tried to bring the genre into the mainstream.

It was during this period, 1981 in particular, that the horror genre, and Jamie Lee Curtis especially, began receiving unprecedented coverage from the mass media. Most of this media coverage could be credited to the Hollywood public relations firm Pickwick/Maslansky/Koenigsberg whose genre clients included not only Jamie Lee Curtis, but also Carpenter, Hill, Brian De Palma, and George Romero. Pickwick/Maslansky/Koenigsberg (PMK) was the PR firm for virtually the entire horror universe, including Jamie Lee Curtis' scream queen career.

Curtis' press agent was Mick Garris, a lifelong horror fan who'd previously worked with Curtis when Garris, who had worked as a genre liaison and production assistant at Avco-Embassy, had produced a Making Of documentary for *The Fog*.

Curtis had also been a guest on a cable access interview program Garris hosted in Los Angeles. "PMK really got into horror after the success of *Halloween* and by 1980, PMK had really become the office for handling horror, as well as Jamie Lee Curtis," recalls Garris, who later became a successful genre film-maker. "I was Jamie's press agent, and in 1980 and 1981, everyone in the media was jumping on the horror craze, and were willing to promote the horror movies, and everyone was interested in Jamie."

As the most iconic and recognized scream queen in film history, Curtis was the face of the horror genre, and her connections to the genre ran deeper than even she could've imagined. The horror boom of 1981 represented the zenith of the post-*Halloween* horror boom, although the commercial success of 1980's *Friday the 13th* certainly can't be minimized in terms of that film's commercial influence. Curtis' subsequent scream queen appearances—in films like *The Fog*, *Prom Night*, and *Terror Train*—had made Curtis Hollywood's ambassador to this most disreputable genre.

In retrospect, 1981 would be looked back on as both the flash-point, in terms of activity, and the end of the Hollywood horror-slasher boom. Even by April of 1981, when *Halloween II* would begin production, the horror craze was evaporating as quickly as it had started. The independent horror films weren't doing good business, *Prom Night* having been one of the few exceptions. Studio genre releases were also posting lackluster grosses of which *Terror Train*'s disappointing box office performance was a prime example.

By the spring of 1981, industry uncertainty about horror's commercial marketability—emboldened by the poor box office receipts from the majority of the genre films released between the summer of 1980 and early 1981—was already becoming palpable and would be exacerbated by a virulent media backlash against horror films that would reach its zenith in 1981. "The horror films just stopped making money," recalls film critic Roger Ebert. "*Halloween* was a big hit, so Hollywood thought horror was the next fad and they made a bunch of films, and none of them did well, and then *Friday the 13th* was a big hit, and then there was a flood of horror films in 1981, and most of them flopped. Hollywood was already ashamed to be involved with this kind of product anyway, and they quickly lost interest, and then they moved from the Dead Teenager movies to the Horny Teenager Movies when *Porky's* became a big hit in 1982."

It wasn't that the horror genre was dead but rather that the independent horror films, aside from *Friday the 13th*, hadn't demonstrated any ability to match *Halloween*'s commercial impact. Horror films were still profitable, in terms of cost versus gross, but they weren't extremely profitable, or profitable enough for mainstream Hollywood to want to become fully engaged. In 1980, twenty-six horror films earned at least one million dollars in domestic rentals followed by twenty-two in 1981 and a record 31 films in 1982.

These robust figures are completely misleading given that in 1980, only three horror films—*Friday the 13th* ($39.7 million), *The Fog* ($21.3 million), *The Shining* ($44 million) —surpassed the $20 million dollar mark in gross domestic box office receipts. In 1981, the list would include *Friday the 13th Part 2* ($21.7 million), *The Final Conflict* ($20.5 million), *Ghost Story* ($23.3 million), and *Halloween II* ($25.5 million). In 1982, *Friday the 13th Part III* ($36.7 million) and *Poltergeist* ($76.6 million) would be the only horror films to surpass the $20 million figure in gross domestic box office receipts.

Considering that *The Final Conflict, Ghost Story, Poltergeist,* and *The Shining* were big budget studio films—and certainly couldn't be classified as slasher films—the list of commercially-successful horror films released during this period is even shorter. The post-*Halloween* horror-slasher films hadn't, with the great exception of *Friday the 13th,* provided Hollywood with the sizzling box office grosses and spectacular profit margins that *Halloween* had seemingly laid the groundwork and commercial blueprint for.

With the exception of *Friday the 13th* and, to a more modest extent, *Prom Night,* none of the legion of *Halloween*-inspired slasher ripoffs released between 1980 and 1981—*The Burning, Funeral Home, Graduation Day, He Knows You're Alone, Hell Night, Maniac, Mother's Day, My Bloody Valentine, New Year's Evil, Night School, Student Bodies, Terror Train*—would live up to Hollywood's inflated and, in retrospect, outrageous commercial expectations. It wasn't that horror films were no longer profitable, but rather that they weren't producing the box-office gold-mines that would entice the big Hollywood studios to hold their noses and stay involved in the horror genre for the long-run.

The breakout commercial success of *Halloween* and later *Friday the 13th* had engendered an irrational, greed-inspired exuberance that the horror-slasher genre simply couldn't justify in terms of trying to satisfy Hollywood's unreasonable expectations. When *Terror Train* had been released in October of 1980, 20th Century Fox executives, emboldened by the blockbuster success that Paramount Pictures had enjoyed with *Friday the 13th,* had projected that *Terror Train* would gross between $40 and $50 million dollars at the box office. When the film grossed $8 million, which wasn't terrible but was far from a blockbuster success, the film's performance was viewed as a colossal failure.

Irwin Yablans, one of *Halloween*'s architects and producers, would be involved with several horror films between 1980 and 1982. *Fade to Black* (1980), *Blood Beach* (1981), *Hell Night* (1981), *Parasite* (1982), and *The Seduction* (1982) were all made with *Halloween* money— literally—and were all attempts to duplicate *Halloween*'s commercial formula. While all of these films performed respectably at the box office, with *The Seduction* grossing more than $10 million in 1982, none of them came close to equaling the success of *Halloween.*

All of the horror films released between 1980 and 1981, especially the post-*Halloween* slasher films, suffered from an overcrowded marketplace, jaded and weary customers, and the plain fact that most of the post-*Halloween* horror films were derivative, sleazy and tasteless. More than that, perhaps all of these films lacked—and this is especially true of a Yablans-produced film like *Hell Night* which featured *Exorcist* star Linda Blair in the lead "scream queen" role—the one additional key ingredient that might've substantiated them and made them successful, and that's the presence of Jamie Lee Curtis.

What Jamie Lee Curtis had that was missing from all of the *Halloween* copycats was an inherent likableness that shone through in all of her horror films. Curtis felt that this was the main ingredient lacking in the other horror films. "The horror films that didn't make money during this period didn't have likable characters," recalls Curtis. "I played normal people in unreal situations and I think that's what made the films so successful. That's what John told me on *Halloween*. He said, 'I feel that Laurie has to be so vulnerable that, in the last two reels, if the audience isn't screaming out loud for you, we've lost them.' Those words stayed with me."

What's interesting about Jamie Lee Curtis' scream queen career between 1978 to 1981 is how Curtis' scream queen career really covered the entire spectrum, both artistically and commercially, of the horror genre during this period. She's the face of the genre during this period in every respect—the good, the bad, and the very ugly. She truly dominated the entire horror genre, and was the face of the horror genre just as she, in many ways, still is today.

As the star of *Halloween*, Curtis has the distinction of being the face of the film that is the unquestioned godfather of the modern horror genre, and one of the greatest horror films in cinematic history, period. With *Prom Night* and *Terror Train*, Curtis was the star of two of the most prominent—and two of the most enduring and popular— of the post-*Halloween* copycats, and these films defined Curtis as the "queen of the slashers." Just as John Carpenter is the film- maker most identified with the horror genre in the period between 1978 and 1981, Jamie Lee Curtis is the actress most associated with the period.

In terms of commercial success, Curtis' scream queen career between 1978 and 1981 reflects the unevenness of the genre, in terms of commercial success and quality, during the period. *Halloween* was, up to this point, considered the most successful independent film, of any genre, in cinematic history while *The Fog* was one of the few box office horror successes to be released in 1980.

Prom Night, also released in 1980, was, aside from *Friday the 13th*, the most commercially successful post-*Halloween* slasher film released between 1980 and 1981. *Terror Train*, although considered a disappointment given Fox's expectations and considerable investment, still outperformed most of the other *Halloween* imitators. *Roadgames* bombed, although *Roadgames* wasn't really a horror film.

By early 1981, Jamie Lee Curtis had more pressing things on her mind than the survival and the state of the horror- slasher genre she so much wanted to escape from. Curtis' career and life were at a crossroads in every way imaginable. She was about to film *Halloween II*, which would be Curtis' swan-song to the genre that had made her a movie star, a scream queen. After filming *Halloween II*, Curtis was going to be married, in June of 1981, to screenwriter boyfriend Ray Hutcherson. After that, Curtis would jump off a cliff into the great post-scream queen unknown.

Like many young stars in Hollywood, then and today, Curtis was also a recreational drug user. Her drug problem, which had begun in 1980 and would extend about three years, festered during the filming of the made-for-television movie *She's in the Army Now* in early 1981. In the film, which would air on ABC in May of 1981, Curtis, Melanie Griffith, and Kathleen Quinlan played three young female recruits going through basic training. Basically, it was a transparent knock-off of the 1980 hit Goldie Hawn comedy film *Private Benjamin*.

Curtis used cocaine during filming, along with co-star and friend Griffith. "It was a weird time in the early 1980s in terms of the drugs and the partying," recalled Curtis. "During filming, we would have to be on location at 5:30 in the morning. Most of the time Melanie and I would be recovering from the night before, from smoking, drinking, doing coke. I was about to get married, but I wasn't happy." Curtis' drug use during this period would also be the basis for a reunion with her father, Tony Curtis, under the worst possible circumstances. Curtis would go over to her father's house where they would do drugs together. It was the type of unhealthy bond that would ultimately cement Curtis' feelings of mistrust towards her estranged father (4). "When he was doing drugs, I also was doing drugs, so we'd go over to his house and have drugs," recalled Curtis. "It was that simple, and it was that sick. It was that whorish."

None of this was fatal, either to Curtis' career or life. Unlike other young stars, Curtis never fell into an unescapable abyss, never missed a day of work, and never looked stoned during filming. This was a testament to Curtis' self-control, as evidenced by the fact that Curtis had pledged to quit smoking during the filming of *She's in the Army Now* although this resolve, like Curtis' eventual withdrawal from drugs, wouldn't take firm hold until the Spring of 1984. "I was the kind of drug addict who would do my last bit of cocaine at one in the morning, but I wouldn't allow myself to stay up past 2:30 a.m. because my work was my life," recalled Curtis. "I was able to stop. It wasn't a situation where I had to institutionalize myself. It was just a real sad time."

Unlike many of her contemporaries, Curtis was able to control her personal demons, to compartmentalize her drug use, to survive. Lindsay Lohan, Curtis' future co-star in the 2003 comedy hit *Freaky Friday*, is a sad modern example of Curtis' own difficult journey in the early 1980s. Like Curtis, Lohan enchanted the public with her charm, energy, and inherent likableness. Unfortunately, Lohan's destructive off-screen behavior has derailed her film career, and made the public forget why they liked her so much in the first place. She's gone now, irrelevant, while Curtis is still alive and kicking, still relevant, still welcomed by the public.

Yes, Jamie Lee Curtis could've crashed and burned during her own rough period, but that wasn't in her character and makeup and if there's one lesson to be learned from Curtis' horror films, it's that scream queens don't die easily. Jamie Lee Curtis is a Hollywood survivor and has proven this both on-screen and off. Scream queens, survivors, outlive people which is how they claim victory in the end. They're still breathing and standing while everyone else is dead and buried. This is true of both Curtis' horror films and the enduring career and life that would grow out of Curtis' scream queen career.

Not only did Jamie Lee Curtis outlive the victims in her horror films—as well as the half-forgotten actors, the Sandee Curries and Casey Stevens' of the world, who surrounded her in these films—but she also outlived most of her acting contemporaries of the period. Curtis outlived the Kristy McNichols and the Tatum O'Neals who seemed so poised for enduring stardom at the dawn of the 1980s but who eventually faded away. Curtis outlived them, just as she's outlived the Lindsay Lohans of today along with the legion of interchangeable scream queens that continue to try and imitate her persona. This is what a scream queen does. They survive while everyone else is killed off. The scream queen, despite insurmountable odds, always wins in the end.

How many of the young stars of the late 1970s and early 1980s—from the period when Curtis began her acting career—are still around today, are still relevant, are still alive career-wise besides Jamie Lee Curtis? Jodie Foster, who'd had a much more substantial acting career than Curtis had by the time Curtis made *Halloween II* in 1981, is one shining example. She made the transition from young actress to leading lady and would later win two Academy Awards. While Curtis and Foster have taken radically different paths to success, namely the fact that Foster graduated magna cum laude from Yale in 1985 while Curtis dropped out of the University of the Pacific in 1977, both have master degrees in Hollywood survival 101.

Melanie Griffith, an old friend of Curtis' and Curtis' co-star, along with Kathleen Quinlan, in *She's in the Army Now*, is a closer parallel to Curtis. Like Curtis, Griffith overcame a drug problem, Griffith's having been much more prolonged and serious than Curtis', and subsequently rebounded and revived her acting career in the 1980s, almost reaching superstardom with her academy award-nominated performance in 1987's *Working Girl*.

Kurt Russell is an example, but he's several years older than Curtis and had been acting for three decades before his adult Hollywood career took off. The list of half-forgotten young stars of the late 1970s and early 1980s—the "dead"—that Curtis has outlived includes such names as Willie Aames, Melissa Sue Anderson, Christopher Atkins, Scott Baio, Robby Benson, Linda Blair, Clark Brandon, Danielle Brisebois, Shaun Cassidy, Leif Garrett, Marilyn Hassett, Kay Lenz, Anne Lockhart, Pamela Sue Martin, Glynnis O'Connor, Mackenzie Phillips, Eve Plumb, Brooke Shields, Rex Smith, Parker Stevenson, Vincent Van Patten.

If the horror films, if Curtis' scream queen career, had served Jamie Lee Curtis in any beneficial way by the time she was ready to leave the genre, other than boosting her bank account and making her a movie star, it was that, by 1981, Curtis had formed a bond, a relationship, with the movie-going public that has endured to this day.

One of Curtis' main qualities as a scream queen, her bread and butter formula for success, was her ability to project vulnerability. By the spring of 1981, after having made five horror films in less than three years, the movie-going public, especially horror film fans, had undeniably formed a bond with Curtis. "I've always given my career to an audience and whatever they buy me in, they buy me in, and I have to accept that," says Curtis. "If the public didn't want to see me in a comedy or drama, if they only wanted to see me do horror films, then that's something I would have to accept, but I had confidence in the audience, and I always felt that if I didn't let them down that they wouldn't let me down."

It was a protective bond, like an older brother watching out for his kid sister who's in peril, that is only clearly visible today when one looks back at the long and varied acting career that Curtis has enjoyed since the height of her scream queen years. By 1981, Curtis would need the public more than ever, not in terms of selling more horror films, but in terms of helping her make the transition into a non-horror acting career.

Surprisingly, given her scream queen persona, Curtis was never the victim of celebrity stalkers or crazed fans during her scream queen career, nor was she the type to live in fear of such things. "I always thought that if someone was gonna get you, they were gonna get you and there's nothing you can do about it, and I really believe that," said Curtis. "That doesn't mean you're not careful. I wasn't frivolous and I wasn't going to run around in a mini-skirt in Watts, but I refused to be paranoid."

Nor was Curtis the victim of crude exploitation in her horror films which is something that Curtis has always been grateful for. Curtis never showed her breasts in any of her horror films, and was never dismembered, raped, or tortured, unlike many other young actresses who began their acting careers in the horror genre. "I never played the bimbo, the slut," said Curtis. "I was never in *The Swamp Thing VIII* getting fucked by a beast from the swamp. I never had to sacrifice my own integrity. I was truly lucky that *Halloween* was a big success. Those films gave me a chance to learn about acting."

If Jamie Lee Curtis was going to be able to make the leap from scream queen to mainstream it would be less due to her own self-determination, formidable as Curtis' was, and more due to the public's willingness to let her make this transition, plain and simple. This is why the thought of making *Halloween II* made Curtis feel hesitant and skittish. "I kept being told not to do anymore horror, because of typecasting and the limitations it imposes," said Curtis. "It wasn't an easy decision, and I really didn't want to do anymore horror films ever again, but it was something that I felt I had to do."

Halloween II had been in serious development since the summer of 1980, a period when John Carpenter and Debra Hill were in St, Louis filming the futuristic action-fantasy film *Escape from New York*. Budgeted at $7 million, it was Carpenter's and Hill's biggest film up to that point, a harbinger for the fact that Carpenter and Hill, and Carpenter especially, were interested in making big-budget studio films (5). By early 1981, Carpenter would be knee-deep in pre-production on his planned $12 million remake of *The Thing* for Universal Pictures while simultaneously keeping one eye on the development of *Halloween II*.

Curtis would later record the opening voice-over narration for *Escape from New York* when the film was in post-production which technically makes *Escape from the New York*, and not *The Fog*, the last film in which Carpenter and Curtis would work together as director and actress. This was of course just a technicality, a footnote, and by early 1981, it was clear that the Carpenter-Hill unit, and especially Curtis' involvement with Carpenter and Hill, was drawing to a close.

The development of *Halloween II* was obviously a no-brainer given *Halloween*'s box office success. The only real obstacles, not minor, involved coming up with a story for the sequel and putting the production elements into place. Both of these tasks would be arduous and painful, more than anyone involved with the project could ever imagine.

For Carpenter and Hill, the motivations to make *Halloween II* were very basic. "It was a chance for me and Debra to make a lot of money and to be able to make a film with complete control," recalls Carpenter. "Making the film was more of a business decision than a creative decision because Debra and I didn't feel that *Halloween* needed a sequel. It was inevitable and we decided that we owed it to the audience to oversee the making of the film, and we didn't want to get sued by the production company for blocking the making of the sequel and preventing the financiers from making money. That's why we did it."

In 1980, when *Halloween II* had been in its early planning stages, Moustapha Akkad and Irwin Yablans sold *Halloween*'s broadcast television rights to NBC for a whopping $4 million which Carpenter and Hill would also share in. Neither Curtis or anyone else from *Halloween*'s cast and crew would receive any profit-sharing from either *Hal-*

loween or the network television deal. For Curtis, there was no back-end, no meaningful residuals, just the $8,000 she'd earned from *Halloween* and the knowledge that *Halloween*—and especially Carpenter and Hill—had given her a career.

Money would be just one of several factors leading to the eventual dissolving of the Carpenter-Hill unit that would largely cease to exist after the making of 1982's *Halloween III: Season of the Witch* which was written and directed by Tommy Lee Wallace. "Yes, I think Jamie wanted to head off on her own," recalls Tommy Lee Wallace. "I know I certainly did. However, let me be frank here: John and Debra could've kept their repertory company going indefinitely, and that includes Jamie Lee Curtis, if they'd valued any of us enough to cut us in on the profits, or at least pay us what we were worth commensurate to their own financial success. Had Jamie been a male, who knows? Look what happened when John ran into Kurt Russell."

Although Curtis had a close bond with Carpenter and Hill, it wasn't as it they were joined at the hip, or were some inseparable trio. Everyone in the Carpenter-Hill unit—especially Curtis—had separate lives, and while they all enjoyed working with each other, they didn't see much of each other socially. "Nancy and I didn't see Jamie socially at all after we did *Halloween*," recalls Wallace. "Making a movie is a mild version of going to war. You're thrown together with a group of people, and during the time of filming, you're very close-knit, and the comradery can be quite intense. Love affairs happen. Deep friendships are born. But more often than not, when the movie wraps, there are lots of hugs and maybe a few tears, but ultimately everyone goes their separate ways."

Everyone in the Carpenter-Hill unit—especially Carpenter, Curtis and Hill—were poised to go off in separate career directions. If Carpenter and Hill had been like an older brother and sister to Curtis on *Halloween* and *The Fog*, they were now more like warm godparents. Jamie Lee Curtis was ready to soar off on her own. "It's not like they were some special trio or anything," says Wallace. "With *Halloween* and *The Fog*, John and Debra simply had a movie to make, Jamie was a smart, smart choice, and they did right by Jamie, fostered her talent, nurtured her performance, and reaped the benefits."

Jamie Lee Curtis viewed *Halloween II* as a personal obligation to Carpenter and Hill, her cinematic benefactors, the people who'd given her a film career. Despite her reluctance to do anymore horror films,

Curtis' loyalty to Carpenter and Hill, and to the audience, won her over. "I had to do the sequel because I felt like I owed Debra and John for giving me a movie career," recalls Curtis. "I also felt I had a responsibility to the fans who were going to watch the sequel. They deserved to see the same actress playing Laurie in the sequel, and I couldn't bear the thought of another actress playing Laurie in a sequel so I said yes. It was the end. I wanted to get it over with."

Carpenter and Hill also viewed *Halloween II* as a bit of an experiment in terms of making a studio film with Hollywood money and with complete creative control. Carpenter and Hill only signed on to produce the sequel, in addition to co- writing the script, on the condition that they would be given complete creative control over the film. "We wouldn't have been involved with the production if we didn't have complete control over the film," recalled Hill. "That meant we had final say over everything to do with the production, along with a bigger budget. John and I looked at *Halloween II* as a challenge, to see if we could actually do it successfully."

Basically, *Halloween II* was a chance for Carpenter and Hill, and the rest of the Carpenter-Hill unit, to make a movie with Hollywood money and little supervision, to play around, make mistakes, try different things. It was the same proposition that had intrigued George Lucas, in 1979, to produce a sequel to his 1973 blockbuster *American Graffiti*. The result was *More American Graffiti*, which would turn out to be a commercial and critical disaster when it was released in 1979 (6).

Lucas would later regret ever attempting the sequel and Carpenter would later have the same feelings about *Halloween II*. Like *American Graffiti*, *Halloween* was, is, a classic American film, and just as Lucas would lament that *More American Graffiti* would somewhat tarnish the luster of his original classic, Carpenter would have similar feelings about *Halloween II*. *Halloween II* would turn out to be John Carpenter's *More American Graffiti*, not in a commercial sense—because *Halloween II* would ultimately become a financial success—but in an artistic sense.

As was the case with Lucas and *More American Graffiti*, *Halloween II* was a gamble that Carpenter and Hill were willing to take, especially since it was with Hollywood money. The Hollywood money attached to *Halloween II* was embodied in the form of flamboyant Italian film producer Dino De Laurentiis. By 1981, De Laurentiis had been well into the process of trying to buy into existing Hollywood properties, having produced would-be blockbusters like *King Kong* (1976) and *Flash Gordon* (1980). After trying, and failing, to buy into the *Superman* film franchise, De Laurentiis set his sights on the *Halloween* franchise. In 1981, Dino De Laurentiis and his company, the De Laurentiis Film Corporation, bought the rights to the *Halloween* franchise from Moustapha Akkad and Irwin Yablans, each of whom received $800,000 for the deal. Although Akkad and Yablans would both remain on *Halloween II* as executive producers, their involvement would be largely symbolic. Having bought the rights to the *Halloween* franchise, De Laurentiis secured a distribution agreement with Universal Pictures for the release of *Halloween II*.

De Laurentiis' attachment to *Halloween II* was a sobering sign of how much the film business had changed, and how much the principals involved with the making of *Halloween* had changed, between 1978 and 1981. This was no longer a group of friends and absolute film beginners gathering together to make a low-budget horror film in Pasadena. Everyone's lives—from Carpenter's to Curtis'—had changed immeasurably since the filming of *Halloween* in the Spring of 1978, as had the film business. *Halloween II* would be the document of this disconnect between these two different points in time.

In 1978, it was possible for a film like *Halloween* to creep across the country, through drive-ins and neighborhood movie houses, and slowly develop—city by city and market by market—into an underground blockbuster. By 1981, these distribution channels were slowly being crushed, with theater screens becoming harder, and more expensive, to book for the independents whose numbers were becoming smaller and smaller. The involvement of De Laurentiis and Universal did mean that *Halloween* would have an increased budget, $2.5 million, which was still modest by Hollywood standards but which seemed like *Ben Hur* compared to the draconian conditions that had existed during the making of the $300,000 *Halloween*. The increased budget would mean more effects, stunts, cameras, a much larger cast and crew. Everything about *Halloween II* was going to be bigger. This was especially true of Curtis' salary which had only been $8,000 for *Halloween* but was boosted to $100,000 for the sequel. It was the largest salary Curtis had ever been paid for a film, $100,000 being kind of a benchmark number for young stars during this period. As opposed to today where young actors can demand up to $10 million for a film, back in 1981, the top young stars were lucky to break the six-figure salary barrier (7). Donald Pleasence, who'd become a kind of "Scream King" since *Halloween*'s release in 1978, was offered $45,000 to reprise his Dr. Sam Loomis character in the sequel and took it. "Jamie was in a much better negotiating position than Donald was for the sequel," recalls Joy Jameson, Pleasence's agent. "Jamie was the star, and I think they felt like they could do the sequel without Donald if they had to. Donald always needed money because he had so many children and ex-wives to support so he took what he was offered."

Along with the increased salary, *Halloween II* would give Curtis something she'd amazingly never received on any of her previous films and that is top billing. By 1981, Carpenter and Hill—and certainly Universal—recognized that Curtis was now a full-fledged horror movie star, a genuine asset, and that Curtis should be recognized as the star of the sequel. "Without Jamie there was no movie so it made sense that she should get top billing," recalled Hill. "Jamie was the reason people were going to watch the movie, and she'd become a star, and it would've been silly to not give her top billing, although Donald was of course very important to the film as well."

Having secured the return of Curtis and Pleasence for the sequel, Carpenter—who was scheduled to begin filming on *The Thing* in June of 1981—and Hill were faced with the maddening challenge of figuring out what to do with Curtis in the sequel. As with the writing of the *Halloween* script, Carpenter would write the body of the *Halloween II* script while Hill would tweak the dialogue. "When I sat down to write the script for *Halloween II*, I drew a blank," recalls Carpenter. "I didn't know where to go with the story after *Halloween*, what to do next, and that's when I realized that there really was no sequel after *Halloween* and that *Halloween* was really meant to be the end of the story."

There were several storylines discussed for the sequel and the way in which Curtis and her Laurie Strode character would be used. One possible storyline took place several years after *Halloween* and involved Laurie Strode living in a high rise apartment building where she finds herself haunted by The Shape again. "There was nothing I could think of to do with Laurie and The Shape that seemed at all believable," recalls Carpenter. "Where had The Shape been since the last film? How would he and Jamie get back together? It was a real grind to write the script, a real struggle to come up with any interesting ideas."

There was also serious talk of filming *Halloween II* in 3-D, which would've been a first in Curtis' scream queen career, but Hill nixed the idea for budgetary and logistical reasons. "It would've been too expensive to shoot *Halloween II* in 3-D and I just felt that it wasn't worth the trouble," recalled Hill. "Also, we couldn't find a 3-D process that I thought was reliable enough to use for the film, and I also felt it would've been a bit too gimmicky."

Ultimately, Carpenter and Hill felt that the only logical thing to do was to have *Halloween II* take place right after *Halloween*, to exist as a direct sequel, a "five minutes later" film. "Setting the film directly after the ending of *Halloween* seemed like the most interesting idea to us because it was a real challenge," recalled Hill. "We'd have to match the look of the movie, Jamie's look, match everything to the first film, and I thought that would be an interesting challenge. It seemed to me like the best of the sequel options we had at that point."

Duplicating Laurie Strode's physical appearance in *Halloween II* would turn out to be a great challenge for Curtis, now twenty-two, and in retrospect it was simply not possible. Curtis had transformed physically and psychologically since the making of *Halloween*, and the sexually-repressed wallflower that was Laurie Strode—a character that had been largely conjured from Curtis' own painful high school experiences—was no longer part of her repertoire.

The differences between the Jamie Lee Curtis of 1978 and 1981 are immeasurable. She had new teeth, and was no longer afraid to smile. Curtis' bone structure had also changed, and her body was now more in concert with her peculiar facial features. She was a wide-eyed novice on *Halloween* and was now a cynical, jaded Hollywood veteran of five films, several relationships, along with the usual off-screen problems that accompany newly-minted stardom. Curtis' eyes, which had once sparkled with an I'm-just-happy-to-be-alive-and-working innocence, were now blooded by all of the things, on-screen and off, that Curtis had experienced between 1978 and 1981.

Laurie Strode, the Laurie Strode that had effortlessly sprung out of Curtis back in 1978, was dead and would have to be resurrected again for *Halloween II*.

fifteen

THE MAKING OF *HALLOWEEN II*

The script for *Halloween II*, Jamie Lee Curtis' swan-song to her scream queen career, takes place literally the moment after *Halloween* ends. The story opens at the moment Laurie Strode is attacked by Michael Myers for the last time during *Halloween's* climax and then continues to where Sam Loomis arrives in the Doyle house and shoots Michael Myers six times. *Halloween II* then simultaneously follows Laurie being taken to Haddonfield Memorial Hospital along with The Shape's escape through the back-streets of Haddonfield. The body of the story finds The Shape at the hospital where he systematically butchers the hospital staff in his quest to find, and kill, Laurie Strode.

The biggest revelation in John Carpenter's and Debra Hill's final draft *Halloween II* script, and probably the most artistically-bankrupt and dishonest element in the sequel's development, is that Laurie and The Shape are revealed to be brother and sister, thus explaining their psychic connection. This brother-sister connection was never in Carpenter's mind when he first created the *Halloween* mythology in 1978, but was a product of his desperation in terms of trying to create a motivation, a raison d'etre, for the sequel. "No, I never planned that Laurie and Michael would turn out to be brother and sister," recalls Carpenter. "It was something I made up on the spot, as I was writing the script. I was desperate for ideas and the brother-sister connection seemed like the only logical explanation for their relationship."

Choosing a director for *Halloween II* seemed like it would be a much easier choice for Carpenter and Hill. As had been the case with George Lucas on *More American Graffiti*, Carpenter had no intention of directing a sequel to his own classic film and would instead choose another director to continue his own vision. This was both an artistic decision, admirably so, and a logistical one since Carpenter was so deeply consumed with pre-production on *The Thing* and was also exhausted from the filming of *Escape from New York*. "I promised myself that I would never direct a sequel to my own film," recalled Carpenter who would later direct *Escape from LA*, a 1996 sequel to 1981's *Escape from New York*. "I didn't want to repeat myself as a director, and I also knew that the sequel couldn't possibly be as good as *Halloween*. I wouldn't have directed the sequel under any circumstances."

Although *Halloween II* would very much be a Hollywood studio film, both in terms of its form and its making, many of the cast and crew who'd worked on *Halloween* would return for *Halloween II*. Besides Curtis and Donald Pleasence, Debra Hill—who would wield the most control over *Halloween II*—would bring back actor Charles Cyphers along with key crewmembers like Barry Bernardi, Dean Cundey and Raymond Stella. In terms of choosing a director for *Halloween II*, Carpenter and Hill also wanted to keep things in-house and pick someone they knew.

This was Tommy Lee Wallace, Carpenter's old childhood friend and unofficial protégé who'd served as editor and production designer on *Halloween*, and was looking to establish his own feature directing career. The suggestion of Wallace as a potential director for *Halloween II* brought approval from Curtis who felt that if Carpenter wasn't going to direct the sequel that it should be someone in the Carpenter-Hill unit.

Tommy Lee Wallace's attachment as a possible director for *Halloween II* was a happy compromise for all parties involved, especially for Curtis. Curtis had enjoyed working with Wallace on *Halloween* and *The Fog*, as well as acting with Nancy Kyes, Wallace's then-girlfriend, on *Halloween*. In 1979, Kyes and Wallace had gotten married and by 1981 were in the process of starting a family while Wallace was trying to kick-start his own directing and screenwriting career. "Back in 1980, Tommy Lee was the first director mentioned and I was happy because I thought he was very talented," recalls Curtis. "He was close to Debra and John, and we all knew each other, and I trusted him"

When Carpenter and Hill offered Wallace the *Halloween II* directing assignment, Wallace—who would eventually make his feature directing debut on 1982's *Halloween III: Season of the Witch*—said no. "I just didn't think it was a good idea for me to make my directing debut on a sequel to John's film, especially one that was going to be a "five minutes later" type of sequel," recalls Wallace. "It was a tough decision because I knew there was a good chance that the sequel would be commercially successful, which would've been good for me, but the thought of following in John's footsteps—and making my directing debut on a sequel—made me nervous."

In retrospect, Wallace regrets the decision not to direct *Halloween II*. This isn't for commercial or creative reasons, but rather because of the missed opportunity to have worked with, as director and actress, Jamie Lee Curtis. "My only regret about passing on *Halloween II* was not getting to direct Jamie," says Wallace. "I have no doubt we would've had a blast together. She's a pro. So am I. It would've been fine. I still look forward to working with her sometime in the future."

JOHN CARPENTER, CO-PRODUCER/CO-WRITER: I wanted *Halloween II* initially to be a fast-paced action movie, and to start the action very quickly with The Shape terrorizing Laurie again very early in the film. The rest of the film would've been like an extended series of chase sequences between Laurie and The Shape, just non-stop action and terror. Debra and I soon realized that all of these ideas would've been too expensive and too-consuming and that's when we decided to move the story to a single location which turned out to be a hospital.

DEAN CUNDEY, CINEMATOGRAPHER: I think Jamie looked at the Carpenter-Hill unit like she got her start there, and it gave her the platform from which to move on and do other things. She was grateful, but I think she also felt it was time to move on. I think we all felt that way when we were about to do *Halloween II*, but it wasn't a conscious thing at that time. In terms of our approach to the sequel, I looked at it as an interesting film-making challenge, given that the story takes place right after *Halloween*, and I think Jamie and the rest of the crew from *Halloween* felt the same way.

JAMIE LEE CURTIS: Everyone around me told me not to do the sequel but I believe in loyalty, and I felt a strong loyalty to John and Debra, who gave me my career, and to the audience who deserved to see me playing Laurie again. If George Lucas wanted to do another *Star Wars* movie with Princess Leia, and I was Carrie Fisher, I would do it for nothing and that's how I felt. You had to love Laurie as much in the sequel as you did in *Halloween* or the sequel wouldn't work and it wouldn't have worked with a different actress playing Laurie. I also looked at the sequel as a great challenge in terms of the sequel taking place right after *Halloween*; to make a whole new film while continuing the same storyline. Doing the sequel meant I had to be a teenager again—a virgin, Laurie—so it was a real acting challenge.

MICK GARRIS, PRESS AGENT: Jamie, Debra, and John all kind of started together and they certainly had their first huge, career-launching successes together. That bonds you. Jamie's career was already starting to change a bit when *Halloween II* was made. *Halloween II* was made at Universal, a major studio, and *Halloween* was such a huge hit that there were more finances available for the sequel. There's no question that Jamie was pretty special, and a terrific actress. Many good actors have made the leap from small-budget genre movies. I think it was a great training ground for Jamie.

KIM GOTTLIEB-WALKER, STILL PHOTOGRAPHER: I think Jamie was at a point in her career where she wanted to explore other genres (she's a great comedienne, for instance) and John strictly does horror and suspense, and that's why I think Jamie was ready to move on.

DEBRA HILL, CO-PRODUCER/CO-WRITER: The original premise that John and I thought of for *Halloween II* was much different than the filmed version. The original idea we had was that the sequel would take place years later in Chicago and would follow Laurie, who's still coping with the effects of what happened in *Halloween*, living in a high-security high rise apartment building, having left Haddonfield to escape the bad memories from *Halloween*. Five years later, Halloween night, Michael tracks down Laurie again, haunts her dreams, and that was going to be the movie.

TOMMY LEE WALLACE: I know through conversations with Debra that she felt Jamie pulling away, already trying to distance herself from the "Scream Queen" pigeonhole, or perhaps just trying to prove herself on her own, away from the umbrella of those who gave Jamie her "first big break." One of the reasons I passed on *Halloween II* was my dismay at the script when John and Debra turned it in. I hated all the gore and gratuitous violence. It seemed the antithesis of the original. I had suggested that we pick up the story a year or two later, after Laurie has had a lot of therapy and gotten a little bit on top of her incredible dreams. Now she's having a go at college, and there's this campus, and lots of security, and—you can figure out the rest. I would've enjoyed that, and directed it with real enthusiasm.

IRWIN YABLANS, EXECUTIVE PRODUCER: The first story I heard for the sequel was that it was going to be that Jamie Lee Curtis was going to move to a new town and would live in a luxury apartment complex. The Shape returns and haunts Jamie again and then Donald Pleasence returns to stop Michael. That was the first idea Debra had for the sequel.

JAMIE LEE CURTIS: I thought they could've gone in a more interesting direction with Laurie in the sequel. It would've been interesting if the story had taken place ten years later and Laurie's living in Chicago and she has kids now and she has an interesting job; maybe she's a teacher or some kind of businesswoman. Then Michael reappears in her life. I think that would've been interesting.

DEBRA HILL: The problem is that if we'd set the story years later we would've had to deal with all kinds of silly questions about Michael Myers and where he's been, how he's survived, all kinds of things that would've been hard to explain. I think John and I both felt that maybe there was nothing more to do with Laurie and Loomis in the sequel, and we actually thought about doing a sequel with new characters. We had one idea where Laurie's dead at the start of *Halloween II* and then we meet a whole new group of characters. Part of the reason we thought of this was because of Jamie and how much she'd grown and matured, both as an actress and a woman, since we'd made *Halloween* in 1978. I didn't think anyone would believe Jamie as a high school kid anymore. In the end, we knew that the audience had identified with Laurie in *Halloween* and that they wanted that story to continue in the sequel.

JAMIE LEE CURTIS: We originally thought it would be better to begin the story four years later and have Laurie live in a very secure high-rise building. Then we thought: What would The Shape have been doing for four years? He couldn't have got a job with that mask on. I thought Laurie should be a catatonic mess, but John convinced me that the character would just not be interesting. Then I wanted her to be vulnerable and always crying, which would have been more fun to play as an actress, but John felt it wouldn't be very interesting for the audience if she just sat in the corner. John would say, "Keep playing it strong. This girl is a fighter." I think he was right.

After Wallace turned down *Halloween II*, Carpenter and Hill found their director when they screened a twenty-six minute short film—a film that also centered on a psycho-killer—entitled *The Toyer*. The film was made by Rick Rosenthal, a 32 year old graduate of the prestigious American Film Institute (AFI) who'd been making documentaries for New Hampshire Public Television. "John and I had the same lawyer as Rick's and that's how we saw Rick's movie, which impressed both of us," recalled Hill. "It was a really great little suspense thriller, very exciting, and you could see that Rick had a real director's eye. After meeting with Rick, we decided to give him the job."

Prior to entering film-making, Rosenthal had majored in economics and government at Harvard before a "religious experience," as Rosenthal puts it, watching shipbuilders provoked Rosenthal to become a metal sculptor. Rosenthal, who eventually turned in his senior thesis on videotape, was also enamored with film noir and German expressionism and these two influences would be visible in his early film- making career, including with *Halloween II*.

Rosenthal, who was also an Alfred Hitchcock devotee, felt that his artistic sensibilities would be compatible with a project like *Halloween II*, especially since *Halloween* had made such effective use of contrast, lighting and shadows. Despite his artistic sensibilities, Rosenthal was also cognizant of *Halloween*'s massive impact. "The approach I took with *Halloween II* was that I wanted to make a suspense-thriller, which was what John had done with *Halloween*, instead of making a really graphic horror film," recalls Rosenthal. "Basically, I just wanted to follow what worked so well in the first film and bring that to the sequel."

When Rosenthal first met with Curtis, they discussed ways to get Curtis more involved in the story, and earlier, since Laurie Strode is virtually comatose and unconscious in much of the Carpenter-Hill script. Since *Halloween II* takes place immediately after *Halloween*, the story for *Halloween II* sees Laurie Strode being taken to a hospital where she's drugged and placed in a hospital bed for much of the film. "Rick and I talked about ways to get me more involved in the film and we decided to move the drugging of Laurie back in the film so I'd have more to do in the film," recalls Curtis. "In the original script, Laurie was drugged right at the beginning and she's totally out of it. I couldn't believe how little dialogue I had in the script, something like ten lines."

Curtis and Rosenthal met at a now-defunct restaurant in West Hollywood to discuss *Halloween II* where they discovered that they had a lot in common, namely the fact that Rosenthal had also attended Choate. "Jamie was very open, warm and friendly," says Rosenthal. "We sat outside cafe-style and talked and it turned out that we'd both gone to the same East Coast prep school—Choate—so there was an immediate connection and common experience to draw upon. Jamie was someone who was aware that she'd grown up in a rarefied atmosphere of Hollywood, but she was curious and open—and great with people."

In terms of Curtis' concerns about her character's lack of involvement in the story, Rosenthal was very understanding but also felt that *Halloween II*'s story structure—in terms of the vulnerability inherent in Laurie Strode being stuck in a hospital bed—had its advantages in terms of creating suspense. "The difficulty/limits of the film's premise—the vulnerability of its heroine stuck in a hospital bed and, therefore, its confining claustrophobia—were also its strengths," says Rosenthal. "I think Jamie found it frustrating not to be more pro-active as both a character and as an actress, but the audience really cared about her—and her vulnerability. I think that was a big part of the success of the sequel."

Besides Curtis and Pleasence, other actors from *Halloween* who would appear in the sequel were Charles Cyphers and Nancy Stephens. Nancy Kyes would also make a cameo appearance in the sequel in a scene where her wide-eyed corpse is revealed to Cyphers' Leigh Brackett character at the start of the film. With most of the key crew positions filled by veterans of *Halloween*, first-time director Rosenthal would be faced with the added pressure of trying to measure up to the example set by John Carpenter on *Halloween*. "The main conflict on *Halloween II* was that all of us who'd worked on *Halloween*, including Jamie Lee, wanted to do things the same way we did them on *Halloween*," recalls Dean Cundey. "Rick had his own way of doing things, his own vision, and there was conflict between the two groups."

A notable exception was Nancy Stephens, veteran of both *Halloween* and *Escape from New York*, whom Rosenthal would fall in love with during the filming of *Halloween II* and would marry almost immediately after the end of *Halloween II*'s filming. Ultimately, this would be the happiest legacy from *Halloween II* for Rosenthal—along with the sequel's eventual commercial success—for whom the making of *Halloween II* would turn out to be a bruising and frustrating experience. "Aside from the production designer, Michael Riva, and the first assistant director, and me, it was pretty much the exact same crew as the first *Halloween*," says Rosenthal. "There were definitely times when I had a feeling I was being compared to John Carpenter and, given the phenomenal success of the first film, those were mighty big shoes to fill, but Jamie seemed genuinely supportive of me as the director, despite my lack of experience."

Anxious to be surrounded by some people he knew, friends, Rosenthal cast several actors he'd worked with at the Beverly Hills Playhouse—where Rosenthal had studied acting under the tutelage of the legendary Milton Katselas—to fill out some of *Halloween II*'s supporting roles. Actors Ana Alicia, Gloria Gifford, Leo Rossi, Pamela Susan Shoop and John Zenda all knew Rosenthal from the Playhouse and were all cast in the sequel. Actress Tawny Moyer was also cast in the film, having appeared in a music video Rosenthal had directed just prior to being hired for *Halloween II*. Actor Cliff Emmich had worked with Rosenthal back at the AFI and was also cast in *Halloween II*. "I wanted to have some people around me that I knew," recalls Rosenthal. "Jamie and the rest of the crew all knew each other from *Halloween* so they had a lot of chemistry together, while I didn't know anybody."

For the part of Michael Myers, Rosenthal chose veteran stuntman Dick Warlock for the iconic role. Warlock would replace Nick Castle who was in the process of starting his own film-making career, having co-written *Escape from New York* with Carpenter. The rest of the cast was filled out with actors Lance Guest, Jeffrey Kramer, Ford Rainey and Hunter Von Leer. Guest would share the most scenes with Curtis in the film. None of these people had any connection or history with the Carpenter-Hill unit.

Halloween II began filming on April 6, 1981 around South Pasadena, California, the same area where much of *Halloween* had been filmed.

The hospital scenes, which are most prominent in the film, were primarily filmed at vacant Morningside Hospital, located near Inglewood and Los Angeles, with additional hospital scenes to be filmed at Pasadena Community Hospital. "The main hospital we shot at looks really creepy in the film, which I'm happy about because, in reality, it was a relatively pleasant place to work," recalls Rosenthal. "It was easy to get to, fast to light, and there was a lot of cooperation from the location people."

The hospital setting was quite suitable for Rosenthal's planned German expressionist vision for *Halloween II*, the mixture of dark and light settings. The hospital's reception area was airy and light—relatively so given that Morningside Hospital, which has since been torn down, was an old and somewhat decrepit place—which contrasts the contorted, darkened, and long hospital corridors that were ripe for grim suggestion. "We were making a film that takes place one minute after *Halloween* so I felt a responsibility to maintain the style of *Halloween*," recalls Rosenthal. "We had virtually the same crew, and so I wanted it to feel like a two-part story. I wanted to do a thriller more than a slasher movie, like *Halloween*, but I had no control over the script which was very gory."

One problem with filming at Morningside, which the cast and crew of *Halloween II* wouldn't fully appreciate until filming was underway, was that the hospital was located in close proximity to Los Angeles International Airport (LAX). The resulting noise from nearby air traffic would distract the cast and crew and ruin many takes of scenes. "When the weather was bad, there was almost a continuous line of jets stacked up on approach, holding just above our hospital," recalls Rosenthal. "This made shooting very difficult, especially long dialogue scenes. We'd do scenes and the jets would roll in and ruin the scene."

The only part of the hospital that Curtis saw during the filming of *Halloween II*, until the end of the film, was the hospital room in which Laurie Strode lay prone for much of the film. Although Curtis could, and would, freely walk around the hospital in between takes and talk with the cast and crew, most of her acting in the film takes place in a hospital bed with Laurie Strode being drugged and semi-conscious throughout much of the story. "It was strange to have so little to do, and so little to say, in the sequel because Laurie had been such a big part of the first film," says Curtis. "Because they set the sequel in the hospital, and that's where Laurie was, there wasn't much for me to do in the film."

Rosenthal's closest professional ally on *Halloween II*, and a person who'd play a major role in Curtis' life at this juncture, was production designer J. Michael Riva. Like Rosenthal, Riva—who'd recently worked on the 1980 Best Picture Academy Award winner *Ordinary People*—was an artist himself who was entirely in-step with the film noir, German expressionist approach that Rosenthal envisioned for *Halloween II*.

Curtis and Riva had more in common than any other relationship Curtis would ever be involved in prior to her eventual marriage to actor-director Christopher Guest in 1984. The biggest thing they had in common was that Riva was, like Curtis, born into Hollywood royalty as he was the grandson of Hollywood screen icon Marlene Dietrich which is probably just as impressive, if not more, than being the daughter of Tony Curtis and Janet Leigh. Unlike with her previous relationships, including her relationship with then-fiancé Ray Hutcherson, Curtis didn't have to be self-conscious of her Hollywood pedigree and her famous last name around Riva.

Although *Halloween II*'s $2.5 million budget was modest by Hollywood standards, it was like *Gone with the Wind* compared to *Halloween*'s $300,000 budget. The increased budget, which was the biggest example of De Laurentiis' involvement with the sequel, was visible during the production of *Halloween II* in many ways. This was no longer a group of friends floating around South Pasadena in the haphazard pursuit of completing a movie. *Halloween II* was a real Hollywood production.

For Curtis, this meant getting her own Winnebago trailer, unlike on *Halloween* where Curtis and the rest of the cast and crew had shared Dean Cundey's lone Winnebago. Curtis also had her own chair with a gold star on the back of it, a clear sign of her value to the production. The exterior of Morningside Hospital was full of Winnebagos, along with catering trucks, production vehicles, and all of the various Hollywood studio trappings that were just a dream during the filming of *Halloween* in the spring of 1978.

One of the most hilarious examples of the sequel's relative excess is present in the film's opening shot, a wildly-ambitious crane shot that hovers over the front of the Doyle house as the sequel recaps what happened at the end of *Halloween*. Meanwhile, The Chordettes chime *Mr. Sandman* over the soundtrack. Neither of these elements—either the crane or the use of the music—would've been imaginable during the production of *Halloween*.

Given that *Halloween II* takes place immediately after *Halloween*, which had been filmed almost precisely three years earlier, one of the most difficult tasks for the crew—especially cinematographer Dean Cundey and production designer J. Michael Riva—was achieving stylistic and visual continuity between *Halloween* and *Halloween II*. To this end, the film succeeds in terms of successfully recreating the feel and look of the Haddonfield streets. Everything from *Halloween* that's in *Halloween II*—from Loomis' appearance to Haddonfield to Michael Myers' William Shatner mask—looks virtually the same. Everything in *Halloween II* looks pretty much identical to *Halloween* with the noticeable exception of Laurie Strode's hair.

Curtis had transformed physically in the past three years, definitely, but her hair was a whole other story. In *Halloween*, Curtis' hair was thin and tomboyish-looking, very much a microcosm of Curtis' own awkward self-image at the time. Between *Halloween* and *Halloween II*, Curtis' hair—as seen in the four other films she'd made after *Halloween*—had undergone so many different frostings and treatments that, by the time of *Halloween II*'s filming, it would no longer respond to her commands.

The real problem, in terms of matching the look of Laurie Strode's hair in *Halloween II*, is that Curtis had trimmed her hair short for the filming of *She's in the Army Now* and so the situation was unattainable. The only solution was for Curtis to don a wig in the film. "Getting her hair to match was a problem," recalls Rosenthal. "Jamie had cut it for a role and there wasn't time for her to grow it out before we had to start shooting, so we ended up wigging her for the role. But, this being Hollywood, we had access to amazing hair people and I think it's hard to tell that Jamie is wearing a wig throughout—especially amazing considering *Halloween II* picks up right where the first film left off. Jamie had to look exactly like she did in the first film—and I think she does."

Despite the production's best efforts, the wig that Curtis wore for the film was bowling shoe ugly, and rather unconvincing, and it's a tribute to Curtis' star quality that she makes the disguise look passable in the film. "Her hair didn't look the same and none of us really knew why exactly," recalls Dean Cundey. "She's so beautiful and such a great actress that I don't think it was really a big issue, unless you'd just seen *Halloween* before you watched the sequel."

In terms of *Halloween II*'s style and tone, the increased budget was most prominent in terms of increased effects and gore. These were two elements that were almost entirely absent from *Halloween* partly because of financial constraints but mostly because of Carpenter's and Hill's insistence on avoiding cheap shocks. The sequel contains no less than ten gruesome killings, most of which involve the hospital staff being dispatched by Michael Myers with various hospital instruments at his disposal—whether it be a scalpel, a Hypodermic needle, or scalding hot water from a therapy pool. The sequel is also full of fiery explosions and stunts. "Everything on *Halloween II* was bigger—bigger effects, more producers, more crew," recalls co-star Charles Cyphers. "We had everything except a good story."

DEAN CUNDEY: Jamie was dissatisfied with her character's involvement in the film and I also think that Jamie, like the rest of us, was frustrated that we weren't maintaining the style of *Halloween*. She wanted more dialogue, more character, and she talked to Rick about that. Jamie and the rest of us—the crew from *Halloween*—wanted to continue the *Halloween* style and Rick wanted to make the film his way. There were two different views of how to make the film.

JAMIE LEE CURTIS: I'm happy I did the sequel—in terms of fulfilling my obligation to Debra, John, and the audience—but I was disappointed with my lack of participation in the film after I agreed to do it. I hardly had any lines in the film, and I didn't like being drugged for the first half of the film. I thought it was a waste of a good character because in *Halloween*, I had a lot of dialogue. Laurie talked a lot in *Halloween* and you got to know her and that made the audience identify with Laurie. I wish I would've been given more to say in the sequel.

GLORIA GIFFORD, CO-STAR: What I remember most about Jamie was that she was very generous, very present, very in-the-moment as an actress, and very supportive of the rest of us. She has a great sense of humor and she was very down to earth, just like she was one of us.

KIM GOTTLIEB-WALKER: *Halloween II* was a much harder shoot. We had an inexperienced director who didn't seem to fully trust our wonderful crew, and Jamie was stuck in that awful wig and hospital gown for the whole picture. It wasn't the joyous experience *Halloween* had been, especially for the crew. I never spoke with Jamie about how she felt, so I really can't say how she coped with the discomforts on that shoot, or what she thought of Rick, who was generally considered more of an actor's director than an overall film-maker. I'm sure he was deferential to Jamie because he had a very rigid pecking order and was nice to those he perceived as higher in status and he was good to the actors he had brought into the project.

LANCE GUEST, CO-STAR: Jamie was always very positive during the filming, even though she spent most of the film in the hospital bed. She was always in a good mood, always up, and very friendly and generous as an actress. With my character, there's obviously an attraction between my character and Jamie's character in the film, and we tried to play that up in the film. I looked at my character, Jimmy, as Jamie's protector in the film; he was the one who would risk his life to protect Laurie from the Shape.

DEBRA HILL: It was a bit nerve-wracking for us—all of us who'd started together on *Halloween*—when we started shooting *Halloween II* because it was the first time John hadn't been there with us. The night we started filming, back in South Pasadena where we'd shot most of *Halloween*, John was about to go to Alaska for pre-production on *The Thing*. I think for all of us it was a big adjustment not having John around.

TAWNY MOYER, CO-STAR: Jamie was very supportive of the rest of us when we were doing our scenes, and very available as an actress. She clearly had a strong grasp of film acting and she had an uncommon ability to get into character, even though she didn't have much dialogue in the film.

RICK ROSENTHAL, DIRECTOR: There was one quite emotional scene with Jamie at her bedside and the jets from LAX just kept rolling in, interrupting take after take. Finally, out of desperation, we put a production assistant with a walkie-talkie on the roof so he could radio down when it looked like there was a break in the line of approaching planes. As soon as we got the word, we started the scene. When it was over, Jamie asked me how I thought the scene was. I said "Fine." Jamie burst into tears, and rightfully so. I'd been so relieved to finally get through the scene that I was completely insensitive to the actors—and after their grueling experience they needed more than just a "fine." It was a worthwhile lesson learned—and I think it served me well. Debra Hill and I, having gotten to know each other during the pre-production period, had developed a pretty good shorthand by the time filming started, and Jamie was very easy to work with.

PAMELA SUSAN SHOOP, CO-STAR: What I remember about Jamie on *Halloween II* is how professional she was and how she would do anything Rick asked her to do without ever complaining. She had a tough job in terms of the physical things she did in the film and the fact that she had to display emotions without much dialogue, with just her eyes. She was always happy, always laughing with us, and yet when it came time to film a scene she had a lot of intensity, and could be very focused. We did a lot of night shooting in the hospital and sometimes we'd go back to Jamie's trailer outside the hospital and just hang out until early morning.

DICK WARLOCK, CO-STAR: I fell in love with Jamie the first time I met her, and I had a mad crush on her throughout filming, and I think she had a bit of a crush on me, although I was married at the time and probably too old for her anyway. Jamie just had a great sense of humor and was very smart and incredibly beautiful.

Halloween II's creative direction and Rosenthal's stylistic approach was the major point of contention between Rosenthal and the members of the Carpenter-Hill unit during the filming of *Halloween II*. "All of us who'd worked on *Halloween*, including Jamie, wanted *Halloween II* to be made in the same way, but Rick had different ideas," recalls Cundey. "That's where the conflicts occurred. I don't think any of us, including Jamie, were happy with the direction the sequel took."

While Debra Hill was an involved and constant presence on the *Halloween II* set, serving as both a producer and line producer on the sequel, John Carpenter only visited the set twice, mostly to offer Rosenthal encouragement and to say hello to Curtis and the other veterans of the Carpenter-Hill unit. Despite his rare appearances, Carpenter's presence was constantly felt throughout filming, especially by Rosenthal.

If Rosenthal wanted to shoot a scene in a certain way, he would be reminded, gently but persistently, by Cundey and Hill of what Carpenter's approach might've been in a similar situation. A typical example of this was during the filming of a scene in the film where Janet (Ana Alicia), a nurse at the hospital, discovers the corpse of Dr. Mixter (Ford Rainey) who's been murdered via a hypodermic needle through his eyeball.

In the script, the dead man's head is propped up by a lamp, but Rosenthal, thinking this illogical, wanted to shoot the scene by having the victim sit in an armchair with his back turned whereby the chair then spins around and reveals the corpse to the nurse. Cundey felt it was a cheap gag and would lessen the scene's chilling impact.

Ultimately, Rosenthal's version prevailed, but such disagreements were commonplace during the filming of *Halloween II*. Although Debra Hill, who barred Dino De Laurentiis and Irwin Yablans from the *Halloween II* set in order to preserve artistic control, maintained that Rosenthal was always in control on the set, there were limits to what Rosenthal could do in terms of making his own creative suggestions that deviated from the script that Carpenter and Hill were intent on following.

By the end of filming, many of the Carpenter-Hill unit would be in rebellion, feeling that Rosenthal didn't understand what had made *Halloween* such a great film. "It was the opposite of working with John because the director on *Halloween II* didn't take his time and wanted to rush everything," recalls co-star Charles Cyphers. "An example was the scene where I saw my dead daughter. The director wanted me to burst into tears, but you have to let that stuff come out naturally, slowly, or it's not believable."

Rosenthal was faced with mixed signals in terms of his creative approach to *Halloween II*, and this conflict would fester right through the film's production. Although Rosenthal was intent on making *Halloween II* as a suspense-thriller, more or less in keeping with the form of *Halloween*, the recent gory trend in the horror marketplace—namely the success of 1980's *Friday the 13th*—would cast a shadow over *Halloween II*'s creative and stylistic direction. "Whereas much of the killing in *Halloween* happens just off-screen, by the time *Halloween II* was made, *Friday the 13th* and various other horror films had veered away from suspense and into the slasher genre," says Rosenthal. "This trend, I believe, shaped Dino De Laurentiis' expectations—he was involved with the financing of *Halloween II*—and he viewed an early cut of the film with impatience. I felt his opinion weighed heavily on Debra and John. The final version of *Halloween II* had a couple of killings in it that I don't believe were necessary, but as a first time director, my opinion didn't carry the day."

Curtis was a conscientious objector to these disagreements, and although several members of the *Halloween II* would voice their disapproval of Rosenthal's direction to Carpenter himself, Curtis wasn't one of them. "I thought Rick did a good job of directing the film under tough circumstances," recalls Curtis. "There were a lot of problems on the film that weren't his fault."

Even though Curtis is the star of *Halloween II*, and her presence is essential for the sequel to exist, Curtis only has—excluding the film's extended prologue sequence—about twenty-five lines of dialogue in the entire film. Most of this dialogue, which totals less than 100 words, is of the monosyllabic variety—a lot of yeses, nos, helps. Basically, Curtis spends the first half of the film in sedation, as a virtual catatonic, and the second half of the film in speechless terror. "Once the decision was made that *Halloween II* would be a continuation rather than a conventional sequel and that she needed to go to the hospital, the die was pretty much set," says Rosenthal. "But her immobility—although certainly frustrating at times for Jamie—preyed on the audience as they felt her isolation and vulnerability, and that added to the intensity of the film."

Curtis would spend most of her time during the filming of *Halloween II* laying in the hospital bed inside the dormant hospital, although Curtis would constantly move around and interact with the cast and crew between takes. It was during this stationery period that Curtis struck up a conservation with production designer J. Michael Riva that would eventually lead to a romance which the cast and crew of *Halloween II* were oblivious to right up until the end of filming.

In addition to being born into Hollywood royalty, Riva was a decade older than Curtis, the same age dynamic as virtually all of Curtis' relationships. Ironically, Rosenthal's closest ally on *Halloween II* had become Curtis' as well. When they weren't working, Curtis and Riva would retreat to Curtis' Winnebago where Curtis would also host several mini-parties with her fellow cast and crew members during filming (1). "We called it Winnebago passion," said Curtis. "No one knew about the romance until the end of the movie."

One of the main reasons Curtis that agreed to do *Halloween II*—aside from the money and a strong sense of loyalty to Carpenter, Hill and the audience—was to close the chapter on her scream queen career. To this end, Debra Hill—who also wanted to leave the horror genre—had decided that *Halloween II* should be the end of the Laurie Strode-Michael Myers saga for good. This meant killing off Michael Myers once and for all.

This happens during the film's explosive finale where Curtis and Loomis conspire to blow Michael Myers to pieces inside the hospital by inciting gaseous fumes inside one of the hospital's operating rooms. It's during this sequence that Laurie shoots Michael Myers in the eyes—both of them—with two perfect shot. "That was a ridiculous scene in the film," recalls Dick Warlock. "It seemed silly to all of us when we shot it. After Jamie shot me, I just flailed around like I was blind. It looked good but the scene wasn't believable. I don't think anyone really knew how the film should end."

One of the most notable features of *Halloween II*, aside from what was going on in Curtis' career and personal life at this time, is the teaming of Curtis and Pleasence. In *Halloween*, they only appeared together briefly at the end of the film whereas in *Halloween II* they have several scenes together, although not nearly enough given what fascinating and iconic characters Sam Loomis and Laurie Strode are. They are the Batman and Robin of the *Halloween* films, and yet they're hardly on-screen together, which is maddening. These characters cry out to have an entire film based around just the two of them—together—and while their joint appearance during *Halloween II*'s lengthy denouement is welcome, it's also painfully tantalizing in terms of what possibly could've been done with these two great characters.

Of all of Curtis' co-stars, none is more elusive and mysterious than the legendary Donald Pleasence, who died in 1995. Maybe poor Casey Stevens from *Prom Night* would be a distant second (2). Curtis and Pleasence spent some time together during filming, but Curtis never really got to know the thespian very well. "Jamie and Donald didn't have much interaction at all during the filming," recalls Dean Cundey.

"Donald was a very professional actor, a very serious actor, but very reclusive. He'd stand off in the corner while the rest of us were discussing a scene. He was a very obsessed actor, and he sort of became a cult actor after *Halloween II*. Donald had the same interaction with Jamie that he had with the rest of us—maybe except for Debra and John—which was very little."

The rest of *Halloween II*'s finale, where Laurie runs away from the operating room while Loomis prepares to blow Michael Myers to smithereens with his cigarette lighter, was filmed at Hollywood's Raleigh Studios. This was the location for the hospital corridor which Laurie runs through just before the explosion occurs. "The idea was that Laurie would run towards the camera from the operating room at the end of the corridor and then, as soon as Jamie cleared frame, she would duck through a doorway and a fireball would come hurtling out of the same operating room," recalls Rosenthal. "We set up three cameras, and after several dry runs with Jamie and the special effects people, we were ready to film. When I yelled "Action," Jamie came charging out of the operating room doorway and raced towards the camera. As soon as she cleared frame and ducked to safety inside the doorway behind us, the special effects team triggered the explosion. There was a giant blast in front of us and a fireball rolled out of the operating room and raced towards us, engulfing the entire corridor in flames."

The end of this scene featured a flaming Michael Myers, played by Dick Warlock, stumbling through the corridor before he collapses to the floor while Laurie watches in disbelief. Although Curtis herself was in no danger during the filming of this scene, thanks in part to how quickly she ran towards the camera during the filming of the scene, the entire set eventually turned into a burning cauldron. "When Dick Warlock walked out and fell to the ground, the fire extinguishers appeared and foam quickly covered Dick Warlock and everything seemed okay," recalls Rosenthal. "The rest of the extinguishers were used for the flames on the corridor walls but the corridor was still burning. I had to rescue one of the cameras that was in jeopardy in the corridor and then the special effects guys got the fire under control."

In the theatrical version of *Halloween II*, Laurie Strode is then taken into an ambulance and scooted away. After that the screen fades to black. However Rosenthal shot another ending where Jimmy, the character played by Lance Guest who's presumed to have been killed in the theatrical version, joins Laurie in the back of the ambulance. Earlier in the film, Jimmy—an ambulance attendant who befriends Laurie in the hospital—concussed himself by slipping on a pool of blood and hitting his head on the floor after making the gruesome discovery of a dead body.

In the alternate ending—also known as the "Rick Rosenthal Version," which has scarcely appeared on television in the subsequent years—Jimmy appears in the back of the ambulance with Curtis. A stunned Curtis sees Jimmy and says, "Jimmy, we made it" and then there's a pause after which Curtis repeats the "We made it" line after which the screen fades to black. This alternate version of *Halloween II* also includes additional insert shots, and several additional scenes where characters discuss what's happening in the story.

For the triumvirate of Carpenter, Curtis, and Hill, *Halloween II* had represented an attempt to make a film that would put an emphatic period to the whole slasher film genre that the success of *Halloween* had ushered in. During pre- production, Hill had agreed that the sequel should build fear and suspense—to apply the classic Hitchcockian techniques that Carpenter had manipulated so successfully in *Halloween*—instead of trying to disgust and shock audiences with gore. Pressure from the marketplace, and especially from Dino De Laurentiis and genre-savvy Universal Pictures, changed the sequel's course. "We tried to follow the *Halloween* formula as closely as we could but we also recognized what was happening in the horror genre," recalled Hill. "We felt that the sequel would have to be more graphic and more violent than the original, and the script was kind of a response to that—the changing tone in the genre. Looking back, I think we would've been better off staying with our principles."

Complicating matters was the deal that had been made with NBC to broadcast *Halloween*. The network was planning to broadcast *Halloween* on October 30, 1981, the same date that *Halloween II* would be released in theaters. This would also be the same week that NBC would broadcast *Death of a Centerfold: The Dorothy Stratten Story*, a made-for-television movie that Curtis would begin work on immediately after the filming of *Halloween II*.

In May of 1981, at the end of *Halloween II*'s filming, Hill met with NBC who expressed concern over some of *Halloween*'s scenes, namely the scene where Curtis and Nancy Kyes smoke pot in a car. Additionally, *Halloween*'s 91 minute running time was too short to sustain a two hour time-slot which meant that there was a need for added footage. "It wasn't a happy experience dealing with the network because they wanted to cut everything from the film," recalled Hill. "Their objection to Jamie and Nancy smoking in the car was ridiculous and most of the other cuts they asked for were just pointless. We just kept going back and forth right up until the movie was aired."

In order to satisfy NBC, Carpenter hastily wrote some additional scenes for *Halloween*, mostly having to do with Michael Myers' motivation, his time at Smith's Grove, and his relationship with Dr. Sam Loomis. The additional scenes—which would come to be known as "The Extended Version of *Halloween*"—also tied-in with the whole brother-sister arc that was in *Halloween II*. "I just wrote those scenes so there was enough material to fill the time-slot, but none of it was very interesting or very good," recalls Carpenter. "Basically, I sold-out in doing those additional scenes, but there was really no other choice."

Only one of the additional scenes Carpenter wrote involved Curtis' Laurie Strode character. It's a scene where Curtis is in her house, and has just gotten out of the shower, when a panicked P.J. Soles, returning in the role of Lynda, arrives at Laurie's house. She tells Laurie that she saw The Shape but it turns out that Lynda's prime motivation is to borrow a silk blouse from Laurie's closet.

Carpenter and a skeleton crew from *Halloween II* filmed these additional scenes during a frantic two-day period in May of 1981. The most interesting anecdote of this, in terms of Curtis' scream queen career, is the fact that Curtis had to wear a towel over her head during the filming of her scene because her real hair was too short to match the look from *Halloween*. It's also interesting that Soles herself looks virtually unchanged from the way she looked back in 1978, while Curtis had unquestionably changed in many ways (3).

Besides the hair, Curtis appears visibly older during her one scene in the extended version, and much more assured, confident, and blooded by life than the young innocent that had first appeared in *Halloween*. There's other interesting little details like the fact that Curtis' teeth were now white and straightened, although still not perfect. It had been over three years since Curtis, Soles, and the rest of the gang had worked on *Halloween*, and the fact they were back recreating history at this moment struck everyone as a bit strange, even though the whole process was very rushed.

Although Carpenter's and Hill's motivation for shooting the additional scenes for *Halloween* was entirely money-driven, the additional scenes aren't without value. Besides Curtis' one additional scene, the other newly-filmed scenes focused on Loomis' relationship with Michael Myers at Smith's Grove and serve to provide interesting back-story into the Michael Myers character. The additional scenes also add structure to *Halloween*; instead of the film cutting directly from Michael Myers' nighttime escape to Laurie Strode walking down the street, there's added texture. "I think the added scenes help the story make more sense, although we never would've done them had the producers not made a deal with NBC," recalled Hill. "The scenes do give insight into Michael Myers' mind before he escapes and so I don't think they're worthless."

In June of 1981, Carpenter—who'd made a conscious effort to leave Rosenthal alone during *Halloween II*'s filming and in the first phase of editing—viewed Rosenthal's first cut of *Halloween II*. He was underwhelmed by what he saw. "It just wasn't very exciting, it just laid there on the screen, it was too slow," recalls Carpenter. "The biggest problem I had was that I didn't think it was scary. It didn't work. The only thing I'd asked of Rick was that he make a scary film and the film just wasn't scary enough."

Perhaps the disconnect between Carpenter and Rosenthal—and Rosenthal's own lack of experience in the horror genre—is most evident in a remark that Rosenthal made in the fall of 1981, following *Halloween II*'s production: "Maybe I am wrong about this, but I don't think you should make films for audiences. I think you should make a film that entertains you, that you want to make, and that you have to hope that the film finds an audience."

Carpenter completely disagreed with this, and was always aware of trying to make a film that entertained the audience, seeing that as one of his main obligations as a film-maker. With *Halloween II*, he felt an obligation to make a film that would satisfy fans of the original film, to give them what they want.

To this end, Carpenter—much to his own dismay—went back and shot some additional scenes for *Halloween II* that he hoped would make the film scarier. "I felt terrible because I thought Rick was a talented film-maker and I know how I would feel if someone took over my film," says Carpenter. "But my first obligation was to the audience and I felt like I had to make the film scarier."

These were primarily shock images, and even the most basic follower of Carpenter's technique and work can spot Carpenter's influence on *Halloween II*. The most direct evidence of Carpenter's fingerprints on *Halloween II* is with Carpenter's signature use of space and the edges of the screen. In one additional scene Carpenter shot, for example, a security guard is killed by The Shape who appears out of the corner of the screen and whacks him in the head with a hammer. The first additional scene of Carpenter's that appears in the film is when a young girl is killed in her home by Michael Myers who leaps out from the bottom of the screen (4).

It was textbook Carpenter, but what wasn't typical of Carpenter is just how gory and violent *Halloween II* turned out to be. Whatever *Halloween II*'s flaws are, the film certainly doesn't lack for action or shocks, not to mention gruesome and inventive kill scenes. Rosenthal would later lament that he may have tried too hard to emulate *Halloween* and may have failed to achieve a stylistic continuity between the two films, and that *Halloween II* might've actually benefitted from more Hitchcockian touches. "My instinct as a director was to push the suspense aspect of the film over the pure horror element," says Rosenthal. "The ending of the first film was so strong and so satisfying that I felt we should start the sequel with a "cool breeze on the back of the neck"—letting the suspense build before leaping into action. But the climate—and the marketplace—was changing."

None of this is to suggest, as has been reported over the years, that there were screaming matches between Carpenter and Rosenthal or that there's any lingering hatred between the two men, although they've never spoken since. For her part, Hill recalled having a very cordial relationship with Rosenthal during *Halloween II*'s filming, and both Hill and Rosenthal would later present *Halloween II* together at several preview screenings.

There were also no suggestions of Rosenthal ever taking his name off the film, and Carpenter never wanted to be credited for his direction of the additional scenes. "It was kind of like I was a rookie quarterback who was taking the place of a legend," recalls Rosenthal. "I was in the huddle with all of these veterans and because they didn't know me they didn't trust me until I proved I could do the job. Then it was okay."

These disagreements reflect the fact that *Halloween II* wasn't really a sequel to *Halloween* as much as it was a reaction to the post-*Halloween* slasher copycats that had invaded cinemas since 1978. *Halloween*

II continued the basic story of *Halloween*—with Laurie Strode and Dr. Loomis and The Shape—but not the magic spell. Whereas *Halloween* had been based on a foundation of artistry and technique, *Halloween II* was a product of cynical Hollywood greed.

This was evident when a rough cut of *Halloween II* was screened for various teenage preview audiences prior to the film's release, the purpose of which was to gauge just what the teenage marketplace was looking to find in the film. "What they said they wanted was just more blood and guts and they were especially disappointed that there weren't any teenagers getting killed in the film," recalls Rosenthal who attended, with Hill, a preview screening at UCLA in October of 1981, just prior to the film's theatrical release. "I think Universal felt the same way, so a scene was included early in the film where a teenage girl is killed by Michael Myers. The scenes that I filmed to establish suspense and tension were all shortened or cut completely if there wasn't any gore involved."

Curtis' reaction to all of this was ambivalence. She had, unlike most of her colleagues from *Halloween*, kept whatever misgivings she had about *Halloween II*'s creative direction to herself. Ultimately, Curtis and everyone else who worked on *Halloween II* understood that there was no amount of editing, post-production magic or re-shoots that would transform *Halloween II* into anything more than what it was: a competently-made, intermittently effective, entirely palatable slasher film that lacked the artistry, care, imagination, integrity and professional camaraderie that had existed in spades with *Halloween*.

After production on *Halloween II* had wrapped in May of 1981, Jamie Lee Curtis wasted no time in making the transition to her post-scream queen career. This was *Death of a Centerfold*, a made-for television film about the life and tragic death of *Playboy* playmate Dorothy Stratten who had been brutally murdered by her estranged husband in 1980. The week after filming ended on *Halloween II*, Curtis had forsaken the terrible wig she'd used for *Halloween II*, had dyed her hair blonde, and had begun immersing herself in the life, and the role, of Dorothy Stratten. "I think Jamie grew up a lot during *Halloween II*," says Rosenthal. "When we first started shooting she was engaged, but she decided not to get married shortly after we finished the film and maybe that change of plans triggered a fair amount of introspection."

For his part, Rick Rosenthal would, freed from the bonds of the Carpenter-Hill unit, prove himself a capable and skilled director with his next film, the gritty 1983 teen prison drama *Bad Boys*. As with *Halloween II*, Rosenthal won the *Bad Boys* assignment on the strength of his acclaimed short film *The Toyer*. *Bad Boys*, which marked Sean Penn's first serious dramatic role, earned rave reviews, both for Penn's performance and Rosenthal's strong direction (5).

Proving the never-say-never adage in Hollywood, Rosenthal would return to the *Halloween* film franchise in 2001, twenty years after the filming of *Halloween II*, when he was hired to direct *Halloween: Resurrection* which was filmed in Vancouver, British Columbia. The sequel, which was released in 2002, would also mark a reunion between Curtis and Rosenthal given that Curtis would make an extended cameo appearance in the sequel.

Halloween II didn't just mark the end of Curtis' scream queen career, it also marked an ending, and a new beginning, in her personal life. Curtis' engagement to screenwriter Ray Hutcherson didn't survive *Halloween II*'s filming, and Curtis had fallen in love with production designer J. Michael Riva. Curtis and Riva would later become engaged before parting amicably in 1983, the same year that Curtis began to take a firm grip on her drug problems, and the same year her non-horror acting career would really begin to take shape.

Calling off the planned June 1981 wedding was difficult for Curtis who had to cancel wedding invitations and call friends to tell them the engagement was off. Although Curtis, in subsequent interviews, asserted that she and Hutcherson had remained friends following the breakup, the reality is that they barely saw each other again. "I didn't want to hurt anyone, and I didn't know if I could make it alone," said Curtis. "Better to go through the embarrassment of calling off a wedding than to do something like marriage which you're not ready for."

In October of 1981, several months after filming on *Death of a Centerfold* was completed, a still-blonde Curtis showed up on the Universal lot to begin a major round of publicity for *Halloween II* that would also send Curtis, who would also do a press blitz for *Death of a Centerfold*, to New York and other major U.S. media markets. For Curtis, the real purpose of this media blitz wasn't to promote *Halloween II*, which she had no feelings for, but to talk about her future ambitions and her post-scream queen career which could only truly begin when *Halloween II* was released and gone from the public consciousness.

Halloween II was released on October 30, 1981 on over 1200 screens across North America. It was quite a shocking contrast to *Halloween*'s 1978 release where Irwin Yablans had basically carried the film from city to city, slowly but surely building word of mouth. In comparison, *Halloween II* was opening wide, all across America, boosted by the Universal marketing machine which invested several million dollars in *Halloween II*'s promotion and release.

What's ironic and kind of silly about Universal's promotion of *Halloween II* is that the studio sold the film as a suspense-thriller. This was a nervous reaction to the swift backlash against the slasher film genre that had fomented between the end of *Halloween II*'s production and the film's release. While Universal's press notes didn't hide the fact that *Halloween II* was a horror film, which would've been ridiculous, Universal's marketing stressed that the sequel was more of a quality suspense film than a "horror-slasher" film.

By the end of 1981, Universal—like every other major studio that had entered the post-*Halloween*, post-*Friday the 13th* horror sweepstakes—would be running for cover from the genre they'd so coveted just several months earlier. This is also embodied in Universal's press notes for *Halloween II* which quoted Debra Hill as saying, "People don't seem to realize that we showed next to no blood in the first picture. You think you're seeing a lot more than we're allowing you. Chopping off people's limbs isn't scary or entertaining, it's disgusting."

Halloween II would prove to be immune from this silly hypocrisy and the looming death of the slasher movie cycle.

On its first weekend, *Halloween II* grossed a robust $7.4 million, averaging more than $6,000 per-screen. The film would end up grossing $25.5 domestically, just over half the business that *Halloween* did, although *Halloween* had the benefit of subsequent re-releases.

Halloween II wouldn't enjoy nearly the kind of cinematic afterlife that *Halloween* continues to enjoy to this day. The sequel was, in Hollywood-speak, a "ten day wonder" that opened big, performed solidly, but didn't have the durable box office legs that *Halloween* had. Still, *Halloween II* was the top- earning horror film of 1981, which was the film's real goal all along: to show the *Halloween* copycats who was king of the mountain. Carpenter's *More American Graffiti* had at least accomplished this much, in addition to marking the end of Jamie Lee Curtis' scream queen career.

Halloween II's nearest gore competitor in 1981, ironically enough, was *Friday the 13th Part 2* which grossed $21.7 million domestically. The other top-grossing horror films in 1981 were *Ghost Story* ($23.3 million), *The Final Conflict* ($20.5 million) and *The Howling* ($17.9 million). *Halloween II*'s box office performance was almost identical to that of Carpenter's other 1981 release, the action-fantasy *Escape from New York*, which grossed $25.2 million upon its release in July of 1981.

Halloween II was released the same week that NBC aired *Halloween* and the made-for-televison movie *Death of a Centerfold: The Dorothy Stratten Story*, Curtis' first post-scream queen project, both of which received solid ratings. "I called it NBC week—Nothing But Curtis," recalled Curtis. "I kept joking to my friends that I was everywhere that week, with *Halloween II* playing in theaters and the movies being shown on television."

Predictably, reviews for *Halloween II* reflected the backlash and weariness for the slasher film cycle while also lamenting the sequel's blood-soaked treatment in comparison with *Halloween*'s artistry and subtlety. Interestingly, Curtis largely escaped notice in the film, likely a result of Laurie Strode's muted, almost cameo-like participation in the film. However much audiences and critics might've hated *Halloween II*, and hated the sequel's gory approach, no one could blame Jamie Lee Curtis. "The plain fact is that *Halloween II* is quite scary, more than a little silly and immediately forgettable," (David Ansen, *Newsweek.*); "It's a little sad to witness a fall from greatness, and that's what we get in *Halloween II*," (Roger Ebert, *Chicago Sun-Times.*); "*Halloween II* is good enough to deserve a sequel of its own. By the standards of most horror films, this—like its predecessor—is a class act. The direction and camera-work are quite competent, and the actors don't look like amateurs. That may not sound like much to ask of a horror film, but it's more than many of them offer. And *Halloween II*, in addition to all of this, has a quick pace and something like a sense of style," (Janet Maslin, *The New York Times.*); "The one big plot development in the story is that *Halloween II* explains why the killer is particularly drawn to Jamie Lee Curtis. Who cares? We want tension and excitement, not explanations. It's not really meaningful to talk about performances in a film such as this; the director is always the star in a horror film. We are supposed to feel locked in his (or her) control. But I watched *Halloween II* from afar, checking off the implausibilities right down to the very last shot," (Gene Siskel, *Chicago Tribune.*)

Curtis was oblivious to any of this, and she claims to have only seen *Halloween II* once more in the subsequent years. In 1998, Curtis watched *Halloween II* when she was in the planning stages for *Halloween: H20* (1998), a sequel to *Halloween* and *Halloween II*. By that point, Curtis' feelings towards *Halloween II* had somewhat hardened. "It stinks, it's awful," said Curtis. "It's a terrible, terrible movie. I should never have done it. I only did it because I was honoring John and Debra because they wrote it, and I was honoring the audience."

For Curtis, the filming and release of *Halloween II* meant the turning of a page in her career, and her personal life, and although Curtis would eventually return to the horror genre—in *Halloween: H20* and several other later genre films—in the subsequent years, the days of Curtis being chased by knife-wielding maniacs were pretty much over. "I was looking for parts that were more challenging," recalls Curtis. "I'd never played a bitch or a completely horrific type of woman, anything other than a normal person in an unreal situation. Not that I was looking to play a bitch or a horrific woman, but I was ready for new acting challenges."

Three years. Six horror films. Endless running and screaming. Now it was all over; Jamie Lee Curtis' scream queen career had finally come to an end and now it was time for Curtis to take off her blood-soaked sneakers and seek other challenges in her acting career. 1981 was a year of personal and professional transformation for Jamie Lee Curtis, of which the end of her scream queen career, her scream queen era, is the most significant element. She would never be the same again. This Jamie Lee Curtis was now dead, and a new Jamie Lee Curtis was about to be born.

1981 was the year the screaming stopped.

sixteen

THE SCREAMING STOPS

The day after completing work on *Halloween II*, in May of 1981, Jamie Lee Curtis began focusing on her post-scream queen career. She'd signed on to play murdered *Playboy* playmate Dorothy Stratten in an upcoming made-for-television movie which was then called *Dorothy Stratten*. Re-titled *Death of a Centerfold: The Dorothy Stratten Story*, the project represented the dawn of a new era in Jamie Lee Curtis' acting career. *Death of a Centerfold* would begin filming in June of 1981.

Although not a horror project, in many ways *Death of a Centerfold* and the story of Dorothy Stratten would represent the ultimate scream queen role for Curtis, but there was a grim difference about this project. The life and tragic murder of Dorothy Stratten represented real-life horror which was something that Curtis had never experienced as a scream queen before.

Dorothy Stratten, who was murdered on August 14, 1980 at the age of twenty, also represented the first pure victim role that Curtis had ever played. Dorothy Stratten was the ultimate victim, not just in terms of her grisly murder but also because of all of the parasites and users that Stratten was surrounded by during her all-too short career and life. Although only Stratten and her killer know what happened during the final seconds of Stratten's life, one can imagine—given the grim details of her murder—that Stratten probably screamed before she was murdered.

At first glance, Curtis seemed like the last actress on earth who should be cast as Dorothy Stratten. Physically, Curtis looked nothing like Dorothy Stratten. Although Curtis and Stratten were roughly the same height, about five-foot-nine, their body types and facial features were completely different. Even after dying her hair blonde for the role, Curtis looked about as much like Dorothy Stratten as Donald Pleasence.

Death of a Centerfold was a Metro-Goldwyn-Mayer (MGM) Television production and by 1981, the company was in dire straits, so much so that the company was desperate for any kind of success. Thomas Tannenbaum—the former head of Universal Television who'd technically given Curtis her first break when he'd endorsed Curtis' seven year contract at Universal back in 1977—was the President of MGM's television division and felt that this project required a name actress to play Dorothy Stratten in order to be successful.

Paul Pompian, *Death of a Centerfold*'s producer, agreed and they both quickly settled on Curtis. They knew Curtis was looking to make a departure from horror roles, and Pompian and Tannenbaum also realized that Curtis was probably the biggest name they were going to attract given the project's $1.7 million budget. For Curtis, who's always been conscious of her physical appearance, a role like Dorothy Stratten represented a bold choice.

Having to fight for roles, as Curtis did with *Death of a Centerfold*, was a new and humbling experience for the actress. Despite having made six feature films in three years, and establishing herself as a movie star and a scream queen, Curtis discovered that, in terms of mainstream Hollywood, she was basically a non-entity and was starting over from scratch.

It was the same in Curtis' personal life. She'd recently broken up with former fiance Ray Hutcherson, and was now involved with *Halloween II* production designer Michael Riva. Curtis had also left the house in Studio City and had moved into a modest house in Van Nuys, California.

In terms of trying to get "real work," Curtis discovered that her scream queen persona was a major handicap, and in the view of Hollywood, it was almost as if none of the work Curtis had done between 1978 and 1981 mattered. "Jamie had no real body of work other than slashers," recalls Pompian. "Doing a role like Dorothy represented a real gutsy choice for Jamie. When I met Jamie, I could see that she was an adventurous and remarkable actress. She told me she was looking for a departure from the scream queen roles so it was a good fit."

Pompian had met with Curtis in May of 1981 to discuss the project during which Curtis expressed doubts about her ability to portray Dorothy Stratten, primarily in terms of recreating Dorothy Stratten's physical appearance which was still fresh in everyone's mind. "At first, I didn't think I was right to play Dorothy," said Curtis. "I don't look anything like her. She was buxom. My chest isn't as large. She had a full face and a sweet, high voice. I have a thin face and a low voice."

Pompian assured Curtis that he wasn't looking for an actress who necessarily matched Stratten's physical look but who could rather embody Dorothy Stratten's character and mostly make the audience feel sympathy for her. "Jamie took the role very seriously and she did a lot of research about Dorothy before we started filming, but she was very nervous," recalls Pompian. "I would say she was game but very reluctant going into the movie. In terms of Jamie's appearance, I told Jamie that I wasn't looking for a visual copy of Dorothy but rather an actress who could capture the soul of Dorothy Stratten. I knew she could do it, but Jamie was filled with doubts."

Curtis was also worried that the film would be exploitative or sleazy, especially since the production of *Death of a Centerfold* was taking place so soon—less than a year—after Stratten's murder. Conscious of the project's exploitative appearance, Pompian had hired esteemed screenwriter Donald L. Stewart to adapt Stratten's story. "I didn't want it to be an exploitation film or anything sleazy," recalls Pompian. "In all of my years as a producer, I never made a picture as sad as this, and I wanted it to be a tragedy with intense drama. I hired Donald Stewart, a serious writer, to write the script, and he wrote a really ambitious script, really lavish, even though this wasn't a lavish movie. The script reached farther than most made-for- television movies, so we really tried to tell a good story."

Aside from the lack of a physical similarity between Curtis and Stratten, their lives had some stark contrasts and some eerie similarities. The biggest difference was in their backgrounds. While Curtis—who was about fifteen months older than Stratten—grew up around Hollywood royalty, and was wise to the ways of Hollywood well before she was twenty years old, Dorothy Stratten was a naive and unsophisticated dove from Vancouver, Canada who'd been working in a local *Dairy Queen* when Curtis began her acting career in 1977. "If there's a sadness to being a celebrity kid, it's not having a romanticized view of this business," recalled Curtis. "I learned what mistakes not to make. Unlike Dorothy Stratten, whose career knowledge only went so far as being Vancouver's *Dairy Queen*, I was wise to the ways of the world at an early age."

The Dorothy Stratten story is the ultimate example of the dark side of the Hollywood dream. It's also a chilling metaphor for the relationship between those who are famous and live in the spotlight and those creepy characters who lurk in the background and the shadows and are full of jealousy and self-hatred that manifests itself into rage. "Having grown up in Hollywood, I was never motivated by the Hollywood dream that people like Dorothy were driven by," says Curtis. "By the time I was Dorothy's age, I was immune to all of that."

Ironically, Stratten's naivety and lack of sophistication was fueled by the one quality she most shared with Curtis which is that Stratten, much like Curtis, never thought she was beautiful. Stratten, like Curtis, was a gangly, tall girl who didn't think she was beautiful, didn't think she was good at anything, and that made her vulnerable. With Curtis, this vulnerability translated to her acting, while Stratten's own vulnerability and lack of self-confidence was embodied in her disastrous choice of men.

In 1977, while working at a *Dairy Queen* in Vancouver, Stratten was approached by a local hustler and pimp named Paul Snider who recognized Stratten's beauty and swept Stratten off her feet. Snider later took nude photos of Stratten and sent them to *Playboy* who were impressed enough to bring Stratten down to Los Angeles. In June of 1979, Snider and Stratten were married in Las Vegas, and in August of 1979, Stratten was named *Playboy's* Playmate of the Month.

In 1980, Dorothy Stratten was named *Playboy's* Playmate of the year by *Playboy* publisher Hugh Hefner. By this time, Stratten had gotten a taste of fame, and the Hollywood lifestyle, and was outgrowing Snider who became increasingly jealous. By August of 1980, Snider and Stratten had separated and Stratten had fallen in love with film director Peter Bogdanovich who had recently directed Stratten in the feature film *They All Laughed*.

On August 14, 1980, Snider and Stratten met at the Los Angeles duplex the couple had once lived in to discuss the terms of their divorce. It was at the duplex that Snider raped and tortured Stratten before firing a shotgun blast into her face, smearing blood all over the walls and killing Stratten instantly. Snider then turned the shotgun on himself.

The details of Stratten's life and murder chilled Curtis and would torment Curtis right through until the end of *Death of a Centerfold's* filming. No other role Curtis had played previously, and maybe no other role Curtis played after, haunted the actress as much as that of Dorothy Stratten. "Dorothy Stratten was a sweet, sensitive, vulnerable girl who was caught in something she couldn't control," said Curtis. "Getting to play Dorothy was a wonderful opportunity for me to grow, but it was a scary movie for me to make. I felt a great responsibility on my shoulders because I wanted to capture Dorothy's inner beauty."

Although the Dorothy Stratten story contained many horrific elements and lots of sad irony, Curtis didn't see any resemblance between *Death of a Centerfold* and her previous scream queen roles. Curtis saw *Death of a Centerfold* as a tragic love story. "Don't forget, Paul Snider was the first person who ever told her, 'Honey, you could be something real big,'" said Curtis. "He loved her a lot in his own way. He made love to her a lot. I have a feeling they had a great sex life."

Although Curtis doesn't recall ever meeting Stratten, Hollywood being a small place, their paths did intersect. The most notable example of this is the fact that Stratten had guest-starred on an episode of *Buck Rogers*, playing Miss Cosmos in an episode entitled *Cruise Ship to the Stars*, that aired on December 27, 1979, almost two months after the airing of Curtis' *Unchained Woman* episode.

Like Curtis, Stratten had, by the age of twenty, begun an acting career in low budget exploitation films and would be trumpeted by publicists as "one of the film goddesses of the new decade." In 1979, Stratten starred in the films *Autumn Born* and *Skatetown, U.S.A.*. In 1980, Stratten starred in what would become her best-known film, the science-fiction spoof *Galaxina*, in which Stratten was cast as a robust robot. Ironically, *Galaxina* was shot by Dean Cundey, one of Curtis' closest colleagues. Stratten's last film, *They All Laughed*, would be belatedly-released in 1981. Sadly, what all of these films revealed was that Stratten—although clearly a beautiful, lively young girl—couldn't act and lacked a compelling screen presence.

The connections between Curtis and Stratten aren't as distant as they first appear, although the films Stratten made before her death were certainly a grade below Curtis' post-*Halloween* scream queen roles, both commercially and technically. Just as Curtis was typecast as a scream queen in her quest to become a serious actress, Stratten found herself typecast as a *Playboy* centerfold in her pursuit of an acting career. The dreary and exploitative films Stratten starred in before her death reflected this.

Who knows, maybe there were times when Dorothy Stratten was sitting in the Playboy mansion, and looking out the window and thinking of Jamie Lee Curtis, and wondering if she could have a career like Curtis'- as modest as Curtis' own film career was by 1980—someday. For Stratten, Curtis' acting career, even as represented in schlock like *Prom Night* and *Terror Train*, certainly would've represented a step-up from the pornography, the seedy car shows, the roller discos, and Grade Z trash like *Autumn Born* and *Galaxina* that defined Stratten's own brief film career.

As Curtis has always pointed out, she was never sexually- exploited in any of her horror films. Dorothy Stratten's entire life was full of exploitation, not just from Snider but from everybody. In this regard, Curtis and Stratten were both looking for something better, although Curtis was much farther ahead in this pursuit than Stratten ever would be, and there's a sense that this would be true even if Stratten had lived. Where would Dorothy Stratten be today if she had lived? Where are all former *Playboy* playmates?

In terms of doing research on Stratten, Curtis didn't have to look far, whether it be the countless tabloid articles about Stratten's death or, more directly, her father, Tony Curtis. Tony Curtis had been a frequent guest at Hugh Hefner's Playboy Mansion at the time Stratten was a playmate, even dating a playmate himself, and had gotten to know Stratten a little bit. "My father was dating a playmate at the time of the murder and suicide," recalled Curtis. "I first heard Dorothy's story from him. She was a kind, gentle, considerate young woman. She wasn't stupid by any means, but she was naive."

Even though she dyed her hair blonde for the film, and was roughly the same height as Stratten, Curtis looked nothing like Stratten, a fact that Curtis was painfully aware of going into *Death of a Centerfold*'s filming. Ironically, the newly-blonde Curtis more closely resembled her mother, Janet Leigh, at this moment, in a way that had never been visible before. "Everyone said I had an uncanny resemblance to my mother when I went blonde," recalls Curtis who would undergo 36 costume changes in the film. "I took it as quite a compliment."

Filming on *Death of a Centerfold* commenced in June of 1981 on a tight twenty day schedule in and around Los Angeles. Aside from marking the beginning of Curtis' post-scream queen career, *Death of a Centerfold* was also the first time Curtis was paired with a female director in the form of British-born film-maker Gabrielle Beaumont. Beaumont, a television veteran, also had a horror background, having directed the 1980 demonic-tinged horror film *The Godsend* (1).

In terms of casting, actor Bruce Weitz was cast opposite Curtis in the key role of Paul Snider, Dorothy Stratten's husband and eventual murderer. Veteran actor Mitchell Ryan was cast as Hugh Hefner and, in perhaps the film's most interesting casting choice, Robert Reed, best known as the star of *The Brady Bunch* television series, was cast as David Palmer, a film-maker who falls in love with Dorothy Stratten. "David Palmer" was an obvious pseudonym for film-maker Peter Bogdanovich (2).

During the filming of *Death of a Centerfold*, Curtis and the film-makers were faced with much resistance from various forces who felt the project would be defamatory and exploitative. *Playboy* was angry, Hugh Hefner was angry, Peter Bogdanovich was angry, lawsuits were threatened. "They were all angry that we were doing the film and they all threatened to sue us," recalls Pompian. "Tom Tannenbaum at MGM was great because he would talk to these people and explain that what we were really trying to do was tell a genuine tragic story that was very sympathetic to Dorothy."

Faced with little or no cooperation from anyone associated with Dorothy Stratten or *Playboy*, the film-makers had to be creative in terms of portraying Dorothy Stratten's short-lived career. The most notable example of this was in terms of recreating the iconic Playboy mansion, a very key place in Dorothy Stratten's career and life. "Recreating the Playboy mansion in the film was our biggest challenge and eventually we filmed at the old Marion Davies estate in Santa Monica which worked out pretty well," recalls Pompian. "We tried to make the estate look as good and as splendorous as we could, but it was really hard. As we started filming, people who knew Dorothy slowly came out of the woodwork and started contacting us and telling us stories about Dorothy."

One of the biggest challenges Curtis faced in terms of portraying Dorothy Stratten was getting her hair to match that of Stratten's. Just as Curtis' hair had been too short for the filming of *Halloween II*, it was now, despite its blonde appearance, too thin. "Getting Jamie's hair to match Dorothy's was a big challenge," recalls Pompian. "Jamie had dyed her hair, but Jamie's hair was naturally thin and brown while Dorothy had unusually thick hair, so we spent many hours working on Jamie's hair for the film."

Curtis' biggest challenge in playing Dorothy Stratten was the emotional part, and Curtis found herself haunted by Stratten throughout filming. Curtis also questioned whether she could do justice to Stratten's memory, so much so that Janet Leigh was called to the set to give her daughter a pep talk. "I think Jamie was haunted by Dorothy and filled with doubts throughout the filming," recalls Pompian. "Janet Leigh came to the set and she talked to Jamie and she shared some of her own acting experiences with Jamie and that gave Jamie the confidence to get through the film. I could see they were very close and that Jamie looked at Janet not just as a mother and a friend but also as an acting teacher."

Another challenge for Curtis was that *Death of a Centerfold* required the actress to do her first on-screen nudity, for the scenes where Stratten is posing for the camera. This is where having a female director helped Curtis, who would grow to trust Gabrielle Beaumont during filming. "Jamie and Gabrielle really bonded during filming and spent a lot of time together," recalls Pompian. "Jamie really trusted Gabrielle and that made the difficult scenes easier for Jamie than they would've been had the director been a man. Jamie was a real treat to work with. Jamie was very unaffected and grounded for someone from such a famous Hollywood family, Hollywood royalty."

Curtis' nudity, which would only be later visible in a European theatrical version of the film, in *Death of a Centerfold* consists of about thirty seconds of Curtis' bare left breast. Curtis shot the scene in one take on a closed set with just Curtis, Beaumont, and a few other crew members present. Additionally, Curtis requested that the set be refrigerated in order to make her breasts look firmer in the shot. "I wanted it cold if they were going to be shot standing up straight," said Curtis. "They're breasts; everyone has them. I wasn't nervous in front of the crew at all, but in front of the camera, I was terrible. I went back to my room and had a good cry."

The film also required Curtis to perform several dramatic scenes with actor Bruce Weitz, who played Paul Snider, as well as several kissing scenes with actor Robert Reed who played Peter Bogdanovich alter-ego David Palmer. Reed, who later died of complications from AIDS in 1992, was a well- known homosexual in Hollywood in addition to being an underrated dramatic actor. "Robert and Jamie got along very well together during filming, and Robert was a very smart actor," recalls Pompian. "Bruce and Jamie worked well together, but Bruce and Gabrielle hated each other, and Bruce actually walked off the set for several days. They never spoke to each other and it was very tense. I told Bruce that he either had to fly right or take off and we didn't have any problems after that."

In retrospect, all of Curtis' trepidations about playing Dorothy Stratten stemmed from the fact that she didn't think she was beautiful enough to play the role. This is the same lack of confidence that plagued Dorothy Stratten and made her susceptible to someone like Paul Snider, the only person who ever looked at her and told she was beautiful, that she could be a star.

Before she was murdered, Stratten had tried to sever ties with Snider which drove Snider to murder her. Curtis identified with Stratten's relationship with Snider, not in terms of the violence which Curtis had never experienced in any of her relationships, but in terms of the challenge of trying to end a relationship. Earlier in 1981, Curtis had broken up with then-fiance Ray Hutcherson. "I remember how difficult it was for Dorothy to break up with her boyfriend because she didn't want to hurt him," recalled Curtis. "I'm very much the same way."

Death of a Centerfold: The Dorothy Stratten Story was broadcast on November 1, 1981 on NBC, on the same week that NBC broadcast *Halloween*, and the same week that *Halloween II* was released into theaters. *Death of a Centerfold* drew good ratings and was, along with *Halloween*, one of the top-rated programs for the week. Reviews were lukewarm. "The film drew big ratings and it was one of the most successful things MGM did during that period," recalls Pompian. "This was back in an era where the Movies of the Week were still big, and there were no cable channels, and you could have a movie get a 35 share. Nowadays that wouldn't happen."

Death of a Centerfold: The Dorothy Stratten Story is a competent, meat-and-potatoes, straightforward, workmanlike document of Dorothy Stratten's life and death that mostly succeeds at detailing Stratten's brief career without being exploitative or sleazy. The message is that Dorothy Stratten was a nice girl, an awkward and gangly girl, who didn't know how beautiful she was, and that her murder was a tragedy. She should be still alive today, and it's a tragedy she isn't, but these things happen. The film portrays this reasonably effectively and basically fulfills its remit of chronicling Dorothy Stratten's last hours. It gets the job done.

If Jamie Lee Curtis' performance in *Death of a Centerfold* and the film itself both seem somewhat lacking in retrospect, it's in comparison to the later 1983 feature film version of the Dorothy Stratten story, *Star 80*. *Star 80*, which was directed by the legendary Bob Fosse and which starred Mariel Hemingway in the role of Dorothy Stratten, was a brilliant, electrifying, searing portrait of Dorothy Stratten's life and death. Fosse's film also contained a powerhouse performance by Eric Roberts in the role of Paul Snider (3).

Mariel Hemingway, who's five-foot-eleven and had previously been nominated for a Best Supporting Actress Oscar for the 1979 Woody Allen film *Manhattan*, gives a brilliant, haunting performance as Dorothy Stratten. Hemingway's performance, and the film itself, makes the viewer feel so much sympathy for Dorothy Stratten that it's almost impossible to watch the film's climax when Snider, in a truly powerful performance by Eric Roberts, blasts Stratten in the face with a shotgun.

This isn't to suggest that Curtis is, or was, any less of an actress than Mariel Hemingway, but that perhaps Curtis was just all wrong for the part of Dorothy Stratten and that no amount of Curtis' effort and determination would suffice. Hemingway so perfectly captures Stratten's personality and physicality in *Star 80* that it's as if she quite simply is Dorothy Stratten. It's as if Hemingway didn't have to try to play Dorothy Stratten whereas Curtis' performance in *Death of a Centerfold* comes across as somewhat of a forced creation, a patchwork, a square peg in a round hole.

In *Star 80*, Mariel Hemingway looks like a girl who worked at a Dairy Queen, while Curtis, who was twenty-two when *Death of a Centerfold* was filmed, appears not as a young girl but as a young woman who looks like she's been in Hollywood all her life. This is where the Laurie Strode character would've served Curtis well as Curtis' eyes lack the sense of awe and discovery that undoubtedly overwhelmed Stratten when she first arrived in Los Angeles. Although Curtis, as always, creates a believable and sympathetic character in *Death of a Centerfold*, it feels like she's playing someone else, someone older, not aw-shucks, wide-eyed Dorothy Stratten.

In terms of advancing her acting career, *Death of a Centerfold* didn't have the effect of turning Curtis into an A-list actress in Hollywood, but it was a necessary first step in a long journey. Curtis took the role of Dorothy Stratten to show Hollywood that she was capable of doing non-horror roles and in that narrow scope, the film was successful. Steven Spielberg wasn't beating down Curtis' door, but at least Curtis now had a dramatic acting reel to show people. "The part showed me in a different light," says Curtis. "I wanted to show I could do more than scream and look scared as I had in my other movies."

Despite having made six feature films between 1978 and 1981, Curtis was in many ways starting over again in terms of establishing herself as a credible and serious actress. In many ways, *Death of a Centerfold* can be viewed, in relation to Curtis' post-scream queen career, in the same way that *Halloween* is viewed in relation to Curtis' scream queen career. It was a beginning, the introduction of a new Jamie Lee Curtis. "I think *Death of a Centerfold* provided a good career stimulus for Jamie and helped to boost her into major features like *Trading Places* and so on," says Pompian. "I think the film got her to that next place in her career."

Perhaps the greatest significance of *Death of a Centerfold,* in terms of Curtis' acting career, is that it made her into a most unlikely sex symbol. The film, along with subsequent film roles, would help to transform Curtis from the Queen of Scream to The Body. "All of a sudden I was a sex girl," recalled Curtis. "All of a sudden people discovered I had breasts. I mean, it was wild."

Curtis' next genre appearance came in 1982 when Curtis hosted and narrated the film *Coming Soon*, a documentary showcasing scenes and trailers from Universal Studios' greatest horror films. The film was directed by John Landis and produced by Curtis' former press agent, Mick Garris. "I'd been developing a romantic sex comedy project and Jamie had agreed to play a small part in it but the project fell through, which I think was a good thing for all of us," recalls Garris. "John Landis and I both knew Jamie, and he just called her up and asked her to do *Coming Soon*. I was doing publicity at Universal at the time, and came up with the idea of selling Universal as "the" horror studio again by doing a documentary look at their horror trailers. Jamie, as the daughter of the star of *Psycho*, and the reigning scream queen at the time, was the perfect choice."

In promoting *Coming Soon*, Curtis paid a visit to the old *Psycho* set at Universal, taking a smiling pose on the steps of the hill leading up to the Bates house. This would be as close as Curtis would get to the *Psycho* franchise for although Curtis would briefly circle *Psycho II*, which *Roadgames* director Richard Franklin would be developing, both Curtis and Franklin wisely agreed that this would be a bad idea. "There are two things I'm trying to avoid emphasizing in my career now—my parents and my horror films—and here they were together, a classic horror film that my mother starred in," said Curtis who'd also been haunted by childhood memories of how her mother had received numerous stalker threats following *Psycho*'s release. "It was time to move on."

Curtis had first been approached by Universal about *Psycho II* in the Fall of 1981 when the sequel's proposed storyline would've had Curtis playing a relative to her mother's character, something Curtis regarded as "the silliest idea I ever heard." The rest of the initial storyline had Martin Balsam returning as the twin brother of his slain character and Vera Miles reprising her character from the 1960 film who subsequentally buys the Bates Motel in the sequel. Two years earlier, when Curtis was loathe to reject any film project that came her way, Curtis might've agreed to such an insipid idea. By 1982, however, Curtis was determined to move as far away from the horror genre as possible, no matter the offer.

Other than narrating *Coming Soon*, Curtis avoided any temptation to return to the horror genre, to scream queen roles, during this period. Meanwhile, in 1982, the *Halloween* series continued—sort of—with *Halloween III: Season of the Witch*, an in-name-only sequel to *Halloween II* that featured a new story and new set of characters. *Halloween III* marked the feature directing debut of Tommy Lee Wallace, who also wrote the film's script. *Halloween III* is probably most significant in that it would mark the last real teaming of the Carpenter-Hill unit.

Except for Jamie Lee Curtis. Although Carpenter, Hill, Barry Bernardi, Dean Cundey, Wallace, and many others returned for *Halloween III*, there were no discussions about Curtis returning. Laurie Strode was now gone, both in terms of *Halloween III*—whose story concerned an evil toy manufacturer—and from Jamie Lee Curtis' life (4). "I didn't ask Jamie to star in *Halloween III*," recalls Wallace. "That would've made no sense whatsoever, since the original plan was to create a whole new franchise each year, on the subject of All Hallow's Eve."

Curtis' work on *Coming Soon*, which was very much a tongue-in-cheek documentary and largely a promotional film for Universal, was significant in terms of Curtis' relationship with director John Landis. Landis was a big horror fan, and had recently directed 1981's ground-breaking horror-comedy *An American Werewolf in London*. In July of 1982, Landis began work on the doomed *Twilight Zone: The Movie*, after which Landis began casting and pre-production on *Trading Places*, a comedy film project with stars Dan Aykroyd and Eddie Murphy attached.

In addition to his own genre credits, Landis was a big horror fan and a big fan of Curtis'. Landis recognized, as John Carpenter had, that Curtis had a lot of untapped potential. In the case of *Trading Places*, which would begin shooting in November of 1982 in New York City, this was comedy. When it came time to cast the part of Ophelia, a savvy, smart prostitute character, Landis brought Curtis in for an audition, liked her immediately, and gave her the part (5).

The part of Ophelia, and *Trading Places* itself, represented a career-changing moment in Curtis' life. In terms of breaking free from her scream queen past, and establishing that she could do good things in other genres, nothing could've been better for Curtis than *Trading Places*. Curtis' sense of humor was a quality that had been visible to almost everyone who'd worked with her on her horror films, but it was unknown to audiences. *Trading Places*, which was later released in June of 1983, not only kick-started Curtis' mainstream film career, it established her as a screen comedienne.

Trading Places was also significant in that it was the first feature film in which Curtis showed nudity—not counting the unseen footage from *Death of a Centerfold*—which in this case was her breasts. It's kind of ironic that the first time Curtis showed nudity on-screen was in a big-budget Hollywood comedy like *Trading Places* instead of one of her horror films because usually the opposite is the case with young actresses. With *Trading Places*, the nudity was largely irrelevant. The success of the film, which would gross $90 million domestically, and the impact Curtis made in the film amongst audiences and critics, did wonders in terms of removing any exploitation labels that might still have been attached to Curtis at this time.

Trading Places also resulted in Curtis' first major acting award recognition when she was nominated for a prestigious British Film Academy Award (BAFTA) in the Best Supporting Actress category. Even more surprising was that at the 1984 BAFTA Awards ceremony, in March of 1984, Curtis won the British Oscar for *Trading Places*, beating out Maureen Lipman for *Educating Rita*, Rosemary Harris for *The Ploughman's Lunch*, and Teri Garr for *Tootsie*. Curtis' co-star in *Trading Places*, Denholm Elliott, won the Best Supporting Actor award.

The award was a great triumph for Curtis in her acting career. Having said that, the BAFTA Awards always have to be taken with a grain of salt given their notorious track record for taking a cheerfully contrarian position to their American counterpart. At the 1984 ceremony, this was evidenced by the fact that the rather middling British comedy *Educating Rita* won the Best Film award over the great comedy *Tootsie*. As well, Curtis' competition in the Best Supporting Actress category wasn't exactly top-drawer, given that she was only up against three other actresses, two of whom, Harris and Lipman, had received scant attention stateside.

Still, the BAFTA award was a great personal triumph for Curtis who felt that the award, and the enthusiastic audience and critical reaction to *Trading Places*, validated her as an actress. Unfortunately, since *Trading Places* came out in June of 1983, a dead zone for films in terms of attracting Academy Award buzz, Curtis had little chance of receiving an Academy Award nomination and, not surprisingly, she wasn't nominated (6).

Curtis' triumph in *Trading Places* gave her tremendous confidence, the same type of confidence boost she'd felt after the first day of filming on *Halloween* when Carpenter had called her and told her how wonderful she was. After *Trading Places*, Curtis knew she was capable of doing good acting in a good film, and she also felt that she was good.

The next genre connection in Curtis' acting career, following the end of *Trading Places'* filming in January of 1983, would coincide with what would end up being probably the best performance, BAFTA Award notwithstanding, of Curtis' early post-scream queen career. This would be *Love Letters*, a low budget drama that would be produced by horror legend Roger Corman and written and directed by Amy Holden Jones, a young film-maker whose only previous directing experience had been on the infamous 1982 slasher film *Slumber Party Massacre*. Like Curtis, Jones—who'd begun her career working as an editor for Corman—was also looking for something better.

Love Letters was about a young woman at a crossroads in her life who discovers, through her recently-deceased mother's love letters, that her mother had been involved in a torrid love affair. The young woman, Anna, learns that her mother had carried on the affair for years, cheating on Anna's father whom Anna despises. As Anna reads her mother's love letters, she becomes infatuated with her mother's affair, and the very idea of affairs, and Anna soon begins a passionate affair with a married photographer.

Curtis read the script for *Love Letters* in early 1983, right after she'd finished work on *Trading Places*. Curtis loved the script, as did every other actress who read Jones' script. Although *Love Letters* was going to be very much an independent, low-budget project, Jones' script attracted a lot of interest from various actresses. If Curtis wanted the part, she would have to fight for it, even though the part only paid $25,000, a figure that business-savvy producer Corman set as his limit for what he would pay the film's female lead.

Curtis was prepared to fight for the part of Anna, and she did, but not before actress Meg Tilly had shown interest in the project. Tilly had just finished shooting *The Big Chill* as well as, ironically enough, *Psycho II* where she'd played the female lead role that Curtis had been briefly considered for. Curtis hadn't been interested in *Psycho II*, but was passionate about *Love Letters*. Curtis sensed that the project could be her dramatic acting breakthrough and that the $25,000 salary was insignificant in that this role would be worth countless times more in terms of credibility.

The problem for first choice Meg Tilly was that Tilly's agent wanted $30,000, more than what Corman would pay, and this opened the door for Curtis who met with Jones and secured the role. "Meg Tilly was wonderful, and she did an excellent reading for me, but she'd just done *The Big Chill* and she wanted too much money," recalls Jones. "Both Meg and Jamie read very well, but I think Jamie read better, and she was very determined to do the film. Having said that, if *Trading Places* had come out before we shot *Love Letters*, there's no way we would've gotten Jamie for $25,000. Jamie wasn't considered a big star at this point in the sense that casting Jamie in a serious drama at this point in her career would've been like casting Neve Campbell in a drama in the 1990s."

Since *Trading Places* hadn't been released by the time *Love Letters* began filming in the Spring of 1983, Curtis was still known mainly for her scream queen roles while Jones was the director of *Slumber Party Massacre*. Neither Curtis or Jones approached *Love Letters* with any preconceptions of each other. "Everyone loved the script I wrote so there was no discrimination because I did *Slumber Party Massacre*, and certainly not from Jamie," recalls Jones. "In terms of Jamie's horror career, the only movie I'd seen of hers was *Halloween*, and what I took from that film, in terms of Jamie as an actress, was that Jamie was a real person, vulnerable, complex, and of course I knew the great reputation of her mother, Janet Leigh."

Love Letters, which had a budget of $550,000, was filmed around Los Angeles and Venice, California, in the Spring of 1983 over the course of twenty days. For Curtis, the role of Anna was very demanding, not only because *Love Letters* was an intense drama, but because the script called for some graphic nudity as well as sex scenes. Much of the film was shot at Jones' own house which is Anna's house in the film. "Roger Corman told me I could make an art film as long as it had at least one of his trademark commercial elements which turned out to be nudity," recalls Jones. "Jamie was a real trooper about doing nude scenes in the film, and it was actually more difficult for me, being a young director, than it was for Jamie. I would describe Jamie as a very energetic and passionate lady, kind of effusive."

The film also made Curtis come to terms with her own strained relationship with father, Tony Curtis, since Jamie Lee Curtis' character, Anna, has an unhealthy relationship with her father in the film. "I think Jamie brought some of her own childhood difficulties to the film," says Jones. "She was just a very professional, proficient actress, and I felt like we kind of caught the bubble with Jamie on *Love Letters* in terms of her career just taking off at this point. She gave a luminous performance in the film."

Love Letters received a limited theatrical release in January of 1984 and although the film did little business, even by art-house standards, both the film and Curtis' performance received strong reviews. "The film didn't get a wide release because Roger didn't want to spend money on more prints because that would've cost more than the film itself, and the first review we got for the film was kind of lukewarm," recalls Jones. "Then Roger Ebert and Gene Siskel gave a great review and we started getting more great reviews, and great reviews for Jamie's performance. Roger Corman himself told me he loved the movie and he said it was one of the most beautiful films he'd seen or made." Roger Ebert in the *Chicago Sun-Times* wrote, "This role, side-by-side with Curtis' inspired comic acting in *Trading Places*, shows her with a range we never could've guessed from all her horror pictures."

With *Trading Places* and *Love Letters*, Curtis had knocked down most of the barriers her scream queen career had created. She'd proved, with these films, that she was both a fine comedic actress and a more-than-capable dramatic actress. It's both hypocritical and ironic that the two films that moved Curtis from scream queen to mainstream, *Trading Places* and *Love Letters*, both required nudity from Curtis while her horror films—which mainstream Hollywood considered to be so disreputable and sleazy—had never made such demands. "For five years, I was called an exploitation queen for doing horror films," recalled Curtis. "I never took my clothes off. I never swore, I never smoked dope. But I had every woman's group in the country after me. Then I do two movies in which I take my clothes off. And now I'm considered legit. You tell me where the morality is."

The closest brush Curtis had with genre-related material during this period came in the Fall of 1983 when director Brian De Palma approached Curtis about taking the female lead in his upcoming Hitchcockian suspense-thriller *Body Double*. Like Curtis, De Palma was also in the process of making a career transition, and *Body Double* would represent the director's unofficial swan-song from the suspense-thriller genre he'd demonstrated such mastery in before he would move on to big studio films like 1987's *The Untouchables*.

The *Body Double* role was that of a porn star named Holly Body who becomes implicated in murder. The film was both an homage to Hitchcock's *Vertigo* as well as a satire of B grade horror movies, two subjects—that being Hitchcock and horror—that Curtis was determined to leave in the dust. Curtis turned down the role which went to old friend Melanie Griffith who gave an electrifying performance in the film, earning a Golden Globe nomination for her performance which subsequently ignited Griffith's film career. For an actress like Curtis, who still wasn't in the position of being able to turn down good movie roles, the decision to reject *Body Double*—which turned out to be a rather brilliant thriller exercise—was a big mistake.

Just as Curtis' acting career was going through major adjustments between 1983 and 1984, so was her personal life. By the Spring of 1983,

Curtis had become engaged to production designer J. Michael Riva, but by the summer, their relationship had, quite amicably, ended (7). Curtis then began dating British new wave rocker Adam Ant who, by 1983, was enjoying minor pop stardom in America thanks to his 1982 hit *Goody Two Shoes*. By the Spring of 1984, Ant's heyday, along with his relationship with Curtis, who was now clear of drugs, would be over.

In May of 1984, while filming Columbia Pictures' *Perfect*, Curtis' first leading role in a big studio film, Curtis' life took a completely different turn when she spotted the May 24, 1984 issue of *Rolling Stone*. Pop star Cyndi Lauper was on the cover, but what got Curtis' attention was an article on the 1984 mockumentary comedy film *This is Spinal Tap* and a picture of the film's co-star and co-writer, Christopher Guest. Curtis instinctively told friend Debra Hill she was going to marry Guest who's a decade older than Curtis. In October of 1984, Guest would begin a one season stint as a performer and writer on *Saturday Night Live* (8).

What Curtis saw in Guest's *Rolling Stone* picture was a smirk, the same kind of smirk that Curtis had used for many years as a mask for her own self-consciousness regarding her physical appearance, especially her once crooked and greyish teeth. Curtis saw the same thing in Guest. "I told my friend Debra Hill, 'I'm going to marry that guy,'" recalled Curtis. "The smirk serves as a bit of a mask and I saw the same thing in Christopher, who I knew absolutely nothing about."

Curtis and Guest had their first date on July 2, 1984, and were married on December 18, 1984 at the home of mutual friend Rob Reiner, Guest's collaborator and director on *This is Spinal Tap*. Both Tony Curtis and Janet Leigh were in attendance, along with Curtis' older sister, Kelly, stepbrothers Benjamin and Nicholas, and stepsisters Alexandra and Allegra. In 1986, Curtis and Guest adopted a daughter, Annie, and in 1996, they would adopt a son, Thomas.

Perfect, the film Curtis was shooting when she saw her future husband, serves as a strong example of Curtis' durability and tenaciousness and the rocky path that Curtis would have to take to eventual mainstream Hollywood stardom. It was a starring role for Curtis—her first in a mainstream Hollywood studio production—opposite John Travolta who, by 1983, was still ranked as one of the top five box office draws in America despite disheveled recent efforts like *Staying Alive* and *Two of a Kind*, both of which had been released in 1983.

Perfect's director and co-writer was James Bridges, a serious film-maker who flirted with greatness in the 1970s after such triumphs as *The Paper Chase* (1973) and *The China Syndrome* (1979). Prior to *Perfect*, Bridges and Travolta had collaborated, quite successfully, on the 1981 honkytonk drama *Urban Cowboy*. *Perfect*, which was to be a satire of the then- booming fitness club industry, seemed like a sure-fire hit, and the perfect vehicle from which to turn Jamie Lee Curtis into a major Hollywood star.

Curtis was cast in the film as Jessie, a former Olympic athlete turned aerobics instructor who befriends, and eventually romances, Travolta's character, a hotshot *Rolling Stone* reporter who's doing an expose on the health club scene. Basically, *Perfect* was supposed to be "*Urban Cowboy* set in a fitness club," with Curtis in the Debra Winger role opposite Travolta. With all of these commercially-designed elements, *Perfect* seemed like a can't-miss enterprise, but the film would turn out to be as shallow and superficial as the subject it was supposed to be satirizing. *Perfect* would be anything but.

Perfect was released in June of 1985, accompanied by a vigorous promotional tie-in with the *Rolling Stone* publication, and was a commercial and critical failure. It was worse than that. The failure of *Perfect* sent Travolta's career into a decade-long hibernation until the actor's electrifying work in 1994's *Pulp Fiction* would resuscitate the icon back onto the A-list. *Perfect* knocked James Bridges out of the upper ranks of American directors, a fall that Bridges would never recover from.

In addition to critically-wounding Travolta, it could also be argued that *Perfect* brought the mid-1980s fitness craze back down to earth, much in the same way that 1978's *Sgt. Pepper's Lonely Hearts Club Band* had driven a stake through the 1970s and leveled The Bee Gees and Peter Frampton. *Perfect* was also a major embarrassment for *Rolling Stone*, and especially its founder Jann Wenner who was cast as Travolta's fictional editor in the film. *Perfect's* failure basically hurt everyone involved, and catastrophically so, except for Jamie Lee Curtis.

Somehow Curtis survived the experience of *Perfect* intact career-wise, largely unfazed from the film's bruising reception. In fact, the film actually served the purpose of branding Curtis as a legitimate sex symbol, for while film critics would mercilessly trash *Perfect*, almost all of them—especially the male critics—were won over by Curtis' sexy movements. Although *Perfect* virtually killed everyone it touched, it made Curtis into an unlikely but undeniable mid- 1980s sex symbol. The nickname "The Body" that Curtis had half-jokingly applied to herself at the end of her scream queen career was now legitimate.

The experience of *Perfect*, both the filming and the painful aftermath, was like a crash course for Curtis in terms of the rules of big-budget Hollywood film-making, especially in terms of inflated expectations. Although *Perfect*'s $12.9 million domestic gross didn't qualify the $19 million *Perfect* as a flop of *Heaven's Gate* proportions, *Perfect* had been expected to be one of 1985's big hits and thus was a colossal disappointment for its studio, Columbia Pictures. Curtis regards *Perfect* as one of her worst films. "It's an awful film," says Curtis. "With *Perfect*, I bought into the hype of what the film would do for my career if it had been a big hit. I had hope, and when the film died, it made me sad because I'd bought into the hype."

The fact that Curtis was able to survive *Perfect*, and even benefit from the disaster, is another example of Curtis' keen survival instincts that she'd learned from her early career and her Hollywood upbringing. It's also an example of how Curtis' film career has always kind of existed under the radar. Curtis' film career, her post-scream queen film career, has never been plagued with any dizzying highs or crushing lows. "When the movie deals with the little universe inside the health club, it's fascinating—especially when Jamie Lee Curtis is on-screen, because of her electrifying performance," (Roger Ebert, *Chicago Sun-Times*.)

Despite the success of *Trading Places* and the acclaim she'd received for *Love Letters*, Curtis knew that she would never be on the same plane as the elite, erudite circle of Hollywood actresses that included Sally Field, Jessica Lange, and Curtis' acting idol, the great Meryl Streep. She couldn't wait around for A-list directors to call her, because they weren't going to call her, and she had to take roles, and find roles, that other actresses wouldn't touch.

Curtis' choice of film projects in the mid to late 1980s reflects this. Following *Perfect*, Curtis would appear in small, intimate films such as *A Man in Love* (1987) and *Amazing Grace and Chuck* (1987). Curtis' biggest triumph of this period was her delightful comic turn as a sexy, smart thief in the 1988 British comic heist film *A Fish Called Wanda*. The film was a critical and commercial smash and earned Curtis both a British Academy Award (BAFTA) nomination, for Best Actress, as well as a Golden Globe nomination.

The Jamie Lee Curtis visible in these films, much like the Jamie Lee Curtis of today, is almost unrecognizable from the scream queen image that had existed less than a decade earlier. Physically, emotionally, every which way, there's a stark transformation here that's almost akin to an awkward, shy girl from high school who reappears at her ten year high school reunion as a completely transformed woman that none of her former classmates, the ones that made her life hell back in high school, can even recognize.

In 1981, when Curtis had departed her scream queen persona, she'd sought to change her image, and transform as an actress. By the end of the 1980s, this transformation is complete and is present in the performances she gave during this era which reveal a much more experienced and versatile actress. Jamie Lee Curtis' post-scream queen, post-1981 acting career had, by the end of the 1980s, been as successful as Curtis could've hoped for when she left the horror genre back in 1981.

seventeen

WHATEVER HAPPENED TO LAURIE STRODE?

A lthough Jamie Lee Curtis didn't appear in any horror films in the remainder of the 1980s, her fingerprints were still all over the genre she'd played such a major role in.

In 1988, the *Halloween* film franchise was resurrected with the arrival of *Halloween 4: The Return of Michael Myers*. Filmed in Salt Lake City, Utah, the sequel contained the premise that Laurie Strode had, following the events of *Halloween II*, been killed in a car accident, along with her husband, and that Laurie Strode's daughter, named Jamie Lloyd, had been sent to live with a foster family in Haddonfield, Illinois (1).

Meanwhile, Michael Myers, comatose since *Halloween II*'s explosive ending ten years earlier, awakes and returns to Haddonfield to track down his blood relative. Dr. Sam Loomis, also a survivor of the explosion at the end of *Halloween II*, returns to hunt him down, as did actor Donald Pleasence, the only returning cast member from either *Halloween* or *Halloween II* to return in *Halloween 4: The Return of Michael Myers*.

Other than Donald Pleasence, and executive producer Moustapha Akkad, who'd recently bought back the rights to the *Halloween* series from Dino De Laurentiis, the *Halloween 4* production had no link to Curtis or any other members of the Carpenter-Hill unit. *Halloween 4*, which was directed by Dwight H. Little, is of course completely unnecessary but on its own terms, the film is respectable to its source material and features sure direction, and even contains qualities that could be interpreted as resembling style and technique.

Halloween 4 grossed $17 million domestically upon its release in 1988 which was a respectable performance, even though *Halloween 4*'s $5 million budget was twice the budgets of both 1981's *Halloween II* and 1982's *Halloween III: Season of the Witch*. *Halloween 4* was quickly followed-up by 1989's *Halloween 5: The Revenge of Michael Myers*, an awful and stupid sequel that definitely ranks as the worst film in the entire *Halloween* film series. Good thing that Laurie Strode wasn't alive to see this.

Jamie Lee Curtis—like John Carpenter and Debra Hill, both of whom had sold their remaining stakes in the *Halloween* series prior to the making of *Halloween 4*—was oblivious to the *Halloween* sequels and has never seen either *Halloween 4* or *Halloween 5*. For Curtis, the *Halloween* films were in the past, ancient history, and Curtis was definitely looking to the future.

In August of 1988, two months before *Halloween 4*'s October release, Curtis began filming on *Blue Steel*, a psychological-thriller that many critics, most notably Roger Ebert, would ultimately compare to *Halloween* in terms of the film's form and technique, if not the film's ultimate achievement.

In *Blue Steel*, which Curtis shot on location in New York City, Curtis was cast as Megan Turner, a rookie New York cop who becomes the object of the affections of a psychotic commodities trader, played by Ron Silver (2). Early in the film, Silver sees Curtis shoot and kill an armed robber in a supermarket and becomes completely unhinged by the experience. When no gun is found at the scene, the gun having been snatched by Silver's character who bears the cryptic name of Eugene Hunt, Turner's put on suspension. The cat and mouse game begins.

The Eugene Hunt character, for whom Curtis becomes the object of his death fantasy, uses the gun to commit a series of brutal murders. He also carves Megan Turner's name into the bullets which briefly implicates her in the murders. Like Michael Myers, Eugene Hunt is a relentless killer who will stop at nothing to force an eventual and unavoidable fatal confrontation with Megan Turner which is manifested in the form of a brutal and extended shootout that ends the film. "Squint a little to see the structure lurking beneath the details, and *Blue Steel* is a sophisticated update of *Halloween*, the movie that first made Jamie Lee Curtis a star. She plays the competent, strong woman who finally has to defend herself because nobody else can. Her life is endangered by a man who seems unstoppable, un-killable: No matter what happens to him, he picks himself up, pulls himself together, and continues his inexorable pursuit," (Roger Ebert, *Chicago Sun-Times*.)

Eugene Hunt, unlike Michael Myers, isn't unstoppable; he's a meek little man in public who harbors a deep sickness. He's made of flesh and blood, which is very apparent when Megan Turner blows him away at the end of the film. Whereas Michael Myers operates under no bonds, no moral or social constraints, Eugene Hunt has enough discipline and foresight to trap Megan Turner in situations where she looks bad and he looks innocent, where she's always portrayed in the worst possible light. In the tradition of the Hitchcockian Wrongfully Accused protagonist, no one believes Megan Turner in the film until it's too late. Unlike Michael Myers, Eugene Hunt doesn't want to kill Megan Turner but rather kill for her, and maybe his ultimate fantasy is to be killed by her.

The clearest similarity between *Blue Steel* and *Halloween* is between Megan Turner and Laurie Strode. Like Laurie, Megan is a sexually-repressed young woman which makes her initially vulnerable to Eugene Hunt's charms. Early in the film, she seems willing to go to bed with him after their first date, until he reveals his true identity to her. Like Laurie, Megan's the only one who has the vision of evil, who can see the evil lurking in the atmosphere.

Although Megan Turner does need the help of a man in the film, in the form of a superior officer—and eventual love interest—played by Clancy Brown, it's Megan Turner who must confront Eugene Hunt at the end of *Blue Steel*, just like Laurie Strode had to confront Michael Myers in the *Halloween* films, with the invaluable support of Dr. Sam Loomis.

Perhaps *Blue Steel* and Megan Turner represent an older vision of Laurie Strode, ten years later. Is it hard to imagine poor Laurie Strode going into law enforcement? Although Curtis was on the eve of her thirtieth birthday when *Blue Steel* began filming, she's effortlessly-believable as an insecure, wet-behind-the-ears cop who's gone directly from the academy to the mean New York Streets. "The film is about a woman cop, so obviously there's a feminist statement in it simply by the nature of there being a woman cop," recalled Curtis. "I never made a decision about a role with feminism as a criterion. I read the story and thought it was very exciting."

The role also required Curtis to fire a gun, to shoot to kill, and although she fired a gun in *Halloween II*, during that ridiculous sequence where Laurie Strode miraculously blinds Michael Myers with two straight shots, playing a cop was different. Curtis spent time at a shooting range prior to filming, in preparation for the film's grueling shootout that closes the film. "I wanted to be convincing in the areas of technical agility and technical knowledge, so I spent time at a shooting range trying to learn the proper techniques of combat shooting and regular standing shooting and marksmanship," said Curtis. "I found that the sport is quite interesting to learn once the moral issue is out of the way."

Blue Steel was directed by Kathryn Bigelow, a former painting student turned film-maker with an obsession for violence. Her previous film was the critically-acclaimed but commercially-ignored 1987 vampire western *Near Dark*. Bigelow, who would marry fellow film-maker James Cameron in August of 1989, was drawn to Curtis by Curtis' uncanny ability to portray ordinariness and vulnerability. It was also Bigelow's belief that Megan Turner should be a somewhat androgynous character in the film, and this made Curtis an ideal choice given that androgyny was one of the key ingredients of Curtis' unconventional— yet undeniable—appeal. "I felt that it was really important that the Megan Turner character had an androgynous quality," recalls Bigelow. "I saw Megan Turner as an Everyman hero as opposed to a Dirty Harry character who's instinctively ready to shoot."

Blue Steel marked Curtis' second feature collaboration with a female director, after working with Amy Holden Jones on *Love Letters* (3). Unlike the *Love Letters* experience, Bigelow and Curtis had creative differences throughout *Blue Steel*'s filming. "I didn't have any confidence in Kathryn when we were making it," recalled Curtis. "It was a very difficult movie, a departure for me. She had a very specific vision. It's very hard for me to buy into someone else's vision because I have such strong opinions and I didn't really trust her all that much. I was quite apprehensive about what this film was going to be until I saw it."

Curtis finally screened *Blue Steel* in early 1990, just prior to the film's release in March of 1990. The release had been delayed for more than a year because the film's original distributor, Vestron Pictures, had collapsed and MGM/UA had since taken ownership of the film. After watching *Blue Steel*, Curtis was ecstatic about the film, her performance, and Bigelow's vision. When the hastily-arranged screening was over, Curtis triumphantly pumped her fist in the air. "I didn't know what we had, I had no idea," said Curtis. "Kathryn is a very stylized director and she likes to shoot in tight close-ups which is very hard on actors because you can't use your tools as an actor, you can't use body language. It was a very challenging process. I wish I had gone to dallies; I wish I had joined her instead of fought her. I really liked the film."

Blue Steel unquestionably represents one of Jamie Lee Curtis' finest screen performances, of any genre. In Megan Turner, Curtis creates a character of bottomless vulnerability who effortlessly grabs the audience's sympathy as she confronts the growing evil that surrounds her world. This is perfectly embodied in the film's final scene where a beaten and exhausted Megan Turner, having just vanquished her tormentor, sits in a police car and just wilts like a wounded flower, body and mind completely numb from the whole ordeal. As with Laurie Strode, the viewer is left to wonder what's left of Megan Turner, and whether she'll able to pick up the pieces of her life, or if the pieces have been irretrievably altered and broken.

Blue Steel was released in March of 1990 with a surprisingly strong marketing push from MGM/UA, given the company's own weakened fortunes at this time. *Blue Steel* was greeted with tepid box office along with lukewarm to modestly-enthusiastic critical notices, most of which stated that Curtis' performance was the strongest ingredient in the film. Still, *Blue Steel's* paltry $8 million domestic gross was a major disappointment for Curtis and probably more-so for Bigelow for whom a lack of commercial acceptance would haunt her entire career and dull the impact of her sometimes brilliant and visionary work (4).

Strangely enough, the failure of *Blue Steel*, much like *Perfect*, had some unintended benefits for Curtis' acting career. Despite the film's failure, the image of gun-toting Megan Turner lodged in the public consciousness and served to both redesign and reinforce Curtis' genre credentials. *Blue Steel* was Curtis' first foray into the thriller genre since 1981's *Halloween II* and if there was any doubt that Curtis had evolved into a mature and older actress, the sight of a gun-wielding Jamie Lee Curtis had certainly put that to rest. More importantly, *Blue Steel* would lead, indirectly, to the next professional high-point in Curtis' acting career.

This most definitely wasn't Curtis' next genre appearance which was *Mother's Boys*, a hysterical, ludicrous, wildly- overwrought psychological thriller that was barely released in the Spring of 1994. The most notable thing about *Mother's Boys*, in terms of Curtis' acting career, is that it represented her first, and last, femme fatale, villainess role.

In the film, Curtis plays Judith "Jude" Madigan, an emotionally-troubled, possibly schizophrenic woman who returns to reclaim the husband and children she abandoned years earlier. Jude Madigan ruthlessly sets out to eliminate anything, and anyone, that stands in her way of achieving this rather unrealistic goal. Despite a distinguished cast—almost disarmingly so for an otherwise shaky production—that included Peter Gallagher, Vanessa Redgrave, and Joanne Whalley-Kilmer, *Mother's Boys* is full of implausibilities. This is most striking in the film's basic premise—Jude's quest to retake her family by any means necessary—which is fundamentally flawed and unbelievable.

It's impossible to believe that Jude Madigan, played with icy menace by a bleach-blonde Curtis, could've ever functioned as a wife and mother given her emotional state. The character is so underwritten—and so hysterical and over-the-top—that it's impossible to take the character, or the film, seriously.

Mother's Boys was a risk for Curtis, a wild departure, and it's kind of fun to watch her play such a crazy character like this, but for the wrong reasons. Watching Curtis in *Mother's Boys* is to watch an actress jump off a cliff in terms of Curtis' relentlessly high-voltage performance in the film. Sometimes such a risk can pay off, as was the case with *Love Letters*, and sometimes it's a disaster which was definitely the case with *Mother's Boys*.

Mother's Boys was a failure on every level, and if Curtis is guilty of overexertion in her performance, the rest of the film fails long before she does (5). "That was a tough shoot," said Curtis. "I felt a real scary vibe on that film. It's too bad it did not hit the mark."

Still, jumping off a cliff can be a good thing if an actress can catch lightning in a bottle in terms of finding the right character in the right project with the right director who can harness her energy. All of these elements would converge in 1994's *True Lies*, an action-adventure epic from writer-director James Cameron in which Curtis was cast opposite then-action superstar—and sometime comedic actor—Arnold Schwarzenegger.

Cameron had met Curtis during the filming of *Blue Steel*, at a time when Cameron had been eying Curtis for a film project. Cameron, who'd gotten divorced from *Blue Steel* director Kathryn Bigelow in 1991, was enamored with Curtis' mixture of physicality and sexiness. *Blue Steel* hadn't been such a failure after all.

For Curtis, the role of Helen Tasker—the neglected wife of Schwarzenegger's super-spy who eventually becomes entangled in her husband's work—represented another career-changing moment in terms of providing the perfect showcase for the combination of Curtis' comedic skills, her physicality, and her sexiness.

With *True Lies*, Curtis—who would describe Helen Tasker as "a grown-up Laurie Strode"—had finally found a project that had, in her mind, supplanted *Halloween* in terms of career significance. "I think *True Lies* is my best film, and James Cameron is the best director that I've ever worked with," says Curtis. "He was a fantastic director, and I think *True Lies* is a comic masterpiece, a great film."

True Lies, which had a budget of $110 million, is still the biggest film Curtis has ever made, and the most successful, eventually grossing $364 million worldwide upon its release in the summer of 1994. Although the success of *True Lies* was no doubt largely attributable to the surefire Cameron-Schwarzenegger connection, the film showed that Curtis could hold her own in a blockbuster. This was validated in 1995 when Curtis won a Golden Globe award for her performance in *True Lies*, in the comedy/musical category. Unfortunately, the Golden Globe award didn't translate into Curtis' first Oscar nomination (6).

Despite the success of *True Lies*, the triumph strangely didn't transfer momentum into the next phase of Jamie Lee Curtis' film career. Maybe this was because Curtis was now in her mid-thirties, and was approaching middle-age status in Hollywood. Curtis was no longer a young woman, and even a character like Megan Turner—the rookie cop from *Blue Steel*—seemed like a distant memory. By the mid-1990s, Curtis was entering a phase of her career where she was now being viewed more as a mother figure, an older actress, rather than a heroine. This is the same thing that had happened to Janet Leigh in the mid-1960s.

Whatever the reasons, whether it be Hollywood ageism or bad career choices, Curtis' follow-ups to *True Lies* were disappointing, both commercially and critically. In 1996, Curtis starred in the domestic comedy *House Arrest*, a flop, and then followed that up with 1997's *Fierce Creatures*, an underwhelming non-sequel reunion of the cast members from *A Fish Called Wanda* that would be derailed by production problems, namely conflict amongst Curtis and her fellow cast members.

As happy an experience as 1988's *A Fish Called Wanda* had been for Curtis and co-stars John Cleese, Kevin Kline, and Michael Palin, it was the opposite with *Fierce Creatures*. This lack of chemistry, lack of togetherness, is evident in the film. *Fierce Creatures* bombed.

Through all of the ups and downs in Jamie Lee Curtis' acting career, it's been Curtis' genre career—her scream queen identity—that has been her bedrock. After the post-*True Lies* flops, Curtis was offered the lead role, with her name above the title and everything, in *Virus*, a $75 million science-fiction thriller about a ship and its crew that are haunted by an alien entity. Curtis began filming on *Virus* in North Carolina in the Spring of 1997. *Virus*, which still represents the most expensive film that Curtis has ever top-lined, certainly appeared like a surefire hit given its impressive pedigree. Based on an acclaimed Dark Horse Comics series, *Virus* marked the feature directing debut of Academy Award-winning visual effects legend John Bruno, a disciple of James Cameron, and was produced by Gale Anne Hurd, who was formerly married to Cameron and whose genre credits included such classics as *The Abyss*, *Aliens* and *The Terminator*.

Despite these impressive credits, and a cast that Included William Baldwin and Donald Sutherland, *Virus* would turn out to be the worst experience of Curtis' acting career. The production, which would eventually last a brutal and whopping five months, was plagued by logistical problems and a scorched earth relationship amongst cast and crew. "It was the worst experience of my acting career," recalls Curtis. "It went on for five months, and it seemed like it would never end, and the whole time I was wishing I'd never made the film. I just kept wondering how bad the film was going to turn out to be and how it would affect my career."

Virus eventually sat on the shelf for a year and a half before Universal Pictures unceremoniously dumped the white elephant into theaters in January of 1999. With scant publicity and terrible word of mouth, including the fact that the film wasn't screened for critics, *Virus* was dead on arrival. The film stands as one of the biggest studio flops of the 1990s (7).

Curtis knew *Virus* was doomed as soon as filming in North Carolina eventually wrapped in June of 1997, and she was eager to move on. In Curtis' case, this meant going back in time. She was approaching her fortieth birthday, her film career had leveled off, and she was a bit shocked to realize that *Halloween*, the film that had given birth to her acting career, was nearing its twentieth-anniversary. "I couldn't believe that twenty years had passed because I wasn't even twenty when we made the film," recalls Curtis. "I was shocked at how fast a life, a career, can go by, and it all really hit me as the film approached its twentieth anniversary. *Halloween* was the film that fans always mentioned when they came up to me, if I was at the mall or walking down the street. I felt that the twentieth anniversary of *Halloween* shouldn't go unnoticed and that's when I got the idea of doing another movie."

In the Fall of 1996, Curtis had met with old friends John Carpenter and Debra Hill at the Hamburger Hamlet in Hollywood, the same restaurant where Carpenter had wooed Donald Pleasence for *Halloween* almost twenty years earlier. Times had changed. Pleasence had died in 1995, after filming the lackluster *Halloween: The Curse of Michael Myers*, Carpenter and Hill were both approaching 50 years old, and Curtis was pushing 40. "When I got the idea for another *Halloween* movie, the first people I went to were John and Debra because we all started out together on *Halloween*," said Curtis. "I said to them, 'Let's do a twentieth-anniversary *Halloween*.' We decided to approach the studio together."

The studio was Dimension Films, the genre arm of Miramax Films who now controlled the *Halloween* franchise and had released *Halloween: The Curse of Michael Myers* in 1995 to tepid reviews and lackluster business. When Carpenter, Curtis, and Hill approached Dimension head Bob Weinstein about the idea of doing a new *Halloween* movie, Weinstein reacted with cautious enthusiasm. The company was about to release *Scream* in December of 1996, a film that would ultimately redefine and redraw the horror genre in the late 1990s. By the fall of 1996, the horror genre seemed lifeless and stagnant.

Still, the prospect of Jamie Lee Curtis returning to the *Halloween* series, to her iconic Laurie Strode persona, was too attractive to pass up. It was a no-brainer, at least in terms of Curtis' involvement. Carpenter and Hill quickly dropped out of the project during these preliminary talking stages. "They didn't want to pay us," recalls Carpenter. "For me, it was a situation where I would've had to have taken a pay cut to have done the film, which would've been fine if there was something on the back-end, but it just didn't work out. We wished them luck and went away."

Carpenter's and Hill's rather unceremonious departure from the project, although it's unclear if they were ever officially attached to it, was very awkward for Curtis. When later pressed on the subject, Curtis would explain, rather unconvincingly, that problematic scheduling had been the reason for Carpenter's and Hill's absence from the new *Halloween* film. Privately, Hill had expressed hope that Curtis might hold firm for the trio, but Curtis was determined to press forward with this project, no matter what. She'd genuinely hoped that Carpenter and Hill would be joining her on this quest, but she wasn't willing to fall on her sword over the matter. After all, it was Hollywood's money, not hers.

In the Spring of 1997, while Curtis was filming *Virus* in North Carolina, Curtis bumped into director Steve Miner with whom Curtis had previously worked with on the 1992 fantasy- adventure film *Forever Young*. Miner, whose extensive genre background included, ironically enough, directing two *Friday the 13th* sequels, was in North Carolina shooting the pilot for the teen-drama series *Dawson's Creek*. *Dawson's Creek* was the brainchild of writer Kevin Williamson who'd written the script for *Scream* which had become a bit hit upon its release in Christmas of 1996, and had reinvented the horror genre. "I introduced Jamie to Kevin, who was a big fan of Jamie's and a big fan of *Halloween*," recalls Miner. "At that point, I was under the impression that John Carpenter was still attached to the new *Halloween* movie."

Also in the Spring of 1997, George Lucas and 20th Century Fox began re-releasing the first three *Star Wars* films into theaters with staggering box office success. In the Fall of 1997, Paramount Pictures announced plans to re-release 1978's *Grease* into theaters in the Spring of 1998. Hollywood was, by the late 1990s, in a retrospective mood that had been ushered in by the massive impact of 1994's *Pulp Fiction* which had triggered a cinematic and cultural earthquake. "When I heard they were going to re-release *Grease*, the same exact movie, I couldn't believe it, and that's when I knew that doing another *Halloween* movie would be a great idea," recalls Curtis. "I thought that we should do another *Halloween* that took place twenty years later; a completely new movie that would celebrate and honor the first *Halloween*."

The timing for a new *Halloween* movie, commercially-speaking, couldn't have been better for Curtis, especially after the bitter experience of making *Virus*. By the Fall of 1997, the new *Halloween* film project, which would eventually bear the working title of *Halloween 7: The Return of Laurie Strode* before changing to *Halloween: H20*, had the green-light from Dimension. Not only would Curtis star in the new *Halloween* film but she would also serve as an uncredited executive producer which reflected the fact that she'd instigated the project into motion. "When we did the film, people would ask me whose idea it was to do this, who was behind this?" recalls Curtis. "The answer was simple. I was. It was all my idea. I made it happen, and I was very proud of that." It was the first time in Curtis' career that she'd ever taken this kind of responsibility for a film project, and her role on *Halloween: H20* would be anything but symbolic or token. Armed with a $17 million budget—more than 50 times that of *Halloween*—and a $3 million paycheck, which was almost 400 times what Curtis had been paid for *Halloween*, and this project was Curtis' baby. She would be calling the shots, in terms of script approval and story development, and she would also be involved with the choosing of a director, once it became clear that Carpenter's return was no longer a realistic possibility.

In this regard, Steve Miner was a happy compromise. He had experience in the horror genre, to say the least, and he and Curtis had worked together previously, and quite happily, on *Forever Young* which was, and still is, Miner's most successful film to date, and one of Curtis' most successful films as well (8). "I'd really enjoyed working with Steve on *Forever Young* and I was very comfortable with Steve which was important because I felt like I was Laurie Strode's guardian angel," says Curtis. "Steve reminds me a little of John in that they're both very laid-back, very calm. Steve also understood the genre and he had some great ideas about the story that made the film better."

In terms of the script for the new *Halloween* film, Curtis and Miner recruited Kevin Williamson, who was otherwise too preoccupied with scripting chores on *Scream 2* to write a screenplay for the new *Halloween* film, to come up with a treatment that would serve as the basis for the new film. Meanwhile, Dimension had commissioned writer Robert Zappia, who would ultimately receive—along with writer Matt Greenberg—final screenplay credit on *Halloween: H20*, to write the film's screenplay which would incorporate many of the elements of Williamson's seven page treatment.

Both the Greenberg-Zappia script and Williamson's treatment would move the *Halloween* story from the streets of Haddonfield, Illinois to a secluded boarding school in Northern California. It's here that a forty-ish Laurie Strode, who's changed her name to Keri Tate for reasons that become obvious, serves as headmistress to a group of teens, including her own teenage son, John Tate, played by a pre-stardom Josh Hartnett. Divorced, haunted by her memories from the first two *Halloween* films, and ravaged by alcohol and drugs, the scream queen formerly known as Laurie Strode is almost unrecognizable from the shy and vulnerable angel that had been introduced in *Halloween*.

This was the idea. Curtis wanted the fans who had grown up with Laurie Strode to be shocked by the older version of the character, as well as to interject some of the personal demons Curtis had experienced since her *Halloween* stardom. "Everyone told me it was too dark, but you have to stop and think and remember that Laurie was terrorized by a psychopathic killer when she was seventeen, and her friends were murdered, and her whole life was destroyed," says Curtis. "She's fighting a demon, and that's Michael Myers, and I don't think somebody with that kind of history would turn out any differently than she appears in the film. I wanted Laurie to be in a position where she has to make a choice to face her demons, to confront her past, and confront Michael Myers once and for all, instead of being scared her whole life."

Halloween: H20, as the project would eventually come to be known, was filmed around Los Angeles, California between February and May of 1998. In the film, Michael Myers, who's played in the film by stuntman Chris Durand, discovers Laurie's identity and whereabouts after killing Marion Chambers (now known as Marion Whittington), the nurse from *Halloween* and *Halloween II*. Nancy Stephens returned to play the role, the only other returnee from *Halloween* besides Curtis to appear in *Halloween: H20*. Stephens' appearance, in *Halloween: H20*'s opening sequence, also serves as the film's only reference to the legendary Dr. Sam Loomis with whom Marion was paired with in the first two films.

The Sam Loomis character is long dead in *Halloween: H20*, a necessary requirement given Donald Pleasence's own death in 1995. In the early scripting stages, there was a detective character, to be played by veteran actor Charles Dutton, who would serve as the pseudo-Loomis.

Curtis nixed the idea, feeling that *Halloween: H20* should focus on Laurie's conflict and avoid any unnecessary subplots. "I miss Donald Pleasence greatly but even though he meant a lot to *Halloween* and to the fans, when you think about it, he didn't mean much to Laurie," says Curtis. "In the first film, I only met him at the very end of the film, in the last three minutes, and it was the same thing in *Halloween II*. Laurie and Loomis really didn't have any kind of relationship to begin with, so I didn't see any point in having that subplot in the film."

Unlike was the case with *Halloween II*, Curtis' last appearance as Laurie Strode, and the horrible *Virus*, the shooting of *Halloween: H20* would be pleasant and virtually uneventful. The filming was made even more pleasant for Curtis given that her mother, Janet Leigh, would make a cameo appearance in the film. Leigh was cast as Norma Watson, Keri Tate's nosy secretary. As with *The Fog*, this mother-daughter teaming would be brief, agreeably nostalgic, if not exactly relevant. "I wanted mom to be in the film in a way that would sort of pay tribute to her own career," recalls Curtis. "I made the writers really work on creating something memorable for her. I wanted it to be scary, poignant, memorable."

Leigh's brief appearance with her daughter in *Halloween: H20*, welcome as it is, is kind of bittersweet in that it serves as a reminder that mother and daughter weren't destined to ever act together in a substantial film project. It's a shame they didn't appear together in something meaningful, something that had meat on it, other than these lackluster pairings in *The Love Boat*, *The Fog*, and finally *Halloween: H20*. Seeing them together on-screen in *Halloween: H20*, and the warm chemistry that's evident between them, only highlights the sense of a missed opportunity in terms of the fireworks that might've been created if mother and daughter had ever starred in a film together.

Actually, P.J. Soles, who was first considered for the role of Curtis' secretary, might've been a better choice in that Soles' appearance would've indicated that *Halloween: H20* contained some history with the film series, with *Halloween*. Amongst the film's many problems, such as the question as to where Michael Myers has been for the previous two decades and how he ended up in Northern California, this one is fatal. *Halloween: H20* isn't really a sequel to *Halloween*, either in terms of Laurie Strode's life or in relation to the 1978 film, but is instead a reaction to the 1990s teen horror marketplace (9).

Much like *Halloween II* was more of a reaction to the post-*Halloween* copycats like *Friday the 13th* than a faithful continuation of *Halloween*, *Halloween: H20* is a reaction to the late-1990s flood of teen-oriented horror films that the success of 1996's *Scream* had given birth to. *Halloween: H20* makes no demands of the viewer, much less the hardcore *Halloween* audience. The story exists separate from *Halloween*, so much so that the film doesn't even require that the viewer have even seen *Halloween* in order to digest *Halloween: H20's* contents. The film is constructed so that if the viewer has no knowledge of the 1978 film, they miss virtually nothing. *Halloween: H20*, though benign and fast-paced, represents a purely cynical type of film-making.

The best scene in *Halloween: H20* is the opening scene with Nancy Stephens' Marion Chambers (Whittington) character. The scene is stylish, taut, dripping with atmosphere, but the scene is effective precisely because the Marion Chambers Whittington character reminds the viewer of *Halloween*, and reveals a history with the characters and events from *Halloween*. For the rest of the film, Curtis only has one scene, this being a moment where Laurie briefly references the murders of best friends Annie and Lynda in *Halloween*, where the viewer feels the impact of Laurie's nightmarish journey. Although Curtis, ever the professional, does a convincing job of showing where Laurie Strode has traveled to in her life, the film itself doesn't show any curiosity or understanding of where Laurie Strode came from.

Ultimately, Curtis would be proven right in terms of her sense of the marketplace and the rabid hunger amongst *Halloween* fans whose numbers had grown exponentially in the previous twenty years. When *Halloween: H20* arrived in theaters, in August of 1998, audiences, old and new, were waiting with enthusiasm. Despite largely negative reviews, *Halloween: H20* grossed a robust $16 million on its opening weekend. Although the film would largely be gone from theaters by Halloween of 1998, by that time, *Halloween: H20* had grossed an impressive $55 million domestically.

The financial success of *Halloween: H20* was a personal triumph for Curtis, if not as an actress than certainly as a businesswoman. The project was born out of Curtis' imagination, and she'd nurtured the project every step of the way until completion. However dubious and shaky *Halloween: H20* may be in terms of its artistic merits, the venture was an unqualified financial success and Curtis deserves most of the credit for that, and she also deserves respect.

As part of her agreement with Dimension, Curtis was contractually obligated to make a cameo appearance in any sequel. This would be *Halloween: Resurrection* and this *Halloween* sequel would be notable for marking the death of Laurie Strode, as well as, by definition, the unofficial end of Curtis' genre career. Laurie Strode, it seems, could escape anything that was thrown at her except for the dark forces of Hollywood greed.

Although only contractually-obligated for a cameo appearance in *Halloween: Resurrection*, Curtis eventually agreed to four days worth of filming on *Halloween: Resurrection*. Curtis was anxious to say goodbye to the Laurie Strode character once and for all, and wanted to give filmmakers the chance to capture the iconic moment of Laurie Strode's death with the dramatic finality that such a momentous event deserved.

In May of 2001, Curtis dragged herself to Vancouver, British Columbia, Canada—during a particularly miserable and rainy period in the city—to film her swan-song to Laurie Strode. In addition to marking Laurie Strode's death, *Halloween: Resurrection* was a reunion of sorts for Curtis, given that it was directed by Rick Rosenthal, Curtis' director on *Halloween II*.

It had been almost exactly twenty years since the *Halloween II* experience, and Curtis and Rosenthal, Los Angeles being the small world it is, had bumped into each other numerous times since. Neither had any lingering memories from *Halloween II* which had been a forgettable experience for both actress and director, in spite of the film's commercial success. "Jamie and I continued to run into each other socially throughout the intervening years and we had remained friendly, so it was great fun to work with her again," recalls Rosenthal. "I don't think the subject of *Halloween II* ever came up when we shot Jamie's scenes for *Halloween: Resurrection.*"

Curtis had traveled to Vancouver to kill Laurie Strode for good, to end the saga. This happens in the first few minutes of *Halloween: Resurrection* which opens at a mental institution where Laurie Strode has been kept since the events of *Halloween: H20*. Dazed, ragged, almost catatonic, Laurie Strode seems almost relieved when Michael Myers appears in the hospital like a specter, to kill her once and for all. They end up on the rooftop where, after a fierce struggle from Laurie,

Michael tosses Laurie off the roof to her death. "I think it was a real kick for Jamie to do her own stunt for her big death fall scene," recalls Rosenthal. "She was great about it, and she was really great in terms of talking to the young actors on the set, and I think she was happy to get it over with, although a bit sad as well."

That was it. Laurie Strode, the invincible one, the ultimate scream queen heroine, was gone. After the scene was filmed, there were no eulogies from the cast and crew, many of whom weren't even alive when *Halloween* came out anyway.

There was no funeral, no retrospectives, nothing like that. Laurie Strode died fairly quietly. In the end, her death, like almost everything else that happens in the *Halloween* universe, was strictly business. It was a rather disheveled and shameful way for an iconic character like Laurie Strode to go out.

Predictably, Curtis' death scene, as brief as Curtis' role was in *Halloween: Resurrection*, was the main point of emphasis in the marketing of *Halloween: Resurrection* when the film was released in July of 2002. Just as predictably, the paying customers, namely the *Halloween* diehards, gobbled up the mixture and *Halloween: Resurrection* grossed a respectable $30 million domestically. This was about half the total of 1998's *Halloween: H20*, which seemed to suggest that the well-worn series, though still profitable, had bottomed-out.

Curtis was 43 when *Halloween: Resurrection* was released, an age when actresses are confronted with their own mortality in ways they've never been confronted before. Curtis had to look no further than some of her illustrious contemporaries—great actresses from the 1980s like Glenn Close and Jessica Lange—who saw their own feature film prospects dim by the time they hit their mid-forties. Or she could've looked back at her mother's film career which had inexplicably stalled by the mid-1960s. Given this environment, it's ironic that 2003 would bring Curtis, who's been very candid about her attempts at self-preservation over the years through plastic surgery, her greatest success, commercially-speaking, as a leading actress.

This was 2003's *Freaky Friday*, a remake of the 1977 Disney film about a mother and daughter who switch bodies with each other with hilarious results. Barbara Harris and Jodie Foster had played the mother and daughter in the 1977 film and for the remake, Oscar-nominated actress Annette Bening was cast as the mother opposite sixteen year old actress Lindsay Lohan for whom *Freaky Friday* would be the ticket to short- lived teen superstardom. However just before production on the $26 million film was scheduled to begin in October of 2002, Bening dropped out, forcing the producers to look for a last-minute replacement.

Enter Jamie Lee Curtis who by this time was more preoccupied with looking after her two children, as well as fostering her burgeoning second career as a best-selling children's book author. For Curtis, this wasn't semi- retirement, not exactly, but she wasn't waiting by the phone either. Still, when Curtis' agent, Rick Kurtzman at Creative Artists Agency (CAA), called with the last-second job offer, it was a nice surprise for Curtis who was in New York on a book tour at the time. "I was on the book tour in New York when my agent called with the *Freaky Friday* offer," recalls Curtis. "I think the call was on a Wednesday, and I read the script on Thursday, and then I was back in LA on Friday. I met with the director, Mark Waters, over the weekend, and we exchanged ideas about my character, and we started filming on Monday."

Being a second or third choice for a film project wasn't a new experience for Curtis, and in many ways, *Freaky Friday* was like a microcosm for much of her post-scream queen film career. Even at the height of her mainstream film career, in the early to mid-1990s, Curtis was rarely the first choice for many of the films she starred in, and certainly was never on the A-list. Curtis relished this underdog role, and she used it in her acting. This resilience also endeared Curtis to producers, along with the fact that Curtis' established salary—which has typically ranged between $1-$2 million—wasn't prohibitive. "It was like if you couldn't get Michelle Pheiffer or Meryl Streep, you ended up with Jamie Lee Curtis," says one producer. "Then you found out how good she really was."

In the context of Curtis' scream queen career, *Freaky Friday* represents the full circle transformation from *Halloween* to the present. Much of *Freaky Friday* is set at a high school, not a million miles removed from Haddonfield High, and Curtis' appearance in the film reinforces the idea that Laurie Strode is now a fully-grown adult. In the film, Curtis' character is inhabited by the soul of her teenage daughter, and the sight of Curtis as a mother figure, in contrast to the lasting image of Curtis as teenage Laurie Strode, is powerful.

Whether it be the audience's nostalgic identification with Curtis, or Curtis' own energetic performance, or the terrific chemistry that Curtis and Lohan have in the film, *Freaky Friday* struck a chord with audiences. Truthfully, there was—and is—no real explanation for the enormous success of *Freaky Friday*. Despite modest expectations from Disney, *Freaky Friday* grossed a whopping $110 million upon its release in August of 2003. It was the surprise hit of 2003.

It was the most successful film Curtis had, and has, ever starred in. This time there was no Arnold Schwarzenegger, and no Michael Myers for cover, and although Lindsay Lohan was unquestionably on the cusp of stardom at this time, *Freaky Friday* was certainly very much a Jamie Lee Curtis film. In fact, the success of *Freaky Friday* was unexplainable. The reviews were mostly positive, and many critics noted the irony of Curtis' completed transformation from younger actress to older mother figure, but no one involved with *Freaky Friday* had any idea the film would become such an unlikely hit. Maybe the simple answer is that *Freaky Friday* is just a lot of harmless fun, thanks in no small part to Curtis' performance which earned Curtis her sixth Golden Globe nomination (10).

The *Freaky Friday* triumph was dulled by two major losses in Curtis' life that occurred between 2004 and 2005. The first, and most significant, was the passing of her mother, Janet Leigh, at the age of 77, on October 3, 2004 at Leigh's home in Beverly Hills, California. Leigh died of vasculitis, a painful inflammation of the blood vessels that had plagued Leigh for more than a year. Curtis was with her mother when she passed away, along with older sister, Kelly, as well as stepfather, and Leigh's husband of more than 40 years, Robert Brandt (11). "We had a year to say goodbye, to say everything that we ever wanted to say to her, and to thank her for everything she ever did for us," said Curtis. "It was nice to say, 'I know you didn't have a lot of help and a lot of guides, and you navigated a lot on your own.' My mother was a very driven and active woman, and letting go of her life was the hardest thing she ever did."

Earlier in 2004, in February, Curtis' friend and mentor, producer Debra Hill, had been diagnosed with cancer which would later result in both of Hill's legs being amputated at the knee. It was a cruel and horrific fate for such a strong-willed woman, and grim evidence that the cast and crew who'd started out on *Halloween* were no longer kids anymore, and weren't immune from real life's killers. Curtis, Hill, and the rest of the Carpenter-Hill unit were at the dawn of their careers and lives when they'd made *Halloween*, a time when things like cancer are an afterthought. Now they were all in their forties and fifties, a time when life stops giving and begins to slowly take everything away.

Debra Hill died on March 7, 2005, having lived long enough to serve as a producer on *World Trade Center*, a film project that Hill was determined to leave behind for posterity. Although the film wasn't released until August of 2006, more than a year after Hill's passing, the film serves as a fine memorial to Hill's career as a film-maker, certainly much more so than the abysmal remake of *The Fog* which was released in October of 2005 and which also bore Hill's name as a producer. "When Debra passed away, it was a real shock for all of us, although we knew she was sick," recalls Dean Cundey. "It was like a cold bucket of water in the face."

Hill was, arguably, Curtis' best friend in the business, a loyal friend and confidant whom Curtis had consulted and trusted all throughout her own career. Like Curtis, Hill wasn't blessed with natural beauty but her colleagues nonetheless had found her to be a very attractive and sexy woman back in the day. In Hill's case, this had been due to her forceful personality, her sense of humor, and her sultry voice. In subsequent years, Hill would gain a lot of weight, and unlike Curtis, Hill never got married and never had children. She was, according to friends, married to her career.

Debra Hill will live on through her films, many of which are cult classics, and not just her collaborations with Carpenter and Curtis, but also later Hill-produced efforts like *Gross Anatomy* (1989) and *The Fisher King* (1991) that have found enthusiastic followings. For Curtis and the others who'd all started out on *Halloween*, Hill's passing was a sad and sobering milestone. "Debra Hill was certainly the most influential woman in my professional life," said Curtis. "She became a dear, dear friend and represents for me the independent Hollywood woman's spirit. She had a wonderful Jersey-girl side to her and loved, loved, loved being in the film business. I owe her my career and will be eternally grateful to her."

The next major milestone in Jamie Lee Curtis' career and life came on November 22, 2008 when Curtis turned 50. Curtis celebrated the occasion with a big breakfast party with some close friends. "I have not one second of anxiety about turning 50," said Curtis. "I want to be older. I actually think there's an incredible amount of self-knowledge that comes with getting older. I feel way better now than I did when I was twenty. I'm stronger, I'm smarter in every way, I'm so much less crazy than I was then."

For most actresses, turning 40, much less 50, is a death sentence in Hollywood where women of this age are considered to be unattractive and worthless. It's a cruel fate that awaits every actress, but for Curtis, the turning of 50 feels like less of a death sentence and more of a crossing of a finish line. The fact that Curtis even made it to 50, and has accomplished so much in her acting career—and has outlived and outperformed so many of her contemporaries—makes this milestone seem like more of an award than a curse.

Perhaps Curtis' film career, as defined in terms of being an above-the-line actress, is over and that Curtis, like many actresses of her age, will have to reinvent herself either as a character actress or an older actress. Maybe she'll quit acting, as she has stated, and devote all of her time and energies to writing children's books. More likely is that she will follow in the footsteps of other older actresses, like Glenn Close and Holly Hunter, and find an edgy cable television series to sink her teeth into. She has, with the exception of winning an Academy Award, accomplished everything in the world of Hollywood that she could ever have imagined when she began her acting career in 1977.

Whatever she does between the ages of 50 and 60, Jamie Lee Curtis always has value, and will always be a welcomed presence. She is one of very few performers who have established a lifelong and special bond and relationship with the public, and this is a direct result of Curtis' scream queen career, and especially her immortal work in *Halloween*.

All of the success in Curtis' post-scream queen career is connected to her scream queen career. The loyal fan-base Curtis' scream queen career engendered certainly will continue to follow Curtis in whatever direction her career goes. Curtis' scream queen career has given her a reservoir of public goodwill, pop culture capital, that she's been spending for the past thirty years, whether it be in her transition to non-horror roles or in the marketing of her children's books. The horror fans have supported her through all of these transformations and this connection will stay with Curtis for the rest of her life.

Although the faded image of Laurie Strode is barely visible in Curtis' current form, the qualities that made Jamie Lee Curtis a great scream queen have been present throughout her career and life. These are an unconventional and unique beauty, honesty, tenaciousness, vulnerability and a million other incongruous and indescribable elements that formed cinema's greatest and most identifiable scream queen.

The legion of starlets and impersonators that have tried, and failed, to follow in Curtis' scream queen footsteps are a testament—along with all of the subsequent remakes of Curtis' films, and the enduring popularity of Curtis' horror films today—to Curtis' influence, her greatness, and sheer uniqueness which makes imitation pointless. Curtis' enduring popularity and relevance as a genre icon, almost thirty years removed from the height of her scream queen career, is compelling evidence that Jamie Lee Curtis has transformed into a living legend, in addition to being regarded as cinema's definitive and undisputed scream queen.

The filming of *Roadgames* (1981) took Jamie Lee Curtis to Australia.
(Photo courtesy of Richard Franklin)

Roadgames teamed Curtis with veteran actor Stacy Keach.
(Photo courtesy of Richard Franklin)

Curtis regarded Stacy Keach as a mentor throughout the filming of *Roadgames.* (Photo courtesy of Richard Franklin)

Promotion for *Roadgames* tried to portray the film as a slasher film.

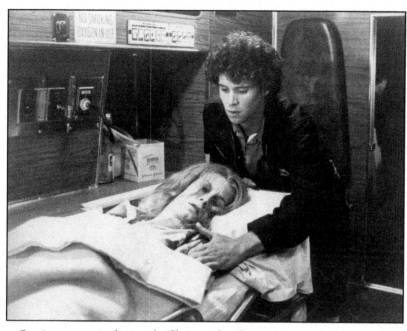

Curtis wore a wig during the filming of *Halloween II*. (Photo courtesy of Kim Gottlieb-Walker www.lenswoman.com)

Halloween II represented the end of Curtis' scream queen career. (Photo courtesy of Kim Gottlieb-Walker www. lenswoman.com)

Halloween II marked the end of Curtis' professional relationship with John Carpenter and Debra Hill. (Photo courtesy of Kim Gottlieb-Walker www. lenswoman.com)

Curtis received top billing over *Halloween* co-star Donald Pleasence in *Halloween II*, as well as more money. *Halloween II* was the first genre film in which Curtis received top billing. (Photo courtesy of Kim Gottlieb-Walker www.lenswoman.com)

Laurie Strode prepares to shoot Michael Myers during *Halloween II*'s finale. (Photo courtesy of Kim Gottlieb-Walker www.lenswoman.com)

Halloween II was the second most commercially successful film of Curtis' scream queen career, grossing more than $25 Million domestically. (Photo courtesy of Matt Hankinson)

Curtis peers into a tank full of piranhas during a segment from the television special *David Frost Presents: The Second International Guinness Book of World Records* (1981) which Curtis co-hosted.

Curtis' portrayal of murdered *Playboy* playmate Dorothy Stratten in the made-for-television film *Death of a Centerfold: The Dorothy Stratten Story* (1981) marked the beginning of Curtis' post-scream queen career. (Photo courtesy of Paul Pompian)

Curtis showed nudity for the first time in *Death of a Centerfold: The Dorothy Stratten Story* although the footage only appeared in the European version of the film. (Photo courtesy of Paul Pompian)

Curtis bleached her hair blonde to play
Dorothy Stratten.

Photo of Dorothy Stratten
reveals the striking
physical dissimilarities
between her and Curtis.
Stratten was murdered in
1980. Ironically, Stratten's
best-known film was
the science-fiction spoof
Galaxina(1980) which was
shot by cinematographer,
and longtime Curtis
colleague, Dean Cundey.

Blue Steel was compared by some critics to *Halloween*. *Blue Steel* was directed by Kathryn Bigelow who would later win an Oscar for the film *The Hurt Locker*(2008).

Blue Steel(1990)marked Curtis' first genre appearance in a decade.

Officer Megan Turner(Curtis)prepares to shoot to kill in a scene from *Blue Steel*.
Although Curtis received good personal reviews for *Blue Steel*, the film itself
was a critical and commercial disappointment.

Despite an impressive cast that included Peter Gallagher (right), *Mother's Boys* (1994) was barely released.

Mother's Boys marked Curtis' first villainess or femme fatale role.

Curtis and her mother appeared briefly together in *Halloween: H20*(1998). Janet Leigh died in 2004.

eighteen

THE MAKING OF A REPUTATION

Q: What were the qualities that made Jamie Lee Curtis a great scream queen—a genre icon? There are many qualities that made Jamie Lee Curtis a great scream queen, a cinematic and genre icon, and while some of these qualities are visible, there are many other qualities that are difficult to put into words.

Beauty. Jamie Lee Curtis' indescribable and unconventional beauty is the most interesting and mysterious of her qualities as a scream queen. The fact that Curtis, with her angular features and crooked smile, was such an unconventional-looking scream queen—in contrast to the stereotypical starlets who are usually cast in heroine roles—made her interesting and unique. The fact that Curtis' beauty and sex appeal as a scream queen was so difficult to classify and define only served to make Curtis an even more intriguing figure. Curtis' unconventional beauty also made her accessible to audiences and made audiences feel like they knew her.

Impact. Jamie Lee Curtis' impact as a scream queen, and her impact in the horror film genre, is powerful and undeniable. She's an icon, a legend, and a vanguard of the scream queen archetype that countless actresses have subsequently tried, and failed, to emulate (1). The fact that most of Curtis' genre films—films like *Halloween, The Fog, Prom Night, Terror Train*—have been subsequently remade is evidence that Curtis' impact within the horror genre remains strong, and that Curtis herself is still relevant as a pop culture icon.

Perhaps more significant is the number of young actresses over the years, aspiring scream queens, who've listed Curtis as a role model in terms of the example Curtis set when she successfully moved from the horror genre into non-horror acting roles. The fact that Curtis is one of the few scream queens ever to make this transition is further evidence of Curtis' impact and the fact that the public recognized her as a true actress as opposed to just being a scream queen.

Vulnerability. This is probably the most visible quality that Curtis exuded as a scream queen in terms of Curtis' uncanny ability to make the viewer care about her and identify with the characters she played in her horror films. While Curtis' Laurie Strode character from *Halloween* represents the ultimate scream queen heroine, Curtis also demonstrated great vulnerability in her post-*Halloween* scream queen roles.

This vulnerability was especially present in a film like *Prom Night* in which Curtis brings a disarming intensity to her scenes that serves to set her apart from the film itself in terms of transcending the primitive material. Jamie Lee Curtis' mere presence legitimized and validated the horror films she appeared in—good and bad—and Curtis' vulnerability was certainly the bedrock quality of her scream queen persona.

MARK A. ALTMAN, PRODUCER, *HOUSE OF THE DEAD*: I think what people loved about Jamie Lee, and continue to respond to today, is that she was real. She wasn't larger-than-life. In *Halloween*, for instance, you believed the character she was playing. She could have been your babysitter or mine. And she cared about the children. She was believable and she didn't act in a silly way. First and foremost, she was empathic, but she was also a good actress and as *Trading Places* proved, as was a prerequisite for any great Scream Queen, she had great breasts too. I think one reason we all think of Jamie Lee Curtis so fondly is she not only had a facility for thrillers, but she could play comedy, drama or suspense and was adept at all of them. Her performance in *A Fish Called Wanda* is genius and it's that ability to slip effortlessly into any role that makes her a film icon.

TOM ATKINS, CO-STAR, *THE FOG*: Innocence and vulnerability.

JAMES BERARDINELLI, FILM CRITIC: Her initial appeal came from her everyday, girl-next-door quality. She was very down-to-earth and you could see her coming over to babysit. After the success of *Halloween*, she became typecast in this sort of role and, wanting to continue her acting career, accepted (perhaps unwisely) many of these cookie-cutter roles. *Trading Places* is probably the first high-profile film where she got a chance to do something other than run away from a guy with a knife.

GILLES BOULENGER, AUTHOR, *JOHN CARPENTER: THE PRINCE OF DARKNESS*: Jamie Lee Curtis became a great scream queen, first and foremost, because John Carpenter and her met at the right time. Being a great aficionado of the American horror classics from the 1950s and 1960s, Carpenter had kept a vivid memory of these landmark B movies filled with screaming, frightened actresses chased by horrible, malformed creatures. Once he had become a film-maker, Carpenter knew he had the frame with which to pay tribute to these sultry female icons from his childhood past. When *Halloween* was proposed to Carpenter, the time had come, and he had to find an actress for the lead who could be both young and tough at the same time. A new breed of screaming queen. Jamie Lee Curtis was the per-fect choice, though she was still inexperienced. She was special, and she had to prove that she could start a career in the movie business. The core of the script, as well as the way Carpenter decided to relent-lessly reduce the escaping space through his camerawork and settings, helped her acting job to a great extent, but above all, Carpenter and Curtis were on the same page, in perfect sync. They both knew that when confronted by your worst nightmare you just scream, scream and scream again.

JOHN BRUNO, DIRECTOR, *VIRUS*: I believe it's a combination of her emotional strength and innate sexuality. It's an alluring combi-nation. Jamie has the ability to project an honest, vulnerable courage that audiences relate to and the camera loves, and it's that pairing that makes women want to be her and men want to come to her rescue. Did I mention how great she looks wielding an axe?

GLENN BYDWELL, PRODUCTION DESIGNER, *TERROR TRAIN*: She had a tremendous capacity for playing a down-home girl who wasn't affected by anything. She was solid, not glamorous, kind of like your sister, like everyone's sister, contrary to the other girls who were starring in the horror films during that era.

LAMAR CARD, EXECUTIVE PRODUCER, *TERROR TRAIN*: She brought star caliber to the horror films and she made you care about her, and those were two qualities that none of the other scream queens had. Her presence gave legitimacy to the horror films she starred in.

JOHN CARPENTER, CO-WRITER/DIRECTOR, *HALLOWEEN/ THE FOG* / CO-PRODUCER/CO-WRITER, *HALLOWEEN II*: When I first met Jamie and we talked about the part of Laurie in *Hallow-een*, I stressed to Jamie that the character had to show vulnerability, so much so that the audience would literally be shouting advice to her when they were watching the screen. At first, I think Jamie saw this as weakness, but I explained that the purpose was to make the audience identify completely with the character. I felt that I needed the audience to fall in love with Jamie or the film wouldn't work. Jamie was able to show tremendous vulnerability in the film, to make the audience care about Jamie, and I think that's the quality that makes her a great actress. In the horror films, she was able to make you care about her and I think that's why she made such a powerful impact.

MARK CERULLI, DIRECTOR / PRODUCER / WRITER, *HALLOW-EEN UNMASKED 2000*: Jamie Lee was exactly what the producers were looking for—she was young, fresh and had that "all American girl-next-door" look. *Halloween* was aimed at teens—and for most teens, their first job was... babysitting. Jamie Lee looked like someone you'd have over to watch your kids, or the girl with the locker next to yours in high school, and that made her character accessible and believable for every kid going to see the film. I know they also liked the fact that her mom, Janet Leigh, was in *Psycho*. That gave them a bit of a pedigree on a shoe string budget! The other thing Jamie Lee had going for her was her talent—she could act. When you saw her running from Michael or cowering in the closet, she conveyed fear—she was the hook around which the rest of the movie was pinned, and it worked! I interviewed her in 2000 and more than any other celebrity I interviewed, I felt that she was really realistic about the business— that's why her career has lasted. She knows what she has and how the business works. Most people go into it with stars in their eyes. Jamie Lee has none of that and she takes nothing for granted. I remember when she left the room I was thinking, "wow, that is one tough lady."

SEAN CLARK, HORROR JOURNALIST: Jamie had an innocence that she played very well, making her the perfect vulnerable-yet-strong female victim. She also had a likable quality to her characters that made the audience really care about what happened to her. That on top of being the daughter of Janet Leigh, the original scream queen, gave her all the right ingredients.

JASON PAUL COLLUM, AUTHOR/FILM JOURNALIST: Most people think it was Jamie Lee's scream that made her a star in the genre, but I think it was her vulnerability. She was the everyday girl. She wasn't gorgeous—and unapproachable. She was simply a plain, average pretty girl who realistically could be sitting next to you in class. She'd even be willing to talk to you, maybe go to a dance. In *Halloween*, she was the epitome of a babysitter at the time. I was five in 1978. Though I didn't see the film until many years later, Laurie Strode was everything I recalled about the teenage girls who'd made popcorn, watched movies on TV, talked on the phone with their friends and read comic books with me. They too carried their school books close to their chests like a piece of protective armor. Walked sheepishly with their heads hung a little low. I knew that in their care, I was safe from the Boogeyman. All said, Jamie Lee made Laurie real. As her other horror films came along, it was the same character, only a little more aged. Kim in *Prom Night* was more confident, but still a gentle soul. Alana in *Terror Train* was stronger, but guilt-ridden about her past, even though she had nothing to do with the prank that resulted in the mayhem. Whether she was fighting off ghosts in *The Fog* or running afoul of maniacs in *Road Games*, Curtis always maintained that soft, pouting lip of concern and furrowed brow of being on the verge of dismay—even though we knew she'd pull through in the end. Horror films today have bitchy, overly make-upped, way-too-perfect heroines. You might even giggle a little if they got knifed. Jamie Lee Curtis made you love her simply by being simple.

DEAN CUNDEY, CINEMATOGRAPHER, *HALLOWEEN/THE FOG/HALLOWEEN II*: She was the ultimate girl-next-door who didn't think she was beautiful even though we did. She wasn't a model type; she wasn't hired for her beauty and you knew she wasn't hired for that and so you assumed she must be smart, which Jamie certainly was. She had great vulnerability, and she had the look of the average girl and she was able to translate the experiences of the average girl into her performances. You feel great empathy for her, and you especially don't want to see her get killed. She was an average girl thrust into a horror situation and that made her more believable and the audience both identified and related to that.

EVERETT DE ROCHE, WRITER, *ROADGAMES*: There's a natural empathy about her—an "every girl" quality that's hard to quantify.

TOM DESIMONE, DIRECTOR, *HELL NIGHT*: To my mind it is probably that Jamie Lee Curtis was never a beauty queen nor did she fit into the starlet role that so many horror films people themselves with. She was your ordinary next door baby-sitter, your sister's best friend or your high school chum. Her predicaments were all the more real in that she conveyed a quality that the audience could most definitely identify with. "Hot Babe Starlets" who soon became the staple victims in subsequent slasher films were nothing more than titillation and fodder for male fantasies. Jamie was our friend; we didn't want to see her in danger.

JON DOWDING, ART DIRECTOR/PRODUCTION DESIGNER, *ROADGAMES*: Jamie had much the same qualities that Greta Garbo and Katharine Hepburn had in the way she could flesh out a character, as well as her tremendous screen presence. There was also a great authority about Jamie in her performance which is very unusual for someone as young as she was. She was also incredibly beautiful.

JOHN FALLON, FILM JOURNALIST: In my world, Jamie Lee Curtis is the definition of a well-rounded actress. She has succeeded, and still succeeds, in every cinematic genre she tackles, in what seems to be an effortless fashion. Be it dramas, comedies or horror films, you name it and Jamie Lee can do it, and better than most at that. To fervent horror fans such as me, she is the premium scream queen and for good reasons. When she burst through to the screen in the 1978 shocker *Halloween* she exuded a distinctive and winning presence. Jamie Lee oozed of inner strength, vulnerability, charisma and sheer sexiness, all wrapped up in an aura of authenticity at that. And it is that endearing mixture which made her a talent to be reckoned with and a sturdy staple within our beloved horror genre. She paved the way for the scream queens to come while setting the bar high for all to strive for. Most horror actresses today owe a little (or a big) something to Jamie Lee if you ask me. Her impact was that powerful and for that alone she will always be remembered. Whether it be within strong pieces like *Blue Steel* or *The Fog*, or even in sub-par efforts akin to *Terror Train* and *Halloween: Resurrection*, the magic that is Jamie Lee Curtis always shines through. She enhanced the quality films she appeared in and made the stinkers bearable.

STEPHEN FARBER, FILM JOURNALIST: Jamie Lee Curtis is an unusual scream queen in that she always emanated strength. She was never one of the fragile maidens. So if she was frightened, you knew there was a good reason to be scared because she was a woman who could take care of herself.

RICHARD FRANKLIN, CO-PRODUCER / DIRECTOR, *ROAD-GAMES*: I never thought of Jamie as a scream queen, never thought of her that way. I certainly didn't cast Jamie in *Roadgames* because of this.

BRAD FULLER, PRODUCER, *FRIDAY THE 13TH/THE TEXAS CHAINSAW MASSACRE*: She had equal shares of innocence and strength.

MICK GARRIS, FORMER PRESS AGENT / PRODUCER, *COMING SOON*: Jamie was very special because she was so real. It wasn't all about a transitory glamour; she was a very gifted dramatic and comedic actress, and her performances didn't seem like acting. She brought a reality, a no-bullshit likeableness to every role she attacked. And she would keep surprising her audience. I think her brief nudity in *Trading Places* took everyone by surprise, and suddenly she was doing more adult roles, relationship roles. She's not like anybody else, and that may be her greatest asset. You think you know her.

KIM GOTTLIEB-WALKER, STILL PHOTOGRAPHER, *HALLOWEEN / THE FOG / HALLOWEEN II*: She has an innate intelligence combined with both a vulnerability and resolve...and a basic sympathetic humanity that makes you want to see her succeed and survive. Her genuine goodness as a person shines through.

WILLIAM GRAY, WRITER, *PROM NIGHT*: Jamie's quality is that she's a great person and that shines through. You watch her and you want her to survive, you want her to do well. Some people become stars and some people don't and Jamie just had that star quality about her. You want her to win, you cheer for her. Who Jamie is shines through on-screen.

LAWRENCE GROBEL, FILM JOURNALIST: A good set of lungs.

DANIEL GRODNIK, CO-PRODUCER/CO-WRITER, *TERROR TRAIN*: Jamie was the girl-next-door; she was accessible to the audience who looked just like her and related to her. Jamie came across as a normal person, normal heroine, not an extraordinary person thrust into extraordinary circumstances but an ordinary person thrust into extraordinary circumstances and that's what made her great.

ALAN JONES, AUTHOR/HORROR JOURNALIST: Jamie Lee Curtis exuded three qualities: attractiveness, capability and assuredness. Each made her the perfect scream queen, but the combination of all three made for a dynamite package. Obviously she was helped by the *Halloween* scripting that felt teen-authentic and believable being uttered by her, but she just had that feel of engaging resourcefulness. It's in all of her movies, *Roadgames* in particular, and why I feel she has become a horror icon is because she didn't care if she did or not. She quite happily moved on to comedy, action etc. without thinking she had anything to prove (unlike Barbara Steele) and therefore didn't come across so desperate. I'm assuming it was something she learned from her mother too.

AMY HOLDEN JONES, DIRECTOR/WRITER, *LOVE LETTERS* / DIRECTOR, *SLUMBER PARTY MASSACRE*: Jamie had a very unconventional beauty that made her unique. Maggie Gyllenhaal of today would be a good comparison to Jamie back in the early days. The only horror film I'd seen of Jamie's prior to working with her on *Love Letters* was *Halloween* and I think what made her special was that she seemed like a real person who was complex and vulnerable.

ROY LEE, PRODUCER, *THE GRUDGE/THE RING*: Jamie Lee Curtis had that innocent "girl-next-door" image that many people could relate to. She played a vulnerable victim who looked believable when she was able to fight back her aggressors.

TIM LUCAS, EDITOR, *VIDEO WATCHDOG*: My answer to that question would probably be short and sweet: She had good acting genes, was a fast learner and resourceful in her own right, but most of all, she was in the right place at the right time. Perhaps I'm showing my age, but I personally have a hard time accepting anyone of her generation as a genre icon, and I tend to think of "great" and "scream queens" as mutually exclusive terms. I don't know that Jamie Lee ever had a role that allowed her to achieve her fullest potential as an actress, and the ones that granted her the best opportunities to stretch were outside the horror genre (*Love Letters, A Fish Called Wanda*). I consider her work in the horror genre better than average, certainly, but not particularly fascinating or iconic. I've never seen her elevate a bad film simply by being in it, which horror's real icons (Karloff, Lugosi, etc) —and even its finest supporting players—are usually able to do.

PAUL LYNCH, DIRECTOR, *PROM NIGHT*: I think she was a great scream queen because she was a great actress. I think she would've excelled in any genre when she was beginning her career, and it just so happened that she became a scream queen. She had incredible emotional depth, and an uncanny ability to be in-the-moment as an actress, and I was amazed, working with her on *Prom Night*, at the emotional places she could get to.

PAMELA MALCOLM, DANCE CHOREOGRAPHER, *PROM NIGHT*: Jamie was very young and I think what made her excel in the horror movies was her tenaciousness which she brought to her acting, and her dancing.

ANTHONY MASI, DIRECTOR / PRODUCER / WRITER, *HALLOWEEN: THE SHAPE OF HORROR*: For me, I've never met Jamie...she's probably one of the few people connected with *Halloween* that I haven't met, but I feel there's only one quality that established her as a modern day scream queen...she was probably the first cerebral cinematic heroine to grace the screen in the horror genre. Even though Laurie Strode tells Tommy the bogeyman isn't real, she has really spent the entire day seeing him all around town stalking her. So it's an illogical thought process to tell a child the bogeyman isn't real when she's seen him with her own eyes. But the thing that catapults her out of normal helpless victim behavior is a strong script. The control she takes when Myers does end up chasing her, and how she protects the kids by locking them—as well as herself—in various places in the house to not be the killer's next victims is what gave Jamie Lee her icon status. Because of the solid writing from Carpenter and Hill, *Halloween* introduced modern audiences to their first real scream queen in the character of Laurie Strode.

JOHN MCCARTY, AUTHOR/HORROR HISTORIAN: It strikes me that Curtis is, if anything, a reluctant "scream queen." Given her three-in-a-row starring roles in *Halloween*, *Halloween II* and *Terror Train*, she could have made a career out of starring in all the slasher films that followed in the wake of *Halloween*'s success and influence, but she didn't – and that was a conscious choice, I believe. Her return to the genre in *Halloween: H20* seems to me less of an attempt to gain (or regain) her status as a "scream queen" than just logical, since it was the first film in the series since *Halloween II* to resurrect the now-grown baby-sitter character she originated. I guess the bottom line, at least to me, is this: Much like her mother, the late Janet Leigh of *Psycho* fame, Curtis is a horror icon for being in the right place with the right role in the right film at the right time, and having the talent (and lung power) to pull the opportunity off.

STEVAN MENA, DIRECTOR/WRITER, *MALEVOLENCE*: Intelligence, beauty and empathy. Her intelligent presence on-screen makes you instantly root for her, whereas most scream queens can just scream well. Because she is a very giving artist, she allows you to identify with her character, so where we tend to objectify most beautiful damsels in distress, Jamie allows us to share and empathize with her characters on-screen. Jamie is also a classic beauty, but never falls back on her looks or uses them to intimidate. Her wit and charm brings you back to her eyes from her breasts. She could certainly impress without ever opening her mouth. As an actor, she endears us to feel of her as more of a sister, and you can't dump your sister, so you have to root for her to survive; it's your damn sister up there, you gotta help her!! Her later comedic roles prove what a well rounded artist she is, and what a great sense of humor she has. However the defining role will always be Laurie Strode. Her performance is what made *Halloween* great and timeless. That's the reason why that movie has never been equaled in the genre. The only comparison is *Psycho*, and it stars her mother! Nuff said. It's in the genes.

TAWNY MOYER, CO-STAR, *HALLOWEEN II*: When we look back, across her many roles, in many genres, I think we can see that her true strength has always been her devotion to the truth, both the best and the worst of it, coupled with her willingness and ability to grace us with it, on the silver screen and beyond.

BRAD MISKA, HORROR JOURNALIST: *Halloween. The Fog. Prom Night. Terror Train. Roadgames. Halloween II.* Six horror movies in three years, all good. Hard to ignore. She's a legend.

DAVID MUCCI, CO-STAR, *PROM NIGHT*: Jamie was a very good actress, and very honest, very up-front in her acting style which magnifies her scenes. She was forward, open, attractive, very good at revealing her emotions.

JOHN KENNETH MUIR, AUTHOR/HORROR HISTORIAN: Jamie Lee Curtis was a successful and beloved scream queen for a number of reasons. Among them: she was attractive without being "unreal" or somehow intimidating in terms of physical appearance. She was believable as a person and "normal" human being rather than as a product-of-Hollywood/glamorous screen beauty. In other words, there was something very enticing, disarming and "real" in her portrayals of characters like Laurie Strode or Elizabeth Solley. A viewer sensed no artifice or smugness in her personality. Thus it was easy to identify with her, and also cheer for her when she became endangered and fought back against the likes of Michael Myers. Curtis projected the aura of an authentic American girl-next-door: someone we all grew up with and who some of us had a crush on in high school. Yet—importantly—she was an *idealized* girl-next-door, someone who was really something of a renaissance (or dream) girl: "book" smart in school, athletic, and not overly hung-up about teenage preoccupations and bugaboos like smoking weed or premarital sex. In her horror films, Curtis exuded intelligence, self-deprecating humor, charm, and again, a sense of realism or naturalism. For women, she was a heroic figure and role model to identify with; for men she was a fantasy figure who did not seem threatening or entirely out of reach.

ROBERT NEW, CINEMATOGRAPHER, *PROM NIGHT*: I think one of her best qualities as a scream queen was her sense of humor. She had a good perspective on everything; she was having fun with life and that helped Jamie create her characters. She was able to step into the scream queen roles and have fun with those roles. She was a hard-worker but she also had a sense of perspective and although she put a lot of time and effort into her acting, and her character, she didn't take herself or the work too seriously and that allowed her to throw herself into these roles.

PHILIP NUTMAN, AUTHOR/HORROR JOURNALIST: Jamie Lee Curtis brought a verve and depth to her role as Laurie Strode in Carpenter's *Halloween*. The other characters were primarily two-dimensional (only P.J. Soles stands out because of her sexy, liberated enthusiasm and on-camera charisma as Lynda, the sexually-voracious cheerleader). Jamie had a girl-next-door quality and warmth—and strength of character—that was founded in her acting ability. When I saw the movie for the first time, back when it was originally released, I "believed" she was Laurie; I immediately bought into her character. With her angular good looks (and the fact she could be beautiful without being conventionally-beautiful) and sense of authenticity in her role, I developed an empathy with her character. And having directed actors, I know that's not an easy quality to manifest on film.

Subsequent films which tried to capitalize on the success of *Halloween*—the original *Prom Night* and *Terror Train* in particular—failed to channel the full range of her talents. Miss Curtis combined a unique blend: she radiated an unspoken sensuality without being overtly sexual; a sense of quiet, calm compassion which, when pushed to the limits of endurance, transformed into action and a desire to protect and defend. She was, and always will be, the original "Final Girl." I wished she'd been my babysitter when I was growing up.

GRANT PAGE, CO-STAR, *ROADGAMES*: Jamie had a great spirit and a great sense of vulnerability. Her looks are part of it, but it's mostly her spirit because there's nothing insipid or phony about her. In the scene in *Roadgames* where she's looking in the van for clues, you're worried about her, and she has a naive energy about her that makes you care about her. You never forget she's a real person.

GREG RICKETSON, PRODUCTION MANAGER, *ROADGAMES*: She is sassy, sexy, strong, funny, can cover a wide range of characters, a great actress. In her scream queen roles, she is as much of a standout as Sigourney Weaver as 'Ripley'. Natural appeal? The audience identifies with the inherent strength portrayed, and just goes with her regardless of the silliness of the storyline. Comedy? One of the greatest comedic roles ever in *A Fish Called Wanda*. Am just waiting for the day when she absolutely blows everyone away in a major dramatic film. I know it will happen. Qualities of a star? That she accepts she is, but doesn't play on it in her dealings with other people. Yes, my work memories are now thirty years old, but ten years ago, I watched her in the foyer at the Emmy Awards as she ever so glamorously moved amongst people, always giving of herself to others. I stepped outside to have a cigarette, and wondered why the gathered crowd, of mixed ages, began screaming and cheering. And there was JLC, in a remarkable blue gown, going out to say hello and sign autographs. Giving. I did not see one other 'star' that night do anything like it. No doubt she gets a buzz out of it, but I suspect the reason she did it was much more for the giving than the receiving.

ADAM ROCKOFF, AUTHOR, *GOING TO PIECES: THE RISE AND FALL OF THE SLASHER FILM, 1978-1986*: I think that Jamie Lee possessed that rare combination of girl-next-door sexiness with a mature, almost maternal, vibe. In both *Prom Night* and *Terror Train*, she was fun without seeming vacuous, both industrious and resilient when necessary. And of course, in *Halloween* and its sequel, she epitomized the headstrong virgin.

RICK ROSENTHAL, DIRECTOR, *HALLOWEEN II/HALLOWEEN: RESURRECTION*: Jamie had a great girl-next-door quality. She was accessible and vulnerable. She was sexy, but she could also be a "pal." And, on top of all that, she also had great comedic timing. So with that range, it was easy to see how she would make the leap from scream queen to leading lady—and she did.

MARY BETH RUBENS, CO-STAR, *PROM NIGHT*: She had an edge about her and she had the ability to make the camera follow her instead of the other way around. When the camera hit her, you could feel her vibrate.

SHELDON RYBOWSKI, CO-STAR, *PROM NIGHT*: I think her physical attributes played a big role, especially her beauty. My buddies and I would have *Prom Night* screening parties and the one scene that really stood out to me and my friends was the scene in *Prom Night* where Jamie sees the broken mirror in the change-room and then goes outside to see if anyone's there. The top of her blouse is a bit open and you can see a bit of her breasts and you're like, "Where can I find a high school with a girl like this?" She was very attractive.

RAY SAGER, ASSISTANT DIRECTOR, *TERROR TRAIN*: She was the girl-next-door and she had that special "something" that you couldn't identify but was definitely there.

JOHNNY LEE SCHELL, FORMER BOYFRIEND: Jamie has a good screen presence and has been believable in her roles in general in my opinion. She did a good job of selling the damsel in distress in *Halloween*. Her greatest attributes were common sense and a down to earth attitude. She knew she had no choice in who her parents were, and although proud of their accomplishments, never had an attitude about the Hollywood stuff.

M.J. SIMPSON, FILM JOURNALIST: Personally I have never thought of Jamie Lee Curtis as a "scream queen," a phrase which usually refers to the scantily clad stars of slightly over-the-top, low-budget B-movies (at least in my dictionary). Curtis has always struck me as a serious actress and, to be honest, I associate her more with bigger budget, often non-horror films like *A Fish Called Wanda* and *True Lies*.

DAVID J. SKAL, AUTHOR/HORROR HISTORIAN: Jamie Lee was the first real embodiment of "The Last Girl" motif. She has a slightly androgynous quality that combines qualities of the female victim and male aggressor, which invites identification with both female and male audiences. Her transformation from suppressed school girl to world-class fighter-for-her-life is probably unsurpassed in slasher films. She aged well with the sequels, becoming a more complex character, especially in *Halloween: H20*. Of course there was always that conscious or semi-conscious association with Janet Leigh in *Psycho*. Also, among all the scream queens of the last few decades, she's the best trained and most versatile actress, never giving a one-note performance. Her acting genes came from two great performers, after all.

ROGER SPOTTISWOODE, DIRECTOR, *TERROR TRAIN*: She had a tremendous grip on character; she had complete belief that if she became the character the lens would see into her and portray the character, so she didn't need to "act" to "become." She had a tremendous sense of where the camera was and what it would see. And she would adjust accordingly. She made few requests; she had grace, modesty, and tremendous integrity. She could lose herself in her character and yet still make it very special to her and to the audience.

ANTHONY TIMPONE, EDITOR, *FANGORIA*: While Jamie Lee had spunk, intelligence and the looks to stand out as the best of all the scream queens, she also had talent.

DANTE TOMASELLI, HORROR FILM-MAKER: She's the quintessential girl-next-door in *Halloween*, the virginal maiden of our collective consciousness. Laurie Strode is such an open book, so good natured and untouched, you just want to hug her and protect her. In the film, she's the polar opposite of the mysterious, deep dark Michael Myers. It's the ultimate representation of Good vs. Evil. Watching Jamie Lee Curtis go up against the boogeyman is as primal as having sex. We all love the sheer thrill of it. Especially with John Carpenter's scintillating, spine-tingling theme brushing our senses. This is horror heaven.

MICHAEL TOUGH, CO-STAR, *PROM NIGHT*: She has a great face with so much expression. What made Jamie Lee Curtis a great scream queen is I'm sure what makes Jamie Lee Curtis a great human being to this day. She is totally real and authentic. I have remained a fan and I admire the career choices and life choices she has made and continues to make.

JOVANKA VUCKOVIC, EDITOR, *RUE MORGUE*: Jamie Lee Curtis represents the beginning of a new type of scream queen. Though not exclusively, in the 1930s and 1940s, women were often cast in horror films to scream and run away from the bad guys. But during the 1970s and 1980s, women began to fight back, and the notion of the "Final Girl" was born—the typically morally-pure, resourceful gal who vanquishes the villain and makes it out alive. Jamie Lee Curtis is one of the original final girls of the North American slasher film. She also belongs to an era of scream queens that didn't take their clothes off, sort of what I call the "classy scream queen." The modern day scream queen is markedly different in that regard. Today, "scream queens" are most often associated with being naked and/or being the final girl—but not always. The final girl and the scream queen are no longer synonymous—as they were in Jamie Lee Curtis' day.

RICK WALLACE, ASSISTANT DIRECTOR, *HALLOWEEN*: Jamie had unconscious generosity. She was very open and honest and down-to-earth.

TOMMY LEE WALLACE, EDITOR/PRODUCTION DESIGNER, *HALLOWEEN/THE FOG*: A fine, girl-next-door quality. A real girl-scout, stand-up kind of integrity. Not overly pretty or even cute, but handsome and durable and smart and serious and wise, which ultimately makes her beautiful. Enough testosterone to avoid victim-hood. Most of all, a damn fine actress. I'm still hoping she'll take a serious part or two that really pushes her. I know she would deliver.

TIMOTHY WEBBER, CO-STAR, *TERROR TRAIN*: She was gorgeous. She had tremendous vulnerability, but at the same time you wouldn't want to cross her because she can take care of herself. She had great inner strength, and she was kind of dauntless, and she was also a great screamer.

FILMOGRAPHY

CINEMA

HALLOWEEN (1978)
Falcon International
Executive Producers: Moustapha Akkad, Irwin Yablans
Producer: Debra Hill
Director: John Carpenter
Screenplay: John Carpenter, Debra Hill
Cinematography: Dean Cundey
Editors: Charles Bornstein, Tommy Lee Wallace
Music: John Carpenter
Jamie Lee Curtis (Laurie Strode), *Donald Pleasence* (Dr. Sam Loomis), *P.J. Soles* (Lynda), *Nancy Loomis* (Annie).
Synopsis: A psychopath returns to his hometown to wreak havoc.

THE FOG (1980)
Avco-Embassy Pictures, EDI
Executive Producer: Charles B. Bloch
Producer: Debra Hill
Director: John Carpenter
Screenplay: John Carpenter, Debra Hill
Cinematography: Dean Cundey
Editors: Charles Bornstein, Tommy Lee Wallace
Music: John Carpenter
Jamie Lee Curtis (Elizabeth Solley), *Adrienne Barbeau* (Stevie Wayne), *Tom Atkins* (Nick Castle), *Janet Leigh* (Kathy Williams).

Synopsis: The town of Antonio Bay is haunted by the vengeful ghosts of murdered mariners.

PROM NIGHT (1980)
Simcom
Producer: Peter Simpson
Director: Paul Lynch
Screenplay: William Gray
Story: Robert Guza Jr.
Cinematography: Robert New
Editor: Brian Ravok
Music: Paul Zaza, Carl Zittrer
Jamie Lee Curtis (Kim Hammond), *Leslie Nielsen* (Mr. Hammond), *Casey Stevens* (Nick McBride), *Michael Tough* (Alex Hammond), *Eddie Benton* (Wendy)
Synopsis: High school students are stalked by a vengeful masked killed at their prom.

TERROR TRAIN (1980)
Astral/Harold Greenberg/Sandy Howard
Executive Producers: Lamar Card, Daniel Grodnik
Producer: Harold Greenberg
Director: Roger Spottiswoode
Screenplay: Thomas Y. Drake, Caryl Wickman
Story: Daniel Grodnik
Cinematography: John Alcott
Editor: Anne Henderson
Music: John Mills-Cockell
Jamie Lee Curtis (Alana Maxwell), *Ben Johnson* (Carne), *Hart Bochner* (Doc Manley), Timothy Webber (Mo), *Derek MacKinnon* (Kenny Hampson), *Sandee Currie* (Mitchy)
Synopsis: Six college students are stalked by a killer during a fraternity masquerade party aboard a chartered train.

ROADGAMES (aka *ROAD GAMES*) (1981)
Avco-Embassy Pictures/Quest Films
Executive Producer: Bernard Schwartz
Producer: Richard Franklin

Director: Richard Franklin
Screenplay: Everett De Roche
Cinematography: Vincent Monton
Editor: Edward McQueen-Mason
Music: Brian May
Jamie Lee Curtis (Hitch/Pamela), *Stacy Keach* (Quid), *Grant Page* (Smith or Jones)
Synopsis: A truck driver matches wits with a serial killer in the Australian desert.

HALLOWEEN II (1981)
Dino De Laurentiis/Universal
Executive Producers: Joseph Wolf, Irwin Yablans
Producers: John Carpenter, Debra Hill
Director: Rick Rosenthal
Screenplay: John Carpenter, Debra Hill
Cinematography: Dean Cundey
Editors: Mark Goldblatt, Skip Schoolnik
Music: John Carpenter, Alan Howarth
Jamie Lee Curtis (Laurie Strode), *Donald Pleasence* (Dr. Sam Loomis), *Charles Cyphers* (Leigh Brackett), *Lance Guest* (Jimmy)
Synopsis: Michael Myers stalks Laurie Strode in a hospital.

TRADING PLACES (1983)
Cinema Group Ventures, Paramount Pictures
Executive Producer: George Folsey Jr.
Producer: Aaron Russo
Director: John Landis
Screenplay: Timothy Harris, Herschel Weingrod
Cinematography: Robert Paynter
Editor: Malcolm Campbell
Music: Elmer Bernstein
Dan Aykroyd (Louis Winthorpe III), *Eddie Murphy* (Billy Ray Valentine), *Jamie Lee Curtis* (Ophelia), *Denholm Elliott* (Coleman)
Synopsis: A successful businessman and a street hustler trade places as part of a bet.

LOVE LETTERS (1984)
Millenium/New World Pictures
Executive Producer: Don Levin
Producer: Roger Corman
Director: Amy Holden Jones
Screenplay: Amy Holden Jones
Cinematography: Alec Hirschfeld
Editor: Wendy Greene Bricmont
Music: Ralph Jones
Jamie Lee Curtis (Anna Winter), *James Keach* (Oliver Andrews),
Amy Madigan (Wendy)
Synopsis: After discovering that her deceased mother had been
involved in a long-term love affair, a young woman embarks on an
affair with a married man.

GRANDVIEW, U.S.A. (1984)
CBS
Producers: William Warren Blaylock, Peter W. Rea
Director: Randal Kleiser
Screenplay: Ken Hixon
Cinematography: Reynaldo Villalobos
Editor: Robert Gordon
Music: Thomas Newman
Jamie Lee Curtis (Michelle "Mike" Cody), *C. Thomas Howell* (Tim
Pearson), *Jennifer Jason Leigh* (Candy Webster), *Patrick Swayze*
(Ernie "Slam" Webster)
Synopsis: A teenage boy falls in love with the woman who runs the
local demolition derby.

PERFECT (1985)
Columbia Pictures/Delphi III/Pluperfect
Executive Producer: Kim Kurumada
Producer: James Bridges
Director: James Bridges
Screenplay: James Bridges, Aaron Latham
Cinematography: Gordon Willis
Editor: Jeff Gourson
Music: Ralph Burns

Jamie Lee Curtis (Jessie), John Travolta (Adam), Marilu Henner (Sally), Laraine Newman (Linda)
Synopsis: A Rolling Stone reporter falls in love with an aerobics instructor while doing a story on health clubs.

A MAN IN LOVE (1987)

Alexandre Films/Camera One/Dolly/J.M.S. Films
Producers: Diane Kurys, Michel Seydoux
Director: Diane Kurys
Screenplay: Diane Kurys, Olivier Schatzky
Cinematography: Bernard Zitzermann
Editor: Joele Van Effenterre
Music: Georges Delerue
Jamie Lee Curtis (Susan Elliott), Peter Coyote (Steve Elliott), Greta Scacchi (Jane Steiner)
Synopsis: A married American actor falls in love with his leading lady while filming a movie in Rome.

AMAZING GRACE AND CHUCK (1987)

Delphi V/Rastar/Turnstar Pictures
Executive Producer: Roger M. Rothstein
Producer: David Field
Director: Mike Newell
Screenplay: David Field
Cinematography: Robert Elswit
Editor: Peter Hollywood
Music: Elmer Bernstein
Jamie Lee Curtis (Lynn Taylor), Alex English (Amazing Grace Smith), Gregory Peck (President), Joshua Zuehlke (Chuck Murdock)
Synopsis: A small-town kid decides to stop playing baseball until all of the world's nuclear weapons have been disarmed.

DOMINICK AND EUGENE (1988)

Orion Pictures
Producers: Mike Farrell, Marvin Minoff
Director: Robert M. Young
Screenplay: Corey Blechman, Alvin Sargent
Story: Danny Porfirio

Cinematography: Curtis Clark
Editor: Arthur Coburn
Music: Trevor Jones
Jamie Lee Curtis (Jennifer Reston), *Tom Hulce* (Dominick "Nicky" Luciano), *Ray Liotta* (Eugene "Gino" Luciano)
Synopsis: A man is forced to decide between leaving home and furthering his medical studies or staying home and watching over his mentally-challenged brother.

A FISH CALLED WANDA (1988)
Metro-Goldwyn-Mayer/Prominent Features/Star Partners Limited Partnership
Executive Producers: Steve Abbott, John Cleese
Producer: Michael Shamberg
Director: Charles Crichton
Screenplay: John Cleese
Story: John Cleese, Charles Crichton
Cinematography: Alan Hume
Editor: John Jympson
Music: John Du Prez
Jamie Lee Curtis (Wanda Gershwitz), *John Cleese* (Archie Leach), *Kevin Kline* (Otto), *Michael Palin* (Ken)
Synopsis: A woman and her boyfriend, both thieves, arrive in England where they plot to steal a diamond collection.

BLUE STEEL (1990)
Edward R. Pressman/Lightning Pictures/Mack-Taylor Productions/Precision Films
Executive Producer: Lawrence Kasanoff
Producers: Edward R. Pressman, Oliver Stone
Director: Kathryn Bigelow
Screenplay: Kathryn Bigelow, Eric Red
Cinematography: Amir M. Mokri
Editor: Lee Percy
Music: Brad Fiedel
Jamie Lee Curtis (Megan Turner), *Ron Silver* (Eugene Hunt), *Clancy Brown* (Nick Mann)

Synopsis: A rookie female cop in New York becomes the object of a psychopath's murderous fantasies.

QUEENS LOGIC (1991)
New Line/New Visions
Executive Producers: Stuart Benjamin, Taylor Hackford
Producers: Stuart Oken, Russell Smith
Director: Steve Rash
Screenplay: Tony Spiridakis
Cinematography: Amir M. Mokri
Editor: Patrick Kennedy
Music: Joe Jackson
Jamie Lee Curtis (Grace), *Kevin Bacon* (Dennis), *Linda Fiorentino* (Carla), *John Malkovich* (Eliot), *Joe Mantegna* (Al)
Synopsis: A group of thirtysomethings take stock of their lives when they gather for a wedding.

MY GIRL (1991)
Columbia Pictures/Imagine
Executive Producers: Joseph M. Caracciolo, David T. Friendly
Producer: Brian Grazer
Director: Howard Zieff
Screenplay: Laurice Elehwany
Cinematography: Paul Elliott
Editor: Wendy Greene Bricmont
Music: James Newton Howard
Jamie Lee Curtis (Shelly De Voto), *Dan Aykroyd* (Harry Sultenfuss), *Anna Chlumsky* (Vada Sultenfuss), *Macaulay Culkin* (Thomas J. Sennett)
Synopsis: An eleven year old girl comes to terms with her widowed father's new romance and her best friend's death.

FOREVER YOUNG (1992)
Icon/Warner Bros.
Executive Producers: J.J. Abrams, Edward S. Feldman, Mel Gibson
Producer: Bruce Davey
Director: Steve Miner
Screenplay: J.J. Abrams

Cinematography: Russell Boyd
Editor: Jon Poll
Music: Jerry Goldsmith
Jamie Lee Curtis (Claire Cooper), *Mel Gibson* (Capt. Daniel McCormick), *Elijah Wood* (Nat Cooper)
Synopsis: A 1939 test pilot is frozen in a cryogenics experiment and doesn't wake up until 1992.

MY GIRL 2 (1994)

Imagine
Executive Producers: Joseph M. Caracciolo, David T. Friendly, Howard Zieff
Producer: Brian Grazer
Director: Howard Zieff
Screenplay: Janet Kovalcik
Cinematography: Paul Elliott
Editor: Wendy Greene Bricmont
Music: Cliff Eidelman
Jamie Lee Curtis (Shelly DeVoto Sultenfuss), *Dan Aykroyd* (Harry Sultenfuss), *Anna Chlumsky* (Vada Margaret Sultenfuss)
Synopsis: Vada Sultenfuss researches her mother's life as part of a school assignment.

MOTHER'S BOYS (1994)

CBS/Dimension Films
Executive Producers: Randall Poster, Bob Weinstein, Harvey Weinstein
Producers: Jack E. Freedman, Patricia Herskovic, Wayne S. Williams
Director: Yves Simoneau
Screenplay: Richard Hawley, Barry Schneider
Cinematography: Elliot Davis
Editor: Michael Ornstein
Music: George S. Clinton
Jamie Lee Curtis (Jude), *Peter Gallagher* (Robert), *Joanne Whalley-Kilmer* (Callie), *Vanessa Redgrave* (Lydia)
Synopsis: A mentally-unbalanced woman returns to take back the family she once abandoned.

TRUE LIES (1994)

Lightstorm Entertainment/Twentieth Century Fox
Executive Producers: Lawrence Kasanoff, Rae Sanchini, Robert Shriver
Producers: Stephanie Austin, James Cameron
Director: James Cameron
Screenplay: James Cameron
Cinematography: Russell Carpenter
Editors: Conrad Buff, Mark Goldblatt, Richard A. Harris
Music: Brad Fiedel
Arnold Schwarzenegger (Harry Tasker), *Jamie Lee Curtis* (Helen Tasker), *Tom Arnold* (Albert Gibson)
Synopsis: A computer salesman who doubles as a government agent tries to stop a terrorist from launching a nuclear attack upon America.

HOUSE ARREST (1996)

Metro-Goldwyn-Mayer/Rysher Entertainment
Executive Producer: Keith Samples
Producers: Judith A. Polone, Harry Winer
Director: Harry Winer
Screenplay: Michael Hitchcock
Cinematography: Ueli Steiger
Editor: Ronald Roose
Music: Bruce Broughton
Jamie Lee Curtis (Janet Beindorf), *Kevin Pollak* (Ned Beindorf)
Synopsis: Children hold their bickering parents hostage in order to prevent a divorce.

FIERCE CREATURES (1997)

Fish Productions/Jersey Films/Universal
Executive Producer: Steve Abbott
Producers: John Cleese, Michael Shamberg
Director: Fred Schepisi
Screenplay: John Cleese, Iain Johnstone
Cinematography: Ian Baker, Adrian Biddle
Editor: Robert Gibson
Music: Jerry Goldsmith

Jamie Lee Curtis (Willa Weston), *John Cleese* (Rollo Lee), *Kevin Kline* (Vince McCain/Rod McCain), *Michael Palin* (Adrian "Bugsy" Malone)
Synopsis: A ruthless tycoon buys a London zoo and tries to generate business by killing all of the animals except for the most ferocious ones.

HOMEGROWN (1998)
Lakeshore International
Executive Producers: Tom Rosenberg, Sigurjon Sighvatsson, Ted Tannebaum
Producer: Jason Clark
Director: Stephen Gyllenhaal
Screenplay: Stephen Gyllenhaal, Nicholas Kazan
Cinematography: Greg Gardiner
Editor: Michael Jablow
Music: Trevor Rabin
Jamie Lee Curtis (Sierra Kahan), *John Lithgow* (Malcolm/Robert Stockman), *Ryan Phillippe* (Harlan Dykstra), *Billy Bob Thornton* (Jack Marsden)
Synopsis: Three losers find themselves caught in murder and mayhem when they take over a marijuana plantation.

HALLOWEEN H20: 20 YEARS LATER (1998)
Dimension Films/Nightfall
Executive Producers: Moustapha Akkad, Jamie Lee Curtis
Producer: Paul Freeman
Director: Steve Miner
Screenplay: Matt Greenberg, Robert Zappia
Story: Robert Zappia
Cinematography: Daryn Okada
Editor: Patrick Lussier
Music: John Ottman
Jamie Lee Curtis (Laurie Strode/Keri Tate), *Adam Arkin* (Will Brennan), *Josh Hartnett* (John Tate), *Janet Leigh* (Norma Watson*)*, *Michelle Williams* (Molly Cartwell)
Synopsis: After a twenty year hibernation, Michael Myers returns to terrorize Laurie Strode.

VIRUS (1999)
Mutual Film Company/Universal
Executive Producers: Mark Gordon, Chuck Pharrer, Gary Levinsohn, Mike Richardson
Producer: Gale Anne Hurd
Director: John Bruno
Screenplay: Chuck Pharrer
Cinematography: David Eggby
Editor: Scott Smith
Music: Joel McNeely
Jamie Lee Curtis (Kit Foster), *William Baldwin* (Steve Baker), *Donald Sutherland* (Captain Everton)
Synopsis: The crew of a salvage vessel are attacked by an alien life form.

DROWNING MONA (2000)
Code Entertainment/Jersey Shore/Mangold Productions Inc./ Neverland Films
Executive Producers: Danny DeVito, Michael Shamberg, Stacey Sher, Jonathan Weisgal
Producers: Al Corley, Eugene Musso, Bart Rosenblatt
Director: Nick Gomez
Screenplay: Peter Steinfeld
Cinematography: Bruce Douglas Johnson
Editor: Richard Pearson
Music: Michael Tavera
Jamie Lee Curtis (Rona Mace), *Danny DeVito* (Chief Wyatt Rash), *Bette Midler* (Mona Dearly), *Neve Campbell* (Ellen Rash)
Synopsis: When an unpopular woman drives her car off a cliff and into a river to her death, everyone in the town where she lived becomes a suspect.

THE TAILOR OF PANAMA (2001)
Columbia Pictures/Merlin Films
Executive Producer: John Le Carre
Producer: John Boorman
Director: John Boorman
Screenplay: John Boorman, Andrew Davies, John Le Carre
Cinematography: Philippe Rousselot

Editor: Ron Davis
Music: Shaun Davey
Jamie Lee Curtis (Louisa Pendel), *Pierce Brosnan* (Andrew Osnard), *Geoffrey Rush* (Harold Pendel)
Synopsis: A British spy is banished to Panama where he meets a local tailor with connections to the most powerful people in Panama.

DADDY AND THEM (2001)
Free Hazel Films/Industry Entertainment/Miramax Films/Shooting Gallery/WMG Film
Executive Producers: Jonathan Gordon, Bob Weinstein, Harvey Weinstein
Producers: Geyer Kosinski, Larry Meistrich, Robert Salerno
Director: Billy Bob Thornton
Screenplay: Billy Bob Thornton
Cinematography: Barry Markowitz
Editor: Sally Menke
Music: Larry Paxton, Marty Stuart, Kristin Wilkinson
Jamie Lee Curtis (Elaine Bowen), *Billy Bob Thornton* (Claude Montgomery), *Laura Dern* (Ruby Montgomery), *Kelly Preston* (Rose), *Andy Griffith* (O.T. Montgomery)
Synopsis: A poor Arkansas family is torn apart when an uncle is charged with murder.

HALLOWEEN: RESURRECTION (2002)
Dimension Films/Nightfall Productions/Trancas International Films
Executive Producers: Moustapha Akkad, Ralph Rieckermann
Producers: Paul Freeman, Michael Leahy
Director: Rick Rosenthal
Screenplay: Larry Brand, Sean Hood
Cinematography: David Geddes
Editor: Robert A. Ferretti
Music: Danny Lux
Jamie Lee Curtis (Laurie Strode), *Brad Loree* (Michael Myers), *Busta Rhymes* (Freddie Harris), *Bianca Kajlich* (Sara Moyer), *Sean Patrick Thomas* (Rudy)
Synopsis: A group of college students decide to try and spend a night at Michael Myers' childhood home which is broadcast live on the Internet.

FREAKY FRIDAY (2003)
Casual Friday Productions/Gunn Films/Walt Disney Pictures
Executive Producer: Mario Iscovich
Producer: Andrew Gunn
Director: Mark Waters
Screenplay: Leslie Dixon, Heather Hach
Cinematography: Oliver Wood
Editor: Bruce Green
Music: Rolfe Kent
Jamie Lee Curtis (Tess Coleman), *Lindsay Lohan* (Anna Coleman),
Mark Harmon (Ryan), *Chad Michael Murray* (Jake)
Synopsis: A woman and her teenage daughter switch bodies.

CHRISTMAS WITH THE KRANKS (2004)
Revolution Studios/1492 Studios
Executive Producers: Bruce A. Block, Charles Newirth
Producers: Michael Barnathan, Chris Columbus, Mark Radcliffe
Director: Joe Roth
Screenplay: Chris Columbus
Cinematography: Don Burgess
Editor: Nick Moore
Music: John Debney
Jamie Lee Curtis (Nora Krank), *Tim Allen* (Luther Krank), *Dan
Aykroyd* (Vic Frohmeyer)
Synopsis: Luther and Nora Krank decide to skip Christmas.

BEVERLY HILLS CHIHUAHUA (2008)
Art in Motion/Mandeville Films/Smart Entertainment/Walt Disney
Pictures
Executive Producers: Steve Nicolaides
Producers: David Hoberman, John Jacobs, Todd Lieberman
Director: Raja Gosnell
Screenplay: Analisa LaBianco, Jeffrey Bushell
Cinematography: Phil Meheux
Editor: Sabrina Plisco
Music: Heitor Pereira
Jamie Lee Curtis (Aunt Viv), *Drew Barrymore* (Chloe), *Piper Perabo*
(Rachel Ashe Lynn), *Andy Garcia* (Delgado), *George Lopez* (Papi),

Cheech Marin (Manuel)
Synopsis: A Beverly Hills Chihuahua finds herself lost while on vacation in Mexico.

YOU AGAIN (2010)
Oops Doughnuts Productions/Walt Disney Pictures
Executive Producer: Mario Iscovich
Producers: Andy Fickman, John J. Strauss, Eric Tannenbaum
Director: Andy Fickman
Screenplay: Moe Jelline, Dave Johnson
Cinematography: David Hennings
Editor: David Rennie
Music: Nathan Wang
Jamie Lee Curtis (Gail), *Kristen Bell* (Marni), *Kristin Chenoweth* (Monique Leroux), *Sigourney Weaver* (Aunt Ramona), *Betty White* (Grandma Bunny)
Synopsis: A young woman tries to stop her brother from marrying the girl who tormented her in high school.

TELEVISION

COLUMBO
THE BYE-BYE SKY HIGH I.Q. MURDER CASE (1977)
Universal Television
Producer: Richard Alan Simmons
Director: Sam Wanamaker
Teleplay: Robert M. Young
Cinematography: Ted Voigtlander
Editor: Jerry Dronsky
Music: Robert Prince
Jamie Lee Curtis (Waitress), *Peter Falk* (Lt. Columbo), *Theodore Bikel* (Oliver Brandt), *Kenneth Mars* (Mike), *Samantha Eggar* (Vivian Brandt)
Synopsis: Columbo matches wits with a murder suspect who has one of the highest I.Q.'s in the world.

SHE'S IN THE ARMY NOW (1981)
ABC Circle Films
Producer; Harry R. Sherman
Director: Hy Averback
Teleplay: Earl W. Wallace
Cinematography: William K. Jurgensen
Editors: Diane Adler, George R. Rohrs
Music: Artie Butler
Jamie Lee Curtis (Pvt. Rita Jennings), *Melanie Griffith* (Pvt. Sylvie Knoll), *Kathleen Quinlan* (Pvt. Cass Donner)
Synopsis: A group of female army recruits go through basic training.

DEATH OF A CENTERFOLD: THE DOROTHY STRATTEN STORY (1981)
MGM Television/Wilcox Productions
Executive Producer: Larry Wilcox
Producer: Paul Pompian
Director: Gabrielle Beaumont
Teleplay: Donald L. Stewart
Cinematography: Emil Oster
Editor: Morton Tubor
Music: Roger Webb
Jamie Lee Curtis (Dorothy Stratten), *Bruce Weitz* (Paul Snider), *Mitch Ryan* (Hugh Hefner), *Robert Reed* (David Palmer)
Synopsis: The life and tragic murder of *Playboy* playmate Dorothy Stratten.

MONEY ON THE SIDE (1982)
Columbia Pictures Television/Green-Epstein Productions
Executive Producers: Allen S. Epstein, Jim Green
Producer: Hal Landers
Director: Robert E. Collins
Teleplay: Robert E. Collins, Eugene Price
Story: Morton S. Fine
Cinematography: Fred J. Koenekamp
Editor: Donald R. Rode
Music: Richard Bellis

Jamie Lee Curtis (Michelle Jamison), *Karen Valentine* (Janice Vernon), *Linda Purl* (Annie Gilson), *Christopher Lloyd* (Sergeant Stampone)
Synopsis: Housewives moonlight as prostitutes to earn extra money.

AS SUMMERS DIE (1986)
Baldwin-Aldrich Productions/Chris-Rose Productions/HBO/ Telepictures Productions
Executive Producers: Larry Konigsberg, Larry Sanitsky
Producers: Robert W. Christiansen, Rick Rosenberg
Director: Jean-Claude Tramont
Teleplay: Jeff Andrus, Ed Namzug
Cinematography: Ernest Day
Editor: Michael Brown
Music: Michel Legrand
Jamie Lee Curtis (Whitsey Loftin), *Bette Davis* (Hannah Loftin), *Scott Glenn* (Willie Croft)
Synopsis: An elderly woman's property becomes a major point of contention when oil is discovered on the property.

THE HEIDI CHRONICLES (1995)
Turner Network Television (TNT)
Executive Producer: Michael Brandman
Producer: Leanne Moore
Director: Paul Bogart
Teleplay: Wendy Wasserstein
Cinematography: Isidore Mankofsky
Editor: Stan Cole
Music: David Shire
Jamie Lee Curtis (Heidi Holland), *Tom Hulce* (Peter Patrone), *Peter Friedman* (Scoop Rosenbaum), *Kim Cattrall* (Susan), *Eve Gordon* (Lisa)
Synopsis: Heidi Holland grows up to become a successful art historian.

NICHOLAS' GIFT (1998)
Five Mile River Films/CBS/Lux Vide/Mediaset/Radiotelevisione Italiana
Executive Producers: Lorenzo Minoli, Judd Parkin

Director: Robert Markowitz
Teleplay: Christine Berardo
Cinematography: Raffaele Mertes
Editor: David Beatty
Music: Carlo Siliotto
Jamie Lee Curtis (Maggie Green), *Alan Bates* (Reg Green), *Hallie Kate Eisenberg* (Eleanor), *Gene Wexler* (Nicholas Green)
Synopsis: An American couple and their two children are attacked and shot by highway bandits while on vacation in Italy. After discovering that their son is brain-dead, the couple donates his organs which saves the lives of several ill Italian patients. Based on a true story.

NOTES

INTRODUCTION

1. Since winning the British Academy Award (BAFTA) in 1984, Curtis has won an American Comedy Award, two Golden Globes, and a People's Choice Award. In 1998, Curtis received a star on the Hollywood Walk of Fame.

ONE / JAMIE LEE

1. Janet Leigh had been married twice previously before she and Tony Curtis were married in 1951. In 1942, at the age of fourteen, Leigh had married John Kenneth Carlyle but the marriage was annulled after four months. In 1946, Leigh married Stanley Reames. They divorced in 1948. Leigh attended University of the Pacific between 1943 and 1946.

2. Prior to becoming an actor, Tony Curtis had served in the United States Navy. During World War II, Curtis served aboard the *U.S.S. Proteus*, a submarine tender. On September 2, 1945, Tony Curtis witnessed the Japanese surrender in Tokyo Bay from a mile away.

3. Curtleigh, the production company Tony Curtis and Janet Leigh formed in 1956, co-produced *The Vikings* (1958), although co-star, and co-producer, Kirk Douglas received 60 percent of the film's profits which earned Douglas $2 million. Through Curtleigh, Tony Curtis helped raise the $1 million budget

for Curtis' next film, *The Defiant Ones* (1958). Curtleigh also produced a one-hour television film entitled *The Young Juggler* which Tony Curtis starred in and which aired on NBC on March 29, 1960. The film was made for just $200,000.

4. Tony Curtis and Janet Leigh first co-starred in *Houdini* (1953) in which Curtis starred in the title role. Curtis and Leigh later co-starred in *The Black Shield of Falworth* (1954), *The Vikings* (1958), *The Perfect Furlough* (1958), and *Who Was That Lady?* (1960).

5. John Gavin was paid $30,000 for his work as Marion Crane's lover, Sam Loomis, while Anthony Perkins was paid $40,000 to play Norman Bates.

6. Tony Curtis was a regular visitor to the *Psycho* set during filming. On March 7, 1979, Jamie Lee Curtis and Janet Leigh appeared together at an American Film Institute (AFI) Salute to Alfred Hitchcock that was held at the Beverly Hilton Hotel in Beverly Hills, California. When Melanie Griffith—whose mother, Tippi Hedren, made her screen debut in *The Birds*—had her sixth birthday, Alfred Hitchcock gave her a miniature doll of her mother in a wooden box that forever traumatized Griffith. Jamie Lee Curtis says she never spent any time with Hitchcock. Hedren later starred in Hitchcock's *Marnie* (1964).

7. Tony Curtis and Christine Kaufmann divorced in 1967. Tony Curtis was later married to Leslie Allen (April 20, 1968–1982), Andrea Savio (1984-1992), Lisa Deutsch (February 28, 1993—1994), and is currently married to Jill Vandenberg. Kaufmann gave birth to daughter Alexandra Curtis on July 19, 1964, Tony Curtis' third daughter, and Allegra Curtis, Tony Curtis' fourth daughter, on July 12, 1966. Leslie Allen gave birth to son Nicholas Curtis on December 13, 1971, Tony Curtis' first son, and a second son, Benjamin Curtis, on May 2, 1973. Nicholas Curtis died of a drug overdose in 1994. Janet Leigh suffered a miscarriage in 1954.

8. *The Manchurian Candidate* received a theatrical re-release in 1987.

9. Other celebrities that attended John Thomas Dye are Lisa Marie Presley and Tori Spelling.

10. *Murder Among Friends* opened on December 28, 1975 and closed on January 10, 1976 after seventeen performances.

11. Janet Leigh entered the University of the Pacific in 1943 where Leigh studied music and psychology. Leigh left school in 1946, the same year she was discovered by actress Norma Shearer and was put under contract by MGM after only a single screen test. On May 14, 2004, Leigh was awarded an honorary Doctor of Fine Arts degree from the University of the Pacific.

12. Chuck Binder would later represent such actresses as Daryl Hannah and Sharon Stone.

13. Monique James died of cancer on January 18, 2001. In addition to aiding Jamie Lee Curtis' career, James was also credited with helping the careers of Warren Beatty and Robert Redford. Thomas D. Tannenbaum died of heart and liver failure on December 5, 2001.

14. Pamela Sue Martin was later replaced in the role of Nancy Drew by actress Janet Louise Johnson.

15. Jamie Lee Curtis is still represented by Creative Artists Agency (CAA) today. In the early 1980s, Curtis was represented by legendary female super-agent Sue Mengers who was based at International Creative Management (ICM).

TWO / INTRODUCING LAURIE STRODE

1. From 1970 to 1978, Janet Leigh appeared in the made-for-television movies *House on Greenapple Road* (1970), *Deadly Dream* (1971), *Murdock's Gang* (1973), *Columbo: Forgotten Lady* (1975), *Murder at the World Series* (1977), and *Telethon* (1977).

2. Besides *The Last Tycoon* (1976), the most commercially-successful feature film Tony Curtis made in the 1970s was *The Bad News Bears Go to Japan* (1978).

3. Robert Carradine is best known for starring in the film *Revenge of the Nerds* (1984) and its several sequels.

4. Jamie Lee Curtis' final episode on *Operation Petticoat*, entitled *Claire Voyant*, aired on May 18, 1978.

5. The Sam Loomis character was obviously named after the John Gavin character from *Psycho* who was the lover of Marion Crane, the character played by Janet Leigh. Another character in *Halloween*, Leigh Brackett, was named after the female screenwriter of the classic films *The Big Sleep* (1946) and *Rio Bravo* (1959), both of which had been directed by John Carpenter's idol, Howard Hawks. Tommy Doyle was named after a character in *Rear Window* (1954) who was played by actor Wendell Corey.

6. Anne Lockhart would gain her greatest fame playing the character of Sheba on the television series *Battlestar Galactica* which ran from 1978 to 1979.

7. *Jaws 2* was released in June of 1978, after *Halloween*'s filming. Anne Lockhart insists that she never met with John Carpenter, and Carpenter recalls that the actress from *Jaws 2* had zero interest in taking the role of Laurie Strode.

8. Donald Pleasence's previous genre credits included such titles as *The Great Escape* (1963), *Fantastic Voyage* (1966), *Eye of the Devil* (1967), *Death Line* (1972), *From Beyond the Grave* (1973), *The Mutations* (1974), *Journey Into Fear* (1975), *Escape to Witch Mountain* (1975), *The Devil's Men* (1976).

9. *Halloween* was just one of no less than ten feature films starring Donald Pleasence that would be released between 1977 and 1978. Pleasence also made many television appearances during this period.

10.   Tina Cassaday, who's roughly the same age as Curtis, currently runs a hair salon in Beverly Hills, California where her celebrity clients include former roommate Jamie Lee Curtis.

THREE / THE MAKING OF *HALLOWEEN*

1.   Peter Griffith's role as Laurie Strode's father, Morgan Strode, was Griffith's lone screen credit. Peter Griffith died on May 14, 2001.

2.   Nick Castle's father was famed Hollywood dance choreographer Nick Castle Sr. which explains Nick Castle's crisp, deft movements in the film.

3.   *The Devil's Rain* (1975) was produced by Sandy Howard who would later collaborate with Jamie Lee Curtis on *Terror Train* (1980). *The Devil's Rain* also marked the feature film debut of John Travolta who would later co-star with Jamie Lee Curtis in the film *Perfect* (1985).

4.   *Halloween II* would explain that Laurie Strode, Michael Myers' sister, was hidden and adopted by another family, the Strodes. There's no mention in *Halloween* as to the whereabouts of Michael Myers' parents.

5.   *The Texas Chainsaw Massacre* (1974) and *The Funhouse* (1981), both of which were directed by Tobe Hooper, are also strong examples of this.

6.   Nancy Kyes was born in Falls Church, Virginia on December 19, 1949. Kyes studied theater at Northwestern University in Chicago. Prior to filming *Halloween*, Nancy Kyes, then known as Nancy Loomis, had co-starred in the family-adventure film *The Sea Gypsies* which would be released in 1978. *The Sea Gypsies* was produced by Peter Simpson who would later collaborate with Jamie Lee Curtis on the film *Prom Night* (1980). *The Sea Gypsies* was directed by Stewart Raffill who would later direct the science-fiction adventure film *The Philadelphia Experiment*

(1984) on which John Carpenter would serve as an executive producer.

7.   P.J. Soles later had a memorable supporting role opposite star Goldie Hawn in the hit comedy film *Private Benjamin* (1980).

8.   *Pandemonium* was written by Richard Whitley who'd previously written *Rock 'n' Roll High School*. Carol Kane played the female lead in *Pandemonium*.

FOUR / THE BABYSITTER AND THE BOOGEYMAN

1.   Ben Tramer was named after Bennett Tramer, one of John Carpenter's classmates from USC. In 1981's *Halloween II*, Ben Tramer burns to death after being hit by a car.

2.   In 2000, Curtis, Kyes, and Soles joined together for a screening of *Halloween* that took place at the Egyptian Theater in Hollywood. They also appeared together at a cast and crew Q & A panel.

3.   The Michael Myers character was named after a British film distributor named Michael Myers who'd championed the successful European release of *Assault on Precinct 13*. This was Carpenter's and Hill's tribute.

4.   Curtis had shown some interest in working with children during her short stay at University of the Pacific. Curtis has also written a series of best-selling children's books, and is the mother of two children herself.

5.   James Winburn had worked with Curtis previously at Universal Studios, and had also worked with Tony Curtis on several film and television projects.

6.   The 2007 remake of *Halloween* shows Michael Myers' childhood and also spends an extended period of time with his family members.

7. Curtis later kissed actor Derek MacKinnon, who played the killer in *Terror Train* (1980), and Dick Warlock, who would play Michael Myers in *Halloween II* (1981). This would be Curtis' end-of-filming ritual during her scream queen career.

8. The heroine in *Black Christmas* was played by actress Olivia Hussey.

FIVE / A SCREAM QUEEN IS BORN

1. Curtis would later list *True Lies* (1994) as her best film and best working experience, although she's also listed *Hallowee*n many times as the best film she's ever made.

2. Janet Leigh played Paul Newman's estranged wife in *Harper* (1966), Leigh's last major feature film appearance. The low-budget, killer rabbit horror film *Night of the Lepus* (1972), in which Leigh co-starred with actor Stuart Whitman, most definitely wasn't a major Hollywood feature film. 1979's *Boardwalk*, which Leigh also starred in, was an obscure drama that was barely released.

3. Sally Field had triumphed in *Norma Rae* (1979), Jane Fonda in *Coming Home* (1978) and *The China Syndrome* (1979), and Meryl Streep in *The Deer Hunter* (1978).

4. Johnny Lee Schell is a Grammy award-winning musician.

5. *Elvis*, John Carpenter's follow-up to *Halloween*, aired on ABC in February of 1979 and received excellent ratings and solid reviews.

6. Chicago film critics Roger Ebert and Gene Siskel would be *Halloween*'s two most ardent critical supporters.

7. In January of 2008, John Carpenter filed suit against producer Irwin Yablans and distributor Compass International Pictures over alleged non-payment of royalties from *Halloween*.

8. In *Halloween*, Jamie Lee Curtis was credited as "Introducing Jamie Lee Curtis" which is something that Curtis had asked for. Subsequent horror films would copy this "Introducing" credit, most notably in 1981's *Happy Birthday to Me* where actress' Tracy Bregman and Lisa Langlois were credited as "Introducing Tracy Bregman and Lisa Langlois." This is another example of Jamie Lee Curtis' impact within the horror genre.

9. When Curtis began her post-horror film career in 1981, she essentially had to start her acting career over again. It's only thirty years later, in retrospect, that her scream queen career has transformed her into a screen icon.

10. John Carpenter's last critical triumph was 1984's *Starman* which was released over twenty-five years ago. *Starman* also represents the most commercially-successful film that Carpenter made between 1982 and 2008, even though the film only grossed $28 million domestically. Besides *Starman*, Carpenter would only have one other film that grossed more than $20 million domestically between 1982 and 2008. This was 1996's *Escape from LA* which grossed $25 million. *Escape from LA* had a budget of $50 million.

11. This is true in the sense that *Halloween* has become to the horror genre what 1983's *A Christmas Story*, which was directed by Bob Clark, has become to the Christmas holidays and to the Christmas movie genre.

12. The only similarity between Scout Taylor-Compton's Laurie Strode and Curtis' Laurie Strode is in terms of Taylor-Compton's own unconventional appearance.

13. The 2007 remake of *Halloween* had a budget of $15 million and grossed $58 million domestically.

14. Prior to *The Fog*, Barbeau had done a ton of television work, including 120 episodes of the television series *Maude* between 1972 and 1979. Barbeau had also appeared in several made-for-television movies. Like Curtis and Leigh, Barbeau had also appeared on an episode of *The Love Boat*.

SIX / ENTERING *THE FOG*

1. *The Fog* would be the beginning of a long film career for Barbeau, especially in the horror genre where Barbeau would appear in such genre films as *Escape from New York* (1981), *Creepshow* (1982), *Swamp Thing* (1982), *Two Evil Eyes* (1990) and legions of other genre films since.

2. Before *The Fog*, Atkins had appeared in the comedy-thriller *The Ninth Configuration* which was written and directed by *Exorcist* creator William Peter Blatty.

3. In the 2005 remake of *The Fog*, the Kathy Williams character was played by actress Sara Botsford who was slightly older than Janet Leigh was when Leigh filmed the 1980 version. Botsford was born on April 8, 1951.

4. Leigh, who was born on July 6, 1927, was a couple of months short of her 52nd birthday when *The Fog* began filming in April of 1979. Jamie Lee Curtis was twenty when *The Fog* began filming, and turned 51 years old on November 22, 2009.

5. This is the only time in any of Curtis' horror films that she was ever romantic with another character or was involved in any kind of sexual situation.

6. Atkins worked with Carpenter, and good friend Adrienne Barbeau, again on *Escape from New York* (1981), a film for which Jamie Lee Curtis would provide uncredited voice-over work. Atkins then starred in 1982's Shape-less *Halloween III: Season of the Witch* in which his character's ex-wife was played by Nancy Kyes.

7. Adrienne Barbeau and John Carpenter divorced in 1984.

8. Curtis says she stopped smoking cigarettes in the early 1980s.

SEVEN / JAMIE LEE CURTIS' *THE FOG*

1. Barbeau and Carpenter would only work together once more after *The Fog*, in 1981's *Escape from New York*. Barbeau and Carpenter also formed a production company that was called Hye-Whitebread Productions.

2. In May of 1979, Curtis presented Leigh with an award at the National Film Society.

3. Avco-Embassy also wanted Curtis' role in the film to be expanded.

4. Janet Leigh appeared on the first *Circus of the Stars* which was broadcast on January 10, 1977. Tony Curtis later appeared on *Circus of the Stars #8* which was broadcast on December 18, 1983.

5. The *Buck Rogers* episode would be Curtis' last episodic television appearance until 1982 when Curtis co-starred in the failed television pilot *Callahan*.

6. Archive footage of Curtis would later be used in the episode *A Blast for Buck* which was broadcast on January 17, 1980.

EIGHT / GRADUATION DAY

1. To be clear, Curtis did *The Fog* re-shoots in late October of 1979. In fact, Carpenter and Curtis recall that filming took place during the invasion of the United States embassy in Tehran, Iran that took place on November 4, 1979. Curtis shot the *Buck Rogers* episode at the end of September in 1979.

2. Carpenter would barely be present during the principal filming of *Halloween II*. Carpenter, Curtis, and Hill saw little of each other socially between 1979 and 1980.

3. Tony Curtis shot the film *It Rained All Night the Day I Left* in Montreal, Canada between October and December of 1978. Tony Curtis shot the film *Title Shot* in Toronto, Canada between January and February of 1979.

4. *Exorcist* star Linda Blair was another queen of the movies-of-the-week during the 1970s, along with Eve Plumb whose own feature film career never gained momentum. Eve Plumb was an acting contemporary of Jamie Lee Curtis' in that Plumb was also born in 1958.

5. Curtis' disco fashion spread appeared in an April 1979 issue of the magazine *Preview*. Curtis modeled a V-neck, crystal pleated wrap dress with fluttered short sleeves ($30), a hot red polyester dress for disco madness ($20), and a blue cascade ruffle wrap dress ($20) that was advertised as a "sure way to create disco dynamite." The clothes were available at Infinity and Phase II fashion outlets.

NINE / THE MAKING OF *PROM NIGHT*

1. Curtis recalls Martin, whose birth-name is Edmonda Benton, as Eddie Benton and says she last saw Martin about ten years ago. Martin had been prevented from using the name Anne-Marie Martin, which incorporated her mother's maiden name, at the beginning of her acting career because another actress had a similar name. Martin was credited as "Eddie Martin" for a 1978 episode of the television series *Switch*. Following *Prom Night*, Martin would star in the cult television series *Sledge Hammer* which ran between 1986 and 1988. In 1987, Martin married author and film-maker Michael Crichton. Crichton and Martin later collaborated on the screenplay for the 1996 film *Twister*. They divorced in 2002.

2. Lynch would follow *Prom Night* with the 1982 mutant horror film *Humongous* which co-starred Janet Julian, formerly known as Janet Louise Johnson, who'd replaced Pamela Sue Martin in

the role of Nancy Drew that Curtis had auditioned for. Curtis and Lynch have never met or spoken since the making of *Prom Night*.

3.   Mary Beth Rubens recalls seeing Curtis in Las Vegas a couple of years after the filming of *Prom Night*.

4.   The escaped child killer in *Prom Night*, whose invention was the clearest copy of *Halloween*, turns out to have nothing to do with the murders in the film. Curtis wasn't aware of any of these re-shoots until she eventually saw the film.

5.   Curtis and Martin were still friends when Curtis filmed *Halloween II* in the Spring of 1981, and Martin would make an un-credited appearance in *Halloween II*, playing a character named Darcy Essmont. Prior to Martin's first date with Michael Crichton in 1984, *Prom Night* writer William Gray helped Martin research some books, Thomas Pynchon's 1973 novel *Gravity's Rainbow* being one of them, so that Martin would be able to make a good impression on the brilliant author.

TEN / *HALLOWEEN* ON A TRAIN

1.   Since *Terror Train*, Roger Spottiswoode has directed such films as *Under Fire* (1983), *Shoot to Kill* (1988), *Turner and Hooch* (1989), *Air America* (1990) and *Tomorrow Never Dies* (1997). *Under Fire*, Spottiswoode's most critically-acclaimed film, was shot by *Terror Train* cinematographer John Alcott.

2.   Bochner and Curtis would later attend the 1981 premiere of the film *Rich and Famous* in which Bochner co-starred. Bochner would later direct the films *PCU* (1994) and *High School High* (1996).

3.   In the script, Curtis' Alana Maxwell character is introduced as "a cute, innocent-looking girl."

4.   Derek MacKinnon, who spells his last name McKinnon, would only appear in one other film after *Terror Train*: 1985's *Breaking All the Rules*. MacKinnon says he was placed under a five year contract by *Terror Train*'s theatrical distributor, 20th Century Fox, following *Terror Train*'s filming which forced him to turn down roles in other horror films like *Happy Birthday to Me* (1981) and *My Bloody Valentine* (1981).

5.   Several of *Terror Train*'s cast and crew consider Caryl Wickman as being an un-credited co-director on the film. Wickman, who died in 1987, would direct the 1987 made-for-television film *Shades of Love: Echoes in Crimson*. Wickman also held an ownership stake in *Terror Train*.

ELEVEN / THE MAKING OF *TERROR TRAIN*

1.   Currie had never done any film or television prior to *Terror Train*. After *Terror Train*, Currie shot the film *Gas* in Montreal in June of 1980. *Gas* was released in 1981. Currie would later appear in such films as *Curtains* (1983), which was produced by Peter Simpson, *The Magic Show* (1983), *Terminal Choice* (1985) and *Street Justice* (1989). All of these films were shot in Canada.

2.   Ray Hutcherson and actress Nora Dunn were married from 1987 to 1995.

3.   Derek MacKinnon and Timothy Webber recall remaining close friends with Wickman until her death from cancer in 1987.

4.   Nadia Rona is currently a casting director in Montreal.

5.   Curtis' character on *Callahan*, the failed 1982 television pilot that Curtis filmed with Hart Bochner, was named Rachel Bartlett. The twenty-five minute pilot was directed by Harry Winer who would later direct Curtis in the 1996 film *House Arrest*.

6. Curtis says she never saw Currie again after *Terror Train*'s filming and didn't know that Currie had passed away.

TWELVE / A KANGAROO SCREAM QUEEN

1. Keach would later team with John Carpenter in *Body Bags* (1993) and then in *Escape from LA* (1996).

2. *The Long Riders* also co-starred Curtis' future husband, Christopher Guest.

3. Franklin's next feature film, *Psycho II*, would be shot by Dean Cundey.

4. Peers, a veteran of Australian film and television, would appear in the 1981 horror film *Alison's Birthday*.

THIRTEEN / THE MAKING OF *ROADGAMES*

1. Jodie Foster was seventeen years old when *Roadgames* began filming in June of 1980, and Brooke Shields was fifteen.

2. Jill Donahue and Stacy Keach were married from 1981 to 1986 and had two children.

3. The "MacGuffin" term, which Hitchcock would later embrace in his own career, was coined by Hitchcock's friend, Scottish screenwriter Angus McPhail. In 1966, Hitchcock defined the MacGuffin plot device as being a detail which, by inciting curiosity and desire, drives the plot and motivates the actions of characters within the story, but whose specific identity and nature is unimportant to the spectator of the film.

4. *Psycho II* (1983) grossed $34.7 million domestically and *Cloak & Dagger* (1984) grossed $9.7 million.

FOURTEEN / THE LAST HORROR FILM

1. Prior to her appearance on *Saturday Night Live*, Curtis' only previous comedic work had been on the television series *Operation Petticoat*. Curtis' big comedic breakthrough would be the 1983 film *Trading Places*.

2. Kelly Curtis would later become an actress, and currently serves as younger sister Jamie Lee Curtis' personal assistant.

3. Curtis directed a 1992 episode of the television series *Anything But Love* which Curtis starred in between 1989 and 1992. The episode was entitled *The Call of the Mild* and aired on ABC on January 8, 1992. Curtis is a member of the Directors Guild of America (DGA).

4. Tony Curtis would enter the Betty Ford Center in March of 1984 for treatment of drug addiction.

5. Not including *Halloween II*, Carpenter's first big studio film was 1982's *The Thing* while Hill's first big studio film was 1983's *The Dead Zone*. Jamie Lee Curtis' first big studio film was 1983's *Trading Places*.

6. *More American Graffiti* grossed $8.1 million upon its release in 1979 compared to 1973's *American Graffiti* which grossed $115 million domestically.

7. Brooke Shields was paid $500,000 for *Endless Love* (1981).

FIFTEEN / THE MAKING OF *HALLOWEEN II*

1. Riva had been previously married and divorced before he met Curtis.

2. Casey Stevens is intriguing because of the way he vanished following the release of *Prom Night*.

3. Aside from Curtis' physical changes, the biggest change noticeable in this scene is with Curtis' voice which sounds a lot deeper and a lot more guttural in tone than it did back in 1978.

4. The victim's name is Alice, played by Anne Bruner. In the scene, Alice is talking on the phone to a friend prior to being murdered. Jamie Lee Curtis was present during the filming of this scene and actually read the phone dialogue to Bruner.

5. Besides *Bad Boys* (1983), Rick Rosenthal's most critically-acclaimed feature film after *Halloween II* was the 1988 Vietnam veteran drama *Distant Thunder*. In the past decade, most of Rosenthal's work has been in episodic television.

SIXTEEN / THE SCREAMING STOPS

1. Gabrielle Beaumont had also produced the 1970 horror film *The Corpse*.

2. Eve Plumb, who co-starred with Robert Reed on *The Brady Bunch*, had been the first choice for the female lead in *Prom Night*. Curtis would later work with Bruce Weitz on Curtis' television series *Anything But Love* (1989-1992). Weitz would appear in three episodes that aired between 1991 and 1992. In 1984, Peter Bogdanovich wrote a book, entitled *The Killing of the Unicorn: Dorothy Stratten, 1960-1980*, that was about his relationship with Stratten and the events that led to Stratten's murder.

3. In *Star 80*, Hugh Hefner was played by actor Cliff Robertson while the Peter Bogdanovich role was played, under the character pseudonym of Aram Nicholas, by Roger Rees. Dorothy Stratten's mother was played by Carroll Baker.

4. There's a rumor that Curtis' voice appears in *Halloween III: Season of the Witch*, particularly in a scene where actor Tom Atkins is talking to a phone operator, but neither Jamie Lee Curtis or Tommy Lee Wallace recall Curtis doing any such uncredited voice-over

work for the film. Nancy Kyes, Wallace's then-wife, appears as Tom Atkins' ex-wife in the film which makes Kyes the only performer to have appeared in each of the first three *Halloween* films.

5. During the filming of *Trading Places*, Curtis and fiancé J. Michael Riva stayed at the Park Avenue apartment in Manhattan where Riva's grandmother, Marlene Dietrich, had lived for many years. Dietrich died in Paris in 1992.

6. Curtis would serve as a co-presenter, along with Carl Weathers, at the 1982 American Academy Awards ceremony that was held on April 11, 1983. Curtis and Weathers presented the Oscar for Best Sound Effects Editing.

7. Curtis would later film an un-credited role in *The Adventures of Buckaroo Banzai Across the 8th Dimension* (1984), a film on which Riva served as production designer. Curtis' work in the film was left on the cutting room floor. Curtis narrated the 2001 documentary film *Marlene Dietrich: Her Own Song*.

8. On February 18, 1984, Curtis guest-hosted *Saturday Night Live* for a second time. The musical guest was The Fixx.

SEVENTEEN / WHATEVER HAPPENED TO LAURIE STRODE?

1. The part of Jamie Lloyd, Laurie Strode's daughter, was played by actress Danielle Harris.

2. Ron Silver died of cancer on March 15, 2009.

3. This doesn't include Gabrielle Beaumont who'd directed Curtis on the 1981 made-for-television movie *Death of a Centerfold: The Dorothy Stratten Story*. Caryl Wickman had also served as an un-credited co-director on *Terror Train* (1980).

4. Bigelow's later films—*Point Break* (1991), *Strange Days* (1995), *K-19: The Widowmaker* (2002) —were all commercial disappointments.

5.   *Mother's Boys* grossed $874,148 domestically.

6.   No, but *True Lies* was the closest Curtis came to an Oscar nomination in terms of Oscar buzz and momentum surrounding her performance.

7.   *Virus*, which had a production budget of $75 million, grossed $14 million domestically.

8.   *Forever Young* grossed $56 million domestically and $128 million worldwide.

9.   Norma Watson was also the name of P.J. Soles' character in *Carrie* (1976).

10. Diane Keaton won the Golden Globe for her performance in *Something's Gotta Give* (2003).

11. Robert Brandt died in Beverly Hills, California on September 5, 2009 after a long battle with Alzheimer's disease. Brandt was 82.

EIGHTEEN / THE MAKING OF A REPUTATION

1.   Besides Curtis, the most notable scream queen in the period between 1978 and 1981 was probably actress Adrienne King, star of *Friday the 13th* (1980). Unfortunately, King was typecast by her role in *Friday the 13th* and was unable to parlay this memorable performance into more meaningful film roles.

SOURCES

The majority of the quotes in this book are taken from interviews that were conducted by the author during the period from 1997 to the present. These transcribed interviews were variously conducted in person, by E-Mail, by phone conversation, by fax, and sometimes by handwritten letter. The author has also respected the wishes of those interview subjects who have asked to remain anonymous and to not be listed here or anywhere in the text.

The author first interviewed Jamie Lee Curtis in the spring of 1998, during the filming of *Halloween: H20*, and last interviewed her in November of 2004, during the period of the release of the film *Christmas with the Kranks*. The author's last correspondence with Curtis was through her publicist, Heidi Schaeffer, in December of 2008.

In order not to burden this book with endless and excessive annotation, the following source notes identify only those quotations related to Jamie Lee Curtis that are drawn from secondary sources—primarily books, magazines, newspapers, press-books—to which Curtis has granted interviews over the years.

INTRODUCTION

3   *The Queen of Crud:* Carol Wallace, "The Queen of Crud," *New York Sunday News*, September 27, 1981.

ONE / JAMIE LEE

14   *I would've done the film for nothing*: Janet Leigh to DG.

15   *After the film came out*: Janet Leigh to DG.

16   *When I first became an actress*: Quoted in Janet Leigh with Christopher Nickens, *Psycho: Behind the scenes of the classic thriller*, p. 190.

17   *Dimmy*: Jim Steranko, "Life is a scream for Jamie Lee Curtis," *Mediascene Prevue* #45, May 1981.

17   *There will be no divorce*: Roberta Downs, "There Will Be No Divorce," *Photoplay*, January 1960.

18   *An emotional tumor was growing*: Janet Leigh, *There really was a Hollywood*, p. 272.

19   *I started seeing Christine*: Tony Curtis and Barry Paris, *Tony Curtis: the autobiography*, p. 201.

20   *I don't remember my father very much*: Quoted in Tom Seligson, "Success Isn't Enough," *Parade*, October 29, 1989.

22   *My career was losing momentum*: Curtis and Paris, *Tony Curtis: the autobiography*, p. 232.

23   *The kids at school would joke*: Quoted in Lawrence Grobel, "Jamie Lee Curtis: Controlled Substance," *Movieline*, April 1990.

24   *designer school*: Neal Karlen, "Jamie Lee Curtis," *Rolling Stone*, July 18-August 1, 1985.

24   *When I grew up*: Quoted in David Rensin, "Checking In," *Playboy*, November 1981.

24   *I was not a Hollywood child*: Quoted in Seligson, "Success Isn't Enough."

25   *I never took many acting classes*: Quoted in Alice Marshall, "Jamie Lee Curtis: Hollywood's Miracle Kid," *Movie Mirror*, October 1978.

26   *My mother learned a lot*: Quoted in Dick Kleiner, "Showbeat," *The Times-News*, February 11, 1980.

26   *Weirdness is a virtue*: Quoted in 1976 Choate yearbook.

26   *I look back on that*: Quoted in Neal Karlen, "Jamie Lee Curtis."

27   *Even though I grew up with Hollywood* all around me: Quoted in *Prom Night* press notes.

27   *I don't think*: Quoted in Tony Crawley, "Jamie Lee Curtis," *Starburst*, June 1982.

28   *I was giving tennis lessons*: Chuck Binder to DG.

28   *He was in Europe when I got hired*: Quoted in Don Shewey, "Horror of Horrors—It's Jamie Lee Curtis," *Rolling Stone*, December 10, 1981.

29   *Tom looked at Jamie*: Chuck Binder to DG.

TWO / INTRODUCING LAURIE STRODE

35   *a superficial casualty*: Quoted in Bob Thomas, "Jamie Curtis is Much Prouder of *Halloween*," *Sarasota Herald-Tribune*, October 24, 1978.

40   *Be yourself, Jamie*: Quoted in Thomas, "Jamie Curtis is Much Prouder of *Halloween*."

41   *Debra didn't think I was suited*: Quoted in Thomas, "Jamie Curtis is Much Prouder of *Halloween*."

43   *The best advice my mother gave me*: Quoted in *Halloween II* press notes.

44   *She was just one of several girls*: Tony Crawley, "Jamie Lee Curtis."

THREE / THE MAKING OF *HALLOWEEN*

64   *threw Jamie off a bit*: P.J. Soles to DG.

65   *The scene where the girls walk home*: Pat Jankiewicz, "P.J. Soles: Cult Queen of *Halloween*," *Femme Fatales*, Vol. 9, No. 3, August 11, 2000.

FOUR / THE BABYSITTER AND THE BOOGEYMAN

74   *I'm sorry, Mr. Cyphers*: Charles Cyphers to DG.

84   *This scene is probably my favorite scene*: Quoted in Crawley, "Jamie Lee Curtis."

86   *John said to me*: Quoted in Bob Martin, "Jamie Lee Curtis," *Fangoria* #15, October 1981.

92   *I think this Jamie Lee Curtis is going to be a really big star*: Joy Jameson to DG.

92   *Who the hell is Jamie Lee Curtis?*: Tony Moran to DG.

95   *a real nice guy*: Quoted in Anthony C. Ferrante, "The Night He Made History," *Fangoria* #138, November 1994.

FIVE / A SCREAM QUEEN IS BORN

104   *I was very nervous about working with Jamie:* The Fog press notes.

115   *I couldn't get a job for seven months:* Quoted in Debra Davis, "Jamie Lee Curtis: Shooting to stardom on her own," *US*, July 22, 1980.

SIX / ENTERING *THE FOG*

139   *I liked the fact:* Quoted in *The Fog* press notes.

139   *In The Fog:* Quoted in *The Fog* press notes.

140   *When I saw Halloween:* The Fog press notes.

141   *The script for The Fog:* Quoted in *The Fog* press notes.

143   *My mother has always been my best friend:* Quoted in Marshall, "Jamie Lee Curtis: Hollywood's Miracle Kid."

145   *My most vivid memory:* Tom Atkins to DG.

149   *It was so cold:* Quoted in Paul Scanlon, "*The Fog*: A spook ride on film," *Rolling Stone*, June 28, 1979.

SEVEN / JAMIE LEE CURTIS' *THE FOG*

162   *I hated my performance:* Quoted in Martin, "Jamie Lee Curtis."

EIGHT / GRADUATION DAY

172   *It was a role that was offered to me:* Quoted in Martin, "Jamie Lee Curtis."

182   *Oh, we're ripping off Halloween*: William Gray to DG.

182   *This Jamie Lee Curtis is amazing*: Paul Lynch to DG.

184   *You're perfect*: Joy Thompson to DG.

185   *Yes, we got it*: Steve Wright to DG.

NINE / THE MAKING OF *PROM NIGHT*

191   *a young Brad Pitt*: Steve Wright to DG.

191   *Isn't Jamie just so wonderful?*: Paul Lynch to DG.

193   *The girl gets killed*: Quoted in Rensin, "Checking In."

194   *I certainly did not have a joyous high school experience*: Quoted in Scot Haller, "Forget What the Song Says—Don't Call Jamie Lee Curtis the Closest Thing to *Perfect*," *People*, June 24, 1985.

197   *Oh*: Sheldon Rybowski to DG.

203   *All that psychopathic killer stuff*: Quoted in Martin, "Jamie Lee Curtis."

206   *For someone my age*: Quoted in Seligson, "Success Isn't Enough."

TEN / *HALLOWEEN* ON A TRAIN

210   *When I read the script*: Quoted in *Terror Train* press notes.

210   *It kept me turning the pages*: Quoted in *Terror Train* press notes.

224   *I want to be a pirate*: Penny Hadfield to DG.

225   *I wish I could just be like you*: Derek MacKinnon to DG.

ELEVEN / THE MAKING OF *TERROR TRAIN*

234   *He feels my work endorses that*: Quoted in Jim Wynorski, "*Terror Train*," *Fangoria* #9, November 1980.

235   *A little sweetheart to work with*: John Wooley and Michael R. Price, "Forgotten Horrors: *Terror Train*," *Fangoria* #222, May 2003.

236   *If I take a drink*: Derek MacKinnon to DG.

249   *Something awful*: Quoted in Crawley, "Jamie Lee Curtis."

TWELVE / A KANGAROO SCREAM QUEEN

275   *Alfred Hitchcock is one of the old directors*: Quoted in Crawley, "Jamie Lee Curtis."

275   *I screened Patrick in Hollywood*: Quoted in Crawley, "Jamie Lee Curtis."

276   *Didn't you used to be my father?*: Everett De Roche to DG.

281   *We were really the first Americans to do a film there*: Quoted in Ted Newsom, "Jamie Lee Curtis: Scream Queen to Femme Fatale," *Femme Fatales*, Vol. 1, No. 1, Summer 1992.

THIRTEEN / THE MAKING OF *ROADGAMES*

290   *I learned a lot from Jill and Stacy*: Quoted in Martin, "Jamie Lee Curtis."

294   *Is that what that thing was beside the road?*: Greg Ricketson to DG.

295   *I always thought of myself as sexy and single*: Quoted in Davis, "Jamie Lee Curtis: Shooting to stardom on her own."

303   *I believe in loyalty*: Quoted in Steranko, "Life is a scream for Jamie Lee Curtis."

FOURTEEN / THE LAST HORROR FILM

308   *cleanliness freak*: Sue Ellen Jares, "On the Move," *People*, December 11, 1978.

308   *I'm boring*: Quoted in Crawley, "Jamie Lee Curtis."

310   *It's my idea and my horror film*: Quoted in Crawley, "Jamie Lee Curtis."

310   *It was more of a disaster film than a horror film*: Quoted in Crawley, "Jamie Lee Curtis."

315   *It was a weird time*: Quoted in Grobel, "Jamie Lee Curtis: Controlled Substance."

315   *When he was doing drugs*: Quoted in Grobel, "Jamie Lee Curtis: Controlled Substance."

316   I *was the kind of drug addict*: Quoted in Grobel, "Jamie Lee Curtis: Controlled Substance."

318   *I always thought*: Quoted in Wallace, "The Queen of Crud."

318   *I never played the bimbo*: Quoted in Grobel, "Jamie Lee Curtis: Controlled Substance."

318   *I kept being told*: Quoted in Dave Smith, "Jamie Lee Curtis As The Tragic Dorothy Stratten," *Photoplay Movies & Video*, June 1982.

FIFTEEN / THE MAKING OF *HALLOWEEN II*

329   *We originally thought*: Quoted in Lou Gaul, "Curtis screams for joy this time," *Beaver County Times*, October 25, 1981.

341   *We called it Winnebago passion*: Quoted in Carol Wallace, "Beware: Soft Shoulders - Jamie Lee Curtis' Career Has Changed Course," *People*, August 22, 1983.

345   *Maybe I am wrong about this*: Robert E. Kapsis, *Hitchcock: The Making of a Reputation*, p. 169.

348   *I didn't want to hurt anyone*: Quoted in Christopher Stone, "Hex, Sex, Creepy, Weepy," *US*, November 10, 1981.

349   *People don't seem to realize*: *Halloween II* press notes.

351   *It stinks, it's awful*: Quoted in Douglas Eby, "Jamie Lee Curtis: Halloween H20," *Femme Fatales*, Vol. 7, No. 6, November 1998.

SIXTEEN / THE SCREAMING STOPS

355   *At first, I didn't think I was right to play Dorothy*: Quoted in Stone, "Hex, Sex, Creepy, Weepy."

355   *If there's a sadness to being a celebrity kid*: Quoted in Michael Lerner, "Zany Jamie," *Interview*, August 1989.

357   *Dorothy Stratten was a sweet, sensitive, vulnerable girl*: Quoted in Bettlelou Peterson, "Jamie Lee Curtis trades chillers for a role in *Stratten Story*," *Detroit Free Press*, November 1-7, 1981.

357   *Don't forget*: Quoted in Stone, "Hex, Sex, Creepy, Weepy."

358   *My father was dating a playmate at the time*: Quoted in Stone, "Hex, Sex, Creepy, Weepy."

360   *I wanted it cold*: Quoted in Ted Newsom, "Jamie Lee Curtis," *Genesis*, April 1982.

361   *I remember how difficult it was for Dorothy*: Quoted in Stone, "Hex, Sex, Creepy, Weepy."

363   *All of a sudden I was a sex girl*: Quoted in Lerner, "Zany Jamie."

364   *There are two things I'm trying to avoid*: Quoted in Wallace, "Beware: Soft Shoulders—Jamie Lee Curtis' Career has Changed Course."

364   *the silliest idea I ever heard*: Quoted in Gaul, "Curtis screams for joy this time."

369   *For five years*: Quoted in Wallace, "Beware: Soft Shoulders—Jamie Lee Curtis' Career has Changed Course."

370   *I told my friend Debra Hill*: Quoted in Rachel Abromowitz, "Hot Mama," *US Weekly*, December 21, 2000.

SEVENTEEN / WHATEVER HAPPENED TO LAURIE STRODE?

377   *The film is about a woman cop*: Quoted in Michelle P. Perry, "Kathryn Bigelow discusses role of 'seductive violence' in her films," *The Tech*, March 16, 1990.

378   *I wanted to be convincing*: Quoted in Perry, "Kathryn Bigelow discusses role of 'seductive violence' in her films."

378   *I didn't have any confidence*: Quoted in Grobel, "Jamie Lee Curtis: Controlled Substance."

378   *I didn't know what we had*: Quoted in Grobel, "Jamie Lee Curtis: Controlled Substance."

380   *That was a tough shoot*: Quoted in Marc Shapiro, "Laurie Hallelujah," *Fangoria* #177, October 1998.

381   a *grown-up Laurie Strode*: Quoted in Ferrante, "The Night He Made History."

392   *We had a year to say goodbye*: Quoted in Johnny Dodd, "Home Body," *People*, November 29, 2004.

393   *Debra Hill was*: Quoted in Anne Thompson, "Producer-writer Debra Hill dies at 54," *The Hollywood Reporter*, March 8, 2005.

393   *I have not one second of anxiety*: Quoted in Nancy Griffin, "Jamie Lee Curtis Turns 50," *AARP: The Magazine*, May/June 2008.

BIBLIOGRAPHY

BOOKS

Anobile, Richard J. *Alfred Hitchcock's Psycho*. New York: Universe Books, 1974.

Ant, Adam. *Stand & Deliver: The Autobiography*. London: Pan Macmillan, 2006.

Barbeau, Adrienne. *There Are Worse Things I Could Do*. New York: Carroll & Graf Publishers, 2006.

Bloch, Robert. *Psycho*. New York: Warner Books, 1959.

Bogdanovich, Peter. *The Killing of the Unicorn: Dorothy Stratten, 1960-1980*. New York: William Morrow, 1984.

Boulenger, Gilles. *John Carpenter: The Prince of Darkness*. Los Angeles: Silman-James Press, 2003.

Bouzereau, Laurent. *The Alfred Hitchcock Quote Book*. New York: Citadel, 1993.

Clover, Carol J. *Men, Women, and Chain Saws: Gender in the Modern Horror Film*. Princeton, N.J.: Princeton University, 1992.

Collum, Jason Paul. *Assault of the Killer B's: Interviews with 20 Cult Film Actresses*. Jefferson, London: McFarland & Company, 2004.

Cumbow, Robert C. *Order in the Universe: The Films of John Carpenter.* Lanham, MD: Scarecrow Press, 2000.

Curtis, Tony and Peter Golenbock. *American Prince: A Memoir.* New York: Harmony, 2008.

Curtis, Tony and Barry Paris. *Tony Curtis: the autobiography.* New York: William Morrow, 1993.

Dika, Vera. *Games of Terror: Halloween, Friday the 13th, and the Films of the Slasher Cycle.* Rutherford, N.J.: Fairleigh Dickinson University, 1990.

Ebert, Roger. *I Hated, Hated, Hated This Movie.* Kansas City: Andrews McMeel Publishing, 2000.

Ebert, Roger. *Roger Ebert's Movie Home Companion.* Kansas City: Andrews, McMeel & Parker, 1986.

Farber, Stephen and Marc Green. *Hollywood Dynasties.* New York: Delilah, 1984.

Etchison, Dennis. *The Fog.* New York: Bantam Books, 1980.

Freeman, David. *The Last Days of Alfred Hitchcock.* New York: The Overlook Press, 1984.

Grove, David. *Making Friday the 13th: The Legend of Camp Blood.* Godalming: FAB Press, 2005.

Hardy, Phil (ed.). *The Encyclopedia of Horror Movies.* New York: Harper & Row, 1986.

Hardy, Phil (ed.). *Horror.* London: Aurum, 1996.

Hunter, Allan. *Tony Curtis: The Man and His Movies.* Edinburgh: St. Martin's Press, 1985.

Kapsis, Robert E. *Hitchcock: The Making of a Reputation*. Chicago: The University of Chicago Press, 1992.

Leigh, Janet. *There really was a Hollywood*. New York: Doubleday & Company, Inc., 1984.

Leigh, Janet with Christopher Nickens. *Psycho: Behind the scenes of the classic thriller*. London: Pavilion Books Ltd., 1995.

Maltin, Leonard (ed.). *Leonard Maltin's Movie Encyclopedia*. New York: Dutton, 1994.

Martin, Jack. *Halloween II*. New York: Kensington Publishing Corp., 1981.

McCarty, John. *Splatter Movies: Breaking the Last Taboo of the Screen*. New York: St. Martin's Press, 1984.

Moore, Roger. *My Word is My Bond: A Memoir*. New York: Harper-Collins, 2008.

Munn, Michael. *The Kid from the Bronx: A Biography of Tony Curtis*. London: W.H. Allen, 1984.

Muir, John Kenneth. *The Films of John Carpenter*. Jefferson, London: McFarland & Company, 2005.

Newman, Kim. *Nightmare Movies: A Critical Guide to Contemporary Horror Films*. New York: Harmony Books, 1988.

Pollock, Dale. *Skywalking: The Life and Films of George Lucas*. New York: Harmony Books, 1983.

Rebello, Stephen. *Alfred Hitchcock and the Making of Psycho*. New York: Dembner, 1990.

Richards, Curtis. *Halloween*. New York: Bantam Books, 1979.

Rockoff, Adam. *Going to Pieces: The Rise and Fall of the Slasher Film, 1978-1986.* Jefferson, London: McFarland & Company, 2002.

Schneider, Steven Jay (ed.). *Fear Without Frontiers.* Godalming: FAB Press, 2003.

Spoto, Donald. *The Art of Alfred Hitchcock.* New York: Doubleday, 1979.

Spoto, Donald. *The Dark Side of Genius: The Life of Alfred Hitchcock.* New York: Ballantine, 1983.

Vatnsdal, Caelum. *They Came From Within: A History of Canadian Horror Cinema.* Winnipeg: Arbeiter Ring Publishing, 2004.

Walker, John (ed.). *Halliwell's Film Guide.* New York: HarperPerennial, 1991.

MAGAZINES AND NEWSPAPERS

Abromowitz, Rachel. "Hot Mama." *US Weekly*, December 21, 2000.

Alberge, Dalva. "Masterly Pleasence recalled as friend." *The Times*, October 5, 1996.

Allen, Tom. "Review of *Halloween*." *Village Voice*, November 6, 1978.

Ansen, David. "Trick or Treat." *Newsweek*, December 4, 1978.

Appleyard, Bryan. "The personification of uncommonness." *The Times*, April 25, 1983.

Breuer, Howard. "Jamie Lee Curtis Drops Her Top to Make a Point." *People*, April 28, 2008.

Carlomagno, Ellen. "*Halloween III: Season of the Witch.*" *Fangoria* #22, October 1982.

Carpenter, John. "On Composing for *Halloween*." *Fangoria* #30, October 1983.

Chin, Paula. "Making a Splash." *People*, August 22, 1994.

Connolly, Mike. "Star of the Month: Janet Leigh and Tony Curtis." *Screen Stories*, November 1959.

Corliss, Richard, "*Halloween*." *New Times*, January 18, 1979.

Crawley, Tony. "Jamie Lee Curtis." *Starburst*, June 1982.

Dangaard, Colin. "This mother-daughter team is in a *Fog* and heavy into horror." *US*, February 19, 1980.

Davis, Debra. "Jamie Lee Curtis: Shooting to stardom on her own." *US*, July 22, 1980.

Dawson, Jeff. "Profiles: Donald Pleasence." *Empire*, February 1994.

Delson, James. "The arts." *Omni*, July 1979.

Diamond, Jamie. "Jamie Lee Curtis faces up to her image." *The New York Times*, December 27, 1992.

Dodd, Johnny. "Home Body," *People*, November 29, 2004.

Downs, Roberta. "There Will Be No Divorce." *Photoplay*, January 1960.

Ebert, Roger. "Interview with Adrienne Barbeau." *Chicago Sun-Times*, February 3, 1980.

Ebert, Roger. "Review of *Halloween*." *Chicago Sun-Times*, October 31, 1978.

Ebert, Roger. "Review of *The Fog*." *Chicago Sun-Times*, February 5, 1980.

Ebert, Roger. "Review of *Terror Train.*" *Chicago Sun-Times*, October 9, 1980.

Eby, Douglas. "Jamie Lee Curtis: "*Halloween H20.*" *Femme Fatales*, Vol 7., No. 6, November 1998.

Eby, Douglas. "Jodi Lyn O'Keefe: "*Halloween H20.*" *Femme Fatales*, Vol 7., No. 6, November 1998.

Eby, Douglas. "Michelle Williams: "*Halloween H20.*" *Femme Fatales*, Vol 7., No. 6, November 1998.

Eby, Douglas. "Nancy Stephens: "*Halloween H20.*" *Femme Fatales*, Vol 7., No. 6, November 1998.

Everitt, David. "Rick Rosenthal." *Fangoria* #17, February 1982.

Ferrante, Anthony C. "The Night He Made History." *Fangoria* #138, November 1994.

Fox, Jordan R. "Carpenter: Riding High on Horror." *Cinefantastique*, Vol. 10, No. 1, Summer 1980.

Fox, Jordan R. "Debra Hill: She Shaped-Up *Halloween.*" *Femme Fatales*, Vol. 7, No. 6, November 1998.

Fox, Jordan R. "Partners in Horror." *Cinefantastique*, Vol. 10, No. 1, Summer 1980.

Gaul, Lou. "Curtis screams for joy this time." *Beaver County Times*, October 25, 1981.

Grant, Lee. "*Halloween* in South Pasadena." *Los Angeles Times*, May 27, 1978.

Greenberger, Robert. "P.J. Soles." *Fangoria* #13, June 1981.

Griffin, Nancy. "Jamie Lee Curtis Turns 50." *AARP: The Magazine*, May/June 2008.

Grobel, Lawrence. "Jamie Lee Curtis: Controlled Substance." *Movieline*, April 1990.

Grove, David. *"Freaky Friday."* *Film Review*, January 2004.

Grove, David. "The Sheriff of Haddonfield: An interview with Charles Cyphers." *Firelight Shocks*, September 2002.

Haller, Scot. "Forget What the Song Says—Don't Call Jamie Lee Curtis the Closest Thing to *Perfect.*" *People*, June 24, 1985.

Hamburg, Victoria. "Dark by Design." *Interview*, August 1989.

Harmetz, Aljean. "Quick End of Low-Budget Horror Film." *The New York Times*, October 2, 1980.

"Talking horror with Donald Pleasence." *Horror Fan*, December 1988.

Howell, Arnesa. "Jamie Lee Curtis Freed from 'Rock of Addiction.'" *People*, June 16, 2008.

Isaac, Doug. "In Progress...*Train to Terror.*" *Cinema Canada* #63, March 1980.

Jankiewicz, Pat. "P.J. Soles: Cult Queen of *Halloween.*" *Femme Fatales*, Vol. 9, No. 3, August 11, 2000.

Jares, Sue Ellen. "On the Move." *People*, December 11, 1978.

Karlen, Neal. "Jamie Lee Curtis." *Rolling Stone*, July 18-August 1, 1985.

Kehr, Dave. "Defiant gravity: Jamie Lee Curtis." *Film Comment*, March/April 1985.

Kenas, Alex. "Review of *Psycho II.*" *Newsday*, June 3, 1983.

Kinder, Gary. "Has Jamie Lee Curtis finally found herself?" *Esquire*, July 1985.

Kleiner, Dick. "Showbeat." *The Times-News*, February 11, 1980.

Koenigsberg, Alice. "A new Curtis shows her '*Petticoat*.'" *US*, October 18, 1977.

Lask, Thomas. "Stars from Britain: Donald Pleasence." *The New York Times*, December 10, 1961.

Lerner, Michael. "Zany Jamie." *Interview*, August 1989.

"The cool, clinical kill." *London Evening News*, March 9, 1978.

Maronie, Sam. "Some Gentle Evil." *Starlog*, June 1995.

Marshall, Alice. "Jamie Lee Curtis: Hollywood's Miracle Kid." *Movie Mirror*, October 1978.

Martin, Bob. "Debra Hill." *Fangoria* #15, October 1981.

Martin, Bob. "Jamie Lee Curtis." *Fangoria* #15, October 1981.

Martin, Bob. "John Carpenter." *Fangoria* #8, October 1980.

Martin, Bob. "John Carpenter's *The Fog*." *Fangoria* #5, April 1980.

Martin, Bob. "A talk with John Carpenter." *Fangoria* #14, August 1981.

Martin, Robert. "Sneak Preview: *Halloween II*." *The Twilight Zone Magazine*, November 1981.

Mason, Avery. "Yablans' *Halloween* may be biggest indie." *Boxoffice*, April 9, 1979.

McDonagh, Maitland. "Guns & Poses." *Entertainment Weekly*, March 16, 1990.

Michaels, Evan. "If Only My Dad Could Have Lived to See You." *Photoplay*, May 1959.

Mills, Bart. "Pleasence's villainy—an act that pays off." *Chicago Tribune*, December 19, 1976.

Mills, Nancy. "Screams like Old Times." *New York Daily News*, July 30, 1998.

Mitchell, Blake and James Ferguson. "*The Fog.*" *Fantastic Films*, May 1980.

Mizell, Mary. "Cashing in on *Halloween.*" *Premiere*, Vol. 11, No. 3, 1980.

Moore, Larry. "In progress...*Prom Night.*" *Cinema Canada* #59, October/November 1979.

"Jamie Lee Curtis: "*Operation* Stardom!" *Movie Mirror*, March 1978.

Nashawaty, Chris. "Final Cut." *Entertainment Weekly*, August 14, 1998.

Newsom, Ted. "Jamie Lee Curtis." *Genesis*, April 1982.

Newsom, Ted. "Jamie Lee Curtis: Scream Queen to Femme Fatale." *Femme Fatales*, Vol. 1, No. 1, Summer 1992.

Nichols, David P. "Irwin Yablans: Fade to *Halloween 2.*" *Fangoria* #8, October 1980.

Olddie, Allan. "Making *The Fog*: An Interview with Director John Carpenter." *Film and Video Monthly Filmmakers*, Vol. 13, No. 5, March 1980.

Paskin, Barbara. "Jamie Lee Curtis – What My Famous Mother Taught Me." *Photoplay Movies & Video*, May 1981.

Perry, Michelle P. "Kathryn Bigelow discusses role of 'seductive violence' in her films." *The Tech*, March 16, 1990.

Peterson, Bettelou. "Jamie Lee Curtis trades chillers for a role in *Stratten Story.*" *Detroit Free Press*, November 1-7, 1981.

"Jamie Lee Curtis: Disco Dazzle '79." *Preview*, April 1979.

Rebello, Stephen. *"Halloween II."* *Cinefantastique*, Vol. 11, No. 2, Fall 1981.

Reid, Gordon. "Donald Pleasence talks to Gordon Reid about his roles past, present and future." *Continental Film Review*, May 1978.

Rensin, David. "Checking In." *Playboy*, November 1981.

Rensin, David. "20 questions: Jamie Lee Curtis." *Playboy*, July 1985.

"Pinup Special: Jamie Lee Curtis." *Rona Barrett's Hollywood*, Vol. 1, No. 10, Spring 1979.

Ronaldi, D.R. *"The Fog."* *Famous Monsters*, May 1980.

Sammon, Paul M. "Review of *Road Games*." *Cinefantastique*, Vol. 11, No. 2, Fall 1981.

Saroyan, Strawberry. "Jamie Lee Curtis Embraces the F-Word." *More*, June 24, 2008.

Sarris, Andrew. "Review of *Psycho II*." *Village Voice*, June 14, 1983.

Scanlon, Paul. *"The Fog*: A spook ride on film." *Rolling Stone*, June 28, 1979.

Schickel, Richard. "Review of *Psycho II*." *Time*, June 20, 1983.

Seligson, Tom. "Success Isn't Enough." *Parade*, October 29, 1989.

Shapiro, Marc. "Donald Pleasence is not a madman." *Fangoria* #80, February 1989.

Shapiro, Marc. "A farewell to *Halloween*." *Fangoria* #89, December 1989.

Shapiro, Marc. "*Halloween* in the dead of summer." *Fangoria* #214, July 2002.

Shapiro, Marc. "Laurie Hallelujah." *Fangoria* #177, October 1998.

Shapiro, Marc. "Profile: Dominique Othenin-Girard." *Gorezone* #11, January 1990.

Shapiro, Marc. "The Shape of better things to come." *Fangoria* #176, September 1998.

Shapiro, Marc. "The Shapes of Wrath." *Fangoria* #88, November 1989.

Shewey, Don. "Horror of Horrors—It's Jamie Lee Curtis." *Rolling Stone*, December 10, 1981.

Silverman, Stephen M. "Jamie Lee's *Halloween.*" *People*, August 26, 1997.

Smith, Dave. "Jamie Lee Curtis As The Tragic Dorothy Stratten." *Photoplay Movies & Video*, June 1982.

Steranko, Jim. "Life is a scream for Jamie Lee Curtis." *Mediascene Prevue* #45, May 1981.

Stone, Christopher. "Hex, Sex, Creepy, Weepy." *US*, November 10, 1981.

Swires, Steve. "The Curse of *Halloween.*" *Fangoria* #78, October 1988.

Thomas, Bob. "Jamie Curtis Is Much Prouder of *Halloween.*" *Sarasota Herald-Tribune*, October 24, 1978.

Thompson, Anne. "Producer-writer Debra Hill dies at 54." *The Hollywood Reporter*, March 8, 2005.

"For Girls Only!" *Tiger Beat's TeenView*, March 1978.

"After the Octopus." *Time*, July 20, 1962.

"Marilyn Beck's Hollywood." *Tri-City Herald*, October 14, 1980.

Vallance, Tom. "Janet Leigh." *The Independent*, October 5, 2004.

"Review of *Psycho II.*" *Variety*, June 1, 1983.

Verniere, James. "John Carpenter: Doing His own '*Thing.*'" *The Twilight Zone Magazine*, November 1982.

Wallace, Carol. "Beware: Soft Shoulders—Jamie Lee Curtis' Career Has Changed Course." *People*, August 22, 1983.

Wallace, Carol. "The Queen of Crud." *New York Sunday News*, September 27, 1981.

Wooley, John and Michael H. Price. "Forgotten Horrors: *Terror Train.*" *Fangoria* #222, May 2003.

Wynorski, Jim. "*Terror Train.*" *Fangoria* #9, November 1980.

Young, J.R. "Dr. Terror Stalks Hollywood." *Chic*, August 1979.

MISCELLANEOUS SOURCES

Blue Steel press notes (MGM/UA, 1990).

The Fog press notes (Avco-Embassy, 1980).

Halloween II press notes (Universal Pictures, 1981).

Mother's Boys press notes (Dimension Films, 1994).

Prom Night press notes (Avco-Embassy, 1980).

Road Games (*Roadgames*) press notes (Avco-Embassy, 1981).

Terror Train press notes (Astral Films, 1980).

Virus press notes (Universal Pictures, 1999).

INDEX

Lightning Source UK Ltd.
Milton Keynes UK
UKOW01f1318101017
310734UK00007B/808/P